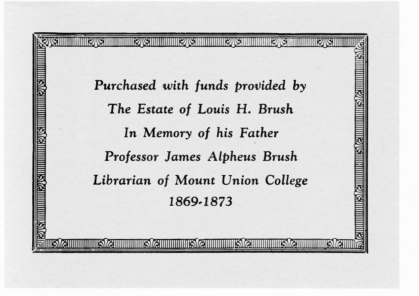

Birdless Summer

I

FIRST AMERICAN EDITION 1968

COPYRIGHT ©1968 BY HAN SUYIN

Library of Congress Catalog
Card Number: 68-25435

PRINTED IN THE UNITED STATES OF AMERICA

HAN SUYIN

Birdless Summer

CHINA
AUTOBIOGRAPHY
HISTORY

G. P. PUTNAM'S SONS
NEW YORK

LIST OF ILLUSTRATIONS

Following page 240.

Part of the steps up from the river, Chungking.
A fairly recent photograph
(*Popperfoto, London*)

A street in a Chinese city in 1939

Third Uncle, Third Aunt and their offspring
and relatives in 1956

Visiting friends in the English countryside

Yungmei, aged three

Pao, with the Chinese Military Mission in
England, winter 1943–4

Reproduced on the endpapers is the painting 'Lotus', by
Fang Chao Ling

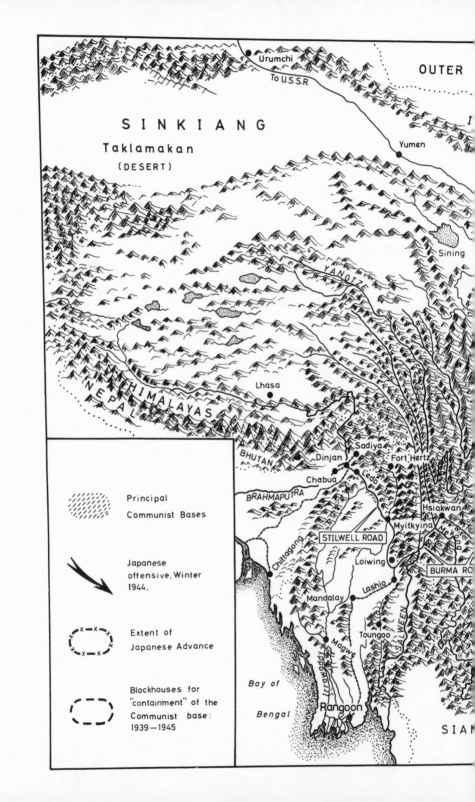

OUTER

SINKIANG

Taklamakan

(DESERT)

To U.S.S.R.

Urumchi

Yumen

Sining

YANGTZE

HIMALAYAS

NEPAL

BHUTAN

Lhasa

Sadiya

Dinjan

Fort Hertz

Chabua

Ledo

BRAHMAPUTRA

Hsiakwan

Myitkyina

STILWELL ROAD

Chittagong

Loiwing

BURMA RO

Lashio

Mandalay

Bay of

Bengal

Magwe

Toungoo

Rangoon

SIA

	Principal Communist Bases
	Japanese offensive, Winter 1944.
	Extent of Japanese Advance
	Blockhouses for "containment" of the Communist base: 1939–1945

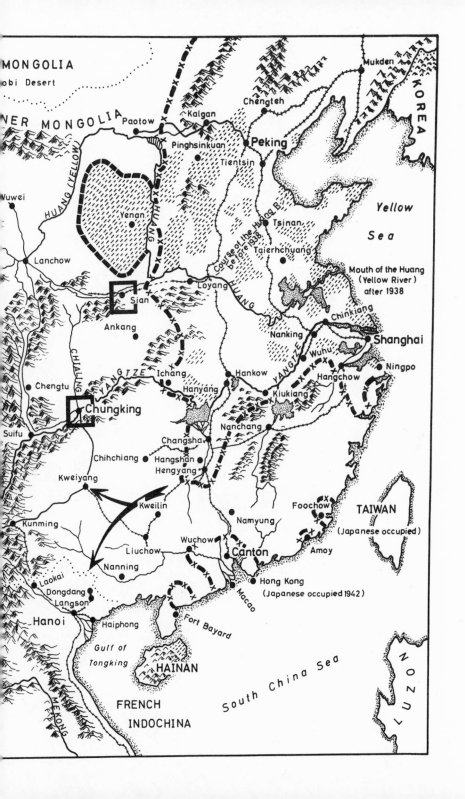

Part One (1938–1942)

One

STANDING on the Canebière of Marseilles in 1967, I re-enter that unsympathetic selfish twenty-year-old girl of deadly ignorance, Rosalie Chou, who stood on this very same spot in 1938, the tears upon her face buffeted by a gritty mistral. Phantom sob, ghostly wind, of a yesterday that chose today, when again the famishing need for a reality beyond the benevolent mummery of success reasserts its raucousness. On the threshold of yet another war, of far larger dimensions, an even more stringent choosing. Today the East is Red, the future has entered our present, has transformed it long before its own advent. The world continues what began in China yesterday. The mistral sings its name and its name is Revolution, World Revolution. Even the Pope knows it, and exhorts the rich to stem, with the miser crumbs of charity, the vast hunger for justice which two-thirds of mankind ready themselves to fight for. Today the thunder in Vietnam exalts Latin America to yet other Vietnams, and the marching songs of thirty million Red Guards in China earthquake the accepted order into a pandemonium of youth. Once again, I have stood on multitudinous platforms, in the United States, in Europe, a hundred platforms in the last two years, and talked of the signs and portents of this convulsion. Today with the mistral singing its song, another beginning lies in wait round the corner of the Canebière. Time has miniatured the tears of my quaint ghost of 1938 into a ridiculous drizzle, grimace of personal woe when the face which they laboured becomes an eyeless windowpane.

Yet another phantom emerges from the welter of the Marseilles street as we – Rosalie Chou of yesterday, Han Suyin of today – stand transfixed, in that small cleft of time where nothing begins nor ends. A tall, aquiline-featured Chinese whom I recognize, Raymond Woo, once a student at the University of Brussels as I was, in 1935–8. I recapture, in his smooth glance, that gleam of a malice so artfully concealed that he stayed on a scholarship for seven years without passing a single examination. I recollect his perpetual escape from his own inadequacy into an inverted racialism, which he deployed upon its natural victim, the Eurasian, me.

When crowd-borne he floats up to me I am not surprised; it is no longer surprising that I should meet the characters in my books. Have I not, only two months ago, while lecturing in the United States, entered a Chinese restaurant and come face to face with the proprietor, Robert Pang, a fellow student of mine at Yenching University in Peking in 1933, also an extoller of patriotic moralism, who now smilingly serves American G.I.s, on their way from the California army camps to Vietnam, their chop suey in Monterey? Have I not met again, on the streets of Peking, of Paris, of Singapore, of London, so many others, so many, until my life's episodes became compounded of the actions, hazards, existences of others?

Raymond Woo begins: 'Of course, you are Rosalie Chou, what is the name Han Suyin for?'

'It is a pen name.'

'Is it true that you go back to China?'

'Yes, I have been back several times.'

'And nothing happens to you?'

'Nothing.'

He is silent, incredulous. It is my turn to question.

'But you, you did not go back to China?'

'I thought of it many times.'

'You talked so much of patriotism, of saving the country ... '

'It seemed preferable to wait ... things were confused ... then the Germans invaded Belgium and von Falkenhausen, the German Military Governor of Belgium, sent us all out, all of us Chinese students ... that was in 1940 ... I came here to Marseilles, some of the others sailed back ... '

'You mean that you stayed in Marseilles nearly thirty years?'

'I am a merchant now, I was thinking of going back to China ... this year for a visit ... I will go if you give me a guarantee that I can return here, to Marseilles.'

I blink. 'You are absurd. No one can use pull or influence, the Chinese government decides.'

'But if you are not connected with them, and have no influence, why do you lecture about China? Why, if you get nothing for it ... '

I shake my head, angry, and begin to walk away, once again baffled by this recurrent trait, among so many, their inability to understand that one acts from personal conviction, not with hope of reward or honour, or even understanding. Raymond Woo pursues me, almost sneering now that he has discovered my unprotectedness.

'It is very courageous ... I have never heard anyone else talk about China, it isn't popular here, nor is the cultural revolution ... the Westerners are all afraid of it ... surely, if you are not *with* them, why are you sticking your neck out? And yet they attack you. Only a month ago, in a Chinese newspaper, your books were attacked ... This cultural revolution you have been explaining has been criticizing your writing, attacking you ... it condemns you ... '

He follows, follows, the cobbles behind me echo the slap of his shoes. 'Give me your address ... I want to write to you ... ' I do not answer, and he gives up following. And now past sorrow regurgitates new pain, wells from the feet up, gurgling and slapping its bilious puddles as I walk.

The next day the sun makes a small flood upon the city, washes the roof gables, pours down the yellow house fronts. The mistral ricochets from the cobblestones, flaps the awnings. The trees twist a landward supplication away from the ocean wind. Revolution, revolution; the whole world bends in the wind of the future ...

'They do not want you, those who fashion the tomorrows you dream of ... that tomorrow is not for you, you belong to the exploiting class, you cannot change this ... ' 'Forward, forward,' shouts the wind.

I think of those who have faltered, renounced. In the newspapers the smiling dulcorous face of Svetlana Stalin waxes its aureate moon ... A million dollars for a book about her father, the great and terrible Stalin ...

Another spectre from the past emerges, this time in Brussels, where I go to lecture on China at my old university. It is Leila, then a fellow student and a communist, now a respectable bourgeoise. Leila scorned my political ignorance, upbraided me for not taking part in politics; for *not* becoming *'engagée'*. 'You are a coward.' Today, pearl ensconced in her oyster life, she criticizes my forthrightness: 'You are a political innocent'; upbraids me for having committed myself on Vietnam, on China, on Asia. 'There must be peace, above everything else – we don't want war ... ' 'But we are already at war, in Asia,' I ·reply – and realize her 'we' is not mine. She talks of the affluent, and I of the others. To Leila, there is no war if she is not personally involved, even if the whole world bleeds.

Leila says: 'I will not be trapped again.' She was caught in Belgium by the Nazis and did two years of concentration camp in Ravensbruck. She will not talk about those terrible years. Few people talk about their concentration camp lives, they shun its horrors. Today Leila repudiates the past, comes to stun me with her new wisdom, and is just as sure now that it is right to be uninvolved as she was sure of the opposite thirty years ago.

'You understand, I live in this socie.y, I depend on it ... It doesn't do to be politically active ... anyway things are so different now ... with nuclear weapons, the most important thing is for everyone to keep quiet ... '

Perhaps, I too, one day shall give myself good reasons for keeping quiet. After all, I am not a revolutionary by nature; I am timorous, unsure, easily frightened; averse and disinclined to take sides, uncommitted to any political party, even today. I cannot imagine joining anything ... but I hear the wind, the Great Wind of tomorrow, sing its tremendous song, and it tells me that we must go once again on a journey, make a choice, Rosalie Chou of yesterday, Han Suyin today ...

And yet Rosalie-me had hoped that somehow, some day, at the end of the last journey (which journey, towards which goal, O traveller?) she would find safety, security and content in a house, her house with two doors, the house she had made a drawing of, when she was a child.

Today, I have unlocked both doors, and know them to be two yawns to the one tremendous horizon. Behind them no lair, no burrow, nor walls nor windows nor a roof to give respite or rest; only the ocean wind, breathing its melody: Revolution, Revolution; your name today Vietnam, tomorrow Bolivia or Brazil or India; and no one can escape, no one, not even Leila, however still and quiet she may keep ...

Although I plod more weary, more wary, knowing the hundred thousand wrong ways I have trod, knowing the stars are eyeless; and so many, so much more gifted than I, discouraged or distraught, with the newspaper smile of Svetlana Stalin in front of me, I can only reply: 'How fine the broad street of your prudent habits, Leila, but neither you nor I will reach the end of its night. You tell me that I shall labour the ocean and sow the sea, you enumerate those who have died, who rot for decades in jails, or who, like you, are wise, and think they have grown up because they have abdicated. But I must go on, for I have heard the singing of the wind, and the birds of summer are not enough shelter, nor weariness nor sloth.'*

A tawdry orange file contains those letters which, on the French steamer *Jean Laborde* sailing from Marseilles to China in September 1938, I wrote with the inevitable backward look to the only person who then seemed to understand; father substitute, mentor of my adolescence, Joseph Hers. He had arranged the scholarship for me in Belgium against his own judgment; he had given me the money to leave Belgium, abandoning my studies, my grandfather, my fiancé, the 'brilliant career' everyone predicted for me, to go back to China, because there was war in China and I could not bear to stay away. I had to go back.

It was April 1966 when that worn cardboard file was handed to me by Hers's son, on an Easter week-end in Brussels. Joseph Hers had died in December 1965, abandoned by the vast corporation for whose profits he had laboured sixty years since his first arrival in China in 1905. A gaunt, eighty-year-old man, some weeks before his death, an administrative meeting of the said corporation had ceremoniously dispensed with him because at his age a man should retire to live on his savings. 'I am jobless and without a pension – why have I lived so long? I live now by selling my books and my curios ... I have no savings.' His bitter letter about the way he had been forced to resign is with me. I sent him some money, he tried to raise more by a circular letter among his friends. In his last hours, semi-conscious, he had thought himself back in China and muttered: 'Hurry up, or we shall miss the sunset.'

The file his son gave me was one of many other such files of students, like myself, provided with scholarships by the Boxer indemnity fund; Hers kept all our letters, and carbon copies of his replies.

Stuck to the inside cover of the file was a typed memorandum, dated December 1952 and written by Hers himself. It purported to be a summary of my life ... but it was a strange summation, with many errors and evasions.

In 1934, Dr J. Heng Liu, president of the Peking Union Medical College said to me: 'I have in my office a young employee, Miss

*Les oiseaux ne sont plus un abri suffisant
Ni la paresse ni la fatigue.
                    Paul Éluard

Rosalie Chou, an extremely intelligent girl ... can't you give her a scholarship?'

It was in 1932, not 1934, when on the front porch of St Michael's church in Peking, Joseph Hers met me for the first time ... why then bring in Dr J. Heng Liu?

What prompted him to this defensive justificatory memorandum when there was nothing to defend? Why was this composed in December 1952 and not before? I knew he was contemplating writing his autobiography, saying: 'I have put something together', yet never getting down to actual writing, although he had accumulated an enormous amount of notes, including letters to his own mother, collected and bound in several large folders, dating from 1905 onwards to her death in the 1930s.

Perhaps Joseph Hers's motive was banal; he felt responsible for what had happened to me, wanted to exculpate himself. But the whole of our sound-and-fury arguments, of our singular and platonic friendship, suddenly becomes a little suspect, precisely because he felt the need to solidify a staid, respectable stance. And the bizarre mistakes in dates, in facts, continue all through this memorandum about me, paragraphs of mellifluous homily which make the living story sound fanciful.

The memorandum continues: I then had an interview with the young girl and her father. Her father was Mr Chou Yentung, born in 1886 in Chengtu, province of Szechuan, China, who had married a Belgian woman. Chou Yentung had studied in Belgium from 1904 to 1913, become an engineer, returned to China with his wife and worked on the railways. I had obtained his first job for him on the Lunghai railway. There were four children of the marriage. The eldest was desirous of pursuing higher studies, but her parents were not enthusiastic. They wanted her to marry a sergeant of the U.S. Marines at the American Embassy in Peking.

Thus abridged, in a last sentence, my mother's ambition for her daughters, resented Rosalie (me), lovely Tiza, beautiful Marianne. 'An American ... you will be at ease then ... Americans are all wealthy ... ' I see my mother smile, the empty gum ridge where her teeth had decayed, the veiling of her brown eyes by a vision of comfort, security; thinking of her daughters marrying Americans ... Today my mother lies in a cemetery in Arizona; the stone above her does not bear my engraved sorrow. It has been omitted, for even after death the tenacious woman would not forgive. I paid for the grave, the funeral and its embellishing rituals. Only now that she is dead can I begin to evoke an almost filial affection for the dour tragic woman, to find the chasm of aversion between us levelled with tardy indulgence. Without perturbation I begin to find much of her in me, her physical toughness, her stubbornness ... also a good bit of her stupidity.

The young Miss Chou insisted on studying, however, and finally her parents gave their consent.

As the young girl's Chinese was not good she first spent two years at Yenching University. In 1935 she left for Brussels via the trans-Siberian railway ...

1935. Summer in Peking. The Japanese rolling into the resilient sullen city ... in the gravelled courtyard of the Grand Hotel de Peking the high-booted Japanese general with his extra long sabre dragging on the gravel, stepping out of a lean wolfish black limousine, extending a white glove to the fat Chinese general, in black boots and white gloves, standing at attention ...

I found her again in 1938 in Brussels ... she was extremely brilliant in her studies, but altogether addicted to giving patriotic lectures under the auspices of the Sino-Belgian Friendship Association.

I remember Hers, sneering: 'Do you think you can stop a war, standing on a platform and spouting commonplaces? What do you know of China, what do you know of war?'

Thirty years later, again I stand on platforms and lecture on China; I do not believe that I can stop a war, for already we are at war, but I believe that keeping quiet is a crime, the crime of silence is unforgivable in those who have a voice to speak ...

She was thinking of marrying a young Belgian solicitor, but estimated that her duty was to return to China.

Thus in one sentence, Louis is disposed of, and Louis is a pleasant ghost, for he too became involved, he did not keep quiet ...

On board the ship she took to return to China from Marseilles, she met a young Chinese officer ... They married in Wuhan ... the marriage had its ups and downs. She had scarcely arrived in China when some Chinese students returning from Europe began to gossip about her. This made her angry and she wrote to all of us that she wanted to have nothing more to do with us ...

The whole picture with its shifting charisma escapes in ready-made glibness, as does also the wider scene, that large time of decay and ruin, slaughter and despair between 1938 and 1948, which was also a time of hope and triumph.

It is of this time that I write; of this war, and what it was in China. Everything I then thought and felt had to be repudiated, rejected, abandoned, like a bad play, and a disillusioned moment of truth, a demarcation line, like an unthought and real death on the stage, altered for ever what was to be. A long parched summer when no birds sang, and yet already, behind the impenetrable mask of heat, the first breath of ocean wind, bringing the timely rain ...

Letter to Joseph Hers
September 7th, 1938   *Port Said*

Dear Uncle Joseph,

Here I am on the *Jean Laborde*; the food is okay, the boat is crowded and it is very hot. We are about twenty, returning to China. Many are from Germany, military graduates, and *so* conceited. Dr Yu who is also here says he wrote to you from Marseilles, and now he sends you his compliments. He is going to Shanghai, to see his father.

Well, here is a big venture, but I am not trying to push myself in the forefront. Anyway nobody among the Chinese except Dr Yu seems to understand why I, a girl, should go back to China now ... everybody is inclined to think that it is for 'mean profit'. I feel sometimes that perhaps I have made a mistake, especially by risking my medical career, but I suppose, should things go all wrong, I could come back, to go on with my schooling, and then I will refund you your money ... I have more confidence in you than in anyone else, and I would like to think you have a little in me too.

PART ONE: 1938–1942

O ship, paltry sanctuary, labouring a conquest of measured miles,
I recapture the sight of the strenuous sea, the restless picketing waves,
the odour of the salt plains rising and falling, of evening coolness on
the deck, of engine oil and tar and human sweat. For when all other
memory fails the power of smell remains, translating us back into re-
living the moment with startled clearness. In the third class are forty
Chinese workmen, half naked, herded together so there is no space
between them when they lie down on their wooden planks. In the
second class, where I am, we are four in one cabin, and the smell is
also unattractive. In a squall I become seasick and Dr Yu comes to
see me, opening my cabin door without knocking, his protuberant
eyes with their thick glasses preceding him. Miss Moss, the English
spinster lady who wears knee-long knickers (and on fair weather
mornings teaches us to dance Morris dances, with waving handkerchiefs and stamping on the deck floor), springs out of her bunk and
pushes Dr Yu out, closing the door with a firm slam. 'Now that's
enough ... I won't have your men friends coming into my cabin ...
It isn't proper ... ' She has grey hair and tremendous springiness in her
stride, wears sandals and hand-woven pleated peasant skirts from the
Balkans, and she is going to India to teach Morris dancing and English
spelling. There is a group of Jews, sixteen of them, who daily occupy
the very small swimming pool; they come from ghettoes in Germany
and Czechoslovakia and Poland, they have escaped and they are going
to Bombay; they shout and laugh and swim and exuberate all day in a
pathetic greasy delight to be alive. There is another Eurasian girl,
Hélène Gee, who is going to Hongkong where her fiancé, a Doctor
Huang, will meet her. Hélène is eighteen; a small well-rounded girl
with very fair skin, Chinese-slanted but green eyes, curly hair; her
Chinese father was a restaurant keeper in France and she was born
there of a French mother. She was training as a nurse when she met
Dr Huang in a hospital in Paris. She speaks not a word of Chinese but
is in love with a China she has never seen but which Dr Huang has
described to her. Dr Yu constitutes himself her protector ('she is young
and innocent, I am afraid others might do things to her') and in the
mornings Dr Yu teaches Hélène Chinese characters in a corner of the
second-class salon.

The seven Chinese in the first class are military cadets, returning
from Germany and from England, and among them is Tang Paohuang. He recognizes me before I recognize him; in the first hour as

19

the *Jean Laborde* makes of Europe a grey fuzziness, and of Louis, planted
on the quay, a waiting anonymous speck, divested of meaning and
movement. Tang Paohuang also lingers on the deck, waving at friends,
and he is the only one of the Chinese students to praise my resolution.
'You are returning to China ... that is good, especially for a woman.'
In the days that follow I do not see him, but the others stray around me,
coming down to the second-class deck and asking me why I am on this
boat. I tell my story, and though I am naive I see that they do not
believe me and I am hurt. Later I realize they expect me to make their
shipboard hours more agreeable.

Those who travel first class are allowed to come to our deck, but we
are not allowed in the first class, except Dr Yu, who as a medical man
has obtained this privilege by courtesy of the ship's doctor. In the
second class a Chinese merchant, his young wife and two children
form an inseparable family group. During a storm the young woman
has a miscarriage, and calls me to help; her husband does not want the
ship's doctor or Dr Yu, who are men, to attend her. There are also
three overseas Chinese merchants returning to Saigon, and several
Vietnamese. The usual shipboard affairs take place, some ship's officer
with the blonde wife of a French colonial businessman returning to
Saigon, the doctor with someone else. Dr Yu, nimble, diminutive,
eyes perpetually indignant behind his enlarging goggles, knows all
that goes on and retails it, with moral unction, to Hélène and to me.
He talks at length of sacrifice for China, promises to help me. 'I have
connections all over China, I can help you to find work in a hospital.'

It takes nearly all of one day to sail through the Suez Canal while on
both sides the pastel and beige sand dunes crouch like waiting centaurs;
camels more antique than the desert sand watch our ship. At Port Said
Dr Yu accompanies Hélène and me ashore. There are women striking
tambourines, others writhing in front of us, calling, shouting; beggar
children with fly-bedecked eyes cornering us for coin, people grabbing
us by the arm to make us enter bazaars. Dr Yu later affirms that some
of the Chinese on board have gone to see women belly-dancing, and
more. He proclaims his own repugnance. 'I respect woman.'

Our ship dawdles in the hot Red Sea and I am disappointed that it is
not red. Dr Yu wears shorts and in the morning paces the deck with
Hélène. There are two priests on board; one of them says he is going
to Tientsin, to teach at the college where my brother taught. He asks
me why I don't go back to Tientsin, to my parents. 'But North China

is occupied by the Japanese, of course I'm not going back to be under the Japanese.' We lie in deck chairs and argue about the war, and the priest says: 'Japan and China will come to an arrangement, you'll see,' and then something hits me on the head. It is a book. Above me, on the first-class deck, stands Tang Paohuang, hand outstretched, 'I am sorry, my book fell ... ' (Some weeks later he tells me that he threw it down to attract my attention.) I go up the steps to return the book to him, and this is the beginning. Pao tells me of our meeting in London when he was a cadet at Sandhurst. 'Do you remember that dinner when someone was arguing about peace?' 'Yes, I remember, you said: "We may love our enemies but we must fight them first." But you shouldn't throw books at people, books are precious.' 'I heard you talk, talk to this white priest. You had better talk with me.'

Thus it began, a relationship which brought me more unhappiness than I had thought could be mine; and yet also joy, moments, days of mirth, as the smiling photographs testify; such lying photographs, when the sum of those years is made, yet true enough when these sunny moments are dissected out of their sombre background; for where are there not happy photographs, even of the most tragic couples? The fundamental ambivalence of our relationship, its extremes of vehemence and hatred, passion and love and cruelty, its obsessional force, hobbled me for a long time. Of such contradictions compounded in wholeness are all emotional ties, reflection of our own multiple selves, and any exact account, cannot tell where love leaves off and becomes hatred, nor where remorse turns resentment into devotion; nor how much tyranny and abnegation go into erecting a smooth surface of domestic content. No one can really probe the variegation of any human situation and not find all description inconsistent.

The emotional stress of those years still claws at me; induces hectic reactions to trivia which trigger off a memory, a scene. It is a predicament similar to those of people who have been in concentration camps and acquire conditioned reflexes, difficult to eradicate, to certain situations. I have often wondered whether those who have managed to give an account of their concentration camp life, did what Hers did with his memorandum: glozed over certain portions and enlarged others; obliterated the more unbearable indignities; trimmed and shaped the unresolved to a purposeful recital; and thus sculptured, from the contradictory and the shapeless, logic and continuity. There must have been humiliations so unendurable that to tell them required a transcendent detachment. The most gruelling and insupportable memories must have been not the cruelties inflicted upon internees, but the survivors' own cowardices, cringing slavishness, the small and large betrayals of the victims themselves, which like vomit cannot be regurgitated; the brutalizing of others to escape being brutalized oneself, the complicitory acquiescence in an order of the camp imposed by the guards, a zeal of necessity to please one's jailers; the acceptance of horror as normal, of bestiality as survival ... Only the very brave, who defied all, or the very unimaginative, who can forget all, are able to survive a more or less exact telling; we can bury in ourselves wordless crimes but their naming kills us ...

It all began on the ship, the *Jean Laborde,* in afternoons and mornings suspended between what had been, and what was to come. Tang Paohuang and Dr Yu, Hélène and myself paced the deck laughing, talking, launched towards a future hopefully unknown. Pao was as full of promises of help as Dr Yu; I felt he meant them more than Dr Yu did, and thought life, or God, or whoever attended to my destiny, kindly, to present me thus with a sincere and spirited friend, who did not make suggestive remarks, who was intensely patriotic, genuinely Chinese. So swift a reward for my good intentions, almost I believed it such. Even in those very early days Pao spoke of duty, his willingness to go on to the battlefield. 'I am going straight to Wuhan, to report for duty ... I am ready to die at any moment ... Who is not ready for the supreme sacrifice is neither patriotic nor even a young man ... The greatest glory is sacrifice for the country against the invader ... ' Even now I hear the words, so marvellous in the wind from the mottled seas, spurring my heart. I hoped Pao would not die too soon, not, at least, before I too would have been able to accomplish something, prove my usefulness, and especially prove myself a Chinese, ready to die for China ... even though, at times, a wince, a twinge, from deep down within me reminded me that to many Chinese I was a Eurasian, and not always acceptable. But Pao did not seem to think so. 'Your blood is Chinese, blood comes from the father, the mother is only a receptacle.' I smiled at his pre-scientific ideas of embryology but was grateful to him for not sneering because I was a Eurasian ...

Thus, carried by a dream, we sped on the Indian Ocean, which bounced its schools of dolphins by the ship's side, and talked of China, and of Pao. Thus Pao became the personification of China to me.

In Saigon, Pao wanted to become engaged; I refused, telling him that I had almost married a young Belgian, and then had left him to return to China. Perhaps Pao did not understand what I meant, which was, that I was not a virgin. Not understanding (and I did not know then that he could not understand), he soberly nodded: 'I am glad ... no Chinese girl should ever marry a foreigner ... '

I sought out Dr Yu and asked his advice. 'Wonderful,' said Dr Yu. 'You should put the past behind you, as I have done, and only look forward. Tang Paohuang is a very estimable young man and from an excellent family, an excellent family.' He then drew me a little farther down the deck, as if seeking seclusion, to emphasize the importance of his confidence, which was that Hélène Gee and he had now fallen in love, that they had made love, that Hélène was going to break her engagement to Dr Huang as soon as the ship arrived in Hongkong. 'Dr Huang is too young to understand her. Meanwhile I would like you to help me, Miss Chou,' Dr Yu said to me.

September 28th   *At sea on the 'Jean Laborde'*

Dear Uncle Joseph,

We left Saigon yesterday and are now en route to Hongkong. I know that you are thinking all kinds of things about me for changing route. You advised me to go via Saigon to Hanoi, then on to Kunming, and you wrote to the Bishop of the Catholic Hospital there to look after me. I shall probably stay two days here in Hongkong, and from thence go inland by rail to Wuhan. I know you advised Kunming because it is safe, but I do not want to get lost among the crowd of refugees who are pouring there. The Chinese newspapers in Saigon warn that there is no space available. I want to be as near the front line as possible, and that is in Wuhan. A big battle is going on there now. And I want to be there ...

Now I have something else to tell you. There is on our boat, a young girl, Hélène Gee, fiancée to a Dr Huang, who returned to Hongkong from Europe last year. Miss Gee during the trip changed her mind. She is going to Shanghai, and she is going to marry Dr Yu. She will tell Dr Huang when she arrives in Hongkong that she does not want to marry him, but she owes him ten

thousand francs for the passage money. Dr Yu says he has no
money to reimburse her passage to Dr Huang; Hélène has none
either. She is likely to get into trouble, she is as innocent as a baby,
and Yu says the only way out is if you will write a letter recom-
mending her as a nurse in the French hospital in Shanghai, where
you have some influence. She is nearly nineteen but a real baby. I
am afraid for her, as Dr Yu says he cannot marry her for a few
months ... There is no question of her changing her mind now.
Dr Yu seems sincerely in love with her. Whatever you may think
of Dr Yu, she is too much of a baby to be hurt ... and she knows
not a word of Chinese ... please keep in touch with my grandfather, tell him I am fine ...

I re-read this letter of mine with stupefaction; and remember that
my first and last postcard to my fiancé Louis, in Belgium, was sent
from Port Said; after Port Said I stopped writing to Louis, as if going
through the Suez Canal had made communication with him no longer
possible. As for my grandfather, he received brief letters or postcards
from me, saying I was fine ... I could not bear to sit down and write
lengthily, for all that was Europe had become so unreal, so vague, and
I could not explain what was happening to me or around me, for what
was around me was Asia, and not to be described with the excited
verve of the tourist – it was too close, too near ... Louis had become
impalpable; I wondered if I would recognize his face, should I meet
him again. While to him I remained the me he knew, and would so
remain, he had become to me a greyish blur, looking towards my
departing ship, confused among others planted like haphazard trees
on the quay at Marseilles ...

Not only Hélène Gee had changed; I too had changed, though my
change had started before I left Europe. Towards my grandfather I felt
much indebted, but when finally I wrote and told him that I was
married and was going to remain in China, he responded with total
rejection. And then war came to Europe, and Grandfather died in
1940.

When we docked at Hongkong a sobbing Hélène rushed into my
cabin as I was packing: 'Protect me, protect me.' Since falling in love
with 'Papa Yu', as she called Dr Yu, Hélène had blossomed; she
looked like a fluctuant bunch of anemones. While I was trying to
disentangle myself from her damp clinging Dr Huang, her ex-fiancé,

24

who had come on board to welcome her, also appeared in my cabin (luckily Miss Moss had departed), tried to pull Hélène from me, and glared at me, as if I were the abductor. 'Miss Chou, Miss Chou, you *must* tell me, what has happened to Hélène?' 'Dr Huang, I am sorry, but I don't know how it happened ... ' 'But she is mine, she is my fiancée,' cried the anguished Dr Huang, 'you must tell me how this happened.' Hélène then shrieked, 'Papa Yu, Papa Yu,' and fled, still sobbing, out of the cabin. I went on deck, followed by Dr Huang, and found Dr Yu leaning on the railing, palely staring at the moth-coloured Peak of Hongkong. 'You must explain to Dr Huang, Dr Yu.' 'Yes, of course I take full responsibility.' Dr Huang went up to Dr Yu and they bowed formally to each other. 'Dr Huang, Dr Yu ... ' I left them explaining. Later, Pao told me that it was Hélène's fault. 'A woman, a good woman, does not change her mind.' I kept quiet, since I had also changed mine.

I was to see Dr Yu once more, very briefly, in a Chungking restaurant, in 1940. He was dressed in army uniform, with a medical unit badge on his arm, and he recognized me. He gave me an evasive nod, and quickly sidled out of the restaurant, for he was very much afraid, as every civilian was, of the military men of Chiang Kaishek, and especially of officers like Pao, graduates of the Whangpoo Military Academy, Chiang Kaishek's elite corps and so powerful. Yu was terrified that Pao might use the story of Hélène against him. To compensate for the corruption and nepotism in his government, Chiang Kaishek ordered 'spiritual mobilization', launched 'morality drives', announced 'purity movements', and it was in this kind of 'movement' that people like Dr Yu, who was neither influential nor wealthy, might get caught ...

Many years later I learnt that Dr Yu's love for Hélène had lasted six months; he already had a wife, whose existence he had conveniently forgotten for fifteen years. He enrolled in the Chinese Red Cross and came to Chungking, but I have no idea how he ended up; I cannot somehow imagine that he is still in China today, but anything is possible. He may even have turned into a communist cadre.

As for Hélène, she lingered in Shanghai, nursing at the French hospital, till 1942, then took a boat back to Europe and married there, and ever after swore that had she known how badly the Chinese treated their women, she would never have left France. Today my letter remains, ephemeral testament of a portion of the blackmailing past, telling of love and calculation, and all of it gone, become the lies of yesterday that compel the truth today around my worn-out youth.

Two

IN HONGKONG, Pao and I stayed at an hotel, and all was made easy by the fact that he had friends. Wherever he went there were friends; linked by class and family prerogative, by ties of school and Military Academy, they formed a cohesive ruling structure, to which he belonged. Always this class solidarity, its more shadowy solder the secret society, has promoted its own seizure of power by its own insiders. Strong, resilient, almost monstrous in its subtleties, the cohesion of the ruling elites transcend even revolutions, go underground to bide their time of return.

Tang Paohuang was a product of the landlord-militarist ruling class. This was the feudal elite, which through its administration, the mandarinate, held power in China until the Revolution in 1949. The moment Pao stepped into Hongkong he was back in it; helped, served, protected, deferred to. Friends came to greet us, friends came to take us out to lunch or dinner, to lend him money, to take us shopping. I who had not been part of anything—the lone one, defiant and isolated—was no longer alone now, nor on the defensive. There is no feeling more flattering than the feeling of belonging to a group, of being *accepted*. This was now happening to me, and through Pao. No longer questioned, reassurance lubricated my conscience, smoothed the ruffled disquiet that was a perpetual accompaniment to my living. And since I knew nothing of class structure, I imagined all China was as the group which now, through Pao, seemed cosily ready to accept me. Today, I can understand the temptations of those who wrest themselves from an inferiority, real or assumed, and 'make good' at last, 'arrive' at last. What sweetness within it must be to them when, succumbing to this succulence, they can exclaim, 'Now princesses will kiss me', and feel that they have 'won'! How often in the past in China the shrewd sons of the poor must have thus been recruited, to reinforce the hierarchic influence of the ruling mandarinate! And in their personal success lay their total betrayal, for the parvenu will more than any other practise the vices and the virtues of the group he has climbed into, and staunchly support its authority.

For me, too, though I did not at the time know it, it was an implicit scheming. Pao was Chinese; engaged to him, I was recognized at last (so I imagined) by China, and it was for China, not for a man, that I had left Europe. This was my grand illusion.

We arrived in Hongkong on the day that the Munich agreement was proclaimed in Europe, and while the headlines of the Hongkong English newspapers screamed 'Peace in our Time', 'They'll have war next year in Europe', said I, and found Pao nodding agreement. Pao said, 'We are not staying a day longer than we need in Hongkong. We are going to Wuhan, to save the country ... The Leader is there, we must go there, to sacrifice ourselves. We shall resist to the last ... ' His young unlined face set in stern forwardness, the future his profile, how infinitely noble then, heroic and glorious, he appeared to me! Pao was attractive, his unbounded faith, his loyalty, seemed in that time of war the right thing for resisting Japanese aggression. That his devotion was to a single person, Chiang Kaishek, and not to the Chinese people, that it was a product of his upbringing and his class, and not love of country, that it was feudal allegiance to a clique, and not real sacrifice, was not apparent to me then. He was such a contrast to the hesitant, the uninvolved, those who timorously hung back! Pao for a long time was to embody, to epitomize for me the best of China because he had returned to fight for China; I fell in love with him because of that, and would have followed him anywhere, and certainly to Wuhan, where the greatest battle of all was going on ...

For the next few weeks, Pao was to undertake my education in 'loyalty'. Until then I had only the vaguest notion about Chiang Kaishek; not enough to call aversion, but no particular liking either. What I had vaguely heard when a child about the way Chiang had massacred his way to power kept me in dubiety; but my fear of communism, and, during the three years in the University of Brussels, the recital of the misdeeds of Stalin, had much influenced me. Though Chiang for so long had refused to fight Japan, he was now fighting her, had become the symbol of resistance. Pao told me that had it not been for the communists, who kept on causing trouble, devastation and misery, China would already be strong and prosperous; that the communists were trying to sell the country to Russia; that they were under orders from Moscow, and that was why Chiang had had to fight them for many long years. It was because of this internal war that Chiang had avoided fighting the Japanese, had been unjustly condemned for giving in to Japan when he was only trading space for time, while making preparation to take them on. The best evidence, said Pao, was that in 1932, Chiang had given a secret speech to selected officer cadets of the Whangpoo Military Academy and officials, elaborating this strategy; a 'vindication' of Chiang's foresight. Actually the full speech was not an anti-Japanese lecture, but a rally call for yet another anti-communist drive to crush the muttered criticism among Chiang's own Kuomintang party members who did not like supine acceptance of the Japanese onslaught, and his enormous 'Red annihilation' campaigns. But I was too uninformed, thinking all politics tiresome and irrelevant, not to swallow, totally, what Pao told me then. 'We resist Japan to the last … The Great Leader has said so.' This, in his young voice, singularly clear and perfect, did much to convince me that Chiang was the sole defender of China against Japanese aggression. To inspire loyalty in such a noble young man, what a great man Chiang must be! There was a thrill, an emotion, in such a dedication which simplified all issues, created a binding link. Pao convinced me all the more as, through him, I too achieved a national identity. I did not realize I merely became an appendage of the powerful militarist clique, the Whangpoo elite, mainstay of Chiang's power.

'Wuhan shall not be surrendered', clamoured the Chinese newspapers in Hongkong. After almost three days of running about Hongkong shopping, and being entertained by Pao's friends, tickets were obtained for us on the Blue Express, and we were to leave for Wuhan, hoping the great battle which was taking place there would not be over before we arrived …

While in Hongkong, I paid a visit to the Belgian Bank, because Hers had given me the address of a friend of his there, Pierre Mardulyn. I gave Pierre a brief note I had written to Hers, telling him that I was going to Wuhan.

Thirty years later, Pierre Mardulyn was still in Hongkong, at the Belgian bank, affable, resourceful and portly. Unchanged.

'I remember well that afternoon,' says Pierre. 'You came into my office wearing a Chinese dress, of that black oily cloth the Cantonese coolie women wear in the summer. You were poorly dressed, I remember.'

'I was going to a war.'

'And you wept. How you wept. Torrents, like a little girl.'

He does not remember why I wept. I had told him that I had left

Belgium and my studies and Louis, in that order, and that Hers had suggested that I go to Kunming in Yunnan province, very far from the war-fronts, and work in a Catholic hospital there. But I had decided to go to Wuhan instead which was now the capital of Free China, and I was going to marry Tang Paohuang because he was so patriotic, so idealistic and sincere. I had never met anyone like him before. And then I asked Pierre: 'Do you think China is going to lose the war?' and he had replied: 'Well, that is quite possible, I think the Japanese are very strong ... Wuhan will be given up ... ' I had then started those torrents. If China lost the war, if we had to knuckle under to the Japanese, I did not think I could live ... Pierre took me out for a drive in his car and this helped, as well as the loan of his handkerchief. 'Things are bad in China. No hospitals, no medicines for the army ... much chicanery and corruption ... all the bigwigs of the Chiang government are making money ... you should ask the International Red Cross here; there is a woman called Hilda Selwyn-Clarke, trying to collect medicines, but there's a huge black market in drugs in China ... of course these stories are not to be spread about ... it would do China much harm abroad ... ' Pierre then gave me the address of Dr R. K. S. Lim, in charge of the Red Cross in Wuhan. His car followed the ribbon road wound round the island of Hongkong, climbed the Peak. I gazed sightlessly at the beautiful landscape; beyond the humped bare hills was China, Wuhan, where a big battle was on ...

During the six-day train journey from Hongkong to Wuhan, my moral education by Pao continued, establishing the pattern of our relationship, at first accepted by me so unquestioningly, later to become so violently resented.

'Our Leader, Generalissimo Chiang Kaishek, keeps a diary. All of us military students abroad keep one, to note down our thoughts, to perfect our moral self-cultivation. You must form the habit of keeping a diary.' A spare diary was produced from Pao's suitcase (he always carried a spare). I wrote my name on it and Pao laughed at my unformed hand. 'You have a child's writing.' 'That is because I was not allowed to learn,' I replied mortified. As soon as I could, I would pick up calligraphy again ... though how I proposed to do this in the heat of battle I really could not explain.

In feudal China and in Japan, intellectuals, scholars and professors kept diaries, as did politicians, statesmen, teachers ... Diaries were intended to be read by others, to be open to inspection, as evidence of one's sincerity.

When the first students from China had been sent abroad, in the latter half of the nineteenth century, they had been commanded to keep diaries, which were to be presented every month to the Inspector of Education, an official attached to the Embassy in the country where the student was being trained. Although the practice had slackened among university students abroad after the Revolution of 1911, it was strictly enforced among the officer cadets of the Whangpoo Military Academy. This device to substantiate, at every moment, loyalty to an oligarchy by writing down one's conformist sentiments was intended as a check on 'poisonous influences', meaning political deviation. It stunted all debate, prevented all discussion. One's 'sincerity' was gauged by what one wrote down, knowing full well it would be read, and how Chiang Kaishek and the young officers loved the word 'sincerity'! The practice was continued, though not officially, by some Chinese Communist Party members, and was again to be found in the universities in China, in recent years. Diaries of new heroes of the New Age were being discovered, admiringly and lengthily quoted; yet Mao Tsetung himself does not keep one, probably having pierced the speciousness of this form of spiritual bookkeeping. And finally in 1966, with the Cultural Revolution, this hypocritical device, stemming from the moralistic propensity so often found in China – even now – of judging people by their *words,* is at last being given up. But even in autumn 1966, on a visit to China, I was still being asked to write down my 'spontaneous feelings' in visitors' books. It was difficult to make the more bureaucratic officials understand that these eulogistic phrases, written by visitors to factories, monuments, or places of interest, are sometimes incense-swinging, on a par with the keeping of diaries in which it is expressly forbidden to write anything but lofty and noble thoughts.

I found very few elevating maxims to write down in the little blue-covered diary which Pao handed to me. No high-sounding phrases were ready in my mind, and this difficulty later became overwhelming. So often in the months that followed, trying desperately to find something to retrieve my abysmal 'wrongness', Pao would skim through my diary ... and discover nothing of worth, nothing indicating a spiritual quality which he could praise, or to convince him that my character-building, which he had so decisively taken in hand, was successful. For he had made up his mind that character-building was what I needed above all. Even in those early hours of our acquaintance he had decided that 'the foreigner' in me was to be thoroughly eradicated, and the only way was a return to all the Confucian feudal traditions of China for me.

And when in 1966, just before the Cultural Revolution, a friend of mine, a communist, also began to criticize my lack of 'self-cultivation' in almost the same phrases as I had heard used by the Kuomintang bureaucrats, I felt catapulted back into the past. For two days I was prey to a sensation of dread, a dazed terror, as I saw, or thought I saw, the oligarchy of the past, the feudal mandarin-official, now in the guise of a communist cadre. Hauntingly it was the same peremptory tone, the same attitude of total righteousness, the same moralistic unction; the same phrases about 'face', about my being too 'head-strong', about my lack of protocol and ritual courtesy to the 'comrade officials' – the almost cabalistic phrases, now smuggled under so-called Marxist theory. And the significance of the Cultural Revolution led by Mao Tsetung lies in the fact that it is precisely this kind of attitude – the return to a hypocritical Confucian tradition, expounded as 'self-cultivation' – which it seeks to eradicate. For two millennia the mandarinate imprisoned the minds of the young in tradition, submission, obedience. Now the young revolted, promoted argument, debate. NOT blind obedience, NOT submission and docility to elders, to teachers – that is the Cultural Revolution.

Into my diary went dreary, reluctant, repetitious sententiousness, copied from Pao; I longed for his sublime undoubting faith, for his glib maxims, high-sounding words: 'Obedience is virtue ... ' 'Filial piety above all ... ' I must battle with myself, to give myself good reasons for acquiring the same sureness in what was right or wrong, overcoming that eternal crossgrain of doubt, compound of my very being. I must learn to conquer my weaknesses, my faults ... but on scraps of paper, I wrote what I really felt, the colour of the sky, the air raid at the railway station of Yochow, our running out of food, and the people, the people, the undaunted and wonderful people of China, streaming out of the cities that were abandoned and bombed, carrying their children, patient and for ever beaten down and so apparently submissive, yet all-conquering in the end. 'You must note down your thoughts about the war, about our Leader.' Feebly, I protested: 'But we haven't reached the war yet, and I haven't met the Generalissimo' (I always avoided the word Leader, it had a nasty taste). To which the reply was: 'You have been abroad too long ... you must be all Chinese now, you must write down your resolution ... your resolution to be a virtuous, true Chinese woman ... '

I wrote it down. Little did I know then what the words virtuous, true Chinese woman, in all their degradation, entailed.

I was full of zeal, ardour, will to do well ... of course I wanted to be Chinese ... just as my brother had, so long ago ... he had given up, I would not give up. Of course I wanted to have noble thoughts. And now guilt began to creep upon me. Reinforced by Catholic guilt, a moral Confucian guilt began to suffocate me, kept my head a prisoner for years until, in a desperate surge of all of myself, I was to wrench myself free.

Of this strangled time, the mildewed anguish still prowls about me on long-drawn evenings, sudden wakings, in front of lovely land-scapes. Fetid, soft, felted terror swoops to seize me when are repro-duced incidents, tones of voice, which bring the past back.

All this, which began with such ample, childish fervour, I was un-able to discuss for many years, and my own self-deceit, in those terrorized days, became the witness of my own folly.

Yet all the time, all round us was the marvellous big land, land of China, people of China, robust and suffering, ruined and verminous and poor and so barbarously treated by their own ruling class, and so magnificent, that the heart swelled with their greatness, a transport and a rush of love which made me know my terrors and griefs trivial compared to the tidal waves of suffering endured round me so stoic-ally. On the great wind of life which coursed and surged through the detritus and crumble and chaos of those years, I survived; and the talismanic gibber of traditional 'wisdom', of Confucian loyalty, re-vered by those who prefer mummies to live men, at last became only gibberish ...

It was on the train trip to Wuhan that suddenly, and despite my lack of diary-worthy sentiments, I was back, back with the smell and the feel of China, all familiar, all dear, alive, alive, people, people, through the stations horrible with beggars and refugees, the gaunt soldiers, yellow with malaria, weak with hunger, shuffling their peasant plod to a war in which more died of disease and ill-treatment than of being shot at; throughout this vastness, this enormousness which is China, opening the heart and the eyes and ears, the people, and from the fields the smell of the great earth and all the known beauty that is so earthy and so human until my heart capsized and I was back.

After six days in the train we reached the Triple City of Wuhan, Hankow-Hanyang-Wuchang; triangle metropolis astride the Great River. Famous city, city of revolution in 1911, again in 1926, city of vast uprising and cruel exploitation, in October 1938 it was a bastion of defiance against the Japanese invader. And what a shock to find this heroic city, which the newspapers said was to be defended at all costs against the Japanese, to find it putrid infection, squalid corruption! I wrote a letter to Hers, the limpid first sight of a child, and true; later increasingly terrified and therefore cautious, I would no longer see what I saw that first day in Wuhan ...

October 9th, 1938   *Wuhan*

Dear Uncle Joseph,

Have finally arrived here yesterday the 8th evening, after leaving Hongkong on the 3rd. We were held up by an air attack once. Life in Hongkong was terribly expensive, just as everywhere in China now. A room for 75 dollars a month, with nothing in it. The hotels were full, the Y.W.C.A. full, refugees from China, especially the wealthy. I may either stay here or go to work in another place, which is probably the best thing as most hospitals have already moved. Wuhan is dreadful, dreadful, everybody only thinks of having a good time, sex apparatus are sold everywhere openly ... as it is The Moon Feast today, Sunday, and to-morrow the 10th of October, everybody eats ... anyway I am glad to be here ... getting in touch with all sorts of people ... I am learning a lot on all sides.

The £60 sterling which Hers had given me before my departure had been spent in Hongkong, between Pao and myself, on the hotel, making purchases; it was with about £10 sterling left that we had arrived in Wuhan. I intended firmly to be no bother to Pao. I would work in a hospital, earn my keep.

On our arrival night we strolled under the full moon; the Great River glittered, and many families walked about, almost as if there was no war. Pao spoke of his noble father; and later, back in our hotel room, showed me what he told me was a photograph of his mother. I could not identify this photograph, my childhood recollections were different; and now I know it was a lie, it was not his mother, but the photograph of a maid-in-waiting to the Dowager Empress Tzu Hsi which he showed me. His father, Pao said, had been a revolutionary, a friend of Sun Yatsen. So was his uncle, General Tang, whom we were to call upon. Alas, his father had succumbed to wealth and influence, smoked opium, had concubines, though admonishing his son not to follow his example.

Pao told me how, as a young student, he had joined a revolutionary cell in school, how it had been raided, and he had escaped ... he told me of the young teacher, so shy, so modest, so good, one day arrested because he was a communist, a real one, and shot ...

'That is how we know that they are communists. They appear honest, they are quiet, they study a lot, they are always reading ... even among us, when we were cadets at the Whangpoo Military Academy, if we found one who read too much, had no defects, we suspected him ... he might be a communist. They put on this show to capture the hearts of the people, but they are actually working for a foreign country ... Our Leader says China has two hereditary enemies, England and Russia ... ' And Pao gazed fiercely at the moon as if perceiving in its blurred opalescence those two enemies, ready to pounce.

I did not know that this reference to books was later to be turned against me; for some years, I would have to hide to read books not 'selected' for my moral re-education by Pao. But in Wuhan in October 1938, on the Harvest Moon Festival, all I knew was that we would get married and both work for China.

In the cool clear sunlight, unshattered tall buildings, in English colonial style, raised their arrogant brick on the Bund in the ex-British concession. Streamers and banners taut against the walls, strung across the streets, proclaimed: WUHAN WILL CERTAINLY BE DEFENDED. The crowds with their laughing chattering children reassured me ... that great serenity, and the waters of the Yangtze, the Great River, rolling silver under the moonlight. Surely Wuhan would stand for ever against the invader. On October 10th, parades, banners, bugles, volunteers marching, Chiang Kaishek appearing, and the acclaim, the tremendous acclaim because WUHAN WILL BE DEFENDED TO THE

LAST. All this fired my ever-ready enthusiasm. Chiang Kaishek was a hero! Pao, his worthy follower, another one! How happy I was to be in Wuhan, in those proud days of a heroic city, resisting aggression, one of the screaming, shouting multitudes roaring their patriotic fervour, their will to fight to the last! I wept tears of joy, and shouted with the best.

At night, we visited friends of Pao's; a certain Commander Wu, very thin, and his wife who had a tuberculous fistula in her abdomen and kept a very dirty piece of plaster on it; she asked me what she could do for it. She was a Szechuan woman; she told me that Commander Wu had given her a disease, which came from much heart of flower (frequenting whores). Commander Wu said he could get me a job in a hospital 'almost immediately'; in fact, he was the superintendent of the military hospitals in the region. That was the Kuomintang hospital for wounded soldiers which the next day I was to be dissuaded from going to. In such hospitals nurses were recruited for the officers' leisure hours. 'They simply do not exist, these military hospitals,' said an overseas Chinese engineer I met some days later. And he told me a few more things about these 'hospitals'. 'But don't repeat this; there is a censorship. You had better work in one of the missionary Red Cross hospitals. But don't say I said it.'

October 10th – letter to Hers

... I am going to have something to do in a hospital here soon. One thing I must tell you; there are young people here who have left everything to come to work for China ... boys from America, from Singapore, and they too are a little foreign, but they want to be Chinese like me. And there are some really pure Chinese who do things for no money at all, but they are few. I am not disillusioned at all, I know I was right to come.

I was continuing the argument with Hers who had prophesied that I would be disgusted: 'All the Chinese think of is money, money, they are not patriots ... your patriotism, it is not Chinese ... ' Every time I was to meet someone who really did things through love of country, the barometer of my ardour rose. And I did meet them, even in putrid Wuhan.

October 11th

Have applied for work at the International Red Cross, will get an answer tomorrow. Am getting offer to work in a purely Chinese hospital for wounded soldiers, but conditions for a woman are impossible ... there is so much sex business, it is awful, and besides this military hospital is not here, but moved to Heng-shan, a country place ... but I may go elsewhere after training for two months at the Red Cross here ...

It was the Red Cross administrator himself, Dr R. K. S. Lim, who dissuaded me from accepting work in a Chinese military hospital. I remember going to his office in great trepidation that afternoon. I did not know, at that time, how much the energetic, bronzed face concealed mental distress. For Dr Lim had to choose between his career and telling the truth about the terrible conditions due to graft and corruption among the officers and officials of the military 'hospitals'. But to criticize was 'treason'; Dr Lim was already accused of 'disloyalty', for in private converse he had whispered that more Chinese soldiers died of neglect and brutal treatment at the hands of their Kuomintang officers than on the battlefield. However, in front of me he was the well-assured, efficient head of the Red Cross and co-ordinator of all the hospitals in China ... 'You want to work? That's wonderful, but we're moving our hospitals to Changsha, to other places ... ' Then he suggested the International Red Cross mission hospital. 'There's plenty to do there, if you're going to stay here for a while ... '

'China is at war, China is fighting for her life ... ' how can one criticize in wartime? This was also the question posed by the mission-aries in the International Red Cross Hospital to which I next went ... How can one *notice* defects, write about them, in wartime? The con-clusive statement came from an English missionary: 'It is already hard enough to get help from abroad ... all help will stop if one opens one's mouth the wrong way ... and besides, it's always been like this in China ... everything's always been a mess ... '

And Pao had the answer, or so he said, when I told him my doubts. Of course China was in a mess, of course there were bad people, corrupt people, and that was precisely why one must follow the Leader, and all this would be cleaned up. The officer corps of the Whangpoo, Chiang's elite students, young men such as Pao, would clean it up. It sounded like King Arthur and his Knights of the Round Table ... high resolve, chivalrous deeds, nobility and loyalty, a brotherhood of perfect knights slaying evil dragons. The mess and corruption, the foulness, the hypocrisies – these were products of the past, to be done away with. Meanwhile we wallowed in them. 'But we must keep ourselves pure.' To keep pure, one had to practise the great and noble ancestral virtues, 'only these can save China'.

Dear Uncle,
  As I told you, I got an offer to work in a governmental military hospital for wounded soldiers, but conditions for a woman there are quite impossible ...
  There are no 'nurses', only prostitutes, kept for the officers, not the soldiers. The soldiers die like flies. There are no medicines, no doctors, no care at all ...
  There is lots more to tell you ... please reassure my grandfather about my being here ... It is most worthwhile for my education ...

In the restaurants of Wuhan, with the menu, another bill of fare comes automatically; a sheet bearing serried rows of small numbered photos, each one the face of a girl. You pick the one you want, tell the waiter the number, the girl will come and sit with you at your table. Later this is also found in Chungking, with additional descriptions of each girl's charms, her name, her price ...

On the night of October 11th, Pao and I are told that in spite of the slogans, the marching, the patriotic speeches, all that glitter of torch-light processions and the brave acclaims we saw and heard only last night, in spite of the government's solemn utterances, Wuhan was not to be defended ...

I cry: 'It must be, it *must* be defended. Wuhan must be defended ... '
Have I not seen the parades only yesterday, the banners: KEEP WUHAN, RESIST TO THE LAST, and everywhere today: WHO HAS MONEY GIVES MONEY, WHO HAS STRENGTH GIVES STRENGTH. And in the parade the schoolchildren, the shopkeepers, the merchants, marching, the floats, the firecrackers, the people shouting, and today the volunteers, hundreds of them, marching out to the front ... this cannot mean nothing ... But it does.

The person who tells us is Pao's uncle, General Tang; a quiet man, shrivelled and reserved, with a thin, aquiline face; in later years he will sink into sadness, neurasthenia, go to his office in Chungking, sit at his desk, a fixed, rigid posture, and close his eyes; he is out of favour with Chiang Kaishek, he is bypassed, for he is honest. In his heart he has given up, he knows the regime is doomed, but he is not ready to sell his country for Japanese money, as some of his superiors are doing. Despair is his, unrelieved by personal cupidity, and he is unsuccessful because he has no tricks. His career wanes and disappears, and he is later impeached by Chiang's secret police for 'lack of loyalty', which simply means that someone wants his job, and he is removed. By 1941, Pao his nephew will be more influential than his uncle General Tang, who is not 'in' with the Blueshirts, with the secret police. Ill-placed, in a disjointed time, General Tang fades away ... only to reappear in 1965, in New China, as vice-governor of a province, for now a man's worth is not judged by the intrigues he can carry out. That day in Wuhan, October 1938, it is General Tang who murmurs with a delicate distant look that 'it may not be necessary to hold Wuhan.'

On October 15th Pao and I were married. The ceremony was performed by the Reverend Dr Kent, a clergyman, also a member of the Red Cross. One of the witnesses is an aircraftman, an overseas Chinese whom we call Ah Huang, who becomes our best man between two bouts of malaria. Another is an officer, all in a black suit with a felt hat, a Colonel Pei, fat and short, whom I later learn to hate for he is from the secret police. All doubts are submerged that day, in the emotion I feel; at least, in the devastation, the corruption, the grimness, we would stand together, Pao and I, we would fight all this together. It was only temporary, a passing phase, an effect of the war ... there are also *good* people, one must have faith ... and then I hear that Canton, too, has become 'unnecessary'. Just as Wuhan is now 'unnecessary' to the prosecution of the war, Canton will fall ...

The offensive of the Japanese against Canton started on October 12th; on the 21st Canton was taken, even though there were two hundred thousand Chinese troops there. On the order of Chiang Kaishek there was no resistance, they were withdrawn.

The Japanese attacked both by land and sea, thirty warships sailed up the Bocca Tigris, twenty thousand men landed. Forty-three thousand Canton volunteers put down their names to fight for their city, but the officials were fleeing, no one would give them weapons. The bridge which spanned the Pearl River in the city was bombed; on the afternoon of the 21st, Japanese motorized units entered Canton. By this action Japan placed her military power in position for a thrust, three years later, upon the British colony of Hongkong.

The newspaper in Wuhan denounced this manoeuvre of Japan as the initial step of a war upon South-East Asia, but no one paid attention, least of all the British. They felt so secure, they were a power, a White Power, and Japan had her hands full in China ... she would not be so foolish as to attack the Empire ...

It now seems odd that I should have begun work at the missionary hospital and continued for the next few days, while Pao left Wuhan. The confirmation of his appointment to the General Staff had come through and he boarded the boat which took the General Staff away towards Changsha on October 16th. Many units of the Red Cross had already left for Changsha on the 15th while we were getting married.

The next day, I remained, Pao left ... even today it sounds incomprehensible. Perhaps because the banners still exhorted the people of Wuhan to fight to the last drop of their blood, because the people were still there, and I simply could not believe that Wuhan was being abandoned. The General Staff was leaving, Pao was leaving, but volunteers with sticks in their hands (they had no rifles, and they were sent to the front to be mown down, unarmed) paraded through the streets on their way to war ... WUHAN MUST BE DEFENDED TO THE LAST still floated in great pennants in the streets. I remember protesting. 'But the people don't know that the High Command is retreating ... the government cannot abandon the people ... not without warning ... '

'There have been warnings,' said Pao. But there were not: definitely not until the 18th; and so I did not leave, I stayed after Pao had gone, working, walking in the streets, looking at the city, now emptying of vehicles. All remaining trucks, lorries, carts, wheelbarrows were being commandeered by minor officers and bureaucrats to transport them and their families to safety. An eerie thing, a city emptying itself. And still at night the families with their children walked in the night air and talked and laughed. The river was high, by day an enormous mile of glistening yellow water furling and unfurling, and the docks were crowded with bales, boxes, machinery ...

During those few days, at the hospital, I learnt a little about the wounded soldiers. How ill fitted I was to care for them, knowing so little about nursing, about really caring for people. Their faces stick in my memory, especially that of one man whose bandage I did so badly that it came unwound, and the way he laughed at me, his broken arm dangling, remains distinct and sharp.

The newspapers on the 17th had leading articles on the heroic battle of Tai Erchuang, won, in early spring of 1938, by General Li Tsungjen, provincial militarist, over the Japanese, and claimed there would be another Tai Erchuang victory at Wuhan ...

'China is finished ... she cannot last more than three months ... Wuhan is the end ... ' so said the missionaries in hushed tones at the Red Cross hospital ... We gather for tea; the International Red Cross committee people here have no connection actually with the International Red Cross of Geneva; they are primarily foreign missionaries, British, American, Canadian, organized in local committees. That is why the missionary hospital where I work is well supplied, has a good stock of medicines and equipment. All foreign relief is received by Christian mission hospitals, the Chinese Red Cross and the Chinese army hospitals get nothing at all ...

The talk is nice, guarded, careful ... no criticism. Malaria is bad in the army ... but everyone has it ... 'Be sure to let down your mosquito net, Mrs Tang' (that is me, I am now Mrs Tang). Malaria decimates the armies, and so does dysentery, but worst of all is 'they don't get enough to eat.' 'Have another cake, Mrs Tang.' There is quinine on the black market. We skirt the issue, genteelly. After all, no one can criticize overmuch in time of war, such things do happen ... The Indian National Congress has sent five Indian doctors, and somewhere up north there is also a Canadian doctor, Norman Bethune, but everyone talks of something else, for Norman Bethune is a communist, is with the Red Army, and the foreign missions do not want to send supplies to Norman Bethune who is 'Red' ... It is dangerous to speak of that other side, that other front, in the north-west ... There is a New Zealander called Rewi Alley, who used to be a factory inspector in Shanghai, he came through here some time ago ... 'He thinks that there's a future in industrial co-operatives in the interior,' says someone, who tries to explain to me about co-operatives ... 'and there is also a woman called Agnes Smedley, she was here, she left for Changsha two days ago ... the day of your wedding, Mrs Tang.' There are only a dozen well qualified doctors in the entire Chinese Army medical services; Dr R. K. S. Lim does his best, does all he can ... but there are no medical supplies and no food; the soldiers die like flies ...

One of the missionaries thinks it is all over now that Wuhan is being given up. Matron carries on, unruffled, splendid, starched, crisply abiding no nonsense. 'Well I must get back to work.'

Again I walk the docks and watch the queues, miles long, waiting for passage on the ferry boats. All night and all day the people wait. Tickets have been sold weeks ahead ... By now all motorized vehicles have been commandeered and the last lorries rumble away with small mountains of furniture, private possessions of government officials. There are no lorries for the people, they will have to walk. On the 18th began the exodus of people, people, walking, walking away from the city, miles and miles of them, walking away. I hear the dry click of wooden shutters slid into place, and the sudden night quietness in the daytime streets. I become a little worried ... supposing Wuhan *did* fall (though I still could not believe it), then what would happen to me? I did not want to spend my life in a Japanese-occupied area ... I dropped a hint about it to Matron. She said: 'Have another cup of tea.' She was not worried. England was not fighting Japan ...

I went to the ward and saw two girls, soldiers; one of them had her leg torn to shreds ... She smiled, her face was round, her round eyes were so full of life ... I wonder what happened to them ... The Japanese bayoneted wounded soldiers whenever they found them. They had done so in Nanking, killing all in the hospitals there, all the wounded, and the Chinese nurses and Chinese doctors too ...

On the afternoon of the 18th I went to the docks and saw Ah Huang, the best man at our wedding, supervising the embarkation of machinery on to a river steamer; factories were being dismantled and shipped away. 'Where are you going?' 'Ichang, Chungking, Szechuan province, and all points west.' When he heard Pao had gone and I had remained he stared, malarial eyes birdlike, the brown iris drowned in an overall yellowish tinge, probably thinking: 'Well, what does she expect? She's probably been had and that's that.' But he was polite. 'Well ... if I had a wife I'd keep her with me. This place is going to be damn unhealthy pretty soon ... '

I bought the newspaper, the *Ta Kung Pao*, October 18tn, 1938. It had a stirring message 'for the soldiers', promising 'resistance to the end'. Inside it announced that the printing presses were being moved to Chungking in Szechuan province, and that this was the last issue from Wuhan.

I told Matron this and she became rather cross. 'The Generalissimo and Madame Chiang Kaishek are still here,' she says ... 'I was having tea with Madame only yesterday, so there is nothing to fear ... '

I think: 'It's all very well for them; they are big shots, they can commandeer any aeroplane, anything ... and the Matron is a European, the British are not at war, nor the Americans. They are neutrals. They are sure to be all right at least for the moment. But I am Chinese. I know what has happened in Nanking. And I do not believe in the protection of the whites. I have just come back from Europe, and I know how Spain was let down.' This is something which excites rancour among the young officers, such as Pao, that the British and Americans are making open deals with the Japanese.

The United States has not seen fit to stop selling arms and scrap iron and petrol and machinery to Japan, nor to declare itself other than 'neutral' in the conflict between Japan and China ... Chiang himself deals, not so secretly either, with the Japanese, but the young officers are angry with the foreigners.

'One day we shall make friends with Japan, and kick all the whites out of Asia.' 'Why should we fight Japan? It is England and Russia we must fight ... ' This kind of talk I hear among the officers, even in those very few days in Wuhan.

I go to see Dr Kent, the clergyman who married me ... 'I do not want to stay if the Japanese come ... I have not returned to China to spend time in a Japanese-occupied city.'

And Dr Kent does help. He goes inquiring and finally gets me a berth on the International Red Cross boat, which is due to leave on the 22nd for Changsha. It is the last boat, and it has, in fact, been commandeered by a government organization ...

'Only when I see the buildings blow up, dynamited so as not to fall in the hands of the Japanese, then it will be really true, that Wuhan is given up ... ' But the buildings are not blown up. The explosives have been defused by British and American businessmen, who remain and hope to do business with the Japanese when they take the city.

On the 21st, after midnight, I am awakened in my hospital room. It is Pao, who has returned to fetch me. Suddenly he has realized what we have done, so unthinkingly. 'But you are mad, Wuhan is being given up, the Japanese will take it, this is retreat.' General Tang, his uncle, said this to him when he saw him without me on the General Staff boat going to Changsha. It then became real to him that he had left me behind in Wuhan, and that pretty soon the Japanese would be there. 'Stop the boat!' he screamed, but already the boat had left shore and could not stop. Two days later, at the first river station where the boat moored, he got off and returned by road to Wuhan. And this foolhardiness – for that it what it was – what he had done, for me, confirmed that he was splendid, marvellous, that there was no one like him, no one so brave, risking his life to come and fetch me ... I did not expect so much ... I expected to get out by my own efforts ... On the night of the 22nd we set off together on the Red Cross boat, the last one to leave before the boom was put across the river to 'stop the Japanese'. But it did not stop the Japanese.

The Red Cross boat had been commandeered by the Three Principles Youth Corps, a government organization, and there was Madame Chiang herself, supervising the embarkation of a host of young girls. At that time I revered her, she was a heroine to me – for that was 1938. And this year, 1967, in America, she has been making speeches calling for bombs upon her own country, her own people.

On October 25th the Japanese entered Wuhan. A motley collection of turncoats, prostitutes and others greeted them with flowers and banners. Wuhan was not a blasted metropolis but almost intact, and the Japanese set to work immediately, proclaimed a 'government' there, and started hunting down communists.

But in the countryside, the Red guerrillas were coming out of hiding, digging up their concealed weapons, organizing the people ... the countryside surrounding the treacherous cities, enveloping them, to conquer them in the end ...

Three

Letter to Hers dated October 28th, 1938
                         Nanyu, near Hengshan, Hunan Province

Wuhan became impossible on the 21st, I stayed on till the 22nd. Madame Chiang Kaishek made the Three Principles Youth Corps evacuate on the 22nd night, we left with them on the International Red Cross boat, going to Changsha, in Hunan province. We had no light and no food for the last two days on the boat. In Changsha bombing went on every day; we did not stay there long, and we shall be here perhaps a month at the most, and then we evacuate again ... The Military Headquarters are in Hengshan, also here in Nanyu ... only a few miles away from Hengshan ... a small place, in the mountains, no electric light, no telephone, no railway, deep in the mountains, but such beautiful scenery, so wonderful ...

On the 22nd, day of our departure from Wuhan, bannered slogans 'KEEP WUHAN', 'SWEAR TO DEFEND WUHAN TO THE LAST', still hung stolidly in the morose, hushed streets, the wind flapping them in a clap clap call to arms; 'volunteers' still marched to the 'front', to death, the wounded were still in their beds, they were not evacuated on the Red Cross boat. A hover of silence lay below the shuffle of feet, the endless shuffle, four hundred thousand feet going away, in long long centipedal files of porters with their bamboo poles and the bundles at both ends, swinging with that eternal rhythmic step that porters had all over China; accommodating their shoulders, their flesh and bone, to the rise and fall of their load. They were like water, like streams, fluid, relentless, untarried, unquenchable. There were no rickshaws. The flags on top of the buildings were being hauled down, one by one.

It took three and a half days by boat to reach Changsha, capital of Hunan province on the Hsiang river. Mooring, on the landing docks one saw only disorder and confusion. The loss of Wuhan had set up a panic here; the refugees who had been in Changsha for a while were now leaving and collided against the refugees coming into Changsha from Wuhan. These would stop and ask: 'What now?' The others would reply: 'Changsha not safe, walk farther, walk farther, farther west ... ' Whole families exhausted with walking lay with their bundles in the clogged streets or by the riverside, mopping their faces, dipping towels tied at the end of a pole in the stream; they lined the roads and the river banks as far as one could see. Yet in the middle of this chaos one could discern, after a while, a direction, a pulsation. A gigantic worm was moving, on and on, day and night, despite those that sat, that waited, that stopped, that lay dying or just too tired to go farther, that ran in contrary directions. There were millions taking to the roads, going out of the city, spreading into the countryside, westward.

I think that there must have been twenty million people then walking on the roads of the central provinces, and the Japanese strafed, machine-gunned them, just as in May 1940, in France, the humanity-clogged roads were strafed by the Germans.

And everywhere in the midst of the clatter and rumble of army lorries and jeeps and trucks going away, the pertinacious silence of people, shouldering this staggering burden, an enormous retreat, and going on, going on living, resisting. For if the generals and officers would continue always to be the first to flee, commandeering all that was on wheels to get out, the people would always be the last, and would have to walk, and even then volunteer corps would remain, to fight on ...

At night the dust was so thick one gorged on it, it became part of one's skin and mouth and hair. We took rickshaws from the landing quay where we came off the boat to the railway station, but the special train in which the General Staff was conveyed to its new headquarters in the mountains at Nanyu and Hengshan had left that afternoon. Pao should have been on this train, but he had returned to fetch me, and now had to rejoin the General Staff on his own. 'There is a train to-night,' said the station master, but there were no tickets. The station was a refugee camp; whole families waited on the various platforms, they had been waiting for trains day after day; there was only room to sit, not to lie down, and the day before yesterday's train would perhaps be in tonight. But there was no train that night. And after waiting some two hours we went back to the town. The roads were ploughed mud and dirt. Carts dragged by men, the ropes biting into their shoulders, went by; trucks piled high with bedding, furniture, wash-basins in netting, oilcloth bundles, all of it rolling and heaving; buses loaded so heavily they overturned; and people, people plodding on, carrying their children and their face-towels and mugs for drinking and a blanket. And of course Pao had a friend here, whom we woke up and who gave us an introduction to another friend, who was asleep but woke and told us of an army lorry, leaving early that morning.

Now I sometimes think that all these friends, all these 'benevolent brothers' (as Pao called them), were underground agents of the Blue-shirts, the secret service. I shall never know exactly, and at that time, of course, I did not ask; and had I asked, Pao would not have told me any more than that they were his 'brothers', meaning schoolmates, members of the same group ... But to me Pao was a hero, who had returned to fetch me, risking his life for me. When I thought of it the tears came to my eyes, no one else had ever done so much for me ... So I followed him happily, while the brotherhood of the Whangpoo clique, or the Blueshirts of Chiang's secret service, found us a way. Later, so many of them remained behind to try to sabotage the Revolution of 1949 – almost three hundred thousand of them.

Our rickshaws pulled us to a hotel. A small filthy room, a huge wardrobe, behind which stood a brown glazed earthenware jar with a wooden lid which was the toilet. There was a bed, with a dirty pink satin quilt and a thick mosquito net which as we shook it exuded dust and singing mosquitoes out of its folds. At five in the morning we were awakened by a truck hooting outside the hotel, and by the hotel waiter who called us. It was an army lorry, covered with olive-green canvas against the insidious wetness. Inside, ammunition – crates of bullets, piles of grenades – and four large men ... We insinuated ourselves under the canvas, and that was when I began to abandon luggage. I had already left clothing and books in Europe. Pao had left four trunks of his belongings at the Bank of China in Hongkong. I had two suitcases with me, but their contents were unsuited to the purpose of running away from an invading Japanese army. As a refugee, I should have had a small enamelled washbasin, two towels, a bar of soap, a small light quilt, some oiled canvas for use as a mackintosh, for rolling my belongings into, and for spreading on the ground to lie on, some rope to tie the lot, or a large net, a change of clothes, two pairs of tennis shoes, a tin mug (for drinking and toothbrush purposes), and of course a roll of yellow straw paper for the toilet; all this in one bundle, weight 20 lb., to be carried by one person, myself. But I had two woollen suits, a fine cotton dress, underwear (bought in Hongkong), a bathing suit (now why did I take a bathing suit with me?), a Cantonese oilcloth Chinese dress bought in Hongkong, my blue silk wedding dress, two blue cotton dresses made in Wuhan by a Chinese tailor who made dresses in four hours; stockings; leather shoes ... One by one, I abandoned these on the roads or in the hotels in the next few weeks. I began with the bathing suit which the hotel waiter received with a sleepy puzzled grin, for it was of no use to him. It was like giving a pair of high-heeled pumps to peasants dying of starvation, or dropping candy to napalmed children – imbecilic gesture of the nightmare unawareness which dogs us all.

There are so many temples all over the mountains here in Nanyu. Some of our *highest* commanders are *meditating* in them

... the place is getting much overcrowded. By great good luck I got a hotel room at sixty cents a day. There is no electric light, no water, but if someone *very high up* is living in a temple, and generals go fighting each other for a five-dollar-a-month village room, why, I feel aristocratic. It is wonderful, and you would have a good laugh, seeing all this and thinking: 'well done'; all these people who had houses in Nanking and Shanghai and what not, running hither and thither; living on the countryside, squabbling for the meanest room ... And their wives? Most of the wives of the highest officers are not here, because they could not stand the conditions, they are too well bred, they cannot 'eat bitterness'. Only the secondary rank wives, and the concubines, are here ... I manage with an extra tip to get hot water twice a day. I wash in two basins of water. I bought white cloth for sheets and some blue cloth for a quilt, the tailors have come here too. I enjoy myself ... the climate is splendid, the scenery is wonderful ...

Yes, Nanyu was lovely.

The great north-to-south Imperial highway paved with enormous blocks of limestone runs through it, for Nanyu was a fair centre on the road from Canton in the south to the Yangtze River cities – a road used by cavalrymen of the dynasties and the chariots of officials for many centuries – and a place of pilgrimage. The beautiful Sung dynasty bridge which spanned the lovely river, with its tributary torrents leaping from the mountains, had seen the tribute of salt and grain pass over it, and silk for the Imperial Courts in Peking from the fertile provinces of central China, and fighting men and refugees had walked it many times. It had served the cohorts of the peasant uprisings in Taiping days, those peasant fighters marching up the road through Nanyu to Changsha and onwards to take Wuhan, a century ago. Above Nanyu towered the many peaks of the Hengshan mountains, among them the most sacred of the southern holy summits, Tu Yun Feng. Large Buddhist temples, red-walled, golden-roofed, of graceful proportions, surrounded by centennial trees, glowed purple and amber, and their magnificence compared to the diminutive and poor village of Nanyu was a perpetual astonishment. The temple nestling at the foot of the slopes had been repaired during the Ming dynasty, and now served as a military training centre. Hengshan, the major town, a few miles away, had a China Travel Service hostel, white, clean, now filled with ministers, department heads and top officials. Among the mountain temples lived what I had called in my letter to Hers 'the Highest', meaning Chiang Kaishek, and the dignitaries of his government and the General Staff. We were glad of a room in the Great Nanyu Hotel, which was in the valley at the foot of the mountains; a rickety sprawl of wooden buildings near a stream, over which were built the public privies. The frolicsome autumn air and the sparkling torrents redeemed their pollution. Our hotel room was dirty; in the three weeks there I cleaned it many times, for some meticulous streak always makes me conduct such forays upon dirt, as if the imposition of housekeeping hands could make the world a more orderly place; but so are many women made, who derive great peace of mind from the mechanical actions of cleaning and scouring. The secondary wives and the concubines in the other hotel rooms, however, were far less obsessed; they looked with astonishment at the freak, me, cleaning her room, then adorning it with pots of fuchsia and chrysanthemum, when everyone knew that very soon, very soon, perhaps next week, perhaps tomorrow, we would have to leave. The reputation I gained was not to my credit; it was accounted 'foreign' and 'strange'. Besides, I was actually doing manual work, and doing manual work lowered one's rank ... was I then of servant origin? The self-esteem of many of these women resided precisely in their infinite capacity for living in slothful filth; they would leave heaps of chicken bones on the table, and churchfuls of flies buzzing litanies round their heads did not distract them from the delights of entertaining. They threw orange peel and chewed fruit over the floor, and taught their children to defecate on the verandas. They would not lift a finger to clean, but called the servant to do it. And here was I, even cleaning the window-sill, and tacking newspaper over the empty window-frames. The wives peered, and played mahjong; expectorated, and laughed, while they pointed me out to their children. But the young waiter, who at first had grinned, was now my friend, and brought us hot water and eggs, and even occasionally swatted flies. I did not care about the laughter, I thought it did not matter and just went on in my own fashion, buying flowers instead of buying food. But Pao was not laughing, and pretty soon I too was not laughing any more.

48

(undated)   *Nanyu, Hengshan*

Dear Uncle,

Now I have to realize with great bitterness that we have lost the war through bungling, treachery, cowardice, and that good wills [*sic*] like mine can do nothing ... No girls dare to go in the wounded soldiers' hospitals. No girls at the front line now, except communists ... And there are no more soldiers, only mobs ... the soldiers are dead ... there are only people running away ... No Chinese administration hospital is working properly. The Red Cross trying to do things for the refugees, but it is a drop of water in a desert ... China needs rightly trained people in the right place ... everybody is in the wrong jobs ...

But the next day, a change of mood occurs.

I thought I would feel strange after three years away, but I feel more at home, being here in the countryside, than before ... I am in excellent health ... I will try to get back in time not to waste a school year. The most important work I can do for China is to study; Pao says that Madame Chiang has asked all who can, to get out ... Write to Mrs Tang if you write. Better not ...

Bizarre as this conflict of moods may seem, and especially the last words, I was only reflecting the confusion of Nanyu.

For it was in beautiful Nanyu that the schizophrenic domesticity of my life with Pao started. We were eating lunch provided by the hotel. I do not remember what we were talking about, but suddenly Pao said, 'Women must not argue. You must not argue with me. You must listen to me. And not answer back.' I stared at him. Had we really been arguing? I did not think so ...

Then followed a long monologue. I was too European, I must learn to become more Chinese. People were talking about me. They called me 'mixed blood'. The country could only be saved by the practice of ancient virtues. Chiang Kaishek had said it. I must also learn these Ancient Virtues, and one of them was obedience. 'A woman of talent is not a virtuous woman.' I must be a 'virtuous wife and an exemplary mother'. And therefore I must never contradict anything he said. 'To contradict your husband is a sign of immorality.' 'Immorality? But Major so-and-so, who came yesterday, brought a sixteen-year-old niece with him ... you said yourself she was his fourth concubine; that's what I call immorality ... '

Pao's hand hit me across the face, from the opposite side of the table. 'Talk about others, look at yourself. You dare to answer me, to answer me.' I said wonderingly: 'You hit me, you hurt me ... ' He said: 'You hurt me too, how do you think I like it, that I have married someone not a virgin?'

I became angry then, at the same time as I felt ashamed, and guilty. It is difficult for a woman not to feel guilty about such a thing, in spite of all the talk of sexual freedom and equality for women. Of course I knew that not to be a virgin at marriage was something shameful, although it did not apply to the factory girls, raped and at the mercy of the foremen; nor to the brothels such as the ones now opening in Hengshan, where eight-year-olds served clients like the generals of the General Staff. The double standard in all its absolutism – chastity for women, and whoring for men – was Ancestral Virtue.

The more the whine of virtue, the bigger the boom in brothels. And the slave girls, bought from the peasants, and the 'borrowed wives' of the quartered officers – these also did not qualify for chastity, for virtue ...

'But you knew it, Pao. You knew I wasn't a virgin before we married. We stayed together for weeks before we married and I told you ... '

'You told me! You had the face to speak of all this; to me, as if it was a normal thing for a *Chinese* girl to have to do with a white man, a "foreigner"! Look at you, you do not keep your eyes down when you look at a man ... Last night Major Chang and Captain Wang came to call, and you talked and laughed with them, as if you did not know the difference between man and woman ... '

'But they are your friends ... '

'My friends, of course they are my friends, but their wives don't behave like that ... '

'That's true ... their wives shout at the servants, and scream, and leave everything filthy and play mahjong all day.' I was angry. 'And you said yourself half of them were only temporary wives, on loan ... '

'But they never had to do with a *foreigner,* with a *white man* ... I don't care if you had affairs with ten ministers, twenty high officials, if they were Chinese. But a foreigner, a foreigner ... ' Xenophobia in full spate, characteristic of the Whangpoo young officers, of Chiang Kaishek himself; on a par with the notion of woman as property. That past of humiliation and despoliation and slaughter which was the imprint of the West in Asia had left an inverse racialist complex among the Chinese upper class, manifest by this tremendous resentment; especially in the domain of sex, where woman is considered as a piece of real estate. But with Pao, as with all the young officer clique, xenophobia was not only resentment, it was also a convenience, for it permitted them to find scapegoats for their own betrayals and to preach 'national salvation' along the lines of a deep and morbid racialism.

The courtyard was quietly blossoming with strolling women, ears pricked upwards. The wooden structure of the hotel was so flimsy, the cracks, both in the walls and the floorboards, so large, that everything could be heard. In spite of my trying so hard to be like others, I could never be like those women around me, and this unlikeness persisted; I liked cleaning things too much, I liked walking about alone, I read, I wanted to work in a hospital. Thus began the pattern of my next seven years, and added to the torment between Pao and myself were the many small viciousnesses, furtive malices, a continual and merciless mosquito buzz, which hardly ever stopped, for since Pao himself had started that endless and uncertain cruelty it was only too easily, too soon, that many others would join in the baiting, the nastiness.

It was only after Pao began to abuse and ill-treat me in front of others that one or two returned students from Europe, who had seen me with Louis, added their dash of colourful venom. Who could or would pity me? Many must have thought I had tricked Pao into marriage; I offered to let him go free, I begged him to let me go, I was not claiming anything, I merely wanted to go. But this he would never agree to. 'I don't understand you,' I cried. 'If you think I am so wicked, why don't you let me go?' But this he would not do.

Now I walked into Nanyu village, climbed the hill slopes, watched people working, away from the malicious 'brother officers' and their temporary wives. There were carpenters, and tailors, and bricklayers, and porters, and haulers of water, and carriers; the young waiter who so painstakingly looked after our comfort, and the heavier older man who swept the courtyard and sang between his teeth:

> 'Arise, who do not wish to be slaves,
> With our flesh and blood
> Let us build a new great wall ... '

And the men who repaired the roads sat nursing mounds of small stones between their legs, the echo of their striking hammers filled the warm translucent air. They did not laugh at me, they glanced, and then went on working, I did not feel they were malicious. And what they sang was not quite the song the benevolent brother officers would appreciate. The officers' wives played mahjong and spat and stared and sneered when I returned from my walks.

The day after this outburst Pao was charming; it was Saturday, and we went walking hand in hand in the golden afternoon. Only a very small numbness in me remained, and then my natural bounce took over, laying forgetfulness, elastic like new skin, over the wounding event. Not long brooding, I do not dwell overlong with sorrow, there is always so much to learn, to do, and I want to go on, to go forward, always. But a few days later it started all over again, more prolonged, and worse. Then again it subsided. Pao spoke mournfully of having to leave me, to lead soldiers in battle. He talked bitterly of defeat, of having to give up. 'There are no more soldiers.'

An important military conference was taking place in Nanyu ... any moment, said Pao, he would be on the battlefield ... my heart winged to him, the hero, suffering for his country in her defeat and her humiliation ... I could forgive everything, in a man so young, so good, so determined. What did a little brusqueness matter? So many had suffered, while I had a good time in Belgium ... and as for virginity, yes, it was my fault, all my fault. Of course it was, why had I not waited till Pao came along and married me? I would strive hard, make up for it, be good, and never complain.

Another day Pao told me that I should go back to Belgium to study. Madame Chiang had made a speech, advising those who could do so to get out, to study, to prepare themselves for 'the re-conquest' of the land, he said. And a few members of Madame Chiang's family had already gone to America, to 'study'. I wrote to Hers that I might have to return and study, since China was defeated, and Madame Chiang advised all those who could to go abroad, study, prepare themselves. Pao himself might now be sent abroad, he told me, to plan and to wait for revenge ... But a day later this was no more the case. We were all staying here, we were going on ... And so from day to day the news changed as the high military conference proceeded, and Pao, reflecting the rumours that went round the General Staff, every day made me a different speech ...

And then another crisis occurred after a picnic on Tou Yun Feng, highest and most sacred peak of those sacred mountains. One lovely day we went to visit the monastery on its top; climbed up the pilgrim stone steps, worn with use and time. The day shimmered with light so pure, so transparent, it was like a song to breathe. We carried oranges; the high blue sky was daubed with a deeper blue as the day wore on, until the violet night came dancing upon the slopes. When I think back to that loveliness my heart still lightens with its beauty.

We had company on our climb; a Miss Lu, her fiancé a Major Chang, and others who worked in the General Staff. We arrived at the Buddhist monastery, ate supper there, a vegetarian meal, while the Abbot discoursed to us. We heard the wind all night mourning among the peaks, and saw the sunrise; and on the road back met strolling towards us General Feng Yuhsiang, Vice-Chairman of the Military Council. Feng Yuhsiang was also at that all-important conference which was going on; accompanied by two bodyguards, he paced the mountains between sessions.

Then Pao became moody, and suddenly he started again, upbraiding me on my behaviour. Why had I begun to speak to the Abbot, to the other men? 'Look at Miss Lu, she never said a word. She was chaste.' ('She's sleeping with her fiancé,' I retorted.) 'But she's going to marry him, there will be no other man in her life,' shouted Pao. (He was to be proved wrong; Miss Lu's fiancé was to change his mind, she became someone else's wife, and lived happily.) Pao had just driven me to tears with his shouting when a drone, at first confused with the sound of the torrent's streaming waters, made the air vibrate about us and the sky was speckled with Japanese bombers. We ran to hide, while they spilt their silvery load and the mountains reverberated with the roar and thud of the explosions. We scrambled for cover, one of our company hiding in a small public latrine; after the bombers swept away we could see the village of Nanyu under a pall of dust and smoke. The large temple which served as a training camp for soldiers had been struck; shattered yellow-tiled roofs, splintered trees, corpses of men, a direct hit, and the dust still hanging its dimness widely in the air, and the shouting and screaming and yelling, raucous, continuous as we left the slope and emerged in front of the temple. I said without thinking: 'Perhaps we can help to carry the wounded.' Pao turned on me, white with fury: 'You are mad ... a good woman would not rush like this ... Do you like men so much ... you cannot bear not to touch

them ... you want to run after them ... your place is with me, to prepare food for your husband ... your husband.'

We walked towards the hotel. Our room was littered with debris
from the bomb blast which had shaken the hotel. I cleaned, finding the
waiter's broom. Pao flung himself on the bed. Later he went out. I
trimmed the wick of the oil lamp, hearing from the other rooms the
sharp click of mahjong and the shouts and laughter of the other
women ...

The next day, there was talk of the General Staff moving, going to
Kweilin in Kuangsi province, since Nanyu was no longer safe. The
Nanyu military conference came to an end.

On November 12th the city of Changsha was in great part destroyed
by fire, not started by the Japanese, but by the Kuomintang themselves.
In their absurd 'scorched earth' policies, with unnecessary destruction,
more harmful to their own people than to the enemy, they laid waste
and desolation about. Thus, in the spring of 1938 the Yellow River
dykes had been breached by order of Chiang Kaishek, to flood the
land and to stop the Japanese. It had not stopped them, though it did
flood the land, and a million Chinese peasants were drowned.

And now again, 'strategic destruction', needless, militarily incomprehensible. Chiang ordered the burning of the city of Changsha, and
a large part of it did burn, and hundreds died and thousands became
homeless in the conflagration. Later the responsibility was placed upon
a man called Hsu Peiken. He had made one big mistake; he had also
fired the aeroplane fuel stores, which were not removed, at the airport.
This enraged Chiang Kaishek; petrol necessary for the aircraft which
conveyed him about was far more precious to him than men. Hsu
Peiken was cashiered, and only escaped because he was a protégé of
Tang Tsung, the No. 2 man of the Secret Service. The Staff was upset,
but chiefly because of Chiang's fury; they did not know whether he
would shoot some of them as 'examples', for the loss of the petrol. Hsu
Peiken was jailed for a short while, but I was often to see him in
Chungking, squat, rolling his eyes, and expectorating loudly.

Actually Changsha was burnt because there was an active communist underground in the city; it was also rumoured that the secret
police wanted to kill Chou Enlai, who was there at the time. The
whole area was alive with clandestine guerrillas; Changsha had been
the headquarters of the underground Communist Party for some
years. And Mao Tsetung had trained a good many people there.

I did not know that not many miles from Nanyu, across the river, was the county of Chaling, where the first local Red government had been established by Mao Tsetung. Beyond Chaling was the massif of Chingkangshan, Well Ridge Mountain,* where the first Red Base had been founded in October of 1927. No wonder the man sweeping the courtyard sang:

'Arise, who do not wish to be slaves ... '

Nor did I know the full significance of the military conference which had taken place in Nanyu. Officially it was announced that the decision 'to continue fighting' was taken then by Chiang, though wispy gossip insisted that peace negotiations with Japan were still going on.

The fall of Wuhan, then Canton, after that of Shanghai, Nanking, left the Kuomintang only two main city bastions, Chungking and Sian, in the western part of China. All the seaboard was lost to the Japanese. Would there now be capitulation? Negotiations?

Chiang Kaishek and his wife, Feng Yuhsiang, T. V. Soong, H. H. Kung, Ho Yingchin, a dozen ministers and sixty generals were in Nanyu, and out of the confused rumours the only clear thing was the wrangling that went on. Why did Madame Chiang Kaishek urge all those who could do so to 'get out and study'? Why had Wuhan been relinquished without much fighting although fifty thousand volunteers were recruited and sent, unarmed and with no food, to the front? Was it true what some benevolent brothers hinted, what Pao came back mouthing one day, 'better the Japanese than the communists', and that there were negotiations with Japan?

Pao would not tell me what was taking place in any coherent manner, but would only make sweeping statements such as: 'We must now all go to die on the battlefield, I am prepared.' This indicated that those officials in the Kuomintang party who wanted peace with Japan were not in the ascendant, and that Feng Yuhsiang had strongly urged continued resistance. When Pao said: 'Better the Japanese than the communists,' on the other hand, it meant that those who wanted to negotiate with Japan were winning. And Japan's terms were the

*See *A Mortal Flower*.

permanent satellization of China, under cover of an 'anti-communist alliance'. I felt that the people of China wanted to fight on; that they would not dream of accepting a 'peace' with Japan; I told Pao and he laughed: 'What do you know of such things? Why don't you care about womanly things instead of bothering about political issues?' and lectured me on my immorality and lack of virtue. 'A woman of no talents is a virtuous woman. Look at history. Whenever women have been in power the Empire has fallen.'

Besides the Kuomintang military and governmental apparatus at Nanyu, there was also present the brilliant, treacherous Wang Ching-wei, holding the sinecure post of vice-president. Wang started as a revolutionary student by throwing a bomb at the regent of the Imperial Ching dynasty in 1909. The revolution of 1911 occurred and Wang Chingwei attached himself to Sun Yatsen; he was credited with having drafted and written some of Sun Yatsen's speeches for him, and also taken down Sun's dictated testament. This gave him the status of 'favourite disciple' when Sun Yatsen died in 1925. He challenged the growing military power of Chiang Kaishek, also a 'disciple' of Sun Yatsen; but Wang's motives in setting himself against Chiang were based on personal ambition and not principle. In the 1920s he was considered left-wing, when he joined the left-wing Kuomintang government in Wuhan, opposing Chiang Kaishek's military coup d'état in March and April 1927. Soon after the Chiang-arranged massacres in Shanghai and in other cities Wang capitulated, and also joined in massacring the communists, ending up by being more anti-communist, if that were possible, than most of his right-wing colleagues. His ambition kept him restive, plotting and intriguing. The blandishments of the Japanese militarists then preparing to conquer China appealed to him; in his opportunist vein, he claimed that Sun had laboured for such an 'understanding'.

The Japanese government, in 1938 and 1939, expounded an 'Asia co-prosperity sphere' in which China and Japan 'together' would rule Asia, after throwing out the white man. Wang adopted this thesis, and came to the Nanyu conference to urge an alliance with Japan.

The Japanese after October 1938 wanted a stalemate on their extended China front, while they prepared for the conquest of South-East Asia. After the fall of Wuhan and Canton they were ready for consolidation; and if during that inactive period they were able to manoeuvre China on to their side, their dream of the conquest of Asia would be infinitely nearer accomplishment. But the Japanese military demanded too high a price for 'peace' – no less than what amounted to unconditional surrender; and though Wang Chingwei and Ho Ying-chin and many others strongly pressed for acceptance, Chiang Kaishek realized that accepting those terms would mean his downfall. Never, as Feng Yuhsiang told him then, would the people of China accept the Japanese conditions.

For the war of resistance to Japan was one which the people of China supported with all their might. Even Chiang had to say it in his speeches: 'This is a war of the Chinese people ... this is a people's war,' adapting phrases from Mao Tsetung. The volunteers who came forward to defend the cities were not sham; they were not Kuomintang-inspired, but United Front, or communist-inspired. To make peace with Japan on the terms offered meant a partition of China into three, i.e. Manchuria (renamed Manchukuo, and under Japanese control since 1931), North China and South China; it meant the Japanese garrisoning all China's main cities, and controlling Hainan island, as well as Formosa. 'This will make my name stink for ten thousand years,' said Chiang. 'The Japanese demands are completely unreasonable.' And some of his generals concurred. In any negotiations Chiang had to take into account the other front, the communist-organized resistance to Japanese invasion, whose heart and centre was at Yenan.

This resistance was one which was continuous, consistent, and which, coupled with social reforms, was rallying the population behind it. Should Chiang appear to capitulate to Japan, it was Mao Tsetung, and no other, who would emerge immediately as the only hope, star and salvation of the Chinese people.

The Kuomintang front had been a wholesale debacle. At Nanking, in December 1937, Chiang had ordered resistance, the only time he really threw into battle his own crack divisions, only to have them slaughtered; after Nanking's fall he would never use his own troops again. At Wuhan in October 1938 another stand to the last had been proclaimed, but the city had been relinquished ... Now the Japanese controlled all the seaboard, all the railways, all the main cities of China, except for the far western provinces and the Red Army bases ...

On the communist front the strategy had been different; though pitched battles were also fought, it was mainly guerrilla war, protracted war, the strategy enunciated by Mao Tsetung. In the north-west, Lin Piao was to gain the most important victory of that early part of the conflict, at Ping Hsing Kuan, in the autumn of 1937. The battle of Ping Hsing Kuan actually changed the course of the war in North China, for it denied to the Japanese entry into the north-west and thus safeguarded a very large area; it also set down a foundation for a long-term plan of infiltration, the building of Red bases in the countryside behind the Japanese lines. Manchuria was to become the key strategic area for the civil war which followed in China at the close of the Second World War in 1945.

By the end of 1938, Yenan, the great Red Base, was more than just a military outpost, it was a shining beacon of fervour and patriotism, attracting students and intellectuals from all over China ... If Chiang gave in to the Japanese, the prestige of Yenan would sweep the whole of China, irresistibly.

On July 7th, 1937, the Japanese, who felt the stiffening resistance, had made an attack at Lukuochiao, six miles from Peking. The 29th Army fought back, on its own, while for days Chiang hesitated, and in a mountain resort debated with his high commanders and officials whether to fight or not. But at the Red Base at Yenan everyone was mobilized for the war of resistance, and all China was ringing with voices demanding full military support for the 29th; demanding a United Front with the Red Army at Yenan. No longer, this time, as in 1931, 1932, 1933, would the Chinese armies that fought Japan be sabotaged by their own Supreme Commander, Chiang Kaishek. On July 17th Chiang issued a four-point statement declaring that 'the final stage' had come, that China would have 'to fight to the utmost, or perish for ever'. This statement was described by Mao Tsetung as 'the first correct declaration on foreign affairs' which Chiang had made for many years. But it was not till September 22nd that the formation of the United Front was ratified, although the suggestion had been made by the communists the year before and was supported by all the people of China. In August 1937 the Red Army was reorganized into the 8th Route Army and 30,000 of its 40,000 men left Yenan to fight the Japanese.

Thus two mutually antagonistic forces had entered the war against Japan. The first was the Chinese Red Army built up by Mao Tsetung, steeled by the Long March, and, since the invasion and takeover of Manchuria by Japan in 1931, the growing symbol of patriotic unity, resistance to Japan, and social change.

The other force was Chiang Kaishek's government, built upon a party called the Kuomintang. An array of bankers, landlords, groups of military men, joined by circumstance into a hegemony, it disposed of large armies, and an ever more formidable secret police.

From the beginning there were two fronts, two battlefields. The two armies faced the Japanese invader in different parts of the country, operated in different ways,, dictated by their distinct composition, political tradition, and military experience. At the end of the war there were still two armies, two fronts, two battlefields; but the balance of power had changed in favour of the Red Armies and against Chiang Kaishek.

The slogan of the Red guerrilla was: 'Get to the rear of the enemy, disrupt his lines of communications, organize the masses, make them politically conscious, so that the guerrilla lives among the people as fish in water, and the enemy does not dare to trust anyone.' The essays on 'Protracted War' and on 'the War of Resistance against Japan' written by Mao Tsetung gave all the elements of the strategy and tactics practised against the Japanese from 1937 to 1945.

Lin Piao's victory at Ping Hsing Kuan not only opened up the way for guerrilla infiltration and a people's resistance at the rear of the Japanese lines, and stopped the Japanese forward movement in the north-west, but also produced a consolidation, at least in appearance, of the United Front; it was impossible for some months for the pro-Japanese group round Chiang to press for negotiations with Japan. Communist-trained cadres poured into the enemy rear; from Yenan mass organizers went into the countryside to form anti-Japanese associations of peasants, students, merchants, women and children, and to create guerrilla detachments of young men and self-defence militia corps of older men and adolescents; 'as fish swimming in the ocean we move about among the people freely, by organizing and training the people we automatically eliminate traitors; we rest in the hearts of the people.'

By October 1938, the 8th Route Army was already pinning down twenty Japanese divisions by its operations.

The United Front was always a precarious affair. Eight months after its inception all progressive youth organizations were made to register; many were banned by July 1938; all students were ordered into the anti-communist Three Principles Youth Corps, set up on June 16th. Chiang lectured on the responsibilities of China's youth; the Ministry of Education proclaimed that university students were too valuable to be expended in war and must 'reserve themselves for national reconstruction'. This was actually a mobilization of the young in order to counteract communist influence.

In mid-October 1938, Chu Teh, commander of the Red Army, together with Chou Enlai, flew to Wuhan 'to obtain a better implementation' of the United Front; Chiang demanded greater control over the communist 8th Route Army by his Military Council, and the talks were inconclusive.

In November 1938, Mao Tsetung, in a warning that the Kuomintang was considering treachery, and had not allowed the United Front to assume an organizational form which could be implemented, made his famous speech on the need for armed vigilance:

> Since 1911, all the warlords have clung to their armies for dear life, setting great store by the principle: Whoever has an army has power. Chiang Kaishek values the army as his very life, he has created a huge central army, for counter-revolutionary purposes. He has held firmly to the vital point that whoever has an army has power and that war decides everything ... in this respect we ought to learn from him ...

This was the crux of the matter; civil war against the communists, or a continuation of resistance to Japan? At Nanyu in November 1938 many were in favour of fighting the communists first, peace with Japan, and a grand anti-communist alliance. 'In a hundred years, Japan and China will be one country, and then we can truly be masters of Asia,' said Ho Yingchin and Wang Chingwei, echoing the Japanese militarists.

But Japan would be sure to favour Wang Chingwei, their faithful disciple ... on the other hand Chiang could not let Mao Tsetung become the sole champion of resistance against Japan. In the dilemma facing Chiang, a policy had to be devised which while seeming to continue the war of resistance, would prepare for an internationalization of the war, and for diverting to himself the fruits of victory, by promoting the attrition of the Red armies, and destroying Mao Tsetung's base at Yenan ...

Hence the slogan was put out of trading space for time. The scheme was ostensibly to go on fighting, but not to abandon negotiations with Japan; and at the same time to check the growth of Red Army power.

This decision was reached at Nanyu on November 12th.

PART ONE: 1938–1942

On November 13th, Chiang and his wife flew to the new bastion, Chungking, 'capital of Free China', together with the higher officials, while the General Staff left for Kweilin on November 14th by train, thence to proceed to Chungking. Heady with enthusiasm at the decision (as it appeared) to fight on, I wrote: 'So long as there remains one Chinese alive to say like Chiang Kaishek: we will not yield to armed force, because we refuse to recognize the power of such force ... nothing can conquer us ... so long will China remain free ... '

I did not know that it was not heroic defiance, but a series of careful calculations, well ordered perfidies ... The joy that was mine was an illusion; it was an illusion shared by a good many, who honestly believed Chiang meant to fight.

Wang Chingwei, apparently defeated in his peace proposal, left for Chungking. There was no role for him there in the shadow of Chiang Kaishek. In December 1938 he was invited to give a lecture to the military academy in Kunming; a plane was provided for him to go there. Tai Lee, the head of the Blueshirts organization and Chiang's Grey Eminence, was at the airport to wish him 'bon voyage'. Wang found it surprisingly easy to flee, to escape from Kunming and to go to Hanoi, where Chiang sent a secret agent, ostensibly to assassinate him. But he only succeeded in killing Wang's secretary. From Hanoi, Wang went on to Shanghai; he was well received by the Japanese, and in 1940 was installed as president of a Japanese-controlled government of South China, with its capital in Nanking. The Japanese had another puppet, Ying Jukeng, as president of a government of North China, with its capital in Peking. Manchuria had been turned into the separate state of Manchukuo in 1934, and there Puyi, the last of China's last Imperial dynasty, dethroned by the revolution of 1911, reigned as emperor.

Wang Chingwei's 'flight' was interpreted by some Western observers as a stratagem, a Chiang manoeuvre to get Wang on the Japanese side, thus letting him carry the onus of 'treachery'. The secret police head Tai Lee would now secure contacts in Nanking and Shanghai through Wang and his friends ... Thus ended the brilliant opportunist, the unscrupulous Wang Chingwei. A photo showed him being received by the Japanese General Toyama, and presented with a sword. He wore a European cutaway with a shiny top hat and white gloves for his inauguration.

☆

The front manned by Chiang Kaishek's armies was to remain quiescent for the next three years; until 1944 there would be no major Japanese offensives, only skirmishes with provincial armies, certainly not fighting between Chiang's carefully preserved divisions and any sizeable Japanese forces. Most of the Japanese military effort switched to the other front, the communist front whose great base was at Yenan.

In spite of the agreement that weapons, money and other supplies would be given to the 8th Route Army, the Kuomintang began to shut off all supplies in early 1939. In 1935 Chiang had posted the officer he considered most promising, Hu Tsungnan, to the north-west province of Kansu. In 1937 Hu Tsungnan was assigned control of the whole north-west, and from 1939 to 1945 Hu was to establish a formidable blockade round Yenan, with trenches, fortifications, and blockhouses – a real Maginot line. The best equipment, the best divisions (500,000 men), the best of supplies (received from Soviet Russia and later from America) went to Hu Tsungnan for the only war that Chiang really cared to fight: the war against Mao Tsetung. Hu Tsungnan's troops never fought any Japanese.

The conference at Nanyu which initiated these long-term plans also reduced the number of steps in the chain of command, as it had proved too cumbersome. This had the effect of bringing into power more of the young officers, the secret service and the Blueshirts, and thus directly affected the careers of such men as Pao, who found advancement far more swift than they would otherwise have done.

A campaign against progressives began again. By early 1939, the political department of the National Military Council formed to 'unify' all patriots, had been purged; the Third Bureau, or propaganda department, employing some left-wing intellectuals, including Kuo Mojo, the writer, was shut down. Chou Enlai, then communist representative acting as liaison officer with the Military Council, was deprived of all real functions. Secret instructions were prepared on how to isolate 'traitors with dangerous thoughts'. Raids on bookshops began again ... In March 1939, some officers of the New Fourth (communist) Army were seized and buried alive ... Families of communist officers, in Szechuan, were killed by secret service men ... Censorship, gradually more oppressive, clamped down upon the newspapers. From that time onwards, the United Front existed only in name.

☆

Two perspectives for China became delineated, and their unity was impossible since one automatically abolished the other. One was the perspective of true resistance to the invading Japanese armies; abandoning any idea of being able to live in submissive peace with the aggressor; mobilization of all land, sea and air forces and of all the people in a people's war, and self-reliance on the strength of the Chinese people themselves, until ultimate victory.

The second was a policy of prevarication, compromise and concessions towards Japan; hope of aid from the Western powers; maintenance of the ruling groups in their immediate moneyed interests; and civil war to 'eradicate communism'. This was the policy Chiang Kaishek followed.

By December 1938 the communists had already set up four major anti-Japanese bases in the north and two subsidiary ones, later to be developed as full bases, or liberated areas, elsewhere.

In North China, two large bases in Shansi and in the Tai Hang mountains had followed the victory of Lin Piao at Ping Hsing Kuan.

In Central China, the New Fourth Army base, of special significance later in the war, was already active.

In the south, the fall of Canton in October 1938 produced a guerrilla anti-Japanese force, to be known as the Pearl River detachment. Their nucleus was formed by guerrillas from the Red Army who had participated, eleven years before, in 1927, in the Canton commune during the heroic days when Chou Enlai, Yeh Ting, Chu Teh and others fought there so gallantly, against enormous odds. The reprisals by the Kuomintang at Canton were frightful, yet some of the Canton fighters had escaped, 'gone to earth' and survived. Now, they reappeared, joined by students, labourers, and overseas Chinese from Hongkong, also stragglers from the Kuomintang armies that had abandoned Canton to the Japanese, and volunteers from the city itself. They dug out of the ground buried arms, took some weapons from the retreating soldiers, and formed the Pearl River detachment. They started off with only eight guns which worked, but they never let up attacking the Japanese. By the end of 1938 they had grown to five thousand men. By the end of 1939 they had liberated an area of two hundred thousand people.

A Red nucleus was established in Hainan island, and maintained all through the war. After the invasion of Hainan island on February

10th, 1939, by the Japanese, it was decimated, but never stopped fighting.

From 1939 to 1945 the conclusive test of strength between the two ideas, the two perspectives, was played out. And the great power of a people's war was proved, where the people, mobilized, educated, become politically conscious, accomplish miracles of fighting by their own volition; where they are the 'water' for the guerrilla 'fish'; where every man, woman, and child is a combatant.

The song of the guerrillas, composed in those years, sang of this power:

> We are all experts with the gun,
> Every bullet gets a foe,
> We are the army with wings,
> Unafraid of high mountains or deep water.
>
> In the thick forest, everywhere
> Are the shelters of our comrades,
> On the highest ridges and summits,
> Are our numberless brothers.
>
> Nothing to eat, nothing to wear,
> But the enemy gives us food and clothes.
> No guns in our hands, no bullets,
> The enemy makes them for us to use.
>
> We are the people who were born here,
> And every inch of ground is ours.
> If anyone wants to invade it,
> We shall fight him to the death.

But of guerrillas there were none to be seen when, in the usual tangle and chaos, laden with equipment, furniture, files, clothing, the General Staff of Chiang Kaishek and their families, including several hundred women, of whom I was one, left Nanyu like a hiccuppy, overladen mob of stragglers. Today, I wonder about those who remained, more vivid to me than the colonels, the brigadiers, the generals – our young waiter, so helpful and so guileless, and the not-so-guileless man sweeping and singing 'Arise ... ' Perhaps they were also guerrillas. I hope they became guerrillas when, in 1944, the Japanese came down to Nanyu at last.

Four

Dear Joseph Hers,

After some bombing by Japanese planes, we left Nanyu on the 16th of November, and reached Kweilin. The trip took a long time, by rail; by great good luck we got a small room here in Kweilin. Everyone seems to be here. People say: 'Consult Chinese history, and you will find the next move.' What does that mean? It usually means Szechuan province; going to Szechuan is probably the next move and that means Chungking ... No way of getting anywhere, communications impossible, but I am fed, my health is good, and I am learning about my country and my people. Luggage is a problem, I am throwing away more clothes, I spend my spare time studying ...

Dispiriting the total disorder during the journey from Nanyu to Hengshan and on to Kweilin, and all its minor horrors piling up to a niggardly miserableness; appalling the amount of space taken by the furniture of officers and their families, while refugees huddled on the carriage roofs in the rain, or fell off in a trance of exhaustion, or were pushed off because they were dying of typhus or malaria, or simply because they tried to relieve themselves and were too weak to grip. At every station were refugees, a flux of close-pressed heads and bodies, a swarm, spreading outside the stations' barricades, moving to storm the platforms and climb on to the trains and beaten off with truncheons, pushed off and still flooding back. The millipedal processions of porters carrying the files and papers of the General Staff in large baskets slung over their bamboo poles went on and on. The train crawled, halted for hours, for days. We spent four days and nights in the barn of a rich peasant (rich by Chinese standards, which was not much), with rats running over us while we slept; all of this but an insignificant detail among millions of such, and we were the privileged ones who would not die on the roads. And the rain, the raw gusty rain, still a boon, for the almost daily bombing raids would now stop. Throughout the four days at the farmhouse, Pao and I had no quarrel, but we had not been an hour in the train – which finally arrived, and which we got into, as well as thousands of others,

assaulting every carriage, clambering and clawing up on to the roofs
or clinging to the windows – when Pao began to shout at me, heedless
of those who listened. Since we were two to a narrow wooden bench,
with two facing us, in a railway carriage which housed eighty-seven
people, with no privacy at all for five days, everyone heard and saw
everything.

Why did Pao make scenes in full sight and hearing of so many? He
later seemed to choose restaurants, parks and other public places to
shout at and even to strike me. He loudly complained now that my
immorality, my unchastity, and the fact that I was a Eurasian would
make him suffer in his career, which – he told the eighty-five others –
was jeopardized by me. He then recapitulated all the virtues: Courtesy,
Uprightness, Integrity, Sense of Shame, Loyalty, Brotherliness, which
were to bring about the National Salvation of China. It was fantastic,
and even then, slightly comical, but I could not afford to laugh. He
then asserted that gentlemen like himself were loyal, that China
needed more like him; that I had 'thrown away the face of China'. It
was people like me who had brought China into her present peril.

After a few hours of this ranting, a refugee on the roof urinated and
the urine trickled on to me: 'Look, there are your people, there on the
roof,' I cried, and Pao became furious and went up and hit them – I
felt really criminal then.

Reviewing the meteoric rise that was Pao's later, I realize now what
nonsense it was; but I was all he feared and disapproved of, all of me,
body and spirit, and yet the hypnosis of hatred and love gripped and
tormented him, and he reacted by extremes of passion and resentment.
He thus suffered awfully, implacably, needlessly, in a grand Victorian
Confucian tragic mode; and since the last thing he had was a sense of
humour, he remained immersed in the abysmal tragedy of his love and
his loathing. When after an excess of brutality, having cried my fill, I
would burst out laughing, he was deeply insulted. And so often, in
spite of my unhappiness, I also thought him pathetic, my own situation
so ridiculous! Laughter hurt him most of all.

He was intensely race-conscious, and I was the perpetual reminder
of a national humiliation which now sought to reassert its pride
through an inverse racism. I provided Pao with the splendid opportunity of working out his complexes through those archaic platitudes
which, according to Chiang Kaishek's feudal precepts, would save the
country. He took it upon himself to reform me, remould me, change

me into a paragon of all these bleary virtues which were only real in their wordage, and this moralism, linked with ambition, and politics, he was to exercise upon me for years, exorcizing out of me wickedness, immorality, foreignness ...

Loyalty to the Leader, unquestioning obedience; 'the relationship of husband and wife is that of superior and inferior, master and servant' – thus says Confucius; all these puerile degradations, erected into virtues by the patriarchal feudalism of China, would, if practised devoutly, save China from the dangers which attended her. On and on went our train to Kweilin, on and on the hours, on went Pao, working himself into a frenzy talking of virtue and tradition, until he subsided through sheer exhaustion.

I was then only at the beginning of this harrowing season, and when the train, five days later, arrived in Kweilin, we staggered out, I nearly stuporous, Pao silent at last; but not for long. Then came two weeks in beautiful Kweilin, capital of Kwangsi, the most lovely landscape in the world with its marvellous mountains jutting sheer out of the earth, scooped out with caves; its extraordinary emerald-and-sapphire river swishing over rocks, its fishing cormorants; and its Miao people, the sturdy working women with silver bracelets and silver necklaces, handsome men with silver buttons on their vests. Kwangsi province was supposed to be a 'model' province; it was run by Li Tsungjen and Pai Chungsi, two warlords, often at odds with Chiang Kaishek but at the moment supporting him because of the war. It had a large proportion of Miao people, whose women were not as oppressed as those of the Han Chinese, because they did not have Confucius upon their backs. Shortly after our arrival the Japanese staged a bombing raid on Kweilin, and in the crowd stampede, crossing the bridge to take refuge in the mountain caves, I was pushed off, and Pao rescued me from falling into the river.

And so again I was captive, and guilty; bound by my own beginning confusion, fettered by Pao's tortuous 'reasoning' in which nothing mattered but correct thinking according to the precepts of Chiang Kaishek, and linked to Pao by patriotism, gratitude, marriage and love.

In Kweilin I roamed, purchased some old books and brought them home; poetry, *The Three Kingdoms* ... I began to practise calligraphy. 'I am learning my own language,' I wrote to Hers. Pao took the poetry books away: 'It is not good for you ... you are already too romantic,' and left me only *The Three Kingdoms*, which he of course knew well, for he often tried to identify with one or another hero of the book, particularly in their loyalty to their liege lord.

After a week in Kweilin we began to be bombed every day by the Japanese, though with the mountains and their natural caves around the city, there was easy shelter; but there was no respite from Pao's lecturing, from his relentless preaching, from his beginning brutality. Changed and remoulded I would be, in spite of myself – but though I bent and swayed and wept and was contrite, and always he would press relentlessly on, expounding, preaching – an interminable loudspeaker that could never be turned off – in the end, I could not be changed.

November 25th   *Kweilin*

Dear Uncle,

I wrote to my grandfather, but I am not writing to Louis, now I will tell you why. I want to go on studying, and be a doctor, and be useful to China, but I was wrong, being a Chinese girl, to have anything to do with a foreigner. In China, a woman alone has no chance at all, especially in war time. You did not realize what I was going into. I have now a chance to acquire again my reputation, Pao says. Pao is not a modern young man, he studied in England, at Woolwich and Sandhurst, and before that trained in the old ways. He believes in virtue and has an old-fashioned family who have a great tradition of morality. He has will power, and he came back from England to join in this page of history, and he tells me, against the will of the people over him, just as I did ... he is doing his best, and so am I. He knows all about my past, my errors, my faults. We can work, we are young, China needs us. He says China needs us, and that whatever our faults, our hearts are pure. He says he wants me to change and to learn ... read the old books, and history. He has no money, but he has lots of things before him. He says we must have plans, and I must be a doctor, and we will eat any amount of bitterness, but we shall win out. He is ambitious too, he says if things go on as they are, people like us will be crushed in China, and all will be hopeless, but if we stand together there is a hope ... He says Chinese youth is looking for leaders and he can be one if he gets a chance. Pao says he wants to send me back to Europe for safety, but I don't want to go; I have too much to learn about my own country ... Of course now we are stranded ... we live in common with a lot of people, there is no means of conveyance, we may have to walk to Chungking, but I am not afraid. I am very strong. Pao says in China I have no chance to stand up, a girl, with my looks, my life story, without somebody to protect me. He is much in love with and wants to protect me. I can help him tremendously because he says he will need a wife who can speak foreign languages, and be taken out in society ... he says he needs somebody who can help him build up China's future armies and comfort for China's soldiers and peasants. We must be an example ... it will be hard for me, very hard ... I wrote to my grandfather but there is no answer ... tell me if he is all right ...

Here, in this confused letter, lies the core of Pao's ambition, the reasons why he kept me on, and a hundred contradictory but dove-tailing details; as I re-read it, I understand his mind, my own bemused bewilderment, and how I was to serve his ambitions, once I had been properly remoulded into a docile, obedient instrument.

In early December we left Kweilin, to proceed by bus on the mountainous roads through Kwangsi and Kweichow provinces, to Szechuan province. 'Szechuan is my father's province, I have a family in Szechuan,' I told Pao. We were now crossing the backward regions, as they were called, the hinterland of China, and very few of the people from the coast cities had ever been there. There were many areas full of non-Han people, those called national minorities, the Miaos and the Hueis, the Yees and the Lolos; living on the mountain plateaux, often at war with the peoples of the plains. Tall and ruddy, buckwheat-eating, with strong direct looks, hunters and not rice-planters; some were at more primitive levels, others possessed relics of the matri-archal system. Thus we crossed the enormous south-west of China, and as we went on, the terrible poverty was so immediate, a physical stunning, a degradation so violent and obvious that even Pao commented on it, but attributed it to 'lack of virtue'. Wrecks of humans, derelict villages amid the mountains, broken by imperious torrential rivers, and everywhere opium.

It was on this journey that Pao's friends began to tease him about me. When we stopped at night they would comment aloud on my looks ... 'There is foreign blood in her, one can see that ... '

'Not at all, she is pure Chinese,' retorted Pao. As if it was not written on my face that I was a Eurasian! I knew better now than to contradict him, but he would be furious with me, as if my face were my fault. 'But why do you tell lies?' I said. 'If you told them to mind their own business, would it not be better?' But this would not do. Pao forgot that his public scenes had given the signal for the corrosive persecution I was now to suffer. My face. My looks. But the journey was so physically trying that in the sheer need for surviving on this contorted road which twisted and careened up and down valleys and slopes, in a bus which pelted along and shook and swayed, the deft insults of other bus passengers were soon forgotten. Instead of becoming exhausted, I now began to thrive; for I was young, at the age when tragedy leaves no wrinkles, and after a good cry, my face would blossom again, and there was so much to see, to know ... A woman grudgingly told me how fine my skin was, and my hair; and this too must have made for gossip.

Pao's 'benevolent brothers', in spite of all the talk of brotherhood, were all vying with each other in order to succeed, trying to give others an evil repute in order to boost themselves. 'There are only two ways to advancement, one is to build your own reputation, like a mountain, and stand on it; and the other is to dig pits for everyone else to fall into, so as to appear the only one without fault.' This was a common saying; 'and the second way is easier than the first.' To have good repute *(min yu)* for oneself, and give others bad repute, or cause them to lose face *(tiu lien),* was therefore the essence of social ability, the technique of power, the strategy and tactics of the protracted war each conducted for his own advancement. With what eagerness did benevolent brothers tell discreditable stories about other absent brothers! Pao would laugh with the rest, and I would think: 'When he is not there they talk about him, about me ... ' My looks, and the fact that I was a 'returned' student, an asset for Pao, encouraged their sniping. Within the bus, hypocrisy, a fetor-like halitosis, was with us all the time, a gagging stupidity, both acceptable and accepted, meat and savour of social contact. It wholly dazed me, so that I felt unreal; only the beautiful, violent, ruined country our bus gouged into was without viciousness, while calculating malice built its wordy citadels of petty pain within the hurtling shaky vehicle. When a kind word was thrown my way, at evening, I clung to it. I could not understand that we should not help each other, but already in the train part of our discomfort was due to the irresponsible selfishness of all, in using the toilet, in leaving bones, fruit peelings, on the floor, in caring only for oneself, not for others. And here, too, it was so. Few would help anyone else. But they would while away the time baiting each other, baiting Pao and me. Their wives would lead me on, amiably, to talk. I would give opinions, be listened to, apparently with sympathy, and then would come the crafty, deadly blow ... How could any woman have so much *strange experience* ... the outrageous phrase, like a slap on a candle, would extinguish my candour and Pao would do the rest.

Thus I knew spirit sapping, and knew it of small dimension, but of disproportionate effect, like the constant drip of water on one's forehead, hour after hour, like torture by pinprick; and thus can understand today the agony of those who, subject to the constant mass-criticism meetings, hour after hour, day after day, week after week, commit suicide. After the first few days the physical discomfort was so steady that in the bus no emotional outburst could be pursued for very long. Pao had to close his eyes not to be violently sick. But at night, in the inns, he would monologue for an hour at a time, calling me names before falling asleep. I thought: 'It will be better in Szechuan ... in Szechuan, I shall find my family.'

During this trip I sometimes vomited out of the bus window, but chiefly suffered from a capricious, intermittent haemorrhage which had accompanied my journey since Nanyu. Yet I looked well, and staring at the mountains that sparkled in the morning sun marvelled at how magnificent China was, how gorgeous; some day, I thought, all this will have to be put right. But who was to put it right?

On our journey towards Chungking one evening we met a truck-load that had gone ahead of us, young officers and their personal effects, on the roadway by their overturned conveyance. The driver had been speeding, in the manner of all drivers, like a drunken cyclone whirling up the mountain road and down into valley villages; at a muddy turn in the sleazy rain this one had overturned his vehicle in a deep pothole. No one had been killed; the young officers inside had merely been shaken; some crockery broken, some of the baskets with their household goods spilt ... but a collective madness took hold of them. They felt the indignity of having been physically upset and thus

71

losing face; it was too much for their querulous dignity. They laid
hands on stones and broken boulders spilt from the weathered rockface, tumbled down the mountain slope, and they stoned the driver to
death. Now his corpse was there, a wilted, quiescent heap, stone for
pillow and coverlet; and the truck was still overturned, sprawled like
some uncouth dead monster; the young officers were waiting for ours.
We could only load up with some of them. The next truck, behind us,
would take a few more.

Fortunately that night there was a village a mile or two beyond; a
dreadful village of opium smokers, derelict hovels, walking skeletons.
The corpse by the mountain road had subdued Pao, made him
thoughtful; he suddenly turned to me, fierce and loving, only to be
interrupted by the shrill laughter of a woman peeping. And this, for
him, was akin to losing face again. Out of the rain and the darkness,
the great night upon the mountains, floated a white nebulous haze. I
dreamt it was the stoned driver floating with the opium fumes about
us, and the nightmare was in keeping with the whole of this fantastic,
grim ride to destruction upon which all of us were engaged. I still
wake up today with this nightmare carrying me back, back to the
mountain slope with the cold night vaulting, and the fatuous murderers
and their giggles. Like an incantation, I repeated to myself in the days
that followed ... 'But it will be better when we get to Chungking ... it
will be better ... '

Then one afternoon, five weeks after we had left Kweilin, we did
reach the Great River, King of Streams, the Yangtze, mighty and swift
and enormous, speeding its bronze tumult through rocky cliffs a mile
apart. High upon its rock, where the two streams that made the Great
River converged into one tremendous water, was Chungking, City of
Recovered Gladness, steep and arrogant on its cliff; and on the almost
vertical sides of the rock, riding two hundred feet above the water,
clambered a multitude of dim dark hovels on stilts, a brood of clams
to the tide-locked boulders. In the afternoon fog the city lay, grey and
nebulous smoke in its winter nest; a myth, a dream; a huge stone atop
some giant corpse. 'We have arrived ... we are here.' Everyone was
glad, happy. Some men sang, the women sighed with relief, kind to
each other, wiping their faces with their small towels and nursing
their babies and dabbing the vomit and the baby shit off their clothes.
'Things will be better here.' I was also cleaning my face, shedding not
only dust and dirt but a mind's stored bitterness. Of course it would be

better now. There would be a hospital, work to do ... Pao would be working, and in a better mood ... I would find my family, my large family in Szechuan ... perhaps they, too, would not welcome me ... but I would try, I would try hard. It was another world to conquer and now I knew how difficult it was. Once more I would try ...

Chungking in the darkness seemed great and noble as we went up the cliff, up four hundred and eighty steps of stone to where its streets began; there was new courage in the stones. This, then, was the centre of resistance against Japan; a noble and beleaguered city. I went up, with hope, also with my jaws set. 'I'll put up with anything, and see this through.' For I was young then, and had much life in me, and I was learning to hold on, just hold on, tight like those hovels clinging to the almost vertical rock. I would not let go.

Today at fifty, knowing how much I was cheated and how I cheated myself during all those years, I still have no regrets that I hung on, clam-like, like those dismal and hopeless hovels to the rocks.

Chungking was phantasmagoria, a monster, brusque chimera, an un-real and thorough freak; a fortress where trees could not grow on the inch-thin soil covering the rock. A city of squalor and filth, and with one of the most impossible climates on earth; a furnace in summer, in winter swallowed by unrelenting fog; and yet, for all its squalor, its rats, its misery, its desolation, its impossible cruelties, it was also mag-nificently, raucously alive, palpitating with the stolid triumph of its million people, whose sufferings seemed endless, whose courage, determination and forbearance towards gross injustice was the cindery mask over the flame that would one day devour all this structure of evil.

We arrived there on January 2nd, Chungking's depth of winter. Thick fog ate up the grotesque accretions of hovels which reminded one of all obstinate things, fungi, claws, moss, all macerated and shredded by ruin and by filth. The Great River was at low winter ebb, the elongated sandbank in its middle, named Shuang Hu Pa, which served as air landing strip for half the year, lay in pale-yellow smother in the middle of the flattened stream. The sun did not exist in the grey-yellow quilted air which wolfed the rock. We spent the first few days not knowing when to get up, as we could not tell the time of day, were exhausted with travel, and I with disoriented weeping. A perpetual greasy dampness clung to one's hair and skin. I had no proper clothes and I shivered much of the time, having discarded so much on the way. The haemorrhages had had their effect, which was to blunt the acuteness of distress, but rendered me incapable of fending off the cold.

The first two weeks were spent at an hotel, where rat hordes pounded the stairs in full gallop at night, and whores also arrived in their packs by day as well. The spitting and hawking, the gargling and expectorating, the raucous cries, the laughter, shouts, the noises of children wailing, the perpetual click click of mahjong games, the pails of dung outside the doors, I got used to within a day or so; but the filth of the jars used as women's toilets, big pots of glazed earthenware, with lids of wood, one to a landing, rather worried me, especially as the whores used them, and syphilis and gonorrhoea were prevalent in Chungking, due to the prevailing 'virtue' in its air.

I preferred the public cloaca, less suffocating because fog circulated through its rotting mat roof, and the pervious walls were clay dabbed on to plaited and split bamboo screens. There was no privacy, but there was none in the hotel either. A semi-diarrhoeic condition partly due to the food, partly due to the nervous strain imposed by Pao's bursts of anger, now afflicted me. I sometimes had to run twenty times or more in a morning, until I became so shaky that I feared, when squatting, a slide on the filthy mud floor of the cloaca might land me into the cesspool below.

By our fifth day in Chungking, Pao had succeeded in hitting me twice publicly, once in the Chungking park, and once in a restaurant.

The scene in the restaurant was bad; even the waiters tried to intercede, but only for a moment, Pao turning on them and shouting: 'I will get you shot,' which sent them away with an absent-minded air on their faces. The one in the park, which was a tight steep assembly of steps with a ludicrous monument in the middle, obtained for us a curious crowd, hastily self-dispersed when they noticed Pao's uniform; the mothers with children calling out, 'What are you looking at, nothing to see, nothing to see ... ' shushing and pushing and towing their progeny away.

January 3rd, 1939   *Chungking*

Dear Uncle,

    I hope you received my last letter ... marriage is awful and also wonderful ... Pao knew my past when he married me but now this is making our life hell on earth, he says he feels all the time deprived, and that he has lost all driving power (so he says) ... I am sorry, I wish it hadn't happened ... Pao's family is extremely virtuous, he says, he himself has a brilliant future, energy, intelligence, but he says that the fact that I have had a love affair with a foreigner is destroying everything. He can't get rid of the idea. He won't divorce me either. I offered to go away, or to commit suicide, but he says that would change nothing. Added to this, he says if ever he became a very great man, my past could always be brought against him. It would not matter if it had been a Chinese, but a foreigner, like Louis, he says it is worse than anything ...

Dear Uncle, I am not going back to Europe. Pao says he will punish me and the best punishment I deserve is to be tied down, with a baby, and not allowed to do anything. He says I have destroyed the face of China ... but he knew my life before we married, but now he says he is going to be sick and die of sadness because he cannot get rid of the idea. So the least I can do is to try to patch things up. He says I will never be able to work for myself, to make money. But I never wanted to make money, I wanted to work for my country, and he says the only way is to work with him. Of course it is hard, but I will try, if this is the way. At the same time, I do have so much to learn about China ...

I have to choose now, and I am choosing China, in spite of all this. But I have studied in Europe and listened to music, and read, and made friends there, and I know that sometimes I shall have times of blackness here, but I have to go on with this. Perhaps this sacrifice, to serve my country with clean hands, will help China one day ... Perhaps it was meant to be hard, like this, so that in the end I can render better service ... I don't know. I don't know. Perhaps I will have a child who will be able to do all that I have not done. Our life will be miserable because it is a soldier's life, Pao says, but I have never thought food or clothing mattered all that much. I know you understand ... Pao says that nobody must know that I have a drop of foreign blood in me. China may have made bad mistakes but for the sake of youth and the suffering and the innumerable lives that have been lost, what is this little sacrifice? At least my life, perhaps, will have contained a little righteousness.

I re-read this my letter, returned to me in 1965, and am wearily nauseated at the blackmail, blackmail of me. Pao took advantage of my feeling for China, and the fact that I was a Eurasian; and he beat me and terrified me and brainwashed me and there was no logic or reason in it; and this hermetic and silly martyrdom, of which even the retelling is otiose and odious, kept me tied down, hemmed in by trivial suffering for a long while, when all around there was so much that needed doing. One can bear a good deal for a cause one deems noble, sustained by the dignity of one's belief, sustained by group solidarity. But all this murky raging and frothing served no worthwhile purpose. I said to Pao: 'How can you deplore the mess the country is in, urge that we must all rally and do something for China, and then spend hours and days sitting here, lamenting your fate at marrying me and hitting me and lecturing me?' But this only produced a longer period of raging, and so I gave up talking and sat, mute, sullen, stubborn, receiving blows, and the effect of all this I was still feeling thirty years later, when, at the beginning of the Great Proletarian Cultural Revolution I once more heard the accents of a hyper-frantic moralism, recognized the tone, and nearly had a nervous breakdown.

Often now I dream of that birdless summer of my existence; hear the screams I heard then ... the shrieks of the pressganged conscripts in the conscript camps, those being beaten till they died; the panting breathing of men hunting the runaway soldiers, screaming, 't'ao pin, t'ao pin' (fleeing soldier, fleeing soldier), stomping away in the bushes, their flashlights eyeing the monster night; the strangely levitating corpse of the stoned driver, and so many others; and I am glad that revolution came, and that all this Himalaya of suffering upon the people, in which my pain was but a speck (and a worthless one at that), was not in vain.

But deep and tenacious are the roots of the past, and even in the New China, until after the Cultural Revolution exposed the pattern of humbug righteousness, I often heard, though in new guise, the accents and moral attitudes of the feudal mandarin; though the maxims appeared absolute contraries, it was the same tone, the same moralistic, Confucian absolutism. And I am glad that there is a Revolution to remake Man, beginning with Chinese man, to shake him loose from those millennial thought-ruts of the Bronze Age. It will be difficult, for even recently in China a communist cadre turned on me: 'With a face like yours, any *Chinese* child would be frightened of you.' And a friend, criticizing me: 'You are too stubborn, you don't bend, you must learn to bend,' using the same words, the same tone, as Pao did so long ago. I then return to the nightmare country, the roadside night, the hours and days when there was nothing real, only the vision of a far city, nebulous smoke, the vision of a corpse on the road.

I see again Colonel Pang, one of our benevolent brothers, tall, hand-some, polished, who stayed next door to us in the hotel in Kweilin, sat in the bus with us through that journey to Chungking. He had a wife, a meek, dumb, dumpy, scared being who had produced for him four male children; yet he beat her and kicked her into a faint almost every week. We could hear him, the noise was like pounding a mat-tress, except that the mattress occasionally whimpered. He tells us so himself, sitting so neatly in a chair, his uniform (made in Germany) sitting so well on him.

'I do not know why I do this. She is a good wife; she has given me four sons, she never answers back; she always waits for my return to eat, even if I have had dinner outside and come back very late. Yet I sometimes feel a mist of rage, suffocating me ... and I have to hit her. She never answers back.'

I listen to him; colour of his voice agreeable; he sits drinking tea, his fine brows slightly puckered, a little worried at this minor flaw in his character.

Pao laughs, points in my direction: 'Brother Pang, why worry? I do the same to her. She never answers back either.'

And there is the other benevolent brother's story, told me with such relish, so often, by Pao, that I might not forget it ... His wife had had a child and had gone with the baby for a few days to visit her own family. While there, she went to the theatre with a female cousin, the husband of the latter and their three children. During the intermission the woman cousin took the children to the toilet; leaving her husband and the woman alone in a theatre full of people, for a few minutes.

Somehow the story went about that this woman had gone to the theatre, alone with a man. It took only some weeks for the tale to reach the dimensions of a full-blown scandal.

One evening while playing mahjong with his benevolent brothers, the officer won a good deal at the game. 'You may be lucky in gambling but do you know that a green hat sits on your head?' said one of his friends to him. 'What do you mean?' 'What, he does not know that his wife is so fond of the theatre?' Loud laughter.

The officer returns home, tears his wife's hair, breaks her teeth, and puts her naked in a cage. These wooden cages, made with bamboo and barbed wire, were only big enough to stand in. They were used in the concentration camps, for communists, and also by the feudal landlords to torture the peasants who could not pay their rents. If one leans against the bars the barbed wire wound round the upright bamboo enters one's flesh. Into this cage he drove his wife and put the cage out in the street, for all to see. It took the woman some days to die of hunger; meanwhile no one dared to rescue her, no one dared to feed her, her baby was not allowed near her but kept shut up in a room with its wet-nurse. Her family tried to go to court but they were not wealthy or influential. 'She is only a borrowed wife,' says the officer, 'and she has thrown my face away.'

For the next three years I was to endure the growing terror, the increasing physical duress, which came in whirlwind fits. I learnt to wait out the hours of beastliness, counting, taking deep breaths, counting: 'There are four hundred million people in China, one, two, three, four, five ... He will get tired ... he will get tired of this.' Even when it lengthens, goes on for six, seven, ten hours or so, and I can neither eat nor drink but have to sit huddled on the floor waiting for the blows, only anxious that I should not be blinded or disfigured, only gathering all of me into a small, small ball inside, I would, as a litany, repeat: 'He will get tired ... he will get tired ... just a little more ... only an hour, two hours more ... he must get tired ... ' Sometimes I become quite weak, especially when I do not eat, but not eating is an advantage for then I float, oblivious to the sound of the loud voice which recites the virtues I lack so outrageously, retailing these phantasmagoric 'moral integrities' of feudal China, which The Leader, Chiang Kaishek, asserts alone could save China from all ills ... (and later, every time Pao said The Leader, he clicked his heels).

One occasion I remember well. It was in 1940, a year after our arrival in Chungking. Pao came home at noon, and I could see something was wrong. 'Come here,' he said. I stood by him. He sprawled on the bed. 'Is your mother a Jewess?'

'A Jewess? No, my mother is not Jewish. She is Flemish and Catholic.' The very thought of Mama being Jewish made me laugh; in that buoyancy which laughter creates, an ebullition which provided its own lightheartedness, I went on, forgetful of danger, 'Sometimes

I *wish* I were a Jew, then I would be so much more brilliant ... '

'What did you say?' Eyes wide open, shirt open, Pao lifted himself, in one of these sudden movements he cultivated which terrified me. 'You *wish* to be Jewish? You, you cheap thing, you don't want any face, you don't want any self-respect, you want to be a Jew?' He began rolling up his shirtsleeves.

'Well what is wrong in being a Jew? They are people like ... '

'Shut your mouth, or I'll beat you to death. You, the wife of a Chinese officer, you DARE to say you'd like to be a Jewess?'

On and on, unrepeatable. The Jews were filthy, vicious, sexual perverts ... they always wanted to defile sexually girls of good family ... I must have had a lot to do with Jews ... It was atrocious, unbelievable, and ridiculous; my breath came and went with much difficulty. I was very frightened. 'Someone today said you were a Jewess, your mother a Jewess from Poland.'

'She is not Jewish.'

The next day he brought me a copy of *Mein Kampf,* which was recommended reading along with Chiang's speeches for the military officers and the Youth Corps. 'Read this ... you'll learn all about the Jews. You must read it.'

And because I do not like to see books polluted, I said: 'I will not read it. You can kill me, but I will not read the book of a monster. I think Hitler is a monster and a pervert.'

This was my first small pitiful victory and it cost me dear; for months Pao would go on thrusting the book at me. 'I will win, you cannot mock me, I will break you,' he cried; but I did not read *Mein Kampf.* Then Pao, evening after evening, read passages out aloud to me; interspersed with The Leader's speeches, and Tseng Kuofan's moralisms, and extracts from a book entitled *The Thousand Virtuous and Chaste Widows.* It was a compilation of a thousand women who had hanged themselves, starved to death, or otherwise terminated their lives to escape seduction, or remarriage, or rape, and no distinction was drawn between these three. Their deaths had given their families and district great face, and memorial arches in their honour had been erected, because they had preferred death to dishonour. Whereas I not only had not done so, but I had *deliberately* made love, and with *foreigners* ...

This incident, many years later, was brought again to my recollection, in 1954, in Malaya, at a party. I was approached by Mr Fenner,

Superintendent of the British Special Branch, later Commissioner of Police, Malaya. He and another Special Branch officer manoeuvred me deftly into a corner, then started to question me:

'Did you ever go to Russia?'

'Russia, no, I never ... oh yes wait, when I was nineteen, I went through Russia via Trans-Siberian ... '

'Ah ha.' The two Special Branch men look at each other significantly, then: 'And did you stop in Warsaw?'

'In Warsaw, why, why should I?' I was puzzled.

Months later I knew the answer; in my files at the Special Branch, my mother was put down as a Polish Jewess; and myself, therefore, as suspect because of my mother's origin ... which only goes to show that the British Special Branch, at least in Malaya, was using the old (and incorrect) Kuomintang secret police files.

January 7th, 1939

Dear Uncle,

I have destroyed the face of China by allowing myself, one of China's best future elements, who should be a standard, and set a precedent, to have an affair with a foreigner ... I will never be able to work by myself as I want to, I wanted to work for my country, but the only way to do it is to work for Pao ... if he ever becomes a great man, he says my past can entirely destroy him; not a Chinese, but a foreigner, is worse than anything ... I have to redeem my wasted youth ...

The cry: 'You have caused China to lose face by what you have done' really hurt, it hurt, it hurt most then; and I wrote 'I have to redeem my wasted youth' as if I was forty-one instead of only twenty-one, as if it was my fault that I had not had a sheltered, protected adolescence, as if the chaos in China was my doing ...

And there was no way out; in Chungking least of all. In between the shoutings and the beatings, my head light with pain, with hunger, with cramps in my stomach, I walked the steep ladder-step streets of the city, up and down, down and up, in a shaky fog-numbed daze. Round the cliffs on which the city was built wound the main roads, on which went the cars of the officials, some rickety buses; and the *huakan* bamboo or wicker chairs borne aloft on the shoulders of two men, one in front, one at the back. And it was all my fault, my fault alone that everything seemed such a horrible mess ...

All around filth, brutality, beggary, the constant ha ha he he of the coolies, man-labour, carrying, pulling, tugging, carrying the war and the festering corruption of their masters on their backs, their flesh wasted, their muscles and eyes bulging with life-devouring animal labour, their breath gasping ha ha he he in the unrelenting sweat of the cannibal fog, exudation of their sweat oozing their life away. And their verminous rags were so appalling that even one used to rags, as I was, felt stunned by these shreds through which so often the buttocks were seen, pullulating with lice, sores of their sores, as if it was their skin flayed in these rags. And when they were jailed for 'immodesty' during the 'spiritual mobilization' drives, the sheer insanity of the whole system made one exhausted with hidden rage. I never saw, all those years, a single coolie in whole clothes, only gaunt faces, broken foul teeth, deformed bodies, bandy thick legs, the marks of lifelong misery, and also the marks of opium-smoking, the thick slow gestures and the heaving flanks, for opium eased their pain, the opium dregs they smoked hungrily, in thickset bamboo pipes.

When an important visitor came the police cordoned off streets to fling the beggars back, for the main roads must be kept clean; and the children, crawling in the tunnels of dirt from the hovels, picking their lice, were as grey as the rats which at night were clustered on the side-walks, and the rats ate the babies, the few mangy cats, and bit adults too.

And yet, in spite of this, in spite of this, what vastness, what sense of power from the grey and teeming life which laboured, laboured; even in the first two weeks, even in spite of Pao, I could feel it, the fierce-ness of the people, the stubbornness of the city, a pent-up strength like the power of the tremendous river, now at winter placid flatness but which would rise, rise, rise forty, sixty, seventy metres and bound and leap and carry all the junks upon it with their tattered tall sails at speed towards the down-river plains! And whirl away the derelict hovels, the piles of filth and garbage accumulating below the city walls in its spring destiny! It seemed to me then that the people too were like that, and upon me lay acceptance for the sake of this intangible tangible power, which at lucid moments appeared only a dream, but which clutched me entrail deep even then, through thick layers of ignorance and fear and delusion. And one day I said to Pao: 'Something will happen, and clean all this up,' in a voice far away. Perhaps he did not hear.

Up and up the steps of Chungking, City of Recovered Gladness, they went, the working people, called *coolies,* bitter strength. Bitter strength, incessant stream of feet splayed with pain, and gasping breath, carrying, carrying, beasts of labour, everything inhuman on their human shoulders, bales of cotton, paraffin tins, household furniture, vegetable baskets, and dung, dung, human dung by the bucketfuls for the fields, and also carrying other people, the officials, the officers, the diplomats, the thick-headed and heavy-bellied, all carried on human shoulders, up and up and down and down the staircase streets of Chungking. On these shoulders grew enormous humps, callouses, as large as clenched fists, and many also dragged large hernias bound with straw within the stringy rags of their misnamed trousers.

For the next three years in Chungking, Pao and I were to become part of the regime, Chiang Kaishek's government. And it is impossible to understand the events that took place without explaining the type of organization it was.

Two names personify the two pillars of Chiang's power: Hu Tsungnan, leader of the Whangpoo young officer clique, and Tai Lee, head of the secret police. Together these two made up the backbone of the overall fascist organization called the Blueshirts, in their various disguises, names, activities, overt and covert, political and military.

The moral philosophy of this fascist elite corps is usually attributed to Chen Lifu, an extreme right-wing man, in 1938 Education Minister and 'philosopher' of the Kuomintang party, whose ideas of personalism were later to be borrowed by Ngo Din Diem. The creation of the Blueshirt organization dated back to April 1st, 1932, when its nucleus, consisting of thirteen of the closest associates of Chiang Kaishek, with Chen Lifu and his brother Chen Kuofu, got together to promote a 'spiritual renovation' body. Some of the thirteen were Whangpoo Academy officers, members in 1926-7 of a revolutionary youth society which later had become counter-revolutionary. Among the thirteen was Tai Lee, himself an ex-Whangpoo Academy man.

In its development, the fascist Blueshirts became a multitude of organizations, bodies, institutions, but the directing control reposed increasingly in Tai Lee, who came under Chiang Kaishek, and was responsible to no one else.

The Whangpoo young officers' clique, though not officially under Tai Lee, were the military side of the Blueshirt movement and relied on him and his organizations for 'political clean-ups' within the military and para-military bodies, especially after the Nanyu decision to fight the communists was taken. By 1942 two-thirds, and by 1945 three-quarters of all the jobs in the enormous military administration were held by the Whangpoo young officers' clique.

Three 'rings' existed in the Blueshirt organization: the centre thirteen, the core; the military Whangpoo clique or inner ring; and an outer ring called the Fu Hsing or Resurrection Society. Fu Hsing was especially active in enrolling students and intellectuals, and providing a large and variegated membership from which selected material for 'leadership' could be picked. It was the Fu Hsing Society which went about recruiting students in the universities in Europe, and many were recruited under various pretexts; very often without knowing they were being recruited. By 1942 every middle school, every university in the areas under Chiang's rule was honeycombed with Blueshirt agents; the students were driven in trucks to an assembly place, where they were enrolled by force in the Fu Hsing Society. By 1943 there were nominally five million 'members'.

Another facet of this many-sided organization was the Three Principles Youth Corps, which was a more direct recruitment and manipulation of the young (under nineteen years old). The Youth Corps was begun in Hankow in June 1938 by Chiang; the young were enthusiastic about the Red Army, and droves of them left their schools to trek up to Yenan, hence a counter-organization was set up to keep them in check. From 1939 onwards, Tai Lee would organize special networks to stop the young students from going to Yenan; and since the road to Yenan passed through Sian, headquarters of Hu Tsungnan, the military commander in charge of the blockade of the Red base, it was at Sian that they ran the gauntlet of both police and military agents. The largest number of concentration camps for the young (dubbed 'schools' or 'institutes') was to be found in and round Sian.

All through the development of the Blueshirts the ideological influence of fascism, of Hitler's storm troopers, brownshirts, was central to their build-up. *Mein Kampf* became required reading for the 'inner ring' people, the elite security guard round Chiang Kaishek. After 1943 Chiang's own book, *China's Destiny*, became their *Mein Kampf*.

Where the Whangpoo young officers' clique was concerned, direct

83

indoctrination in fascism was achieved for the more 'promising' ones, singled out for leadership, by trips to Hitler's Germany. Chiang Kaishek's second son, Chiang Weikuo, went to Germany for several months, and among the young officers who went there for a six-week 'holiday' was Pao. A snapshot of Pao with Chiang Weikuo, both in Berlin, was stuck in Pao's photo album for some years. At least sixty military cadets during the years 1934 to 1938 were made acquainted with Nazi doctrine and methods. Not surprisingly, they admired Hitler; but then so did many of the 'democratic bourgeoisie' of Europe before 1939.

The efficiency, the cleanliness, the strident hyper-nationalism of Germany appealed to the hurt pride and humiliated chauvinism of these young officers. Their anti-semitism, borrowed straight from *Mein Kampf,* and irrelevant in China (where the only Jewish community, dating from the sixth century, in Kaifeng, had long been assimilated) was a reflection of their grounding in Hitlerism.

Numerous and bewildering were the ramifications of the Blueshirt set-up. Tai Lee and Chiang Kaishek, as well as the brothers Chen Lifu and Chen Kuofu, were also members of Chinese secret societies, such as the Triads. Chiang during his young days in Shanghai had become the adopted grandson of the head of Shanghai's largest secret society; his induction into the Shanghai underworld was due to the two Chens' father, himself an important secret society chief. Chiang could thus rely upon gangster armies for support; Tai Lee, also a secret society man, kept in touch with the Triads in the Japanese-occupied city of Shanghai all through the war. Chiang had utilized the Triad Society gangsters during the massacres of the workers in Shanghai in April 1927, and again during the massacres of the Canton commune in December of that year. The chief gangster of Shanghai, Tu Yuehseng, for his services in helping to slaughter the workers, was dubbed a philanthropist, decorated, and sat on the board of the Chinese Red Cross, an office which permitted him extensive and profitable deals in medical supplies, such as quinine, as well as in the traffic of opium and heroin. While the army was decimated with malaria, quinine stuffed the godowns ... to be sold on the black market by the gangsters of Tu Yuehseng, and these godowns and these transactions obtained the protection of the secret police of Tai Lee. Tu Yuehseng accompanied Chiang to Chungking and helped the Blueshirts infiltrate the local secret society, the Kelao, or Elder Brothers, hostile to the newcomers as it meant competition on their own stamping ground, Szechuan, in the commerce in opium and the control of brothels.

A synthesis of the secret society brotherhood rites, the Confucian teacher student loyalty, and a fascist philosophy based on racial purity – this was Chiang's idea of a personal organization, of which he, the Great Leader, became the absolute head. Tai Lee was the man who held this structure together.

Unlike Hitler, Chiang would never officially recognize the Blueshirt organization, since it also was a 'secret' brotherhood. But in order to advance rapidly in the hierarchy of power one *had* to be a Blueshirt, favoured by Tai Lee, and for many a young soldier, such as Pao, the way to Tai Lee led through Hu Tsungnan, at Sian.

Hu Tsungnan was the acknowledged head of the Whangpoo young officers' inner ring. Many thought he would become the heir to Chiang's military dictatorship; and thus he was often spoken of by sycophants as 'the young knightly leader'. To 'walk the Hu way' was to climb to power.

Tai Lee and Hu Tsungnan loved each other more than brothers. Though Tai Lee could not be accused of homosexuality (his many affairs were well known, including his habit of employing the husbands of his mistresses on black-market deals), Hu Tsungnan is thought to have been a homosexual. Tai and Hu when they met spent all night talking, walking back and forth. They wrote to each other very often. None dared to disturb this friendship or come between them. When a marriage was suggested between Hu Tsungnan and the second daughter of the Finance Minister, H. H. Kung, Tai Lee wept, and flew to Sian to dissuade Hu. Second Miss Kung was well known in Chungking for her pistol-packing exploits. She dressed as a boy, and strode about, pistol on hip, whip in hand, accompanied by gambolling wolfhounds. She was said to be extremely direct in manifesting her displeasure, and people were chary of encountering her on the roads to the imposing South Bank mansions of Chungking where ministers, ambassadors, the top military, and Chiang Kaishek lived.

Tai Lee considered these plans disastrous, in spite of the Kung millions, and even though it would have brought Hu into Chiang's family circle (since H. H. Kung, the Finance Minister, was Chiang's brother-in-law). He therefore, it is said, recruited a Miss Yeh, a starlet, who was doing intelligence work reporting progressive students in the University of Chengtu by pretending to be herself a progressive in the department of political science. He sent Miss Yeh to Sian as a gift to Hu Tsungnan. Although it is not reported whether Miss Yeh was successful or not, Hu Tsungnan did not marry Miss Kung.

Tai Lee and Hu Tsungnan became allies against the influence of the Chen brothers and their followers, despite the fact that the latter had been among the initiators of the Blueshirt movement. Chiang kept a balance between these contending elements and also maintained in place the pro-Japanese Minister of Defence, Ho Yingchin, whom Tai and Hu both disliked. In this way Chiang remained master, playing one subaltern off against the other; even Hu Tsungnan, Chiang's most trusted general, could do nothing against Ho Yingchin.

In order to pay for the 600,000-odd agents of all kinds in the Blueshirt organization, Tai Lee conducted, through 50,000 'specials', an active trade in narcotics – opium and heroin – with the Japanese. Heroin factories in Shanghai, Tientsin and Nanking, now under the Japanese, found outlets for their products in the rest of China, and the crude opium necessary as raw material was supplied to them by Tai Lee.

After the fall of Wuhan, Szechuan province, now the bastion of Chiang's power, saw the Blueshirts come swarming in. Daily commodities, including foodstuffs, came under their control, as well as transport, by air, river and land.

To compete in power and influence with Tai Lee, Ho Yingchin, the Defence Minister, also had his private rackets, concerned with supplies for the army. Many a division was mown down by starvation, the men dying of hunger and disease while their food and clothing was being sold at black-market prices by their officers. Ho amassed a vast fortune by selling command posts, reporting non-existent divisions and drawing pay and supplies for them, and black-marketing in cloth, rice, leather and petrol, as well as medical supplies for the army.

When Chungking became Chiang's capital, the Blueshirt organizations clashed with the local secret society, the Kelao, and the provincial warlords. Pitched battles were fought between Tai Lee's gangs and the Kelao, and Tai Lee blackmailed the Szechuan feudal landlords and gentry. In 1939 Chiang proclaimed an 'opium eradication' campaign in Szechuan, and also at regular intervals campaigns for 'the moral improvement of the nation'. This was done to enable Tai Lee to seize the opium districts from the Szechuanese warlords, and to blackmail them through their private morals. The Kelao were so incensed that they threatened to cut out the livers of Tai Lee's agents and eat them should he force them to relinquish the opium, but by 1943 many of the opium districts had been wrested from the Szechuanese and were controlled by the Blueshirts.

Chiang knew that to maintain his power he must have the support of the young. Universities and middle schools were infiltrated with Blueshirt recruiters. In 1940 training courses for teachers, throughout the schools and universities of Szechuan, were held for 'moral uplift'. The subjects forbidden to be taught were not only communism, but also inflation, any study of 'corrupt practices' or 'ills of the peasantry'. Concentration camps, called 'family reform hostels', were set up and manned by the Blueshirts for the progressive students and intellectuals who were caught going to Yenan. They were given 'family correction', indoctrination, calisthenics and beatings. The converted were sent out as agents to spy upon others.

In 1937 the Blueshirts started the supervision of the embassies abroad, and by 1939 all embassies had their Tai Lee man who reported on the 'thoughts' of the Ambassador and his staff. With the consolidation of the Whangpoo clique, after the Nanyu conference, all appointments of military attachés abroad had to be sanctioned by Tai Lee.

The *crème de la crème*, the pick of Chiang's pyramid of control, was the 'Obey and Serve' service, a government in microcosm with almost absolute power. Its structure was based on the 'inner ring' – but not entirely, since even there Chiang kept some rivalries going by giving a few posts to Ho Yingchin's clique and also the pro-American group of T. V. Soong and H. H. Kung, ostensibly to remain impartial, actually to refine his control and intelligence work.

The Obey and Serve was predominantly pro-Axis, pro-German, and when Germany invaded Soviet Russia in the summer of 1941, the Whangpoo cadets of the service were elated. After Pearl Harbour they became ostensibly pro-American as more Americans came into China with military missions, and as Chiang became increasingly dependent on the United States.

It was in 1942 that the Office of Strategic Services (O.S.S.) organized a branch in Chungking, under Major Miles, an American Naval Intelligence officer; it soon spawned an office of Sino-American

Co-operation (SACO), of which Tai Lee was the head and Miles the 'chief adviser'. This was the Asian kernel of the Central Intelligence Agency of today; Tai Lee-trained agents manned SACO, and the Chinese staff was supplied with information concerning suspect liberal Americans, and in return supplied information to the Americans on Chinese suspects. Thus many features and refinements of the Blueshirt organization were utilized by American 'special' officers, who later contributed to forming the C.I.A.

SACO's budget, like the Blueshirt and the C.I.A. budget, was not subject to audit by any instituted authority. The C.I.A. is not responsible to anyone save the President of the U.S.A.; Tai Lee's Blueshirt organization was responsible to Chiang Kaishek alone.

Because of this type of organization which found its highest executive expression in the Obey and Serve, the pronouncements of the latter outweighed the advice of all ministries; as the war went on, the power of Obey and Serve and of Tai Lee was reinforced in the army: every divisional staff had its agents.

Contracts for the import and export of tung oil, cotton, foodstuffs and minerals, after 1944, came under the Obey and Serve, and so did all transport. Only a portion of the Obey and Serve staff had had the advantage of foreign study; and those were regarded as qualified for the much coveted posts of military attachés abroad, becoming Tai Lee's 'eyes and ears' in the outside world.

The Obey and Serve officials were in charge of the collection of internal intelligence against 'communist subversion'; they dealt with foreign intelligence and foreign missions; they searched for 'intellectuals with dangerous thoughts'. They screened all persons who had appointments with Chiang Kaishek and all material intended to reach him; they dealt with the files of the thousands of teachers, students, intellectuals and others kept in concentration camps; they kept checks on all personnel in the embassies abroad and in the various civilian offices in China. They spied on ministers, heads of departments, field commanders and generals, foreign correspondents and missionaries. They had on tap a corps of agents for 'special services', such as the assassination of unwanted people. They formed the Praetorian Guard of Chiang Kaishek; they knew the 'thinking of the Leader' before it was made public.

At military conferences, when Chiang harangued his Whangpoo officer, the Obey and Serve staff turned out in full array, notebook in hand, to record the words of 'The Leader'. In their spick-and-span uniforms and white gloves, they looked what they were, the Praetorian Guard of a tyranny.

Since Chiang Kaishek's idea of saving China was a return to medieval moral tenets, the gabble of precepts of virtue took the place of any positive thinking on how to conduct the affairs of the country.

'The way of father and sons, husbands and wives, elder and younger brothers, and friends; the order of upper and lower, superior and inferior, man and woman, old and young.' A 'natural hierarchy' with absolute obedience. A return to absolute authoritarianism both in personal and in public life; feudal 'loyalty' with strong overtones of Nazism. No wonder that, as in Germany or Italy as far as women were concerned, the precepts of 'absolute obedience to the father when young; to the husband when married; and if left a widow, suicide to prove one's fidelity and chastity', were held up as ideals.

I had thought that upon our arrival in Chungking all would be well; that the quarrels were only due to the hard conditions of our travel; that now in the city, we would settle down and I would be able to work at something useful. I was soon to find out how wrong I was.

For Pao was singly devoted to making his way to the top; the veneer of Sandhurst rubbed off as soon as he was back; the vicious system in which he was caught destroyed him as a person, and all that he mouthed was utterly false, as he himself became more actively involved in 'loyalty' towards Chiang. His ambition would carry him up, up, through the 'inner ring' to the Obey and Serve, to the top ...

I did not know what I now know – that I was on the wrong side, on the wrong front; that it would be impossible for me or for anyone else to do anything useful or valid; though many clung, as I did, to the mistaken belief that somehow, out of the sordid mess and chaos which was the China of Chiang Kaishek, which was the Chungking of Chiang Kaishek, some good could be retrieved.

Five

ON JANUARY 12th, 1939, a letter reached me from my parents in Tientsin. I had written to them from Kweilin, telling them that we

89

were now going to Szechuan, to Chungking, and giving Pao's office postal box address, P.O. Box 132, Chungking; each of the military departments and bureaux had a post-box number assigned to it. I had written that I was married, and asked my father for the address of our family in Szechuan. My father corresponded regularly with his family in Chengtu, but he told us very little about them. It was a portion which he cloistered from that other segment of life endured with us in Peking; all that had to do with the Chou family in Szechuan was unpleasant to my mother; she was so afraid that Father might go back.

My parents lived the war under Japanese occupation in Tientsin, and in Peking. My father was arrested for a few days by the Japanese in 1937, then released and ordered back to work on the railway. I found among his notebooks one filled with Japanese words, for the Japanese made all the railway staff learn the language. Mail between the Japanese-occupied zone and Chungking never ceased to be delivered throughout the war; the postmen in the one zone would leave, at certain specified towns, the mail for the other zone, which would then be picked up by the postmen of the 'enemy' regime; and this accord ·was not surprising, considering the intense and open traffic in goods of all kinds and also in narcotics which went on between the two zones, and also the contacts among the higher officials of Chungking and the Japanese all through these war years.

A total of forty-two generals, seventy high-ranking officers and officials, and half a million troops of the Kuomintang went over to the Japanese during the war; with the tacit agreement of, and by arrangement with, Chiang and Tai Lee. This was part of the double game being played; in accordance with Chiang's policy of fighting Red power, and making deals with Japan. It was also a gamble of Machiavellian subtlety, sizeably to reduce the army bill for Chiang. The Japanese would have to feed, pay and equip the Chinese troops on their side. In 1942 and 1943 the rate of desertion to Japan accelerated, precisely at the time when Joe Stilwell, the American commander deputized by the U.S. government to China, following Pearl Harbour, wanted to reorganize the whole of the Chinese armies, to turn them into an efficient combat force for a land-based invasion of Japan. Chiang feared the United States would force him to relinquish some of his power; by sending half a million troops to the Japanese side he subtracted them from American emprise, balked American plans for turning China into an American arsenal, and rendered a service to the Japanese, at that time hard pressed for manpower in South-East Asia.

After 1942 the Japanese delegated certain operations on their China front to these puppet Chinese troops, certain that only the communists would be engaged in fighting, while on the Chiang side, the tactics of withdrawal and retreat were scrupulously maintained. Ninety-eight per cent of the puppet troops by 1944 were engaged by the 8th and the new 4th communist armies, only two per cent engaged in nominal fighting with the Kuomintang. At an armistice, Chiang calculated, both these puppet troops which he had so obligingly loaned to the Japanese, and those on his side, could combine to fight the communists, using a vast pincer-like movement against the Red bases from North to South China.

This mathematics of craftiness was typical of Chiang; as was the whole strange accord, which permitted letters, goods, cosmetics and narcotics to circulate under the aegis of the Blueshirt 'mercantile organizations', the Ming Hua and the Fu Hsing monopoly enterprises, from one side of the front to the other. Throughout the war the Japanese foreign minister was in constant touch with Chinese officials of the Obey and Serve service and thus with Chiang Kaishek. It was not surprising that I very quickly got a reply from my parents in Japanese-occupied Tientsin.

My father's letter was a happy one. He was obviously pleased; he gave me the business address of my Third Uncle, his younger brother, in Chungking, and also the family home address in Chengtu. He assured me that he was well, and that I was not to worry. Strangest of all there was also a note from my mother, not long, but amiable, saying that she had 'at last' been able to tell her friends that I had married! My marriage seemed to reconcile her to me. It vindicated her whole life. 'At last I could tell *them* all that my daughter is now *married*' she wrote, underlining the words, not mentioning who 'them' was; it was the others; the 'they', the 'them', always invoked by my mother, and in this she was like millions of others who speak of mysterious 'they' as forces in their lives, when they feel at odds with the rest of the world.

Together with these letters my parents had sent photographs of myself when a child; with my mother, next to my horse, Balthazar; with my sister and my mother holding her last baby; of my parents together ...

Some weeks later, Pao was to extract these photographs from his pocket while we were walking round the Hot Springs of Peip'ei, a health resort a few miles from Chungking, where in one of his bursts of fondness he had taken me for the day, and was to gouge out my mother's face from each of them, then tear them up, and make me swear I would never have any more to do with my parents. He then wrote a letter to my father while I cried, for I did not want to hurt my father. I never knew what he wrote, and my father never replied.

The day after I received my father's letter I went in search of Third Uncle at the address given to me.

The Meifeng Bank was my Third Uncle's business address: an imposing building, eight-storied, with brass-and-glass doors, and a large and busy hall with many counters inside. Opposite it was the Szechuan Salt Bank, also with a large façade. The Szechuan Salt Bank and the Meifeng Bank together held most of the capital of the Szechuan landed gentry, lately become businessmen and capitalists. Before 1921, the Meifeng Bank had been the American Oriental Banking Corporation, but after the uprisings of 1923 and 1925 American capital had fled, and the Szechuanese capitalists had the bank in their own hands.

When in 1956 I went back to Chungking both banks had become nationalized; the Meifeng was now the Chungking branch of the People's Bank, and the Szechuan Salt Bank had become the People's Agricultural Bank.

At nine in the morning, I reached the Meifeng Bank, and stood at first outside the main gate, too shy to enter, but peering through the opened doors. Then I edged myself into the hall. An attendant asked me what I wanted. I said I was looking for Mr Chou Kiensan. At that moment I saw a man who looked very much like my father, but with more prominent cheekbones, more bounce and assurance to his walk, entering the hall. He was dressed in a long fur-lined brown silk gown and wore black velvet shoes, and his eyes were bright and assured. I stared towards his back, and the attendant moved towards him, but already Third Uncle (for it was he) had felt someone was looking at him, and turned and was staring at me. I said: 'Third Uncle.' He said:

92

'You are my niece.' I bowed and said: 'Yes.' He said: 'I thought so, you have something of your father in your face, and also something of your sister, Moon Orchid ... Do you know that she came here some two years ago?' 'No,' I said, 'I did not know.' I had not been told that Marianne, my youngest sister, had come to Szechuan.

Third Uncle now turned back and walked briskly ahead of me, his step springy, noiseless in his cloth shoes. He opened a door and took me into his office, a room with large leather chairs dating back twenty years to American influence, carved Szechuan tables and screen, and calligraphy hangings on the wall. He called for boiling water, went to a large cupboard whose glass doors were screened with white silk, and which contained many boxes, cylindrical, square, octagonal, of bamboo, of lacquer, of pewter, each one containing a different kind of tea. Third Uncle was a tea connoisseur, and had the servant pour the boiling water into a teapot while with sleeves rolled up he let drop the required amount of tea-leaves from one box, meanwhile explaining where this particular tea came from, the manner of its picking, the season and the day and the cost; all this in between asking me questions about my doings and why I was here and throwing little sharp glances at me and then looking away at the wall opposite when I answered, as it was rude to stare at someone when they talk. I told him I was married, told him Pao's name and wrote it down for him, and he said: 'You must come and stay with me, in my house here in Chungking, not at the hotel.'

That afternoon, when Pao returned from the General Staff Headquarters where he worked, I told him about meeting my uncle and about the invitation, and took him to call upon Third Uncle. When we alighted from our huakans in front of the large black-lacquered gate in Woodcutter Lane, the gate of Third Uncle's house, I saw Pao straighten his face and put on his serious, responsible air, to impress Third Uncle with the good manners of his virtuous family.

The gate opened into the first courtyard, leading to a second, and to a third; the house of Third Uncle was one of the better ones in Chungking, luxurious in the prevailing poverty, though by Western standards it would be reckoned cold, uncomfortable, and of medium size. The drawing-room was oblong and, like all the other rooms, stone-paved; because of the winter weather, the chairs, draped in white covers, were covered with furs, snow leopard of Szechuan with butterfly markings; bear skins and goat skins were laid upon the floor.

In the cold stillness the scent of winter orchids at my Third Uncle's writing desk was discernible and exceptionally pleasant.

Third Uncle, precisely because he had never been a scholar in his young days, practised calligraphy every day; and was sitting at his desk, ending his self-imposed afternoon sheet. He was a fanatic for cleanliness; could not stand dirt or disorder round him; had everything, including his numerous boxes of tea, labelled and arranged with punctilious neatness, would keep a soft cloth in his drawer, and himself always clean his study, and also brandish a feather duster about the house, hunting for dust, and giving long lectures to relatives and servants on hygiene, health, and cleanliness. He had also bought a car, a black Ford sedan, but kept it in the entrance courtyard and never used it. He would, however, go to see his car every day and with a cloth polish the mudguards and flick dust off the body with a special feather duster. Everyone knew about Third Uncle's car, and when they laughed at him he said: 'Laugh all you wish, but I am not going to be blackmailed because I have a car.' Our affection, clear-sighted and enduring, dated from our first meeting and has never changed.

Third Uncle received us by crying; 'Exceptional guest, exceptional guest,' and beaming at Pao. Again tea was poured, while Third Uncle examined Pao, handsome in his English-made uniform (he had eight of them), and lauded him with appropriate and flowery compliments. I think he was glad about my marriage. I had not, after all, married a foreigner, which would have made difficult the social courtesies and protocol concerned. I had married a Chinese officer. Excellent, thought Third Uncle, and looked with keenly appreciative eyes at Pao, while gathering from him his native place and lineage, and remembering meeting Pao's father at the Paoting Military Academy; and beaming effulgently as the conversation proceeded.

Third Uncle could appreciate the advantages of such a marriage in these times of turmoil, when Szechuan was being invaded by about forty million 'outlanders', 'underfoot' and down-river people from the eastern seaboard, people whom the Szechuanese in their proud seclusion despised. It was a contempt that the sophisticated Shanghai and Nanking officials heartily returned, calling the Szechuanese 'Szechuan rats'. The local gentry were apprehensive of the intruding powers of the Central Government ... having someone 'in' with the Central Government might help, for already the exactions of the Kuomintang were being felt at all levels in this once isolated province.

In Szechuan, as everywhere else in China, family relationships counted a great deal; and in that withdrawn inland state perhaps to a greater degree was enterprise of any kind grafted on to feudal clan and blood-tie connections, not to mention the all-pervasive local secret society, the Elder Brothers, the Kelao.

In the Meifeng Bank, of which Third Uncle at that time was general manager, three of the directors were brothers to each other, the fourth a cousin; Third Uncle was in the bank because of his reputation as a financial expert, he having for a long while managed the financial affairs of Szechuan's biggest warlord, Liu Hsiang. Within the bank sons, daughters, nephews, cousins, and other relatives of the directors occupied numerous posts, mostly in the cashier, accountancy, and other vulnerable departments. Third Uncle had placed many of his nephews and nieces in the bank in Chungking, in Chengtu, in Neichiang and other smaller cities and towns. Today, when the bank has been taken over, these employees, my cousins and relatives, remain in their posts; they have not lost their jobs and I find them at the same place, doing the same kind of work, as thirty years ago.

The day after our meeting Pao and I moved to Third Uncle's house. Third Uncle gave us a very good room, with silk hangings round the enormous carved bed, and coverlets as light as swan feathers, filled with silk waste, embroidered with flowers and birds. We had a bathroom with an enormous glazed bathtub, in which every evening the servants poured hot water for our baths. The toilets were clean; servants cleaned them every time we had used them. At the black-lacquered gate, every time Pao went in or out, the gateman would shout: 'Honourable Third Junior Master is entering', or 'Honourable Third Junior Master is going out'. There was always scented fresh tea; the floors were clean, the spittoons (which we did not use but which were there) were of flowered porcelain and had clean water poured inside them every day; the lacquered furniture was carefully dusted. The window curtains were of pure white silk; it was the best room in the house, and Third Uncle was spoiling us.

A succession of dinner parties followed, at which Pao and I were introduced to the Szechuan notables; the K'ang family, the Ch'en family, the Teng family, and many others. Lights were hung and glittered in the courtyards during these feasts; upon the round tables the best dishes of the province were exhibited, and Third Uncle expounded about their cooking, eating with relish and gleefully commenting

upon our appetites. I received presents from everyone; piles of embroidered coverlet tops, dozens of lengths of silks for dresses. 'Third
Uncle is treating you as his own daughter,' said Pao, impressed.

For ten days Pao was all charm; he brought quite a few 'benevolent
brothers' back to Third Uncle's house to show them what kind of
family I had; it gave him great face. But it also excited their envy. I
remember one evening when he brought a fellow-officer and his
fiancée, the latter a pretty young woman from Nanking whose father
was in some ministry, and well-connected. The young officer was very
proud of his fiancée, and Pao was happy to show them that I was at
least as well up in the gentry class as the other man's bride-to-be;
although she had the slight advantage of coming from a wealthy com-
pradore and banker family of the coast, whereas I belonged to the
'backward' Szechuan gentry. But in Chungking very few of the in-
coming horde of officials had connections with the local gentry, and
such a connection was deemed an advantage, especially as far as
housing and servants were concerned, and being able to purchase land
and to enter into local commercial life. 'You have solved the problems
of living in an hotel,' said the young officer, casting sidelong glances
round him. But he hastened to add that his fiancée's father had obtained
land through the government agency, and that he was building a
house for himself in the privileged enclave of the South Bank. Airily
he remarked that his father-in-law-to-be had evacuated about twenty
houses belonging to Szechuanese small fry for the purpose of erecting
his own mansion. This was not a boast; there were forcible expulsions
which greatly added to the rancour of the local people. It may have
been true that a 'large house' was being built for the newcomers and
that poor villagers, unable to get rid of their debts, had been deprived
of their domiciles.

The fiancée was obviously put out that she was no longer the 'star',
the pick of the lot; for I was a 'western-returned' student, I had been
abroad; which in the balance where every person was weighed as an
asset or a liability, was an asset; however, she soon found something
hurtful to say. Noticing some daisies in a glazed pot, she threw in, just
before leaving: 'White flowers ... how very foreign.' For these were
daisies, cheap flowers, not orchids or plum blossom. I had loved their
sunny look, so brave in those sunless days; I had put them in a large,
cheap, blue earthenware glazed pot, which I had found at the market
for a few cents. And now they gave notice of my difference.

Pao was angry, not with them, but with me. I had to throw the daisies away, although I kept the pot; it became to me an emblem of resistance, and until I was bombed I used it, defiantly. It became of value well beyond its monetary worth. However, Providence, if such there be, arranged a revenge a few months later; the next winter a notice appeared in the newspapers; it was from the fiancée's family:

Termination of engagement contract

Mr ——, who by devious means ingratiated himself, and by misrepresentation as a person of good morals and integrity entered into a contract for engagement with Miss ——, of good and noble family, whose virtuous untainted life is an example to all of her age and breeding, was found to be unworthy of this confidence and hereby the engagement is terminated.

The reason for this serious step is that Mr —— was found in the company of a person of the female sex and of low degree in an hotel on the 13th of November at an unrespectable hour in the night. When interrogated he without shame and unbashfully confessed that this person of low degree was his mistress who had followed him to Chungking and that he had entertained illicit relations with her for several months.

From now on let not Mr —— lay any claims against the family he has thus wronged; and all relations are terminated upon publication of this advice.

It was Pao who brought this printed repudiation to my notice; in keeping with the times. Perhaps he too felt some satisfaction at the outcome of what had been advertised as an outstanding and exemplary romance. 'Well, I hope the girl gets married to someone else,' I said. 'But she is now tainted,' exclaimed Pao. 'She is no longer pure as a blank sheet of paper, she will find it very difficult to obtain a good husband ... ' Pao was either deceiving himself or deceiving me, for the girl got married within six months to a similarly worthy gentleman, of good morals and integrity. However, when the Revolution came, her husband left for the United States, abandoning her and two children in Taiwan. Finding her chances for remarriage slim, her family then arranged for her a pseudo-marriage with an American G.I., for the sum of U.S. $5,000, in order to get her into the United States. It is difficult to get permission to leave Formosa, and when a husband is sent out on mission abroad, he has to leave his wife and children behind, to guarantee his return. But every year young women leave, and one of the ways is by 'marrying' an American G.I. When they reach America, a residence permit is arranged; after that a 'divorce' occurs, again for a little cash. But an American passport has thus been procured, and all is well ...

For the Chinese New Year, which occurred in the month of February, Third Uncle took me and his concubine Yao Niang (who managed his Chungking household, while his wife, my Third Aunt, managed the Chengtu household) back with him by air to Chengtu. Third Uncle returned at least three or four times a year to Chengtu, and in the next three years I often availed myself of these trips to go with him, as it was possible to obtain an air ticket through the Meifeng Bank more easily than if one were a private individual, since transport was controlled by the Blueshirts. But all banks had their special transport bribing agent, who invited the Blueshirt in charge to tea ...

Pao did not go to Chengtu with me; I was to be introduced to my own family, and Third Uncle named it 'the return visit of the new bride', thus putting it in traditional terms. Pao remained in Third Uncle's house, looked after by a bevy of servants. The morning plane to Chengtu took off; soon we were out of the fog into the clear sky of beginning spring. Below us the terraced hills seemed to rotate and shift and then we were into the Chengtu plain, the sun shining and everything sparkling in the clear cold air.

Of the New Year visit with my family, I have written previously, and to say that I enjoyed the large feudal family I discovered is still true, though it is no longer admissible in today's revolutionary China. Although in the months to come I was to find out that like all families, mine had its untellable tales, its murky rivalries, its inarticulate intrigues, its feuds and greeds and bickerings, that it was also, by today's standards, an exploiter, yet the relief I enjoyed with the Family, away from Pao, was in itself enough to explain why I found them all so very wonderful. And they were good to me, particularly Third Aunt; all of them did whatever they could to amuse me, interest me, help me. And the deep, if clear-sighted, affection for the members of my family which then began, neither time nor revolution can efface or destroy.

New Year was a time of rejoicing; the ritual of joy itself a talisman for happiness to come; mirth, kindness, good cheer, pleasantness the tenor of those weeks; no unkind word or deed to mar the delight of a new beginning, and my elastic self forgot, or rather minimized, the quarrels with Pao. Plunged into the zestful crowd of my numerous relatives, I overflowed with happiness, with desire to please them; I even felt sorry for Pao, wrote to him that I missed him. With the family I forgot the sorrowful moments, and gave myself to the enchanted hours (for they were enchanted, lovely days, if only because the sun sparkled so gaily, and everyone seemed so happy). I found it easy, for a short month, to restrain my impetuous and restless self, to adopt the dawdling timelessness and leisurely pace of the family, to do nothing but trivial things with great punctilio and thoroughness. Perhaps it was play-acting, but it was also genuine affection which made all such restraints willing, so that for once I did merge into a group, and desired it greatly, and wept secretly with joy to have discovered my wonderful Big Family in Szechuan.

There were many houses to visit; uncles and aunts, great-uncles and other relatives, whose exact relationships have exact names in the Chinese family system, but nothing corresponding to their accuracy in English. Patiently I learned them, visited and bowed, ate and bowed, drank tea and bowed, followed Third Aunt meekly, like another daughter. So many festivities, so many elders to bow to on New Year's day! The crisp sun-sprayed air was balm upon the courtyards, the plum trees opened their pale-pink and pale-yellow blossoms in all the gardens. All was richly transfigured with laughter. So beautiful the sedate old city of Chengtu, with its twisty lanes, its dark rickety lath-and-plaster houses with their grey-tiled roofs, its parrots grey and pink swinging on their pewter stands in front of shops; its black lacquer gates framed with red paper with New Year calligraphy; its tea shops, memorable, famous, unnumbered, and the fine smell of fresh tea in the morning coldness! Boisterous the children running about, their cheeks rouged, their hair sleek, red strings tying their small pigtails, their bright new cotton clothes making splashes like flowerbeds in motion! The oleander-lined walks of the Shao Sheng park, with its monument to the Szechuan railway struggle of 1911, which had started the Revolution of that year, were thronged with saunterers; its lotus ponds, tea pavilions and banked rows of scented winter orchids, pale green, pale mauve, were all made new with loud praise of their beauty. Haunting and poetic the Tu Fu park with its

99

bamboo groves and the memory of the greatest poet of Szechuan; it was one of our favourite picnic spots. The temples and courtyards of Wu Hou Sze, gaudy with fresh paint, were crowded with families, fathers pointing out to their children the statues of the heroes of the Three Kingdoms. Their names at night the story-teller would make alive again, miming their scheming brains and clever deeds by the light of a small linen wick dipping in rape-seed oil in a cup, so similar in shape to those lamps used by the Greeks in their own heroic days. The thousand pungent odours of Szechuan dishes, morsels of crystallized fruit and sweetmeats, the fresh, fresh tang of oranges and cumquats, and a host of cousins, linking arms with me (the girls only) and calling me Third Sister ... I absorbed the Szechuan way of talking, let the mannerisms seep into me, imbibing by osmosis what was around; lost self-consciousness, floated in the ease, the reassurance of a Big Family, almost as if this magic enchantment would never end.

It was at the close of a family dinner that Third Uncle announced that he had now found a correct family name for me, and put me down in linear rank, by age, among my generation in the book of generations.

Third Uncle kept records of all the generations, and later gave me a copy of this book. My generation consisted then of twenty-five: four children from my father, four from Third Uncle, twelve from Sixth Uncle, and five from First Uncle; these my twenty-one first cousins all counted as my own brothers and sisters, and all were aligned in the book of generations according to age, the first male child born being called First Son, the first female child First Daughter, irrespective of which brother's offspring it was. Thus my own brother was called First Son, and all my generation called him First Brother, although my father was the second male child in his own generation; whereas his elder brother produced Second Son, a year later. Third Uncle's sons ranked third, fourth and sixth according to age, while Fifth Son was again sired by First Uncle. By noting down the dates of birth, and assigning numbers in chronological sequence, one kept track of one's immediate first cousins and also of the immediate generation above oneself, that is of all those issued from one grandfather, and who have the same family name. This patrilineal system also extended to great-uncles, for one of my grandfather's brothers was still alive, and he had sired twenty-odd children, some of whom were only ten or twelve years old at the time I was there, but who were, by definition, my uncles and aunts. My father's sisters, of whom two survived, also had numerous offspring, producing ten children among them; but since they belonged to their husbands' families, and their children were not named Chou, they did not go into the Chou family book of genealogies but into those of their husbands' clans. And these cousins of ours were not 'same clan' but once-removed cousins, although biologically of the same level and generation.

In this patrilineal system of recording and descent, the family name was all-important, because it was a clan name, and in Szechuan it was accounted impossible that two people with the same family name should ever get married, even if it was clearly proven that they were not related by blood. Thus no Chou could marry a Chou, nor any Liu a Liu. And since in all China there were only about 286 family names for 500 million people, the occasions when a Chou wanted to marry another Chou would have been quite numerous had not another feudal device made this impossible. Since all marriages were arranged by the families, and the families would never agree to a marriage with a 'same name' because this was equivalent to incest, and made one a shunned laughing-stock, the terrible misdemeanour could not happen. No matchmaker would undertake such a monstrous deed.

The origin of this habit was probably, like so much else, due to the fact that the patrilineal clan system, based on male supremacy, implicit in the Confucian dogma, had destroyed the primeval matriarchal system which had existed in China, and laid down strict rules on incest. Many villages remained based on the clan system, most of the inhabitants owning the same name, and these villages would contract alliances in marriage with neighbouring villages of different names, never within their own name groups; all such marriages were arranged and never left to the young themselves; and the word 'love' was shunned, and brought blushes and giggles and indignant cries of shame if ever used ...

On the other hand, it was perfectly possible for two first cousins (in the European sense) to marry, provided they had different names. The idea that the male seed predominated, that 'blood' was transmitted by the male, the mother being merely a nourishing receptacle for the child, was another feudalism which even Pao held true.

Today, at last, this has changed: children may adopt either the father's or the mother's name if they so wish, and this in itself is a Cultural Revolution.

At that time some of the very old families in Szechuan possessed a motto: 'Our sons and daughters are not for common blood', and practised an active system of consanguine marriage between the children of brother and sister; spurning marriage with non-related clans, saying that this was 'lowering' to their status: 'The flesh of swans is not for common geese.' In the Chou family such cousinly marriages were common, for when all the cousins got together, including the children issued from different grandfathers, there was a wide choice of consanguine pairing available and regarded with favour, provided the family names were different, as being easier to handle than pairing with unknowns, with all the attendant expense of marriage-brokers (and their inflated mendacity in 'selling' a bride or groom).

There were also 'kinship' clans with whom there was a tradition of marriage; thus the Hou, the Hung, the Teng families were ones which, automatically, when an eligible daughter or son came of age, would think of an eligible son or daughter of the Chou family, and vice-versa. Business and commercial relations followed these family relationships closely and were inextricably intertwined with them.

Third Uncle explained all this to me, or rather not to me, but to us all, for he loved to discourse at length on the Family, and no time was better than the New Year to commemorate, by word, the traditions that were the solder of the system, the Big Feudal Family of China, with its tentacular hold upon each and every member.

Thus I was proclaimed Third Daughter, my name put into the book of genealogy; displacing slightly my Third Uncle's daughter who was born ten days after me; we decided to be called Tall Third and Fat Third; for she was round-faced and merry, and rather better fleshed. All the family called me Third Daughter, and the servants called me Third Miss; and thus I was adopted into the Family at last, and my family name was given to me.

Previous to this ceremony, I had been introduced to the soul tablets of the ancestors, in the minor commemorative hall which Third Uncle kept in his house in Sheep Market Lane in Chengtu. Every morning Sixth Brother, my Third Uncle's youngest son, went round the hall and the tree- and flower-filled courtyard in front of it, with a bundle of lighted incense sticks, striking the gongs and putting the sticks in selected corners, and doing obeisance to the soul tablets of the ancestors; food and drink and fruit were laid in front of them; and Third Aunt would beseech them, saying; 'Grandfather, Grandmother, Great-great-uncle, please eat.'

My grandmother, who had died two years before, also had her place laid at table on certain days of the month; and when Third Aunt sat down to meals she would first call Grandmother's spirit to eat and place some choice morsels on her small plate, and a little tea in her cup.

I liked Third Aunt immediately, and so much; she had hair polished like black jade, a smooth white skin, beautiful small hands. Even today, at sixty-seven, she has those lovely hands, though her skin is darkened with the sun and her hair is beginning to turn white. She had tiny bound feet, and she wore mourning for Grandmother for three years. Third Aunt was so small that when she sat in a chair her feet dangled off the floor, and this is how I remember her, sitting in a chair too high and too large for her, patient and folded patiently upon herself. She knew all that had to be done for a large house and clan, and though she was never anything but gentle, she was also capable. She did not mind Yao the concubine, who was insignificant-looking, rather ugly, did not push herself forward, and as long as she had opium to smoke was able in her own way. Yao the concubine ran the Chungking house easily, for she was a Chungking woman; Third Uncle had found her in a house of pleasure, and she had nursed him through an unspecified illness whose symptoms and signs she related to me most gleefully, but which I could never identify. He had bought her out, and she became his housekeeper. He had very little to do with her, but for thirty years looked after her needs, chiefly in opium, and never stinted her for money to buy clothes. Yao was not profligate, but careful, and sober, as was Third Aunt; she did not drink nor did she bring disrepute upon the house, and her opium habit was discreet, she did it in secret, and never cooked more than three pipes.

Several months later Yao the concubine and Third Aunt were to become active allies, the reason being a temporary infatuation which Third Uncle underwent for a film star. The film star was beautiful; she was an 'outlander', from Shanghai (or so she said), and very expensive; it was this last point, and not the fact that she might or might not lavish her favours upon Third Uncle (and this was never made clear), which alarmed Third Aunt and Yao the concubine. They both went about with glum faces, Third Aunt muttering that Third Uncle was under a witchcraft spell, had been given a love philtre by that 'foreign' woman from Shanghai: then sighing and going on with her duties,

with dour mouth and knitted brows; Yao more explicit, more garrulous, being a coarser person, terrified that her source of opium might
be cut off, saying that the 'star' was a prostitute, and that she knew
who was the procurer, that it was a racket, of which the star was the
bait, to destroy Third Uncle and blackmail him. But soon all was well
again; the star did cost too much, and became more and more demanding; Third Uncle put an end to it.

His office at the bank and his living-room in Chengtu and also the
rooms in the hill house at Ta Erh Wo in Chungking, where he went to
stay after the house in Woodcutter Lane in Chungking was bombed
later, in May 1939, had blossomed with photographs of the star,
generous-busted, dimple-cheeked, dreamy large eyes raised to heaven,
and the lot coloured by hand. 'So expensive,' grumbled Yao the concubine. Third Uncle would take these framed likenesses down and
discourse lengthily on the precept of good looks, making it sound like
a philosophy of pulchritude. 'Consider this face, for instance. You
notice the proportion of forehead to chin, indicating a moral character
of considerable strength ... Notice also the eyes, how they are set ...
the astrologers say that the breadth between the eyes must be as much
as the eye itself ... ' He was never lewd, or immodest, but rhetorical
and long-winded in these disquisitions on the favoured features of
what, at the time, Yao Niang called 'That cheap bone' and Third
Aunt 'Star what?' And suddenly there were no photos, no more lectures on the laws of good looks; Third Uncle shut himself up in his
study and practised calligraphy; then came out, called for his sedan
chair, and that very evening all the photos disappeared and no one ever
heard mention of the star again.

Apart from that slight episode, in all the years I knew Third Uncle
and Third Aunt, there was no rift to their harmony and that tolerant
companionship which is marriage; Third Uncle made fun of Third
Aunt's lisp; Third Aunt would blush like a young girl when Third
Uncle spoke to her. She would sit up, waiting for him; she would
hover, listening to him, as we did, for hours. Today, they are both
old, but together; after the Revolution Yao the concubine was cured
of the opium habit, and died of tuberculosis after some years. Third
Aunt looked after her, and now Third Aunt, who in spite of her small
bound feet can walk miles and is full of zest, goes every day to a lecture
on politics, on the Thought of Mao Tsetung; she is so interested and
avid for more that she arrives half an hour before the group is due to

meet. Third Uncle nurses his bad knees and stays at home, waiting for her. And Third Aunt is as happy in the comparative poverty which is theirs today, as she was when she had so much more, so many houses and so many relations to look after, when Third Uncle was a rich man.

Sixth Uncle and Sixth Aunt were also a happy couple; theirs was a love marriage. All unknown to their respective families, Sixth Uncle had briefly perceived Sixth Aunt at the park on a festival and fallen in love; and behold she it was who was chosen for him! They never got over this good luck, it enriched their married life for all its years. Sixth Aunt was very beautiful. Even after twelve children, six sons and six daughters, she remained slim-waisted and doe-eyed, her skin pale and even. Her body was completely hairless, even at thirty-five; for many a mature woman in Szechuan is thus hairless, nothing on pubes or in armpits, but with most luxuriant heads of hair.

Sixth Aunt, who was 'modern' (had she not married for love?), had herself sterilized after the twelfth child, as she said it was enough. She remains slim, smooth-faced and dark-haired even today, and Sixth Uncle is still so much in love with her he cannot do anything without first running to tell her about it. They shocked a good many people because when Chengtu was bombed by the Japanese in 1940, they let their children go to the shelters by themselves, while they walked behind them, hand in hand, something never seen in Szechuan before the Revolution.

First Uncle, on the other hand, did not get on well with First Aunt, and their children witnessed many family quarrels but bore them philosophically, for a large family has enormous resilience. First Uncle was a spendthrift, unsuccessful in business, and First Aunt accused him of much philandering; she was a thin, perpetually complaining woman, and used to come, her loud voice preceding her, to smoke her water pipe with Third Aunt and Sixth Aunt and talk of her woes.

But at each New Year the family came together, Third Great-uncle, brother to our grandfather, with his numerous progeny, with Third Great-aunt and his concubine, a most hardworking, painstaking woman, devoted to Third Great-aunt. First, Third, and Sixth Uncles and their families, other cousins, of varying rank and degree, for whose relationship there is no adequate English word; cousins of Great-uncle, the Great-uncles of my maternal grandmother's side, widowed and married aunts of second, third and fourth degree. To all of them we of the younger generation kowtowed, and all through the New

Year, which in Chengtu lasts a month, nothing but soft words, pleasant faces and smiles were shown, for as the year began so would it continue, and it must begin well.

On the eve of the New Year itself we all stayed up, talking, as was the custom in the past, when the family had a tobacco trade and used to spend the night awake to do the accounts, wind up the year's business, pay all debts and receive all monies due ... But now there were no debts to pay and no monies to receive, only the family, sitting round, and the voice of Third Uncle, talking of all the many customs and traditions of Szechuan, talking of the tobacco trade which had been the family mainstay for a hundred and twenty years in the past, talking ... until we all yawned and then Third Uncle gave the signal that we could leave and so we went to bed.

After the first ten days of New Year in Chengtu, Third Aunt and an assemblage of the younger generation including myself departed for Pihsien, a small townlet only fifteen *li* or about seven miles from Chengtu. Our small procession went through the West Gate; the road was a morass of sticky, red mud which clung like glue to the feet of the rickshaw coolies. It was a sunny day, that porous sunshine which soon, with the spring advancing, would turn the plain into a damp, humid hothouse, a ceiling of swelter shielding the whole of the Chengtu basin area, keeping it a perpetual steam bath, always a little moist. This quality of dampness also came up from the fields, cloyed with dung, dark, oily, fertile; only at spring's beginning, which was New Year, and for a few weeks in the mild short winter, was it comparatively dry. And from this constant dampness came the fine fair skin of the girls, even the pale and toiling women, squat and small and undernourished, had skins like magnolia petals. The feet of our pullers in their woven straw sandals squashed through the mud of the roads, and soon we were out of the city, going briskly towards Pihsien. I watched the bulging back muscles of the man in front pulling me. He was stripped to the waist, sweating, though it was cold; he had a piece of cloth round his head to prevent the sweat from dribbling into his eyes. I would have liked to walk, but this could not be done, as Third Aunt would not allow it.

Third Uncle had already told me much about the small medieval town of Pihsien, the first spot where our ancestors had settled to become farmers; like so many of the Szechuan inhabitants of today, like Kuo Mo Jo and Pa Chin, the writers, and Chu Teh the commander of the Chinese Red armies, our family came originally from Hakkas who had trekked southwards from the Yellow River basin in the eleventh century, away from the ravagings of the Mongols and the Tartars, to settle in the southern provinces of Fukien and Kwangtung, and there they had been late-comers; the best fields were already possessed; their villages had remained poor, on a tenant-farmer basis, and this had produced a continual migration of the males, in search of better land. Many had become pedlars, or load-carriers, or salt-smugglers, and also rebels and revolutionaries. After the Manchu invasion in the seventeenth century, Szechuan, which had resisted the Manchus for forty years, had been almost depopulated through massacre and plague. The Manchu dynasty began a policy of population shift, urging Hakkas to settle the unpeopled regions. In the nineteenth century they utilized the Hakkas as military units, to suppress local uprisings. Hakkas migrated from Kwangtung north-westwards to Szechuan, following the salt boats which plied the inner waterways, and the mountain paths of the salt-smugglers. They settled in the fertile river valleys and in the Chengtu plain. And Pihsien was the best spot of all, most fertile and rich, with two and sometimes three rice harvests a year.

The rickshaw men joked between themselves as they paced, almost at running speed, the fresh morning road. Third Uncle joined in their talk, saying how lucky they were not to be in Chungking, where all the streets were staircases of stone, climbing the city from level to level; so that the huakan bearers and the rickshaw pullers had much to do to keep their balance in the greasy rain and the winter fog, and when the sweat poured down and blinded their sight in the savage summer heat; if a man's foot slipped there could be broken bones, and a broken bone meant a broken rice-bowl, a stomach caving in from hunger, and no way out. And the men laughed and one said yes, he had heard of Chungking, a brother of his was there, he was a huakan man and there huakan men did not last long, their life ran out of them both summer and winter, for the summer was a cauldron and the winter a river of ice, and where were the poor to get the clothing they needed in such weather? And so they were lucky to be in the fair city of Chengtu, where all was plain and even, the roads flat like pacing a palace floor, and much water about so that there were many tea-houses

107

where a man could quench his dry mouth's thirst. Chungking was so dry the trees would not grow on its rock, and the sun was like a whiplash on the shoulders, not to mention the bamboo poles which bit into the flesh, especially when the chair was atilt on those almost perpendicular staircase streets ...

And another man said it was a better life than being conscripted into the army, and he had seen the officers come to conscript; they were fierce as wolves, and armed; and they rounded up people sitting at tea-houses and working in the fields, just roped them together, and took them away; and that was not all – they also loaded them with bales of firewood and barrels of oil and rolls of cloth and many other things, which they themselves were taking to the city to sell; and they dragged them and whipped them; many died, because they forgot rice-time and made them walk thirty *li* a day, or more, and they shut them up at night, and the living in the morning propped up the dead and dragged them on the road before the officers deigned to look their way. So it was better to be a huakan man and to have a gentleman to carry than to carry a gun for these down-river people; his brother had been taken two months ago and now there were many mouths to feed at home. Thus by indirection, as a tale, they voiced their misery, and in tones so that one could only guess at the anger seething below ...

And this was so much like what the great poet Tu Fu had described, even the man's words, so fiercely beautiful in the Chengtu singsong with its drawling at the end of sentences:

Travelling on the Hsin An road,
I hear lamentation, and the call of conscripts' names.
I question the officer, who says:
The village is small, and there are no more men,
Yet again we need men for war.
None are left
But half-grown boys, absurdly short and small.
The well-fed ones have mothers walking with them, weeping;
The hungry ones are alone, none bid them good luck.
The tumbling sunset waters flow east,
The hills echo with the screams of the wounded ...
No mercy for them, in heaven nor earth ...

As we sped on I could see that eternal trudging of the people, for ever toiling and dying, and nothing but obedience demanded from them, and their leaders leading them to disaster and to death; and breaking them when they rebelled ... their names unknown – was there none but an eighth-century poet to tell of their plight?

Fields were all about us, twinkling their capture of heaven and sun; small black pigs grunted in and out of the mud-floored unkempt houses; then the grey-and-black clusters of more solid brick habitations that was Pihsien, with its battlemented parapet wall, its narrow gate, its main street densely built up with shops, its large-roofed temple with sky-running eaves where the secret society men of the 1911 Revolution had assembled, to fight the imperial Manchu dynasty. In the main hall of the temple, behind dusty curtains, were deities which were carried out once a year to inspect the city and its walls and battlemented gates. Outside the town was the great shrine and clan house, the family ancestral hall my great-grandfather built; next to it the ancestral graves, some mounds in the earth, others great with stone.

From Pihsien where the first pedlar ancestor had staked out a piece of land the family had radiated throughout the province of Szechuan,* establishing secondary clan houses, selecting good funeral sites, rising from agricultural labour to landlordism and the gentry, and here, at Pihsien, all this was clear as the large house lorded it in a landscape of fields, and the graves of future generations were prepared for by the tall grove of lanmu trees whose wood was earmarked for the coffins to come. Here at the festivals Third Aunt and other aunts would be busy, preparing paper money in stacks, in the shape of silver ingots, to burn at the graves. And here in the fields, on the 15th of the New Year, a great ceremony took place, the dragon procession. From the temple came the great, writhing, glittering dragon; long as a hundred men, held aloft on poles, down the streets and about the fields and round the town wall; to conjure disease away the men let off tubes of gunpowder close against their own bodies and did not fear the burn; this made them remain strong in the coming year. Dipping and rearing, writhing in the dragon dance, with the hiss and jet and sparkle of firecrackers, the men carried the dragon to circle the town and the fields of rape and rice, jade-green rice and dandelion-yellow rape, tobacco and bean and also opium, and the million small canalicules glistening with the water of life to the fields.

Four times in the next three years I was to return to Chengtu, and twice more to Pihsien, to accompany Third Aunt on her resolute

*See *The Crippled Tree*.

jaunts there and back; to help her perform these rituals of duty and reverence which held the feudal Big Family together. Every time I fell back into malleable, putty slowness, half reverie, half lassitude, absorbed into a way of living which absolved from independent thought or action and followed the seasons, the rites and the customs; the performance of these rites unquestioned. Had it not been for my family, for the kindness – not individualized but collective, not particularized nor peculiar because it was me, but because it was all-of-us-together – I think I could not have endured so long. I learnt in these years more about the interior of China, about the feudal system and what it meant, than I would have in a coastal city such as Peking or Shanghai in a lifetime; I put myself to study Chinese seriously and it stayed with me, through the years, so that I was no longer incompetent in my own language. I learnt to think round and about a question rather than straight, to gauge the feudal mind, a knowledge valuable to me, for it enables me to understand how much work is left still to be done, to untrammel minds, to destroy the bonds of the past, emotional attitudes and atavistic cravings grounded in millennia of ritual. If I can understand the Cultural Revolution today, in all of its importance, it is because of these years in Szechuan, a generation ago, a Revolution ago.

The district round Pihsien still grew tobacco, though in small quantities, and tobacco had been the chief commercial venture of the Chou family from 1799 to 1917, when their enterprise, known as Kuanghsing, was declared bankrupt. Uncle took us to see the tobacco barns in Pihsien, large airy sheds where the leaves were stored in bundles. The seedbeds for tobacco were prepared in October, after the rice harvest had been gathered in September. The seeds were sown, and the beds, watered with liquid manure, covered with rice straw left over from the harvest. When the tobacco stalks reached half an inch, the straw was removed, the stalks protected by tents made of stalks from rape put astride the seed beds. Thus they spent the Szechuan winter, so mild the swallow does not leave the plain. In April water from the irrigation canals was let into the seed beds by removing the temporary blocks of earth and stone which separated from one another the hand-dug canalicules, and every five days liquid manure was sprayed upon the plants. In May the tobacco shoots were a foot high, and beginning to flower, when their tops were snipped off by hand to prevent flowering and to divert the sap to the leaves. In June the leaves were harvested by hand and placed on bamboo screens to dry in the sun for four to five days, then bound between two bamboo screens when not yet completely dry so that they did not shrivel. Finally, they were spread out to dry again, tied in bundles of three-and-a-half catties each, each bundle containing approximately one hundred and thirty leaves. This was the best tobacco, the finest grade. Smaller leaves came in boxes about two feet square and six inches deep, some rape oil was poured between the layers, the extra oil squeezed out in a wooden press, until they formed a solid block which was sliced two inches apart and again pressed into smaller blocks, hard enough to be shredded with a knife. This was second-grade tobacco. Finally, there was cord tobacco, consisting of leaves hung for twenty days below the eaves of roofs, away from dew and rain, until they turned brown, when they were bundled for sale.

Third Uncle showed us the fine shredded silken tobacco for the water pipe, pale blond in colour, so fine it felt like silk in the hand. Everyone smoked the water pipe in Szechuan, and the pipes were made of pewter and decorated with carvings, with silver, with jade. Today no one smokes the water pipe any more.

Beside tobacco, the family also had dealt in salt from the Tze Liu Ching salt-mines, which had been worked since the Han dynasty. The rock salt from these mines, said Third Uncle, was the best, indispensable for good cooking and much valued; and the salt monopoly had been a government monopoly for many centuries, under control of salt officials, of which Great-grandfather was one. There was also some commerce in preserved cakes from the southern provinces, made with fine flour and dates, sprinkled with sesame seed. Then timber for export and tung oil had also been items of commerce, but never to a great extent.

A few miles from Pihsien, going westward on the road, was Kuanhsien, the beginning foothills of the large ranges running north to south between Szechuan and Tibet; and to Kuanhsien I went several times, and also to the Tsingcheng mountains farther than Kuanhsien, where there were famous Taoist temples and monasteries. All this region was now an opium-growing area; the opium belt extended through the foothill districts into Sikang province. The poppy grew in vast pink-

and-white fields in secluded valleys, and Pihsien was an opium-collecting centre, almost every other man a smoker. The glazed yellow skins, the bleared hooded eyes, the set of the gaunt bodies showed it; the wealthy smoked too, but they also ate well, and opium did not leave its traces upon them, but it quickly destroyed those who relied on opium for strength, for 'breath' as they called it, and those were the toilers, the load-carriers, the huakan men, the pullers of junks, who had not enough to eat. Our family had not trafficked in opium, said Third Uncle, and apart from the concubine Yao, no one in the family smoked. Certainly no one in my generation did, for we had been brought up with the memory of the Opium Wars and the depredations of the Western Powers, all through the nineteenth and early twentieth centuries, and their barbaric violence.

In the brothels and opium houses of Szechuan, all sorts of opium could be had, from the very fine Yunnan quality to the dross the huakan bearers smoked; and the sordid story of opium was linked with the greed of the warlords, their need for money to finance their private wars. Szechuan, the wealthiest province of China, had the poorest people, multitudes in rags, because of decades of tyranny and decades of opium-growing.

Many of the family, including Third Uncle, had lived through the warlord period in Szechuan; even in 1939, during the Sino-Japanese conflict, it had not quite stopped. The warlords of Szechuan had arisen earliest of all after the Revolution of 1911; they had been the first opposed to Yuan Shihkai and his ambition to become an emperor after the downfall of the Manchu dynasty; but very soon had become embroiled in internecine warfare. From 1915 to 1939 the province had not known peace. There had been four hundred and ten warlord wars in Szechuan; and the worst of these were in the fertile basin of Chengtu. Besides the provincial wars, the Szechuan militarists carried on inter-provincial wars. From 1917 to 1923 Liu Wenhui of Szechuan fought with the warlords of Yunnan province; once for seven days and seven nights within the closed gates of Chengtu itself. Most of the victims were the local population. Liu Wenhui then fought Tai K'an of Kweichow province who had invaded Szechuan, for eighteen days and nights, also in and about Chengtu. The Kweichow and Yunnan provincial warlords withdrew; but warfare within Szechuan continued and went on without stop for twenty years. Yang Sen and Teng Hsihou, Tien Sungyao, Liu Wenhui and Liu Hsiang all indulged in what was euphemistically named 'family quarrels'.

The streets of Chengtu were divided by rival factions; crossing from one side of the street to the other involved paying 'custom duties', because it meant crossing into another territory. Like the feudal barons of old they made fortresses of the cities, and pressganged peasants for their armies. In 1934 Liu Hsiang fought against Liu Wenhui (they were nephew and uncle) and with Teng Hsihou, Tien Sungyao, invested the city of Chengtu once again, each taking a quarter; fighting at regular hours in the central streets. Having heard of tanks, one of them, I forget which, requisitioned all the human dung carts, covered them with tin plate, and installed his soldiers in them to assault 'the enemy'. The unhappy manure coolies had to push these loads of soldiers to battle, as they were accustomed to push the manure in these carts along the roads to the fields outside the walls. Most of the victims were manure coolies.

And for these ruinous wars the Szechuan militarists needed men, money and weapons. Of men, hauled off the fields, off the roads, off the streets, there were plenty. The saying in Szechuan was: 300 *li*, 300,000 conscripts. Almost a million men were thus herded into the civil wars of Szechuan and 400,000 were perpetually under arms. Not counting what they spent for their wars, seventy-one warlords altogether amassed in personal wealth in Szechuan alone almost six billion dollars between 1915 and 1934.

With weapons from abroad, from France, the United States, England, through their enclaves in China, the concessions of Shanghai and Hankow, the Chinese warlords were plentifully supplied. Most of the surplus equipment of the First World War was off-loaded into China by the European import-export firms of Shanghai, among them Jardine Matheson. It was from gun-selling and its corollary, opium, that the 'Princely House', as it was called, derived its wealth; from opium and gun-selling the Sassoons had made much money in the Shanghai of the 1920s and '30s.

By 1917 Szechuan was already a bankrupt province; there was very little silver left and the silver dollar coin was getting thinner and thinner, was alloyed with lead and finally disappeared, to be replaced with baked clay coins which crumbled in the hand. The Szechuan militarists were not worried by the disappearance of money; they had with them the gentry, the landlords. They were great landlords themselves and collected land rents in kind. It was the peasant who found his labour and his crop gone for a handful of mud.

The militarists paid for their wars out of taxation and opium. On the matter of taxation, Szechuan was notorious. For the half million men under arms during those twenty years, 86 million dollars a year were required before the 1930s, 140 million afterwards; after the entry of Chiang's government into Szechuan in 1938-9 more men were conscripted, and more money was required. The system of collecting money by taxation and by trafficking in opium remained substantially the same as during the preceding warlord period, but the load was even heavier for the peasantry.

Taxes consisted of land rent in kind, fifty per cent of the harvest crops, and after that a multitude of other taxes, of a range and variety almost unbelievable, which remained in force in one form or another till 1949. There were, among others, a general tax, tobacco tax, wine tax, transport extra tax, education tax, commercial tax, rent tax, festivity tax, mining tax, equalization tax, winter protection tax, ammunition tax, monthly tax, street number tax, New Year pig tax, tooth tax, head tax, winepot tax, market inspection tax, road tax, stricken people tax, red lantern tax, banquet tax, cleaning village tax, police tax, sugar tax, paper tax, rice tax, extra salt tax (there were five salt taxes), boat tax, getting away from conscription tax, getting let off from forced labour (corvée) tax, ticket tax, iron tax, coal tax, salt cellar and stove tax, rolling tobacco leaf tax, special lamp tax, embroidery and printing tax, northern expedition tax (collected since 1925), municipal tax, length of door tax, breadth of window tax, hair and blood tax, tax on weights and weighing machines, bandit tax, bandit suppression congratulatory tax, suppression of communism tax, extra pacification tax ...

The warlords' ingenuity in devising taxes had no limits; new taxes with bewitching names were devised: compassion tax, soldiers' welfare tax, soldiers' rice tax, water tax, temporary tax. The 'social welfare' tax collected in Pihsien alone amounted to twice $300,000 in two years ...

The burden of these taxes fell most heavily on peasant, small craftsman, and petty shopkeeper. The land tax to be paid by the landlords was passed on in the land rent paid to them by their tenant farmers; the rich in the cities had no window tax to pay, since they surrounded their houses with windowless walls; and no lamp tax, since no light showed outside their heavy black lacquer gates. They were automatically spared conscription, being educated, and corvée, since they were not manual workers.

Often the tax on articles was far in excess of the cost of the article itself; to transport medical herbs from Pi Kou to Chungking there were eighty-three taxations stands; sugar from Tsechung to Chungking, about 200 miles, had to pay tax twenty-one times. From Lohsien to Chungking, 400 *li* (130 miles) there were 134 taxation stands for commodities ...

The manure tax, tax on human dung and public cloacae was very much resented by the wealthy, for it directly affected them; they owned the public cloacae. But this was the only tax which affected them. The 'happy' tax which was imposed in order to promote a cheerful countenance from those who paid tax was the subject of much talk in the tea-houses. Some clever subaltern, pressed by his warlord master to find some new sources of money, also devised a 'laziness tax'. The laziness tax was imposed upon those who did *not* grow opium. The warlords instituted 'opium eradication' bureaux, and the laziness tax was scaled on the number of poppies grown; the less opium poppies, the more tax. The laziness tax was even enforced in districts where no opium could be planted, as around Neichiang, the city of sugar and sugared fruit and sweetmeats, which had to pay ten thousand dollars of laziness tax because no opium could be planted there, there was no suitable ground for it.

The peasants were thus forced to grow opium. Opium eradication campaigns, and opium eradication enforcement bureaux established by the various militarists, were only to make sure that the peasant grew the opium, and inspection teams went out to 'eradicate' and came back to report on the harvest prospects. The warlords even sent their soldiers to guard the opium crops against other warlords; over the peasants, busy collecting the thick dark sap from the poppy heart, stood a soldier with a gun. So greedy for the harvest of opium were the warlords that often the opium collector would stand his men near the peasants with orders to feed them rice with a spoon while they went on with their work, incising the poppy heart for the juice to spurt, thicken and darken; a delicate operation, to be repeated thousands of times upon whole fields of poppies. In relays the peasants were pushed to harvest the coagulated crude brown sap as swiftly as possible, and then it was all taken away, under armed escort; and what was paid to the peasant was a very low rate, a few coins for his day's labour, lower than grain, but if he did not grow opium, he paid a tax higher than land rent ...

Taxes had been collected thirty-nine years in advance by 1935; after 1935 the collection of tax in advance accelerated and reached seventy years in advance and since inflation set in rapidly in 1940, taxes in kind, the squeeze on land and on grain, became even more oppressive as money dwindled to nearly nothing.

It was in 1939 that, through the Blueshirts the Chiang regime sought to 'nationalize' all commodity articles, establishing monopoly companies for everything Szechuan produced. And since there was a limit to these products, again it was opium which became an enormous source of funds for the secret police.

The Blueshirt organization started to wrest from the local militarists the control of these sources of money. With the accumulation of functionaries and agents, the rivalry between the locals and the Blueshirt agencies, the opium crops in the known districts dispersed very rapidly, as many new strata of middlemen appeared to sponge off 'residue money' from the crops. The Sung Pan region, Mao Hsien, Li Fan, Wen Chuan, Yu Kong and Tsing Hua counties in Szechuan had all been producers of opium; after 1938 many areas which had not produced opium started producing it, since the demand was even greater than before. Transport was now a Blueshirt monopoly, and this affected the carriage of the drug. Local Kuomintang Party offices served as storage godowns for medicines, textiles, tung oil, and opium in bulk; long lines of carriers could be seen, lining up in front of various government offices with baskets to transport the stuff, labelled 'government files' or 'war material', to the shipping centres. The Great River was the Great Opium road, from Szechuan to Shanghai, as was the road from Yunnan to French Indo-China. All through the war the traffic between the Kempetai, or Japanese secret service, and the Blueshirts under Tai Lee was never interrupted; the crude opium got to the refineries in Shanghai and Tientsin, and from there went out, in the form of heroin and morphine, to do its work of poisoning the people of the cities in the Japanese-occupied zones ...

On this subject, as on others, Third Uncle was prolix. He mimicked the opium grower, the technique of the small hooked knife incising the poppy, during the hurried gathering of the crop. He told of violent

clashes between the traditional gangs, the Kelao, and the new in-
vaders; of the Blueshirts kidnapping minor local warlords, subalterns
of the great ones, in order to get their 'co-operation' in the opium
game. As a way of settling scores with the 'down-river gangsters', as
the Szechuanese called the Chiang government, the local Kelao
secret society heads occasionally gave protection to liberal-minded
intellectuals. One of these local headmen was even persuaded to erect
a 'university' in his domain; and in this university a small communist
cell began to function ... Tai Lee's agents kidnapped the man, accused
him of carrying weapons illegally and forced him to pay a large bribe
to get out of jail. Elsewhere pitched battles were fought, at opium-
harvest time, between Blueshirt and Kelao ...

Third Uncle, like all the gentry and even some members of the
Communist Party itself (such as the old veteran revolutionary Wu
Yuchang, and Liu Tsetan, who had formed the north-west Red
base), was closely in touch with the Kelao Elder Brothers Society. He
occasionally let fall the more obvious phrases by which members
recognized each other. Thus the words 'opening a mountain' meant
collecting new adherents, and 'Have you had your eyes carved in
yet?' meant, 'Are you a "brother" or member of the Kelao yet?' The
Kelao had been a patriotic, anti-Manchu brotherhood, and had had a
good deal to do with the peasant uprisings of the nineteenth century
and with the Revolution of 1911. But they had degenerated into
organized crime, the control of brothels and opium, as well as providing private bodyguards for the warlords. Chiang had sent Dou
Yuseng, the Shanghai gangster, to break the Kelao with his own Triad
gangs, but the Kelao resisted until the end. Mao Tsetung had written
them a letter, in July 1936, in the name of the Central Committee,
seeking to awaken their patriotic feelings, to remind them of their
better days, of the seriousness of the Japanese aggression, to rally them
to a united action against the common enemy. In 1941 some of the
8th Route (Red) Army documents revealed the difficulties they en-
countered in a countryside dominated by secret societies. In 1949 the
Kelao decided not to help Chiang Kaishek, and the Szechuan warlords
went over to the communist armies without resistance. There was no
military campaign to take Szechuan. It is reported that the affair was
transacted through an influential Kelao man, also a member of the
Communist Party, who lived in Hongkong, but there are no longer
any Kelao, or warlords, or opium in Szechuan today.

☆

The rise of Third Uncle to wealth, the regeneration of the Chou family fortunes, were due to the warlord system, as Third Uncle himself was to recognize when in 1956 he wrote his own self-criticism. A copy of this he sent to my father, and thus it came to me, and in it Third Uncle, having followed courses in Marxism, proclaimed himself enlightened as to the role of his class, the gentry, in the exploitation of the people.

After 1917 when the tobacco trade was ruined, the Chou family went bankrupt. At that time Third Uncle was an officer in the Szechuan armies, and the warlord wars had begun. Third Uncle withdrew from a military career in order to wind up the bankruptcy, and for a time, as he described it: 'I stayed at home planting flowers and bamboo, and reflecting what next to do.' In 1919 war started between Yunnan and Szechuan, and Third Uncle went into the army again, under the Szechuan warlords. His abilities, not so much as an officer, but as a shrewd and efficient organizer, came to the notice of Liu Hsiang, the top militarist. Liu Hsiang made Chungking his capital city, and asked Third Uncle to manage his financial affairs. In 1924 Liu Hsiang began to have serious money difficulties; he needed cash for a big war on a host of other warlords, and asked Third Uncle to take charge of the 'bureau for the control and eradication of opium' in order to pay his troops ...

'Now that was a beautiful name,' wrote Third Uncle sarcastically. 'Control and eradication indeed! In truth, we had to stimulate the production of opium, fine the peasants who did not plant opium (that was the laziness tax) and thus get money to pay the soldiers and buy the ammunition for Liu Hsiang. Liu Hsiang made use of me and the connections I had, through the previous commerce of tobacco, my personal friendships, and some ability for figures.' Third Uncle ran the bureau successfully; Liu Hsiang then asked him to manage the collection of the tax on the opium coming into Szechuan by road from Yunnan. Yunnan opium was prized above all, being of a finer quality than Szechuan opium. 'Thus, after a year, Liu Hsiang was able to win the war against Yunnan. I then desired to withdraw, as I did not like my work; I myself never traded in opium, though I managed the accounts of the bureau for Liu Hsiang. As soon as I could I gave it up, and turned to industry and commerce. I have never touched the traffic of opium since then, and never personally made money out of opium.'

But Liu Hsiang would not let an able administrator like Third Uncle go, and in 1929, when Liu promoted himself governor of both Szechuan and Sikang, and was contemplating war against his uncle Liu Wenhui (again for opium, for when Liu Hsiang drove Liu Wenhui out of Szechuan, Liu Wenhui withdrew to Sikang where he planted opium in huge quantities and had a total monopoly over the harvest in the whole province), he recalled Third Uncle to serve him. Third Uncle was to reflect with acerbity on that period. 'I thought the most important thing then was provincial autonomy, independence for Szechuan under Liu Hsiang, for Szechuan is a kingdom enclosed, a small paradise, producing all its needs and more; it is the trump card of China: the great western bastion, all-sufficient heart of the land; so long as Szechuan is safe, all China is safe.' Third Uncle thought that once war was over Liu Hsiang would be able to do something for the people; 'it would be better than the things I had seen in the down-river cities, second-rate imitations of foreigners; and the foreign extortions, which were less open, but even more ruthless.'

So Third Uncle again obliged Liu Hsiang, and set up tax stations (for the control of opium and commodities) both in Wanhsien and in Chungking. 'This device further crippled, instead of aiding, trade and commerce.' Then in 1934 something happened which struck terror in many a warlord in Szechuan; the Red armies, on the Long March, came through Szechuan, and everywhere the peasants rose and many joined the Red armies.

'Joining with sticks only,' said Third Uncle. 'And how frightened we were when the peasants rose! And the landlords and the militarists called up their troops and their armed retainers, and started massacring the peasants again. How they killed! As easily as swatting flies.'

Liu Hsiang, dreading the Red armies, flew to Nanking to confer with Chiang Kaishek; he came back to be named Chairman of the province, both its civil and military governor; this gave him increased power. He then imposed another 'pacification' levy to fight the communists, and thus collected more money for himself. Chiang Kaishek gave him German weapons, and Liu Hsiang pledged allegiance to Chiang. 'And thus', wound up Third Uncle, 'the Nanking lot, Chiang Kaishek and his followers, were able to gain a foothold in our fair and beautiful province of Szechuan, and to plant spies in the warlord councils, and thus Chiang knew all that went on. It was all because Liu Hsiang panicked when the peasants sang: "The Taiping are back," because of the Red armies crossing Szechuan on the Long March, and

burning the land deeds and distributing land ... The Taiping were defeated; the last of them was killed in 1868 trying to cross the Tatu river
that flows between Szechuan and Tibet. The Red armies were cleverer;
they crossed the Tatu river, and though they suffered incredibly they
survived, and today China is liberated ... ' Thus wrote Third Uncle
in 1956.

And reading Third Uncle's self-criticism, I remembered, too, that
Liu Wenhui, the warlord, ended up as Minister of Forestry under the
Communist Government in Peking ...

After four weeks in Chengtu with the family, Third Uncle and I flew
back to Chungking. Pao was at the airport to meet us; absence seemed
to have mellowed him; for a while there was no quarrel; but soon he
was to return to his foolish agony, and monumental trivia began to
gnaw away the hours, the days, that could have been so much better
spent. Though at first Pao did nothing to involve Third Uncle, later
he was to waylay him one afternoon and tell him how he, Pao, had
saved me from a fate worse than death, which was marriage to a
foreigner ... Third Uncle listened and smiled and kept his own counsel.

Only in 1966, twenty-seven years later, when I went to visit Third
Uncle and Third Aunt in their now so modest house, beyond the
South Gate in Chengtu, he suddenly said, while I sipped the tea he had
so carefully preserved for me: 'Tang Pao Huang was not good to you
– he was a very ambitious young man.' And then he looked round him,
and sighed; for the past was more than decades away, it was a Revolution away, and Pao was no more, and the ancestor graves had been
moved to a common cemetery, and Great-grandfather's clan house,
and the ancestral hall, were now a nursery school for the peasant
children of Pihsien.

Six

THAT TODAY I am a writer is fortuitous, an accident determined
by my return to China in 1938, my marriage with Pao, and the
anguished clash of our lives.

In the spring of 1939, when I returned to Chungking from my New
Year visit to Chengtu, Pao was awaiting orders to go to Sian, which

he called 'the fighting front', a terminology which kept me deluded for a long while. The complaint, whenever he and his friends met, was that 'good' people did not get on, whereas those who had tricks, pull, and influence did. Much gossip about higher ranking officers occupied Pao's time, about Hsu Peiken and his exploits at Changsha, about Ho Yaotsou and Tang Tsung, titular head of the Intelligence Bureau, about Ho Yingchin, Minister of Defence. So-and-so had requisitioned a wagon full of so-called war material; so-and-so was cashiered, and would probably be sent to the front as a punishment because he was caught falsifying accounts. There was restlessness among the pushy young officers because 'the old ones glue their backsides to their chairs.' The competition for advancement was intense, covert and perfidious. Pao's cousin, Tang Paohua, was a frequent visitor, much in awe of Pao. A minor officer in charge of supply and transport, he was very useful to us, and as a result Pao's remaining luggage turned up from Hongkong, including a smart and brand-new portable typewriter which he had purchased before leaving England.

In late March, what seemed to Pao a most important event occurred. Together with some other cadets recently returned from Europe, he was to be received by Chiang Kaishek. For a week before this audience, Pao was wistful, dreamy, gentle, almost pious; his whole demeanour one of solemn cogitation. He was absorbed in the study of Chiang's speeches, and recited them to me; his devotion became almost infectious; he was much nicer to live with and even promised that after a few months of my imbibing 'virtue' through the same pious meditations, I might be allowed to work in a hospital. Meanwhile, I should write to Hers and get back my clothes and books which had been left in Europe. Once Pao was settled with a position where he could 'prove his loyalty', I could study while he went 'on the field of battle' to devote himself to his country. Now his whole future was in the balance, it would all depend on the first impression he made upon The Leader (click).

I wrote to Hers, and asked for my things to be sent back, and also wrote again to my grandfather. I had sent him a long letter for New Year, dated January 3rd, telling him that I was married and was not returning to Belgium, but that I did love him and I was doing the right thing, because I was Chinese. I have the letter, returned to me by my grandfather, in front of me today.

There was no problem about the clothes and books left with Grandfather; he sent them to Hers with a note that he had disinherited me (the usual Denis reaction). But I had also left a suitcase, with a few clothes, a painting done of me by a fellow student, with Louis. Suddenly Pao asked me whether I had written any letters to Louis and I said yes, of course. So he said that I should get them back; I said I will write to Louis and ask for them, but Pao would not let me do so. He said I must ask Hers to get them back. I tried to explain to Pao that Louis would greatly resent this, but he would not listen; and thus a fairly simple thing became an extremely involved and bruising one. Louis refused to hand over anything except to me personally; said he would not give my letters to Hers or to anyone else. All he wanted was a note from me to the effect that I wanted my things back, and that I had broken with him. He would accept this, he said, 'for the sake of China'. He had a suspicion that there was some degree of coercion present, which accounted for the strangeness of my behaviour and my silence. His intentions had been honourable, he felt he was the injured party. Hers suddenly became moralistic, and wrote a letter showing that he too, could not grasp what was happening.

I cannot understand the wish you have to forget the past, your origin ... just as if you had committed a terrible crime, just as if your former connections were dishonourable. In my opinion, you have committed only one sin ... you have lied to yourself ... wasted your best years trying to prove that your theory, your ideas were right, now you know they are not ...

All these stupid slogans of campus life were only for school-children, spoilt children. And you have been spoilt ...

It was a continuation of our political argument; Hers thought that I should have done nothing but study, ensconce myself in indifference, refuse involvement, never left Belgium. He sought to prove by this epistolary homily that he had all along sought to restrain me. According to him, to make patriotic speeches was to 'prove a theory'.

'Even if I had no affection for you, no feeling,' wrote Hers, 'I cannot help the fact that I am the one that took you away from your family, from China, who sent you to Europe. A terrible responsibility indeed ... ' This letter, dated May 16th, 1939, reached me in July, in Chengtu.

And all this about a few clothes, a few letters. Pao behaved as if his whole future depended on it; became frenzied, raved, beat me, and said that one day when he (Pao) was a great man, Louis would use my letters to blackmail him. It was impossible to tell him that this was highly improbable as he instantly reacted by shouting: 'You dare to defend him, to contradict your noble husband!' and rained some more blows upon me.

Finally Louis gave in: everything was duly sent to Hongkong, to be stored in the vaults of the Bank of China, and recovered by me in 1950, when both Louis and Pao had disappeared; and none of it was valuable or important. But Hers did send me my diplomas from the University of Brussels separately, by registered airmail, and they fortunately arrived when Pao was away. His cousin, Paohua, handed them to me, having received no instructions to withhold parcels from me, only letters. The diplomas thus escaped destruction at the hands of Pao; I handed them to Third Uncle, who kept them in his private box in the Meifeng Bank vault for some years.

Came the day of Pao's interview with Chiang Kaishek; in a glow, looking glossy and sleek, wearing his best uniform, and white gloves, Pao went. We had bought some powdered chalk to get the gloves even whiter, after I had washed and washed them, but the dubious coloured Chungking water was not the appropriate fluid for whitening gloves. I hoped that Pao would not shake hands too ardently, lest some of the powdered chalk should shake off ...

The results of the interview were a large picture of Chiang Kaishek with Chiang's autograph, inscribed to Pao; it was hung in the bedroom; a few days after that another star appeared on Pao's collar badges; he was no longer a major but a lieutenant-colonel.

This white-glove mania, which was Chiang's idea of how a smart officer should dress, occasioned Pao much distress one day when he forgot to wear them, and was suddenly called to Chiang's presence; the lack being noticed, he was reviled and shouted at, came back pale and shaken ... To lose a campaign and a million soldiers was nothing, but to appear gloveless was almost a crime ...

A few weeks later Pao left, as he told me, for an inspection tour of 'the north-west front' in Sian. He wept, murmured that he might be killed; I became filled with remorse; promised to write regularly; he was the hero, sacrificing himself to duty, I would be the faithful wife, waiting for him – these were the personae of the traditional tales; and we cast ourselves in their roles ...

☆   123

The month of April was now with us, the blanket fog dispersed; the sky cleared to be swiftly replaced by a white dimness of glare, the glare of rising heat from the rock; the glare of water. There were a few Japanese plane alerts. One read in the newspapers about battles in which towns were retaken and then abandoned for 'strategic redeployment'. The seesaw of news about 'the front' conveyed nothing; actually nothing occurred except on the Communist front, which was the only one where real battles were being fought against the Japanese. But not a word about that front appeared in the Chungking newspapers.

I walked about the city, did calligraphy, read *The Three Kingdoms*, the classics, listened to Third Uncle, wrote to Pao. He had promised that when he returned I might be allowed to work ... I saw very few people, apart from the K'ang family.

The K'ang family lived in a very large mansion across the street from Third Uncle's house. The K'ang brothers, Sinjoo and Sinchih, were also directors of the Meifeng Bank as was Third Uncle, and likewise immersed in many business enterprises. K'ang Sinjoo had two concubines; his wife had died, and he had not officially married again. One concubine was called Mantsun, a thin and small woman with a rather ugly skin, but quiet manners and a good mind. We became friends and I visited her often. She had been sold to the K'ang household as a *yat'ou* or slave girl when she was eleven, and she had not yet had her periods when already she was being made use of; and to this she attributed her sterility. She ran the large household, looked after every member, and went to many doctors, hoping to bear a child. K'ang Sinjoo had had children by his first wife and also by his other concubine, and this distressed Mantsun. Here too, in the younger generation, among these sons and daughters of a very wealthy household, one girl had run away to join the Red Army when it had gone through Szechuan on the Long March. Whole villages had risen in revolt and followed the Red armies, until some people said that the Red armies seemed entirely composed of Szechuanese.

Mantsun told me, in whispers, about this girl, who was otherwise never to be mentioned; told me that 'almost every good family has one such rebel' and added: 'Sometimes I, too, feel that my fate has been too hard, and would like to run away.' She had learnt to read and to write, took singing lessons with a teacher who brought his violin, the strident, high-pitched *er-hu*, and played and played while she sang, back turned to him, some Szechuan operatic air.

Mantsun asked her hairdresser, who came every morning to comb the heads of the women of the household, to do my hair also. We had dresses made of the same cloth and pattern, bought sprigs of jasmine, and freshened the bedroom air with them. In late April she departed to the hot springs at Peip'ei for a week, urging me to accompany her. I refused, alleging that I was waiting for a letter from my husband, but actually because although I liked Mantsun I also liked being alone, walking as in a trance about Chungking, looking my fill. Sometimes the nerveless, formless but continual small talk, the incessant chatter about food and meals, the gossip about other people, the shopping expeditions with their drift and petulance, though a distracting pastime, wearied me into restlessness; for all this surely was not living, merely a diversion from living. When I was alone, I could at least go in a trance, be not-there and plunge into looking, looking at everything around me, absorbing it, almost becoming the other, the object perceived rather than the perceiver. However much I liked Mantsun, I could not achieve this profound and satisfactory vision when she was about; for then all my attention would have to be given to our mutual talk. Silence was impossible.

It was in my eleventh year, that the waking trance had first taken hold of me; making me much ashamed, since no one else was similarly afflicted. I felt it to be some dread peculiarity, some abnormal defect, linked up with wickedness. I did not know that such states are essential to the writer, the creator. Among the people I grew up with, the word 'artist', like the word 'actor', or 'poet', denoted unsolidity, fecklessness, something to be ashamed of, and to be caught 'dreaming awake' was almost to be an idiot. So when this strange lapse came I tried at first to break it, as I had broken myself of my left-handedness. But accidents occurred; I would be overpowered by that otherness from inside. A dialogue would begin, a story unfold, a waking dream wrest me from my surroundings, so that I knocked myself against objects in my way. 'You dream standing up,' shouted my mother.

And now in Chungking, the waking trance grew upon me, a saving grace, away from the obsession with my own state, with Pao, away from anguish which might have scarred me for ever.

'He learnt not to care, even if a willow tree grew from his arm, and birds made a nest on his head.'

I read this line in one of Third Uncle's books, and it seemed to me

justification for the waking trance; and now that Pao was not there I
dawdled, revelled in it, forgot everything but these timeless hours of
staring, then shook myself and went back to being normal, to converse
with Third Uncle, with Mantsun, to repetitive hours of attention, to
the empty courtesies that were so essential, it seemed, and by themselves constructed their own system of obligations and worries and
social and domestic chores. The merciless diminution of spirit to which
so many women, engrossed in this extraneous life, voluntarily submitted; which they enforced upon themselves, I watched, and though
I seemed also captured by it, and repeated the gestures and did all that
was done, yet all the time I sought escape from it. And managed to
escape.

Often I would walk down to that great cleft between the mountains
where the Chialing river and the Yangtze met, the promontory upon
which Chungking was built, and gaze for hours at the brimming
waters with their disarray of junks lifting their chequered sails; the
taut gaunt landscape worked its spell of greatness as the eye followed
that twist of water and rock which was the Great River, a curtained
tunnel leading on and on to the gorges, the famous gorges of Szechuan.
Nearer, just below the point where I stood, four hundred and seventy-
eight steps below, was the river edge, inextricable tangle of bales
and boxes and people struggling to lift them on to their shoulders.
And then they would carry their loads, up, up, up, the steps, a file of
men coming up and up, endlessly; and one saw the veins stand out
on their necks and their legs, and heard their breath whistle through
their barrel-chests. Up and up they came, everything carried upon their
shoulders; an endless procession. I saw the huakan men struggle,
step by step, the bamboo poles biting deep into them as the chair
swayed, while in it reclined the officials in felt hats and collared but-
toned uniforms. And of this endless, endless work, carrying and lifting
and hauling, I never had enough, and longed, somehow, to *be* them,
however absurd it sounds; and bought straw sandals which the coolies
wore, and stood at ambulant stalls to drink the sour, strong tea which
they drank, and paced the steps, but alas, with no load upon my back.
Twice in two books, I was to describe this scene, so much it haunted
me.

Now came May, and the rumour that there would be much bombing, since the sky was clear. Third Uncle left with Yao Niang for
Chengtu, giving orders to the servants to pack all valuables in the

house and place them in the bank. The servants and I began to pack; and there was an air raid on May 3rd. But it was May 4th, in the late afternoon, that the most devastating bombing of the populated districts inside the city occurred; the all clear had already sounded, or so we thought, but the planes which had appeared to go away returned, and bombs rained down upon the thickly built parts of Chungking, and then fires began everywhere. There was a direct hit upon Third Uncle's house and I was buried under the debris for a short while, together with two of the servants, but we extricated ourselves and ran out as the fire started. The planes continued to bomb; panic spread as people came running out of the burning houses. I was to describe all this; how the people, almost the whole population of the crowded centre of the city began to trek out of the city that night; and how I went to the Meifeng Bank and met Second Brother there, and of the crowds seeking shelter in the large stone edifice, while streetfuls of houses burnt about us; how there was no light, inside the bank, save for the pinpoint trembling of small oil wicks, but outside oh, the immense conflagration! How that night the bank employees and I, about a hundred of us, walked out of the city, to take refuge in a countryside branch of the bank at Ta Er Wo, because there was a rumour that the Japanese would return to bomb us until all Chungking was but a pile of charred ruins. How the crowds streamed out and by the light of the great fires that were lapping the city we could see this enormous human tidal bore, of which we formed part; how we walked all night, half-carried by the crowds, and at dawn scaled the small gravelly hills which formed the outskirts of the city and at seven in the morning Second Brother and I reached Ta Er Wo and the bank building there, and we were fourteen girls and thirty-nine men.

The next day the exodus was still continuing. From where we lay, on the slope which formed part of the terrace upon which the Ta Er Wo bank storehouse was built, we could see the stream of people, unending, coming out of Chungking carrying their belongings. But I wanted to return to the city, I was afraid that Pao might think me dead; I wanted to send him a telegram to tell him I was safe. Second Brother could not understand this; he thought I was mad; he was just going off to sleep, and here was I insisting on returning when I had just arrived! But I felt it my responsibility to reassure Pao ... had he not, discarding everything, returned to Wuhan to fetch me? 'At least eat some lunch before you go,' said Second Brother, very angry. I did, and then walked the fifteen *li* (about seven miles) back, and the sensation of going in the opposite direction to everyone else was eerie; but I kept on, though some people cried to me: 'Who is that one turning back?' But I thought that if Pao heard on the radio about the bombing of Chungking and did not find me, he might think me dead, and that I must send him a cable ...

I reached the Y.W.C.A. about three in the afternoon, still carrying Pao's overcoat, the only thing I had saved from the fire; and at last came to the Meifeng Bank and looked for water. I found water in the taps, drank and washed, then set out for the telegraph office and arrived to find a small crowd there, and no cables being sent. So I returned to the bank and slept on a settee, then went back to the telegraph office the next day. I fed myself from ambulant pedlars of tea and food, and how kind they were, giving me tea, giving me rice, helping me, they and their families – coolies, coolies, but they remained, and were there, and I shared another meal with a family, and never knew their name.

The second afternoon Second Brother returned. There was no light and we made torches of twisted withes, of old boat-towing rope; thus we went on living for a week, while life returned to the city, people returned, families began to search for each other, a small tabloid newspaper was distributed (the newspapers' printing presses had been hit, and by pooling together their staff and machinery, the three main newspapers produced this tabloid sheet); street criers went about with gongs, chanting out the names of lost children; the green-clad postmen on the third day went their faithful rounds taking note of the houses that had been destroyed and sometimes there would be a box with a label: This is where No. 4 of East Cloth Slippers Street was. The post office would give letters to those who came to ask for them.

I never thought of going to Pao's Military Headquarters nor to any of his benevolent brothers. I stayed at the Meifeng Bank. Another escapee shared the small room I had discovered at the top of the bank building. It was the Miss Lu who had been at Nanyu with me, a tall prim girl, engaged to a fellow officer of Pao's. She always made a great point of being exceedingly proper, and scolded the bank amah who cleaned the upper floors for 'lacking in virtue' because the amah sat and talked with a man on the flat veranda roof of the bank in the cool evening breeze, sat and fanned herself while below her one could see the ruined city still emitting a lazy bluish smoke from some of the burnt quarters. Then came a letter from Third Uncle, asking me to return to Chengtu; Mantsun, back from the hot springs, also urged me to live at the untouched K'ang house. I stayed with Mantsun for two days and she gave me some clothes, for all I had was the dress on my back; then I flew to Chengtu. Third Aunt took me to the doctor, as she was certain that I must be ill. The wholeness of Chengtu, the lack of littered wreckage, the spectacle of unconcerned people, strolling, not picking their way in the rubble, not calling and crying for their children, seemed strange.

It was only when I reached Chengtu that I had fear reactions. At night, hearing an odd plane, my heart would start beating very fast, even before I *knew* I was afraid. What was that strange mechanism called 'dread'? The ransacking heartbeat woke me at night, but by autumn it was gone.

It was June before Pao returned from the 'front', and spent three weeks in Third Uncle's house in Chengtu, since we no longer had a home in Chungking.

I was very happy to see Pao; during his absence, I had forgotten all his faults, only remembered how noble, how patriotic he was, risking his life for his country. I asked Pao naively whether he had seen much fighting on the Yellow River front, where he had told me he was. 'Of course,' he replied, looking fiercely, and fixedly in front of him. But he did not elaborate. I asked again, timidly: 'Were the Japanese very brutal, did you actually see them?' He brusquely said: 'An officer cannot discuss military matters with women.' So I asked no more. Soon, however, some friends came to call on him, and then the name of Hu Tsungnan came up repeatedly. Pao spoke about Hu Tsungnan to them, mentioned how well Hu Tsungnan had received him, how there had been a horsemanship contest which Pao had won, although Hu Tsungnan kept a body of Kansu Muslim cavalrymen, all famous horsemen, in his headquarters ... Pao seemed very pleased with himself, and spent some time in the next few days composing letters to Hu Tsungnan.

It was much later that I knew he had spent these months at the Sian headquarters of Hu Tsungnan, and the armies of Hu Tsungnan never fought the Japanese at all since their task was to blockade Yenan. And by that summer a triple barrier of blockhouses, trenches, machine-gun strongholds, had been erected round Yenan. It was this 'front' which Pao had visited, and with him some other young officers, including Chiang Wei-kuo, Chiang's second son, who had joined the staff of Hu Tsungnan.

About ten days after his return, the first amiability wearing off, Pao's favourite demon started to fret and torment him again. Morality and virtue. Virtue and morality. I was totally without either. His task was to save me by inculcating these, by force, into me. The next day it came out that Hu Tsungnan had enquired about me in a letter, hearing I had a family in Chengtu, and had expressed the desire to call on me and my family, and Pao was afraid that Hu Tsungnan might not approve of me; might look at my face and deduce some 'foreign' blood; and Hu Tsungnan's xenophobia was notorious. This might spoil the good impression Pao had made; he wrote to Hu that I was 'so shy' that I refused to see anyone; I lived in the bosom of my family, from which I could not be extricated, and besides, I was pregnant …

Thus began a long series of equivocations, lies and fabrications. Pao not only lied about me, he also lied about himself. To impress me he fabricated stories about engagements he had fought; he claimed to be of the eighth batch of Whangpoo graduates instead of the eleventh, to give himself seniority; as his inner tensions built up, the situations he created by his own boasting went awry, but he would merely fabricate another 'explanation'. Confronted with evident self-contradictions, only the strenuous asseveration that he was 'sincere' would serve, and he professed total indignation that anyone should dare to doubt his word, even if he was saying something palpably false. In the medley of illogical fictions he thus set up, the breakdown of reason and logic accelerated, truth became what he made himself believe was true, and a whimsical tyranny superseded any semblance of coherence or discussion. I must tell everyone that I was pregnant, and refuse to go out. I must not use the name of Chou any more; I must say I was born a Tang, and not a Chou … This became known to Third Uncle, who was angered as well as puzzled by such foolishness, and almost took it as an offence to the Chou clan. But being wise, he held his peace, and pretended not to notice.

This incoherence varied from day to day, hour to hour; Pao dawdled in Chengtu, saw friends, talked and talked with them … All were terrified of Chiang, all wanted advancement, all practised a verbal mumbo-jumbo of virtuous precepts, totally absent in practice.

All told gleefully tales of corruption, bribery, nepotism, chaos, and then did exactly what they deplored in others. For the execution of what was preached was certainly not required; it was dangerous, indeed, to be honest, hard-working, incorruptible. It was 'unnatural' not to be corrupt, eager for bribes – in fact it was being a communist. Only the communists took no bribes, worked hard and were 'stupid' enough to fight the Japanese. Reading, investigating a problem, trying to redress evil-doing was also reprehensible, it led to being 'talked about', it meant some official might 'lose face', and so the idea was to do absolutely nothing, especially nothing which might show up some-one else. To do anything outstanding would risk offending the others, and that again meant a loss of face, and one could not expect their support when one needed it. Reports would seep back by capillary osmosis until they reached the level at which one could be destroyed should one commit the offence of being zealous in one's work. There-fore one mouthed formulas, kept out of trouble by strict application to doing nothing; one entertained one's friends, thus solidifying a small clique of supporters to oneself; one tried to get three, four jobs at once and concurrently, which meant three, four salaries – it was not really necessary to be present at one's office more than occasionally, hence many of Pao's friends managed to be 'in three places at once'.

The Leader of this grotesque and moribund farce, Chiang Kaishek, was himself subject to destructive fits of temper, to whimsical delu-sions, to the most incomprehensible manias and obsessions. He had no clear purpose other than to remain in power; in the attainment of this aim he did not keep faith with anyone, had no principles to found policies upon, but played off one man against the other, laid cunning traps for all, and had spies to spy on spies; would suddenly order some-one's execution, brooked no suggestions, no discussion, only total loyalty, total obedience. With such a master, how could Pao be other than he was?

Stilwell, the American general, would later experience Chiang's irrationality; Chiang would order (going as always above the head of his Minister of Defence, General Military Staff and Bureau of Military Operations) by telephone a divisional commander to advance, and a few hours later order the same to retreat. The words 'Shoot him!' issued so frequently from his mouth when he was in a rage (he was also addicted to throwing vases and tea-cups and even hurling spittoons at visitors who had displeased him), that people invited to dinner with

the Most High usually made their wills in case sudden demise occurred
during dinner. It was this perpetual havoc, the presence of the Gestapo-
like organizations, the twisting and warping of all fact and event into
a pattern of personal spite, the sinister absurdities which passed as
judgment, which demolished the personalities of many able and
reasonably honest young men.

At times Pao and his benevolent brothers bemoaned the miasmatic
disorder in which they were involved; they described it as 'battling
with manure in a cesspool'. Yet they would not have existed without
it; and they always blamed 'dishonest' so-and-so, or such-and-such,
round the Leader, but never dared to say anything about Chiang himself, though they must have known. Their sudden flashes of consciousness were quickly extinguished in the egotistic pursuit of their careers;
and their careers depended on Chiang's whims and moods and fancies
and suspicions. How could they not become fragmented, incoherent
beings, subject to sudden cruelty and fits of violence, with all this going
on all the time?

One could occasionally detect in their talk a sneaking respect, an
envious fear, of the 'Red bandits', as they called the communists. A
phrase would drop from them, ambiguities, about Yenan – how 'they
do fight, we just sit and talk … ' Communists were accused of 'pretending' to be honest, but since it was true that they were so, and also
true that the hearts of the peasantry were with them (and even then, in
Chengtu, Pao and his brother officers acknowledged that 'the stupid
peasants are with them'), only one accusation could be flung at them
safely, and that was, of course, sex. Their greatest crime was 'free love',
and therefore 'dangerous thoughts'! They preached 'equality of
women'! Appalling crimes which threatened the salvation of China!
Though even the most rabid anti-Red newspapers could not accuse the
communists of corruption, of letting their troops die of starvation (as
happened on the Chiang side), of trafficking with the enemy, they
could be accused of practising orgies! They actually had women in the
Red armies, girls dressed as boys and carrying guns! They encouraged
slave girls and concubines to revolt against their masters! Their widows
remarried! They did not insist on 'chastity'! They incited the peasant
women to stand up and denounce their husbands' misdeeds! Little
girls of eight were sold to brothels and that was as it should be, but Pao
would talk of virtue, integrity, the duty of obedience, discipline
saving the country, while the conscripts walked by us on the roads, a

stinking, swaying mob of men, gaunt with hunger, roped like beasts, while the girls lined up outside the restaurants, in the streets, waiting for clients, while three out of four of the Chinese soldiers that died, died of hunger and disease because the officers pocketed the money for their food ...

Third Uncle, seeing Pao so moody, now suggested that I should take him to Pihsien, to show him our ancestral hall, and on to Kuanhsien, that spot in the western foothills where the plain begins, and the great construction works of Li Pin the engineer can be seen, who two thousand years ago had cleft the Min river in two here, and turned the unprofitable stream into a web of water to ensure for ever the fertility of the Chengtu plain.

Third Uncle was a fervent lover of his province; almost Swiss in his devotion to the superiority of its sun, mountains, air and waters over that of every other province in China, or of any land on earth. No vegetables in the down-river lands tasted as good as those of the Chengtu plain; for here the soil was heady with all that was good, and manure, its main ingredient, both pig and human, more ample so that the soil glistened, black and greasy with this precious worth. On the subject of manure, as on the subjects of tea, and tobacco, and opium, and warlords, and taxes, and customs, Third Uncle was unquenchable; his speech flavoured with all the deft turns of phrase and imagery of Szechuan.

But Pao was not captivated by Third Uncle, for as Third Uncle spoke, Pao watched his own face in the mirror. He told me Third Uncle was too materialistic, probably because he was politely but obviously hostile to Chiang and 'interference' in Szechuan's affairs by outsiders. Pao would for ever measure people by the standard of 'personal loyalty to the Leader'. Landscape, book, person, all had to be brought into an object lesson related to that theme, and this was his only yardstick. To this topic Third Uncle would listen with an air of distant politeness which annoyed Pao, so that he took it out on the servants, ordering them about and reviling them; they shrank away in silence, and Third Uncle was angry but kept his brow smooth and his speech courteous.

One fine morning we set off for Kuanhsien, Pao and I. The temple of Li Pin raised its multichromatic roofs; blue and violet whorls and ribbons of amber and purple cavorted around emblematic beasts, up and down the spines of its sloping eaves; inside the great engineer and his son sat in a solemn fixity; contemplating their work, the plain of Chengtu with its glistening jade and golden fields, its incredible capacity for producing food, and the incredible poverty of its peasants who were not entitled to more than a fraction of this food. It was a lovely day; and strolling by the upper stream of the Min river in its summer turmoils; noticing the eggshaped stones wrapped in their nets of wicker which protected the banks; seeing the boats so swiftly rushed past by the headstrong current, all made a great enchantment. Like an incurious eyeball the sky was pale with the young heat above us; and I remember so well, hearing them still curl about me, the shouts of the boatmen like bird cries, and the stallion noise of the galloping water, snapping and biting into the stark pillar of stone called Elephant Rock, which finally one day collapsed so that when I returned in 1964 it was no longer there; and the curlew call of the wind, which threw itself about the hills with their sombre cloak of forest ...

Here was where rich legend and its cavalcades had begun, yesterday's reality become wondrous tales, their home these waters that ran, bounced, slithered, shaped like the bumping backs of prancing mythical animals, varicoloured in the sunlight like the sun-flecked roofs of Li Pin's temple, all scale and slide and restlessness. The reckless boatmen swirled and shouted past us, and behind the great grey foothills of the first mountain ranges, where the rivers came from, were the ranges of Tibet.

But none of this, to Pao, was occasion for delight; merely occasion for another lecture, another spell of ranting, and the usual accompaniment of blows thudding upon my hostile set face, my mouth, which would utter: 'You have no eyes, no ears, nothing ... all you think of is you and your career ... there is only rottenness in all this government of yours, thinking only of your career ... '

After that he hit me so hard that I vomited, and then I had an attack of diarrhoea (a common accompaniment to life in summer in Chengtu) and was so upset that I fainted. Like many untutored in medical care Pao was very afraid of a faint; he thought that I had died, right in the pavilion overlooking the Min river, face to face with Elephant Rock. In sudden remorse he propped me up, chafed my hands, wept, promised not to begin again, then said that I could study, I could do what I liked, I could hit him back. I lay with my eyes closed, uncomfortable because I had dirtied myself, not answering, not moving ... We went on, the next day, to Tsing Chen Shan, beyond Kuanhsien.

A very ancient and famous Taoist monastery is found at Tsing Chen Shan and it is still one of the scenic resorts of Szechuan. The graceful, millennial beams lay among their gingko trees, and the sound of water from many torrents was about, one of them making music as it poured itself in variously shaped natural rock hollows, scooped out by time and water-wearing. There were rooms for guests, large caged beds with mosquito nets; they were full of bedbugs, and that night I caught and killed sixty-four of them, chiefly from between my toes, and with ferocity. There is nothing like a bedbug bite between one's toes to turn one into a semi-sadist; I laid them in neat rows upon the bedroom table. There were scrolls from famous painters hanging on the walls; the temple went back in time over a thousand years, and though rebuilt several times, every time the original layout had been exactly reproduced. Above us in the cool azure air towered many rocks and beyond we could glimpse the beginning peaks of the great ranges.

We paced the mountain pathways, Pao ranting, and I feeling dazed and sick. When we came down the mountain our huakan men who had carried us up stopped every two hours, as they had done before, for an opium pipe; they were short of cash and demanded advance payment, for they had smoked the daily money we had given them going up. Pao now threatened them, ordered them harshly to go on without opium; they downed their bamboo poles and stared menacingly. He read them a lecture on the evils of opium, called them degenerate, but gave them the money. And all about us in the sheltered valleys were the fields of opium poppies, pink and white.

In 1964, I was to return to Tsing Chen Shan. Nothing had changed in the Taoist monastery's appearance, though much had changed inside, for though priests were still in charge, and there were still rooms for guests, now the monastery was part of the Tsing Chen mountain commune, and the priests did part-time labour; in the afternoon, at the sound of a bell, the whole monastery, young men and boys, assembled and marched off to climb the mountain in sweltering rain, chaffing each other meanwhile; 'militia training and fitness' said the Taoist priest who remained with us. And he poured some more of the monastery's famous tea into our cups. When I remembered the opium-smoking, the gambling, that had gone on in 1937, it was quite a change. There was no opium about at all, but fields of rice extending far beyond their previous scope, and everywhere militia training.

Pao was no longer there, he and his young hard fury. But the monastery was still there, as good as ever. I asked: 'Are there any bed-bugs? Last time I was here, I had two or three between each toe, biting me.'

'Oh, there are no more bedbugs,' said the priest proudly, 'we now have D.D.T.'

I went to the courtyard, remembering it all, and stood transfixed by seeing it again, and this time without the distraction of Pao's voice, ranting on and on about virtue, loyalty; seeing the everlasting beauty which made men choose this rockface in the cliffs, there to hang the temple between sky and precipice; thousand-year-old gingko trees dropped their fruit on the thick moss. The pine trees were old and gnarled, poets dead for centuries had sung about them. The peaks were shrouded in rainmist, the clear laughter of the pool called 'The Listen to the Nine Sounds of Music Pool' had not altered. All round the square paved courtyard, with its Triad emblems (for the temple had been a fortress for the Lord of the Mountain of the secret societies which centre round Taoism), was a carved balustrade with pillars, each pillar children playing, some of the games sexual, for Taoism was never prude or puritan. And the great gong in the main hall, its back against the straight high mountain, could be heard for fifty *li* around. This was an old and vital place, moss-grown, hoary, but tremendously vital, a dark, amoral world, where evil and good had no meaning, where innocence and what is called vice were children's games; not mystic supernatural but earth earthy, with the smell of the rotting gingko fruit and the clear call of the water; a self-deriding quietness was about, and here the miasma of virtue had no meaning, for this was older, much older, eternal in youth like the stone children of the court-yard.

On our return to Chengtu I had a fever; the doctor was called and after taking all of my twelve pulses, he said that I had 'not enough breath in my body'; that my living essence was being choked in my heart; I needed a medicine to open the heart. My knitted brows indicating a snake coiled in my brain, I had to have an uncoiling medicine. I think that doctor who diagnosed all this merely by taking my pulse, asking not one question, was a superb psychologist. The temptation to lapse into chronic invalidism became mine; I pondered it, after taking the ginseng draught the doctor prescribed which induced a calm euphoria, but my natural spirits were too strong.

In two days I was up again, but I had frightened Pao. He began to bemoan his hard fate; the way 'to the top' was hard; he was doing his best; a hindrance to his career was that he had not been in command of troops, and therefore had no 'foot' support in the army (meaning subalterns to serve his purpose, and also a ready access to a source of funds, since the army was one gigantic racket). I could help him, only I must be patient. I replied that he had promised to let me work, and I wanted to work; I could not sit doing nothing at home; and suddenly he was willing. Yes, here in Chengtu, I could study if I wished to, he himself would go with me to the university and inquire ... This sudden volte-face left me abashed. It is not possible, I thought, he will change his mind ... but the next morning we did go to the West China Union University, outside the South Gate of Chengtu.

West China Union University had now become vastly swollen; it was six universities, with staff, students and teachers from the Japanese-occupied areas who had trekked here to continue their studies. Pao insisted upon seeing the dean of the medical school, a Canadian missionary called Dr Kilborn. Dr Kilborn received us; a friendly muscular man, who spoke excellent Szechuanese. We inquired about the requirements for entrance to the university. I then began to feel that going back to a university to study was not what I wanted. I wanted to do something of immediate value, some work connected with the situation. Besides, I was not certain of Pao's next change of mood, and all depended on his mood. Now Pao let out that Hu Tsungnan had some 'female relative' studying at the university. Did Pao want to utilize me to meet her? I told Dr Kilborn I wanted to work, and it was he who suggested that I might go to see Dr Marian Manly, a missionary doctor who ran a maternity hospital and midwifery school very near to the university. I might be able to do something usefu.l right away.

Pao now suggested that we should be photographed as a memento of our imperishable love; we had already done this several times, and each time to celebrate some reconciliation. We now proceeded to a photographic shop. The photographs came out well; he thrust them in front of my eyes and started again; he had been to an astrologer on the way back from collecting the photographs. The astrologer had taken one look at my photo and said that I was romantic, and must be curbed. And my ears were unlucky. I was destined to a bitter life because my lobes were too small ... I retorted that with all the dreadful things going on in China, with the conscripts being tied up and dragged off to the front, it was a pity that he could find nothing else to harp about except me and sex and my ears; and 'You are blackmailing me,' I said, throwing out the words before I thought of the result. He said, 'Me, I am saving you, I am trying to save you ... ' 'But you are not, you are killing me, take care, you may go too far ... ' He laughed angrily. 'You dare to threaten me; what can you do to me?' 'I can do nothing, I know it, but if I die, I don't think you will find it easy to explain my death.' 'Let me tell you,' he said, 'a woman is only an existence in relation to a husband, to a family, she has no person of her own ... ' 'And you are born of a mother,' I replied, 'you are insulting your own mother, and all mothers when you say that.' I was breathing hard with anger, and walking fast and when I saw his fist clench, I said: 'Go ahead, hit me, that is all you can do, why don't you go and fight the Japanese instead? What have you been doing in Sian except racing on horseback with your friends? And you told me you had gone to fight the Japanese and here is half of China gone, and you can find nothing better to do than to hit me.' 'Shut up,' he said, 'shut up.' But he was strangely quiet all of a sudden. From that time on he did not talk about Hu Tsungnan any more to me.

I went alone to the midwifery school in Little Heavenly Bamboo Street outside the South Gate of Chengtu, to meet the American woman doctor, Marian Manly, whom Dr Kilborn had told me about.

Marian Manly was a short, vivacious woman; her face would never grow old, for it was always half set in an urchin grin. She was an active but nonconformist missionary; and both she and her sister, Grace, and their parents had worked in China all their lives. There were many such: the Endicotts, the family of Chester Ronning, today a high Canadian diplomat. Their parents had been missionaries in China and these were the second generation, feeling more at home in China than in their own countries, and sentimentally attached to it;

and this was to be the greatest psychological obstacle to some of them accepting a New Order, for they had become utterly convinced of their own importance and the God-given quality of their work within the framework of Old China. Endicott spoke Chinese like a Chinese; so did Kilborn and William Sewell; the latter was to write a book describing the changes at the university in 1949, when the communists came to Szechuan. The Canadian missionaries in Chengtu were reputed liberal-minded; among them were some whose secret sympathies were with the Chinese people, with the Red Army. But among the majority of the American missionaries reigned a blissful blindness; right up till the end, in their beautiful grey brick houses, with lovely Chinese furniture, paid in hard foreign currency, they were to live well and eat well, while round them their Chinese colleagues and their students grew haggard and wan with starvation ... Marian Manly knew little of politics, and was to remain naive in that respect; she was very afraid of communism, and firmly believed in a China enlightened, democratic, and converted to Christianity 'after the war', under Chiang Kaishek, because Chiang and his wife were Methodists; it was this 'conversion' of Chiang to Christianity which for so long contributed to the delusion of missionaries.

Our first meeting was friendly. Marian immediately agreed to train me. The hospital was a modest, unpretentious wooden building with typical Chengtu-style grey-tiled roof, a two-storied quadrangular structure with a courtyard in the middle and a well. Half of it was residence for the midwives of the midwifery school and for Marian. The other half was the wards for the patients, the operating rooms and the outpatients.

There were three small first-class rooms, holding two mothers in each, and two wards for second class with ten beds to a room. Altogether twenty to twenty-five patients could be accommodated at a time, and there was also a nursery for the babies which held an average of thirty babies. In the winter months it was crowded, and once in a while the baby room had to hold thirty-five to forty babies. Each crib was a box with a lid, the sides and top made of strong netting, because of the rats. All the furniture, the beds, the coir mattresses, the cotton sheets, were locally made.

The midwives were all from Szechuan; they trained for three years; were taught in Chinese as none of them knew any English; and Marian lectured to them in her American-Szechuan dialect, reading from a prepared romanized script or talking from memory. There were three to five fully qualified midwives and instructors in attendance, living on the premises, and a small dormitory for the student midwives, about twenty of them. Most of the cases were delivered in their own houses, and not at the hospital, but some of the better-off patients liked to have their babies here as it was less trouble for them.

I felt that training as a midwife would be more useful than going on for five years, to train as a doctor; here, in a few months, I could be useful; and five years before I could do anything seemed an unbearable stretch of time ... I was ready to start immediately, and so I told Marian, and returned to swallow ginseng, lie in a faint, and threaten Pao with my instant death if I could not work; my pallor, due to my bowel condition, helped. Pao said tragically that he would go on alone, to endure 'hardship' in Chungking; that perhaps he would be ill, and we might never see each other again ... By now I was so flayed raw that I reacted emotionally very easily; there is nothing more searing than unshared paranoia. I wept, I fainted, but did not relinquish my aim. He came to see the midwifery school, and to call on Marian; there was nothing he could find fault with except that it was 'too small'. 'When I am a great man I shall build you all the hospitals you want, and you can become Minister of Health,' he said, grandiose. But right now all I wanted was not to be a Health Minister but to get down to some reality, to do something in the crying desperate need I felt all round me, and within myself.

So Pao departed, alone, and not too unhappy in spite of his 'sacrifice', for he was going back to get into the Obey and Serve office directly under Chiang, and my absence in Chengtu would be the removal of a possible hindrance; he had told so many lies about me, including the one that I was pregnant, that my disappearance for a while was welcome. Besides, Hu Tsungnan was now going to Chungking to a military colloquy there, and Pao was eager to be ready at all times, at all times showing himself, so that he might not be forgotten in the struggle for advancement. It was late November before he came to fetch me to return to Chungking, and by that time the war in Europe had started; there was a new situation in the world, Pao's overvaulting ambition had met with success, and I had become some sort of a writer – though it took me twenty years to recognize the meaning of that word.

☆

Of that baleful summer of 1939, when war was being consciously prepared throughout Europe, of the hopes and surmises of the internationalization of the war which gripped Chiang's entourage, of the balancing act that he practised with the Japanese, a total look has not been achieved from the Chinese side. Most historians consider the play and counter-play of the European countries at that epoch, including Soviet Russia, central to the Second World War. But a geographical displacement entails a different view, and for us in China the Second World War had started on September 18th, 1931, when Japan invaded Manchuria; was confirmed when on July 7th, 1937, their invasion of China began; and its internationalization was a logical corollary when it spread to Europe in 1939. But few would subscribe to this view in the West; China under Chiang Kaishek was still an 'object', to be submitted to outside pressure, a pawn in the eyes of the Great Powers; passive and to be coerced. No one foresaw that in the tremendous upheaval which was taking place, the humiliating role assigned to China was already breaking down; the decision to resist Japan forced by Mao Tse-tung upon Chiang Kaishek in December 1936, even though unwillingly implemented, was the turning point at which the history of China was to begin its change.

But the door to the future turned slowly on its war-oiled hinges. On March 10th, 1939, Neville Chamberlain spoke of a five-year 'peace plan' in Europe. Right up till December 1941 the British maintained active and amicable relations with Japan, in spite of Japanese encroachment upon British commercial privileges in Manchuria and in North China. They were convinced that the Axis could be disjointed; that Japan had her hands full in China; that an entente could be achieved, at China's expense, with the Japanese in Asia; a 'partition' of China's markets, with Britain dominating South China and relinquishing some rights in the North. The Foreign Office strove for appeasement in the East, though appeasement was failing in the West. The five-year peace plan aired in Birmingham by the British Prime Minister was shattered the very same day, for Hitler's armies walked into Czechoslovakia on March 10th, and on March 14th the Czech Republic was incorporated into the Reich; Poland and Hungary receiving small bits of Czechoslovakia, thrown to them by the victorious Hitler.

Nevertheless, the United States and Britain were still exploring the possibilities of 'negotiations' between Japan and China, which really

meant negotiations between themselves and Japan. But these concessions were to both Japan and Hitler evidence of weakness. The New
Order, announced by Japan on December 22nd, 1938, had been a
clear challenge to white domination in Asia; it was on this racialist
basis, replacing white imperialism by their own, that the Japanese
were to launch their conquest of South-East Asia.

In the spring of 1939 Japanese 'businessmen' and secret police agents
began to pour into Hanoi and Saigon. Welcomed by the French, at
the time concerned with local nationalist uprisings, they helped to
launch brutal repressions to destroy the Vietnamese independence
movement. Pham Van Dong and Ho Nguen Giap, its leaders, fled
to China, where they were to meet Ho Chih Min, who after some
years in Moscow had arrived in Yenan in August 1938, and was in
South China in 1939 and 1940. Ho Chih Min was to spend almost
two years in jails under Chiang Kaishek, with irons on his legs and
festering sores. Dragged on marches of thirty miles a day, from prison
to prison; chained to sleep above the cesspool, he wrote many of his
best-known poems during those months.

The surrender of Spain to Franco (March 29th, 1939) marked
another gain for fascism; Japan, not to be outdone, seized the Spratly
Islands, 700 miles west of Manila, 300 miles south of Saigon, 1,000
miles from Hongkong, a strategic base for a jump-off towards South-
East Asia. Then it was Mussolini's turn; he invaded Albania on
April 7th.

The Western democracies remained supine; still clutched by the
hallucination of coming to terms with the Axis powers to forge a
mighty 'anti-communist alliance'. Chamberlain's 'peace plan' was
merely a disguised offer of enlargement and reinforcement of the anti-
Comintern pact elaborated between Germany, Japan and Italy in
1936, in tune with the 'grand anti-communist alliance' offered by
Japan to Chiang Kaishek in December 1938 ...

April 1939. Hitler denounced the Anglo–German agreement. Von
Jodl, Chief of Staff of the Reich armies, lectured on 'the favourable
strategic premises of the Polish problem' after the 'satisfactory solution' of the Czechoslovakian 'problem'. The political games were
further dichotomized into multiple self-contradictory movements.
Talks began in Moscow between the British Ambassador there and
Mr Litvinov, the Russian Foreign Minister, on April 15th. 'Considering how Soviet Russia had been treated, and how she was still being

treated, there was not much to be expected from her now,' writes Churchill. Poland, Rumania, the Baltic States did not know 'whether it was German aggression or Russian rescue which they dreaded more,' and 'this hideous choice paralysed British and French policy' – a picturesque Churchillian phrase; but what paralysed both countries was the dilemma between alliance with Germany and Japan, which implied a piecemeal sharing of their own colonial possessions all over the world for the price of an anti-communist front, or an alliance with the hated socialist state, the U.S.S.R. ...

As far as American policies were concerned, the same schizophrenic ambivalence was evident; America, self-declared 'neutral', went on sending ninety-two per cent of the war material required to Japan for her war on China; American pro-German groups were active and the Hearst press, until December 1941, was to exert itself to keep America 'neutral'. Public opinion, however, was slowly changing; Japan's actions caused increasing apprehension, especially the move into Indo-China in the summer of 1939.

What would the U.S.S.R. do? Stalin, wrote Churchill, was an 'enigma'. Actually the shrewdest statesman of them all, Stalin knew well what was going on in the minds of the Western politicians. In February 1939, small feelers had already been put out to Germany. In May, Churchill made a strong speech in the House of Commons pleading for an alliance between England, France and Russia. 'No time must be lost'; but the hostility to communism at the Foreign Office and at the Quai d'Orsay was too strong, and conversations with Moscow languished.

Stalin manoeuvred adroitly and prudently to have the possibility of a move both ways. In this subtle game of Twixt, the Russian sphinx stayed hermetic and sphinxlike until the last moment, and who can blame him? It was the future of the world's first socialist state which was in the balance.

In China all these moves were followed and understood, both by the communists at Yenan, and by Chiang Kaishek in Chungking. The latter saw them in the same light as the schemes of politicians of the Three Kingdoms era of China two millennia ago. There was nothing new in these games of *Realpolitik*; Churchill's ploy was 'forming friendship with the State farther off, to combat the nearer danger'; that of Stalin was to make a temporary alliance with Germany in order to stave off the greater danger of an all-encompassing alliance

143

against the U.S.S.R.; both were logic itself.

The warning given by Chiang Kaishek to the British that summer, that their seeking for an 'Eastern Munich' would turn against them, was not based on a decision to carry out the war against Japan, but on a fear that the deal would be foreclosed without him, and that Stalin would be successful in deviating Hitler's war machine towards the West. The worst mistake Hitler had made, Chiang said, was to choose Japan instead of China as his ally. Ever since 1933 Chiang had sought German advisers, such as von Beck, to help him in his anti-communist campaigns. And there were still German advisers in China in 1939.

June 1939. The French in Indo-China, at Japan's request, suspended all material sent to China via Haiphong and the railway to Yunnan.

July 1939. The British signed an agreement with Japan, reinforcing (so they thought) their stand with the latter. The 'grand anti-communist alliance' sought by the European colonial powers against Soviet Russia was denounced by Mao Tsetung in Yenan; and as summer advanced the world moved swiftly towards war.

On the evening of August 19th, 1939, Stalin announced his intention to sign a pact with Germany. On August 22nd, Ribbentrop went to Moscow; saw Stalin on the evening of August 23rd and that very night a non-aggression pact was signed. 'This was the result, not the cause, of the failure of the French and British policies,' said Mao Tsetung. The non-aggression pact was for ten years. Twenty-two months later, in June 1941, Hitler invaded Russia. But two years had been gained.

August 30th-September 1st, 1939: Poland was invaded by Germany; war was declared against Hitler by Britain and France on September 3rd, eleven months after Munich and 'peace in our time'.

In Chungking, the news, long expected, of a Second World War was greeted with intense satisfaction.

Now the war in China was to be recognized as part of a world conflict, and this was a further step towards what Chiang had hoped for: American involvement, and American money, in *his* war, the war against Mao Tsetung ...

In Europe the peace movements were confused; fed on a diet of paradisial propaganda, conviction unbolstered by a healthy knowledge of the difficult and dolorous calvary which the Long March of humanity represents, intellectuals left the ranks of the European communist parties; and yet from the Marxist point of view, there was nothing to choose between the rank fascism of Hitler, practised at home, the horrors inflicted upon six million Jews, and the barbarism and genocide inflicted for decades upon colonized peoples by the so-called democracies. But Europocentrism would always make, even for Marxists, what happened in Europe infinitely more important than what happened elsewhere in the world, and still today the Communist Parties of Europe suffer from this purblindness. Mao Tsetung's analysis on September 1st, 1939, of the issues at stake, was the most lucid and penetrating appraisal of the development of the war, and stands, monumental in its validity, even after thirty years.

The effect of the pact on Japan was a certain coolness in German-Japanese relations. Among militarist circles, preparations for a thrust into South-East Asia were already far advanced; more dovelike politicians in Japan were anxious to make concessions to Britain, U.S. and France, and establish a joint partition of China. But the militarists won; it only remained for Japan to sign a four-point neutrality pact with the U.S.S.R., thus securing Japan's rear, in April 1941, while preparing for the invasion of South-East Asia. Since Hitler had not consulted with the Japanese concerning his moves with Russia, the Japanese were to repay him in kind; and this also had an effect on the course of the Second World War.

It was a drizzly September afternoon, damp and muggy. I had already been nearly three months at the hospital, studying and working. I went into Marian Manly's drawing-room to return a book which I had borrowed from her. Here, with Pao away, I could read, without having books snatched away or torn to pieces in front of me.

Marian was seated at her typewriter; she typed nearly every day long letters to her family, but she also wrote short stories, and had written a long poem based on a Chinese legend. Some of her short stories on Chinese themes had been published in American magazines such as *Woman's Home Companion*. She had also attempted a book on China which had not found a publisher. She wanted to write a novel on China. 'I know I can write, I know it,' she said.

I cannot remember why she seemed separate, a little aloof, from the rest of the missionaries at the university and at the large hospital in

Chengtu; it was not some schism of religious thought, but an individual non-conformism which made her prefer to be thus alone, running her own little midwifery school and hospital, independent from the rest of the missionary body. Or perhaps that spark of solitude which all writers need. I found her congenial, and friendship grew between us.

On that September afternoon, Marian looked up from her typewriter when I came in and asked me to stay and have a cup of tea and some of her freshly baked cookies. I sat down gratefully; soon she talked again about writing, read out to me a few pages of the short story she was working on. Her eyes, when she took off her glasses, wore the sleepy look of all short-sighted people; and she polished the lenses energetically. She looked young, almost childish, as with her legs tucked under her chair her voice ran on in its soft American way. My mind wandered out to the veranda, with the sun slanting across the wooden pillars with their resinous touch; into the evening opal sky went the smoke of a thousand charcoal fires, and from the kitchen downstairs where Marian and her sister Grace had been making marmalade from the famous Szechuan oranges, so abundant, so cheap, came the mouth-watering smell of orange peel.

'Well, what do you think of it?' Abruptly Marian took off her glasses to polish them again, a way of bracing herself for remarks about her writing. I felt awed by anyone so clever, so capable as a writer.

'It is a wonderful story ... '

Marian shrugged and laughed, polishing vigorously. 'I hope my agent will like it ... Oh I do wish he'd get my book published, but he doesn't seem able to get a publisher for it, yet I *know* I can write, I *do* write well ... '

Marian Manly said I *know*, I *do* with emphasis, the same emphasis as the stamp of her foot when something went wrong at the hospital, and then followed her outburst with a little apologetic chuckle which immediately restored the childhood grin to her face. And it is true that she had a beautiful style, a flow and evenness which carried one along with her sentences.

'I think this is a very good love story.' It was about the concubine of a warlord, a young girl married against her will, escaping and marrying a young man she was in love with ... a total improbability in Szechuan in 1939. 'I'd like to write a real good story about China,' said Marian, 'I think the American public are just getting interested in China.'

There had been war in China since 1937, but America was not involved, America was neutral; and now the war in Europe, in September 1939, found America similarly uninvolved ... Even the Jews in America were keeping quiet, silent about the pogroms in Germany ...

I said to Marian, 'I have jotted down some notes, about my return last September, the fall of Wuhan, our journey from there to Chungking ... impressions of the journey. They might give you some ideas for a short story ... '

'Do show them to me.'

I went to my room and got the notes: only three or four pages, very little. Not the obligatory diary which Pao made me keep, which he consulted with puckered brow, striving to find some improvement in my thoughts, but what I had wanted to record – physical impressions, random jottings on small slips of paper, tucked in the inner pocket of my dress, along with the toilet paper one always travelled with; and I suffered some pangs of guilt at having hidden this from Pao. Arrived at the hospital, in the evenings, I had worked at them, expanding the stray notes into coherence. I fetched these pages and brought them to Marian. She was typing again, so I put them down on her table and went out. Half an hour later, there was a knock at my door. It was Marian, my notes in her hand.

'But this is good ... so vivid ... I just wanted to tell you, I got so excited, reading your notes. Well, if we could put this together, if there was more of this, I feel, with *your* notes, and with *my* writing, we could make a book ... '

We began almost immediately; I wrote down in three days the draft of a chapter, putting it down as it came to me, and then I gave it to Marian. Ten, twenty pages at a time. She rewrote, polished, reshaped, changed, taking out whatever was considered offensive, or could give rise to squeamishness, or was even downright dangerous, given the circumstances in which we lived. And there was a fair amount that just could not be written about.

Today, reading the book which emerged out of this co-operation, *Destination Chungking*, I can pick out the parts that are mine; the immediate, concrete detail, the drag and drift of people, the smells and the heat, the landscape and the exactness; but, as the writer Nora

Waln, whom I met later in England and who reviewed the book, rightly observed, a veil of beautiful writing had been cast upon events, softening into a beautiful patina, nothing protruding, what was ugly and raucous and crude. The squalor, the sufferings of China, the horrors and the injustices were neatly polished with smooth compassion and diminished in their enormity. All frenzy went out, and a good deal of indignation. This was not censorship, but safety, and it had to be; at that time even Rewi Alley wrote about George Hogg's book, *I see a new China,* 'there was so much that was dangerous to mention,' that he, too, took out many things; 'pages too hot to have around' were removed and hidden or destroyed. The 'thought police' was everywhere and few were idiotic enough to say what they really felt.

From the very beginning, the book had an intention; to please and to interest the American public which would read it, to incite affection and admiration for China at war, for the heroic resistance of the Chinese people, and its legal government. If one had really written the truth, that would have been to help the Japanese against China, to be a traitor; even the communists kept silent, for the sake of the United Front, even they held back many of the atrocities committed against them, because the war against Japan was their foremost concern, and anything was better than to have Chiang openly ally himself with Japan ...

All letters were opened and censored, suppressed if they contained 'dangerous rumours likely to influence the public adversely'. Marian and other missionaries were always very careful not to pass any comment on the government in their letters. A book was far more dangerous. 'I'm afraid we can't use this,' Marian used to say. 'I'll see what I can do with it.'

Where 'our book', as Marian called it, was concerned, 'the last thing we must do is to shock American women ... that would be wrong, with China at war ... the women are getting interested in giving money for China ... but American women are a bit puritan ... we mustn't make the book sound as if you and your husband had been together in the same hotel in Hongkong ... ' Delicately Marian explained, no love before marriage for pure American women (that was in 1939). 'A shipboard romance – well now, that might lead to misunderstanding ... ' We rearranged the romance.

My remarks on prostitution disappeared. 'Certain things are inevitable ... it might make people feel: Well, why should we help

China if things are so bad out there? Why not let Japan have a go at cleaning it up?'

There was also Marian's status as a missionary. 'I couldn't associate with a book that would be controversial or crude ... I don't think we need to mention that ... ' I acquiesced all the way, only too grateful for Marian's advice. We also simplified. After all, this was not a true autobiography, only a story, to do good 'for China'. Marian is enthusiastic. Marian knows best; and I myself still believe that Chiang is a national hero, only badly advised, badly surrounded. Marian also believed Chiang is China's salvation. 'He is a Methodist, a Christian.' That made all he did more acceptable.

The first chapters written, Marian sent them off to her agent in America. The response was enthusiastic; she told everyone on the university campus about it. But now I became worried about Pao; what would he say to this new eccentricity of mine? Had I not again been reminded that a woman with no talent is virtuous, whereas a talented woman is a freak against Nature?

Pao when he appeared in November to take me back to Chungking looked more prosperous, slightly fatter. He wanted me to work under Madame Chiang Kaishek, he said, where I could be of great use to him. I had no interest in working under Madame Chiang, I only wanted to go on at the midwifery school; but suddenly I saw how I could utilize the writing of a book as an opening. Pao called on Marian, and Marian talked about the book, astutely very little, merely telling him that she thought it would enlighten American public opinion. Pao was delighted. 'This is right, this is good,' he told me. 'It will be good for you to write all these things down, to write about your noble husband.' He thought of it in terms of propaganda effectiveness for himself; and besides, everyone knew that Madame Chiang always listened to American missionaries. 'When your book is finished, perhaps the government will publish it, you must send it to Madame Chiang, she may even recommend it. Then you can truly be said to have helped your husband a little, and this may redeem your errors in the past.'

I tell myself that we are at war, and I have to believe that Chiang is right, Pao is right, the mess will be cleaned up by incorruptible, fierce and loyal young men, like Pao. I must believe this (and sometimes I think I am losing my mind).

Now I return to Chungking with Pao; he has found a place for us

149

to live, and he takes me to see Hollington Tong, who runs the Information Service, who is very close to the Soong group, the American returned group, which is behind Madame Chiang Kaishek.

Things are changing, the 'international aspect' of China's struggle is to be intensified. Pao is in the section doing liaison work with England and increasingly with the U.S.A. Pao wants to go to America, he is now hoping to make a good impression with the missionaries. He even asks me about religion; would it do any good if he were converted? He talks to one or two missionaries and buys a Bible. We even go to a Protestant (Methodist) Church service, and to Hollington Tong's Christmas party ...

From stray talk I learn that the U.S.A. is somewhat more worried about Japanese intentions than the British appear to be ...

Pao now tells everyone that I studied in England. 'I don't want you to mention Belgium, such a mean, small little country ... you must say you studied in England.' He writes an essay which I have to translate for him into English, on the virtues of the Chiang regime. He arranges an interview with Pearl Chen, Madame Chiang's private secretary. Pearl is an American–Chinese girl, a very efficient secretary, who scarcely considers me worth talking to. She keeps looking at her watch, and makes other signs of great restlessness. We leave with nothing conclusive. Pao wants me to obtain an interview with Madame Chiang, to show her my book. I tell him it is not my book, that Marian is writing it based on my drafts, and that it is not ready. I do not see Madame Chiang and I don't try to. What would I talk to her about, anyway? Pao says I must imitate Madame Chiang Kaishek in all ways, for she is a paragon of virtue. 'Even when she talks to a mixed crowd of men and women, she only looks at the women's side, and never turns to the men's side.' He urges me to keep my eyes downcast, because I look straight at people, which is all wrong. The women he admires are those who commit suicide when their husbands die ... 'The chastity of a woman', says Pao, 'is the only worth that a woman has.' He tries to make me promise to commit suicide, should anything happen to him. I do not promise, though he keeps at it for some days, for Pao cannot bear any dissent.

During that winter my drafts went to Chengtu, to Marian. *Destination Chungking*, gentled and smoothed, only nice things put in, to safeguard sensitivities, to project an image of China which would arouse the sympathy of the American people, was growing. In the early spring of 1940 I went back to Chengtu with my cousin, Kuangchu, Third Uncle's cheerful daughter. The journey was effected by bus, and took us ten days instead of the usual two. Again a bout of midwifery, some work, some relief from the stifling life in Chungking ... four times I was to go back and forth, between Chengtu and Chungking, back to the little hospital. Through the summer of 1940, in Chungking, between the air raids, now very heavy, I typed and sent the concluding chapters to Marian. Finally I dared one last chapter, slightly critical, and for me the writing ended with the end of summer 1940.

In 1941 I began, with the suddenness of a tropic storm, to realize at last what Chiang was really like. In early 1942 *Destination Chungking* was published in the United States. By that time, because of Pearl Harbour in December 1941, the sympathy of the American public was with China. *Destination Chungking* never sold well, and quickly went out of print in the United States. I received half of the 1,000 dollars advance minus thirty per cent, which brought it to 350 dollars, and that was all.

For the next ten years I did not write again, except for a few short sketches and stories, which were not published and which I have still in a suitcase.

Destination Chungking did not convince me that I could write, but instead gave me an inferiority complex; I was convinced that I could *not* write. Today, I am grateful to Marian for keeping so much of it mine.

Because of this inadvertent lapse into writing, authorship was to remain for me an outside avocation, a release valve, something I almost deprecated, while medicine was my life. It was to become a doctor that I fought long and bitterly. It was a doctor I became and remained through fifteen years of active practice, till 1964. Only today, in 1967, I surrender to the evidence that I am a writer; with all the involvement, commitment, moral responsibilities, ambiguities, torment and contradictions which the word implies.

The sequel was not pretty. It happened in England, in 1943.

Jonathan Cape had published *Destination Chungking* there in autumn

1942; despite the praise of Chiang Kaishek and his wife, despite the idealized version of a brave young Chinese couple, struggling to serve their country, despite the fairy-book fabulation of the narrative, someone among the keen-eyed Chinese embassy staff, acute at detecting dissent even when couched in eulogy, had hinted to Pao that the book was 'not satisfactory'.

There was not one copy at home, of course. Pao purchased a copy at Bumpus's. He returned with it and said: 'Dorothy Woodman [of the *New Statesman*] told us what a good book it was. But someone at the embassy says it is not good. I am going to read it now.' It was true that Dorothy Woodman, Kingsley Martin, J. B. Priestley, Nora Waln, Stafford Cripps and Isobel Cripps, active in the China Campaign Committee to gather money and medical supplies for China, all had praised *Destination Chungking*. They considered it helpful to project a favourable 'image' of China at war. Pao, who never read anything except official dispatches, Chiang's speeches, and *Mein Kampf*, had felt this praise sufficient guarantee. But now doubts had been raised.

It was evening, Pao settled down to read; I crept into bed, shivering with dread ... waited, frozen stiff with terror. In the next room, quietly Pao read on ... Several hours later, he had reached the last page, the only lines where I had let pierce something of my hope for the future, something of my despair with the Chiang set-up; *not* the one he envisaged. And the future I hinted at, however nebulously, was not one where Chiang and his young officers had a place ... It was a hymn to the coolie.

We are not the important ones in China, we who ride in sedan chairs, while you bend to lift, to carry us. The officials, the bureaucrats, the would-be intellectuals – without you we are nothing. We are sterile and without power to create the future. The important one is you, coolie. You do not know how important you are, you who toil and fight and die dumbly, scarcely asking to know why. The significance of your gesture, coolie, when you raise your finger to trace the words on the wall ... it shows me that something curious is awake in you, is beginning to ask questions. It is a gesture of profound meaning, and I who watch am suddenly happy and confident of the future, because I see you, in the mist of dawn, lift your finger to read ...

This I had written, the end of the book, sting in the tail of a long innocuous story. Pao's mind, trained to detect 'intellectual subversion' in all its forms (and what a long tradition of dissent, hidden in eloquent praise, there is in China!), took in the implication of that final chapter, that last page. He strode towards me in the bedroom. I heard him come. He pulled the blankets off me. I sat up, shivering, while he started hitting, then he threw me bodily off the bed, kicking me and shouting: 'You are a communist, your brain is rotten with communism ... this is communist propaganda, this book ... how dare you, how dare you write that one day the coolie, the peasant, will lift his head to read? To lift his head means to revolt. How dare you say the coolie will revolt against us?'

On the other hand, from the real communists the book was to draw violent and bitter attacks; they only saw in it praise of Chiang, despicable reaction; violently, publicly, it was denounced; but I knew it not until, in 1965 in America, a member of the U.S. State Department informed me of this. He had been in China in 1948, 1949, at the time of Liberation; he had then been a lecturer at my old university, Yenching. 'The Chinese Reds don't like you, they are only trying to make use of you, and one day they'll turn round on you and use this book as evidence against you and get rid of you,' he told me. And again in 1966 and 1967 others were to inform me of 'a group of people' in Peking, who were denouncing me all over again, during the Cultural Revolution.

But with all of this I cannot concern myself; for the business of a writer is to grope and search, in agony and dismay, in despair and in discovery; and whatever was said or done, it was with *Destination Chungking* that I had begun on this long road, not knowing where it led.

Seven

BESIDES STARTING on a writing career, my attendance, even if discontinuous, at the hospital in Little Heavenly Bamboo Street, and the work I was able to do as a midwife, although patchy and interrupted, taught me more about China's countryside, about the conditions there, and among the poor in the city, about the feudal system in Szechuan, than I would otherwise have learnt had I remained, as Pao wished, a housewife in Chungking. A passionate, uneasy, physical experience, unformulated for a long time but all the more essential to my being. Like a carrier pigeon winging home, every time I could I went to Chengtu and to the small hospital. There was relief, friendliness, kinship and also work, work of the most satisfying kind; human contact, thawing my fear-frozen spirit, keeping me alive through torpor, dismay and guilt. And though it took years to learn the apt lesson, I learnt there that the real guilt was not to enlarge, with all the freedom in one's possession, the narrow strip of our existence with concern, care, and action for others. But how long that lesson took to bring forth its harvest of deed! And deeds like spilt sand in the sea disappear, leaving only an empty hand ...

It was a profound emotional experience, the first little round head, topped with its glistening dark hair, issuing forth to life from between a woman's thighs, the first cry, almost unbearable in its joy, and I wept for hours, but not in sadness, at the wonder and mystery of this act of faith, for ever repeated in its millions everywhere, the most common and singular miracle of mankind. The first case I tended was that of a small patient countrywoman and her first baby; she never uttered a word all through, and the broad smile upon her face afterwards was the most lovely thing to see. I began to understand the special joy of being a midwife, and why, for so many, it seemed reward enough to bring forth other women's babies without having their own – for they identified, as I later began to do, with the woman in labour, pushing and straining with her, managing her strength for her, sweating with her, urging and coaxing the womb and the muscles to the final orgasmic climax, the triumph of the small head winding free, the body slipping out, slippery and sleek, and the cry, the cry of the child; and perhaps this satisfaction was enough, since so many of them remained spinsters.

Marian Manly gave me special tuition so that I could catch up more quickly. I then realized that my personal insecurity hindered my studying, in a way which had never happened before. I no longer learnt easily; it took work and application now. On the other hand I was ill adapted to many of the techniques that my fellow-midwives were so good at, for mine had been book-learning rather than manual dexterity, and now I longed for dexterity, and even took to knitting, and envied those whose hands, small and capable, wrested with seeming ease grand victories in grievous cases. There was, indeed, a gap between book knowledge and what was required in the conditions in

China, in all their immediacy, the urgency of giant needs, the vast welter of necessity at all levels, in all its forms. For all this I was ill prepared with the book lore that had been poured into me in an organized society, in Europe, quite useless here where the most simple technical instrument, a pair of surgical gloves, scissors, a scalpel, needle, catgut, had to be imported from thousands of miles away. Here the human quality, assiduousness, care, real sympathy were more powerful than technical equipment because they innovated new ways of achieving results.

Through every day and night the triumph and terror of life, producing a human being in such a glory of distress and joy, was the rhythm of our exaltation, and the midwives I met were a dedicated, untiring, uncomplaining group, many of them with stories of suffering and stubborn endeavour behind them. My woes became insignificant in comparison.

The midwifery room was small, it was hot, a pressure-cooker steaming heat; in summer during the progress of a case a student with a fly-swatter was always posted to swat the flies that crawled in through door and window chink. It was equipped with Chengtu furniture, obstetric tables and scrub basins of local handicraft. The surgical instruments were purchased by Marian or donated from various missionary foundations. Rubber gloves were always a great difficulty, and the difficulty became greater as time went on for supplies were delayed many months as they came over the Burma Road. Later, when Chengtu was raided by Japanese bombers, the midwives had to deliver in darkness, as the electric current was turned off. Heavy black curtains on the windows trapped the faint glow of our small oil lamps and the electric torch used to light the proceedings. A small slit-trench was dug in the courtyard within the hospital compound for those expecting patients not in the last stages.

And now I was so much happier, even able to forget Pao, to forget my many crimes, to make friends, though at times grievously plunged into depression, misery, when Pao returned, when he wrote long letters retailing my misdeeds. In spite of this there grew up for me a range of activities which Pao was never to know about; and since he was unconscious of anything that did not directly affect him, I thus led a double existence. When he was with me, and we walked in the streets of Chengtu, my greatest fear was that we might meet someone from the university or from the hospital who might greet me; and if

155

it were a male doctor or the husband of a patient, such a simple courtesy might be the excuse for another pitiless beating. Pao tolerated the hospital because it was an all-woman outfit, because Dr Manly was an American missionary, and the policy of making a good impression on American missionaries (knowing that they fashioned public opinion in the United States) had the blessing of Chiang Kaishek, himself a convert to Methodism.

A peacock streak of charm for older women revealed itself in Pao; later in England he utilized this well and a host of elderly ladies were greatly impressed by his frank face, his nobility of talk, and his mythomania. With Marian Manly he was always at his best. Marion smiled at him and made him feel welcome, but I never found out what she really thought of him. She was too tactful, even when she knew I was unhappy, to probe, and I was reticent.

Pao also never knew that during my training I went, once or twice a week, to the university campus to attend certain Bible meetings at the homes of missionaries, which were built within the university enclave. I was starved for exchange of ideas, discussion, for books to read. These social get-togethers were not always religious, however, though they began with readings of the New Testament and the expounding of religious themes. They had a way of turning into discussion of political events, and the houses of missionaries were the only safe places where such discussions could be held, indirectly critical of the Chiang regime. At that time Protestant missionaries had two hundred and sixty-eight mission hospitals, with seventy-five per cent of the total civilian beds in China, and they represented, therefore, a considerable influence which Chiang hoped to turn to his account.

Finally, it was also through the hospital that I acquired my daughter, Yungmei. There would have been no Yungmei in my life, with all the happiness the word Yungmei makes to blossom in me, had I not been a midwife at Little Heavenly Bamboo Street.

The hospital had a school of twenty-five to thirty student midwives, six graduate midwives and three teachers; Marian Manly herself, a Miss Hsu, and a Miss Wang. Most of the midwives, once qualified, went away to work on their own in smaller towns, but some remained to staff the hospital.

A graduate midwife, with a student midwife, sometimes two, were always on call, at all hours of day or night, to go to patients' homes. Some patients were known to us, and had come for ante-natal care, others had no preliminary visit recorded, and of the latter a few were difficult, even serious obstetric problems, but it was impossible to know exactly what one was going to until one got there. Sometimes we walked, or rode by wheelbarrow to our destination, depending on distance. Years later I was to do two months of midwifery in Ireland, at the Rotunda, and also in the district of Cabra, one of the poorest of Dublin. There we rode on bicycles to our cases, and it reminded me very much of Chengtu. Same odour of poverty, same prolificacy of babies, even the fleas and the lice were the same ...

The hovels where we delivered were very dirty. More often than not we had hens round our legs, piglets to be shooed away; and there were rats to be worried about, for the smell of blood attracted them. They came and watched us at work. Once, turning my head from the dank body on its mattress, I saw one on the shelf, next to the small ancestral altar. In the quivering dimness of the rape-oil wick lamps placed in earthenware saucers, its hairy snout moved, and the shadows made it seem monstrously large.

We sometimes delivered cases in appalling decayed shanties, where there was no bedding, no clothes, no light, no money for oil, even for one wick; where the patient lay naked on a rotting plank set on stones in the churned red mud, and all was fetor and filth, a destitution worse than animal. The winter was not icy, but the dampness of Chengtu made it unpleasant for the poor, undefended from the constant wetness. And there was always the mud taste in everything, the smell of dung, the steaminess of water and the greasiness of dirt, and the darkness; often we saw little except the pale blur of faces and thighs and belly. We carried torches, to light our way and the performance; in bad weather a hurricane lamp supplemented them. We carried basins to wash our hands, basins we sterilized with flaming alcohol; sterile gloves, instruments, sterile gowns and face masks, towels in two heavy bags. When we went far at night a male servant of the hospital came with us.

Most of the cases we went to were poor, but there were also wealthy ones; though they lived in what were called mansions, the noisome neglect and dirt, the spitting and hawking, were almost less bearable, coupled with the satin hangings and carved beds. But there was

157

boiling water, light, space, coverlets, food for the woman, and tea for us.

Among the wealthy patients I remember one, the sixth or seventh concubine of a warlord whose name was Liu. Many of the Chengtu smaller warlords were related to the Three Lius, Liu Hsiang, Liu Wenhui and his brother Liu Wentsai, the last known as the terror of the countryside at Ta Yee, thirty miles from Chengtu, where he had enormous palaces. Liu Wentsai was the greatest landlord in the Chengtu plain, and the most cruel and exacting to his tenants. To rejuvenate himself he sucked the milk from the breasts of young mothers, whose babies died of hunger. Today his palaces at Ta Yee, which I visited, exhibit their torture chambers, dungeons full of water and rats, the cages where a man could only stand ...

Claiming to be descended from the great Liu Pei, Emperor of the West Han dynasty, famous hero of the Three Kingdoms, whose domain was the alluvial basin of Szechuan, whose tales are known to every child, the Liu warlords dominated Szechuan for twenty years. And this particular concubine, when pregnant, came to the midwifery hospital for an examination. She was most exact in her ante-natal visits, and remained to chat with the midwives, and particularly with Miss Hsu, the senior teacher, an able, cheerful, round-faced and diplomatic woman, who was very popular with the students.

'Spring Wave', for such was the name of the Liu concubine, was beautiful, with a lovely face, which she daubed with rouge and caked powder, making it nearly an actress's mask. Her make-up stopped at the high collar which topped her long silk dress. Her sleek black hair, the pride of the women of Szechuan, she wore with little bangs on the forehead and a large bun on the nape. Her hands were small, as were her feet; she was self-assured but not arrogant in her pride of place as the favourite of the moment. The warlord, in a large pelisse lined with fur, with a fur cap on his head, under which he sweated copiously, came with her, and there was a flutter of zeal and too many smiles when he was about, for his presence, whose porous benignity did not conceal a habitual snarling temper, evoked obsequious trepidation and unacknowledged fear. He let it be known that this concubine was highly favoured and we worried lest something should go wrong. Another of his concubines accompanied Spring Wave for her examination, when the warlord did not come in person. Thus pampered, with many strengthening broths and much soothing talk, Spring Wave declared that she would have no other but our hospital deliver her, and this gave us all, and particularly Miss Hsu, who was to perform the delivery, great face.

Came the day when Spring Wave felt the first pains. The baby was to be born at the Liu palace; the best-qualified midwife, with two aides, and Miss Hsu proceeded there. The four sat for three days in the palace, well entertained, with good rooms, padded silk coverlets on their beds, an army of servants to do their bidding, an array of succulent dishes at every meal. The days passed, nothing happened, but no one dared to leave. Suddenly labour started in earnest. And on that very day, some hours before the baby was born, and while Spring Wave was beginning to moan with the long stretch of hours, warlord Liu came back with his latest caprice, a new concubine.

How and why this sudden change? Perhaps the disfigurement of Spring Wave's body, in the last weeks of pregnancy, had displeased him? From the room where she was giving birth, Spring Wave could hear, in the adjoining bedroom, separated only by a screen, the giggles and the little screams of her rival, in bed with the warlord; and when her child was born it was a girl.

Spring Wave lay exhausted, a fine tremor shaking her legs and her mouth, under the silk coverlet embroided with phoenixes and peonies; the servants covered her with yet more silk eiderdowns; the slave girls poured her strengthening broth; the warlord's snores could be heard, above the cooing noises the midwives made purposely while they cleaned the baby. 'Such a beautiful daughter, see, beautiful like her mother,' said Miss Wang. Miss Hsu clucked and chattered gaily, all pretended not to notice and Spring Wave smiled and thanked them with great dignity.

A month later she was back at the hospital for her post-natal check, as sprightly, beautiful and slim as before, but a little haggardness had webbed very finely her thin temples, where pale blue veins showed, and there was new shrillness in her loud voice. The warlord did not come with her, and a year later it was the next concubine who had a child delivered by our midwives at Liu the warlord's mansion ...

And then there was the case of the warlord, who only two hours after his concubine had given birth insisted on intercourse with her ... We were called in haste, but she died bleeding to death.

Most of the births took place at home, and though the custom of asking for a trained 'Western-type' midwife was spreading, the old-type midwives still prevailed, and did immense harm. They would use hooks and tear the mother and the child to pieces, they had no notion of cleanliness, and their dirty, claw-like hands would go searching, searching for an undescended after-birth. Most of the mothers-to-be who came were young or fairly young, but older women would also come, to be examined and delivered of their fifteenth or sixteenth 'joy'; they would refuse the anaesthetic, for they were terrified that it would steal their souls.

Whether in hospital or at home, the women made little noise; some did not utter a sound, even when birth was prolonged and painful. The ones who screamed and shouted were usually the pretty concubines of rich men, or Westernized 'down-river' young women; but this behaviour was considered immodest.

There were different grades of fees to pay for deliveries; the rich paid more, the poor very little, or not at all. When inflation began in Szechuan in 1940, it was only possible to reckon such services in grain, and no longer in money, and the fees never covered anything but a small portion of the expenses of the small hospital.

The very poor would also call at the hospital. The husband usually came to fetch us, standing at the door, not knowing whether his demand would be accepted. But we went all the same. I remember one such case; a young girl, so young, so thin, biting her lip, making no sound, during the painful first birth, in a lean-to against the city wall, on a cold rainy night of January; only a mat rent with holes for ceiling, kept upright by two bamboos; we held an oilpaper umbrella open above her and our heads while the delivery went on. The stones of the city wall were her pillow, a grey rag flapped behind us in the wind and threatened our sterile equipment, and that was the door; only the darkness, probed by our torches, defended and concealed her on the wooden plank on which she lay; there was no blanket, no sheet, no mat, no pillow, nothing.

Her husband was a rickshaw coolie and he helped us by sheltering us with his body from the rain, he held her in his arms when the pains were strong, and murmured words of endearment to her; when the child was born there was no piece of cloth to wrap it in, only the tattered dress the woman wore on her nakedness, only the tattered top and trousers of her husband; and so the man took off his trousers to wrap the baby in them, but he would need his trousers to work, to pull his rickshaw the next day, so what would they do? We left a towel (though towels were precious) for them to wrap the baby in.

They would have to sell the baby as soon as the cord dropped off; perhaps the mother would hire herself out as wet nurse.

The midwife who did the delivery fumbled in her inside pocket and gave the new mother some money, and muttered it was to buy the *tzaotze,* the gruel given to women after parturition, which is supposed to stop bleeding. The young girl thanked her, nestled her baby close with heartrending tenderness, her husband saw us off; he was young and lean, and very quiet. My heart burned within me; oh surely, for these, a better day must come, a star must rise in the east ...

Another time we were called to a case, far out in the country. It took us two hours to reach the place, some of the way by walking and the rest by wheelbarrow. A farm, a landowning peasant family, a young woman. The single large room where she lay, in a poster bed, was crowded with thirty or more people; outside it a host of neighbours and curious children pressed close, almost glued to each other, poking their fingers through the paper that covered the latticed windows and peering through the holes. A week the young woman had been lying there, while from between her thighs protruded the cord, now dried and shrivelled, and attached to the cord the skeletal baby between her feet. And these were rich peasants, of the rare five per cent who owned their own land, fields, three acres, perhaps employed hired labour; they had a house, bedding, furniture ...

All that week, the after-birth had not come down; the local untrained midwife had tried to bring it down by massaging the stomach and later by introducing her hands within the girl's body. Meanwhile the cord had not been cut to release the baby, for according to the old way in Szechuan, the cord was only cut after the placenta had been expelled.

That the girl was dying was obvious; she was quite green, could not speak, could not swallow; lockjaw, tetanus, was very common in Szechuan, and many babies died of it after the cord had been cut with dirty knives or scissors, and it was customary to plaster the umbilicus with rice straw and with mud ...

All over the bed, on the clothes of the rigid girl, sitting up like a pole, wadded blankets rolled as bolsters in her back, were strewn rice grains, scattered in handfuls as placatory offerings to the evil spirits that had locked the after-birth inside the girl's belly; hanging outside the door and the room were streamers and untied knots of straw, signifying the untying of the 'lock' within; on the woman's stomach had been painted some signs and also on her feet; there were feathers about, perhaps from sacrificed fowls. And so many people in the room that peered over our shoulders, and pressed forward, and when we started to undo the obstetric bags, tried to touch what we had brought so that we had to be rude and order them out; an order which of course was not obeyed; and so many more punctures of the paper windows and more eyes and eyes and eyes peering and peering from outside to look at the doctors who had come, and the strange things they had brought. Miss Ma, the qualified midwife in charge of the case, was very upset by all this, and after she had examined the girl remained a long while frowning furiously, cogitating within herself, for this was indeed a perilous occasion.

Miss Ma was round about forty, and had had a very bitter life; sold as a child because her parents were dying of hunger, she was pock-marked so badly from smallpox that her face was darkened and never looked clean; someone had tried to bind her feet, they had been un-bound and she hobbled on semi-stumps, but walked miles indefatig-ably. As a slave girl she had run away, twice, from mistresses who beat her with thin split bamboo, so that she still had the marks down her back and on her legs. She had been forcibly married, as a concubine, to a small shopkeeper who could not afford a prettier woman; an old widower with daughters, who wanted a son from her. It had taken a week before he could force her, she fought so bitterly. After two years she was still not pregnant and was going either to be thrown out or sold to a brothel. She ran away again. By then it was the great fer-ment of 1919, the May 4th movement, women cutting their hair short, girls leaving their parents' homes to study, and committing suicide rather than be forced into marriage, and all crying 'Down with Con-fucius and the oppression of women.' For a while Miss Ma, too, was lifted, carried by the tornado of the Great Revolution, in the years between 1919 and 1927. Then came the massacres of Chiang in 1927, and all through Szechuan also the White Terror raged. There, too, the peasant uprisings had taken the form of a massive agrarian revolution, the peasants fighting the landlords, and sharing the land between them. Miss Ma nearly died of hunger, became a servant, ran away again, and was fortunate enough to find at last a kind mistress, an old lady half blind, who could not walk properly, one side of her being paralysed. Since Ma was strong she carried the old lady on her back, and looked after her, and was not afraid of doing anything that was needed, such as emptying the toilets. The old lady engaged a teacher to teach Ma to read, and after that she became a midwife, which because of money difficulties took her ten years. She hated men, and all to do with marriage, and would remain single always, her experiences having given her a horror of sex. And now, by the bedside of the dying girl, she drew off her sterile gloves, after the examination, and muttered: 'It's all a mess inside, decomposing.' The glove was covered with black filth when she had withdrawn it.

Miss Ma looked at her gloves, then told me to repack, and asked who in the family was responsible, and where was the husband. The clotted mass of relatives heaved and swayed and shook and finally out of it were squeezed an old woman and a young boy, the mother of the husband and the husband. And to them Miss Ma said: 'You can buy the coffin, there is nothing else to do.' And then the old woman wanted us to drink tea but we did not drink it, Miss Ma was so angry that she strode out without the usual courtesies.

Outside the wheelbarrows were waiting. We mounted them and they creaked and wobbled along the narrow paths between the fields, jade green with their young rice, or bright yellow with flowering rape, and the sun glistened daintily and the air was soft like a soft stroking hand, like silk, and all was fair to look at; but in her big loud voice Ma growled all the way, cursing the family for calling us so late; cursing the fate of women; cursing the men who imposed such suffering upon women ... The words rang in the sumptuous fields about us where there had been, where there was so much agony, so much pain; we rode on the narrow paths and on each side, in a million tendrils, lay the sweet gurgling water, a fallen sky under our feet, and Ma went on cursing, the bitterness of her own life welling out of her, and the wheelbarrow men heaved and sweated as they pushed us into the beautiful day.

There was the countrywoman who came a long long way from Chingsien, eighty *li* or more, to be delivered of her tenth child, because all the others had been daughters; and a neighbour of hers had been to the hospital and had acquired a son; this woman thought she too could obtain a son by coming to be delivered at our hospital. She rode in a rickshaw all the way and this must have cost a good deal; and as she lay on the obstetric table in labour she told Miss Hsu what had happened to her baby daughters: the first was alive, and also the third; but the second had been strangled at birth by the husband and so had the fifth and the sixth; the seventh had been born in a bad year, a year of famine when her belly skin stuck to her spine, and the husband had smashed her skull in with his axe; at the eighth female child the husband had been so angry that he had hurled it against a wall; the ninth was a year old and had been given away to a neighbour and now here was something in her belly ... oh let it be a son, a male child.

As the pains came and went, Miss Hsu, stethoscope upon the woman's belly, asked: 'What happened to the fourth?'

We went through the whole list of infanticides again and again, and every time the woman missed one out – the fourth. As the pains became worse (and labour was not easy, for her flesh was exhausted; her belly muscles had parted so that the womb could almost be seen under the skin; and we were prepared for a haemorrhage which is usual after many births), the woman began to sob and told us how the fourth had been killed. She had been so frightened when it was born and it was a girl that she herself had pushed it in the big toilet jar, and there it had suffocated.

And now we hoped, we all hoped. All the midwives by now had heard the woman's story, and all the other patients, and some sat up in bed straining with the woman straining on the delivery table, turned in spirit towards it, waiting, waiting for the miracle, for the son which would truly consecrate the hospital as a miracle-working place. But this did not happen; the tenth was another girl.

'Such a beautiful little sister, look,' said Miss Hsu as the woman lay mute, her eyes fixed on the ceiling, in a frozen stare. 'Look at her. She is so pretty.'

'It is a girl, another girl.' Perhaps she had not paid enough; she unwound the belt round her which she had pushed up under her breasts so as to free her belly for the work it had to do. And there was another twenty dollars in paper, and she said: 'All, that is all I have, for a boy.'

'But a girl is just as good as a boy,' said Miss Hsu to her; and for the next few days we all told her how good it was to be a woman, and how a woman now could do so many things, even become a doctor, or a midwife, and how pretty her baby was. After five days the woman went home, and she wanted to leave the baby behind, but this could not be. Miss Hsu placed the baby, wrapped tight in its swaddling clothes in the approved Szechuan fashion, in its mother's arms and said, 'Take care of her, she will bring you luck.' Then she walked with her to the door, still trying to persuade her, while the hospital servant went to call a rickshaw. Many rickshaw or wheel-barrow men would not carry a woman that had given birth to a child only a week or ten days before. They would only take a mother if the baby was a full month old, thirty days, when all evil was reckoned purged away. Often Miss Hsu would send out the servant to call a rickshaw, only to find the man pick up his shafts and go away when he realized that he was to carry a woman with a week-old baby. Then Miss Hsu would get angry and cry out: 'And where did you come from? Did not a woman bear you? Have you no mother?' to the back of the departing man. But in Little Heavenly Bamboo Street there were rickshaws who were used to carrying pregnant and new mothers, and laughed at the refusal of the others. So a rickshaw was obtained for the woman, an obliging smiling man, who also persuaded her to keep the baby, and told her: 'These are new days, a woman child is also good, look at all those doctors here.' Afterwards the porter told us that all the way home the woman was telling her story and that she did not dare to go back to her husband with yet another girl, and that on the way home she would find a convenient ditch, and throw the baby into it; but we never knew whether she did this or not, for neither the porter nor the rickshaw man would tell us. And some of the midwives thought we should have kept the baby; someone might have turned up to adopt it.

They well up, life after life, life of woman, countless women, one half of humanity, so long oppressed, too long exploited, an inhuman condition still obtaining today in many areas of the world, even among the advanced nations where forms of dominations are less openly cruel, but still exist; where being a woman still means not quite being a full citizen, not quite an entire person; conditions which I found in Ire-land ten years later when I did midwifery in Dublin and its environs for two months; and the treatment of this wonder of birth and preg-nancy, the whole relation of sex, the meaning of woman, a sordid and tragic enslavement, the identity of woman not honour but degradation.

So many lives, each the life of a woman, a mother, of so many mothers throughout the centuries; sometimes my skin seemed to burst off me with the awareness of injustice, with the burden of this collective wrong, fashioned into the very marrow of a society, an era, lauded by pompous Confucian precepts as Destiny, Heaven-ordained.

From this degradation attendant upon her being, no woman, however high in that kind of social context, was exempt. And Pao used to nail into me this lesson: 'Woman does not exist as such ... she is not a person ... she has no place in society save through her father, her husband, or her son ... '

And so many, so many women's lives were an embodiment of this non-status, an acceptance of this servility cloaked with smiles, scented with a false gaiety which broke into distress at the smallest occasion, which masqueraded as disease, illness, to escape consciousness of debasement. Pao called it 'an immutable principle of Nature' that woman should be inferior. 'A woman without talent is a virtuous woman.' 'Above is heaven, underneath earth; between is Man, and woman is to obey Man.' Confucius had established for ever the position of Woman. The very ideogram for 'woman' denoted subjection, the bar across, horizontal burden of her heavy breasts, the protuberant hips and the crossed bow legs, not quite quadripedal, but almost. Since then I have often thought that in today's China, with the Cultural Revolution which compels all to weigh in the light of reason our secret clingings to primeval devices of subjection, the first thing that should be done is to eradicate totally, to change totally, some of those odious ideograms, which are exact pictures of two millennia of feudal oligarchy, four millennia of woman's inferiority.

Even among the so-called educated upper class, I found the relentless tentacles of the past, like the grappling-iron hooks of the midwives that tore the entrails, the bellies of the mothers; even there, to forestall a true liberation of the mind, the eternal engraven classic phrases chained down the longing to be otherwise, to see and to feel and to know in other ways than the ferocious ways of the past.

I remember a case that Marian Manly herself had to deal with. Marian dealt mainly with cases within the hospital, and complications that could not be handled by midwives, and for which it was best to bring the woman to the hospital for the operation. At the ante-natal clinic held in the small hospital, Marian examined every patient in the course of pregnancy at least twice. And then there was also gynaecological work to do – Wassermann tests for syphilis, etc. A very common complaint was discharges due to various causes but mainly a torn or infected cervix. Very seldom, a woman demanded sterilization. Of such rarities was my Sixth Aunt, who had had twelve children and had the thirteenth removed and her Fallopian tubes tied. This case I remember illustrated the tenacity of old structures, in spite of the new emancipation: a young girl, a university graduate, who had just married a university lecturer. The morning after the marriage, the son's mother went to the newlyweds' bedroom to inspect the sheets of the bridal bed. (Until very recently, even in Singapore, that supposedly modern city, a special towel was provided for this purpose and brought ceremoniously to the mother by her daughter-in-law on the morning after the wedding night.) Finding no blood upon the sheet, mother-in-law became indignant, raised a great shouting, and ordered her son to divorce his wife on the grounds of unchastity. The bride protested that she was a virgin, her parents supported her, and accused the other family of slander. Finally it was decided to have the bride examined by a woman doctor (for no one would allow her to be examined by a man doctor). Marian Manly was chosen and found the hymen still intact. She explained to the assembled parents that in six per cent of all women, a lax hymen was unbroken by marital intercourse. Marian talked and talked obstetrics, drew charts, dragged books out of her shelves, showed pictures. In some women with very elastic membranes, even childbirth could not tear the hymen ... But it was impossible to convince the mother-in-law. And though her son himself said he was well content, that he loved his wife, and entirely believed her, yet it was impossible for the young couple to stay with the family as was the custom, they had to go elsewhere. Both families were affected for some years; the sisters of the bride felt that their chances of marriage were lessened; the husband was condemned for keeping his unchaste wife; the mother of the latter became ill with anger, unable to go to her usual mahjong games with her friends. It took a good while for the affair to simmer down; had society been stable, it might have taken much longer. But the system was already breaking down; with the war, with inflation, with general economic insecurity, people had much more to think about than a lax hymen. Yet even after the Revolution of 1949, these patterns of puritanism persisted, and the remarriage of widows, though protected by law, took another decade to enforce as normal behaviour ...

Nevertheless, among the poor, unable to indulge in these expensive habits of chastity-keeping, the customs of wife-renting and wife-selling, female infanticide and sale of female infants, forced upon them by cruel, compelling need, starvation and total denudation, were accepted, and though the upper class reviled them as 'immoral' and 'unchaste', yet they profited from them, imposed these vile and heart-rending cruelties in order to preserve their own 'high virtue'. Who else would have provided the slave girls, the concubines, the prostitutes, the temporary wives for the officials of the Kuomintang government, for the landlords – who else but the defenceless poor?

The rate of syphilis and gonorrhoea infection, due to the double standard, was very high in the cities. I saw women, of so-called good family, so riddled with syphilis and gonorrhoea, contracted from their husbands, that they were horrifying to look at. One of them, purulent and groaning with pain, came to see us; she had a peritonitis due to the extension of the disease from the ovaries into her abdominal cavity. At that time sulphonamide drugs were few, the black market made it impossible to administer them in adequate quantities. Penicillin did not exist. One had to be careful, when purchasing sulphonamides, that they were not pure chalk made into pills. This woman knew that her disease was contracted because her husband 'liked the heart of flower game'. She was only twenty-four.

Sterility was often due to venereal disease; and always women took it upon themselves to think it was their fault if they had no children. Marian and the midwives would talk themselves hoarse explaining that sterility was *both* male and female – still the women went on feeling perversely guilty, would moan and implore. One felt soaked in woman guilt, as in a glue bath, unable to wrest free. It became a desperate threshing about in a web of torment. And all was made worse by the total absence of retaliation, for there seemed no way to shake this penalty imposed upon woman by immemorial custom. And why women had ACCEPTED this psychological guilt, how they had been inveigled, seduced, tempted, decoyed, wheedled or beaten into thinking everything connected with sex and breeding was their fault, remains an inexplicable astonishment to me. Millennia of oppression, whole cultures built upon the guilt of Woman ...

And so into the hospital flowed a fervid and agonized multitude like a great river. And the pure, creative exaltation of birth, which made all else seem unimportant (for without this act humanity would perish) was diluted by such a vastness of pain, that one was torn by the perpetual ambivalence of so much platitude and so much splendour, so much tedious and trivial routine and so much drama, repetitive uniqueness, universal rarity, fragile glory and unending contempt. One wanted to cry as they did: Heaven, why have I been cursed to be born a woman?

Once again, before this pitiless, pitiful unending story of suffering, my own dwindled into nothingness, so long as I could believe that I was really useful in Little Heavenly Bamboo Street doing something to cure, to alleviate, to relieve, and one day perhaps to change all this for the better. It seemed to me that the only way was to become a doctor, as I had wished to be since I was twelve years old.

Many of the midwives in the hospital did not want to get married; the spectacle of what went on about them was enough to make them shun the thought. A few had, behind them, years of struggle to get an education, to *become* a midwife. But this was not a nest of sour embittered spinsters, but a group of thoughtful, independent women; making a choice animated by sound ideals. Some did marry, men of their choice, through love; this in itself was an innovation. I remember one, a fresh-eyed round-cheeked bouncy girl with beautiful eyes and hair, who came back to have her first baby among her friends; married to a young bank clerk with whom she was in love, she glowed in her motherhood. He learnt to mind the little baby girl, carried her every-where in his arms, looked after her when his wife was away on a case. But there were others, like Shen, the little wizened midwife, so scrawny and small that she looked like an eight-year-old child, yet she was a forty-year-old woman who had suffered much as a widow, with a son to bring up. Other women's babies were her whole life now, for of course she could never marry again – widows who remarried were considered unchaste and immoral ...

So many other lives come to mind; the woman who brought us her ten-day-old baby whose nose had been eaten away by a rat; the couple, the husband a 'returned student' whom I had seen vaguely at a conference in Paris; the wife a meek quiet schoolteacher who obvi-ously worshipped her 'returned from the West' intellectual husband. When the baby was born it was a macerated syphilitic cadaver. 'You ought to go to the hospital and have your blood tested,' said Miss Wang bluntly to the man. There was the girl baby with a terrible harelip and cleft palate; and all the midwives spoke at supper of the tragedy, for it was a little girl. 'If it was a boy it would not matter,' said one. 'She will find it hard to get married,' said another. 'Who wants a woman without a nose? Who wants a harelip?' In spite of their sure knowledge and repudiation in talk, and even in their life, of sex as servitude, they still contemplated the state of marriage as an inevitable if melancholy aim.

And it was in the dilemma between the fierce but painful independence of the single state, and the servitude of the wedded one, that the charming and clever Miss Hsu, our head teacher, became trapped without issue; for in the spring of 1941, when once more I found myself back in Chengtu, all over Little Heavenly Bamboo Street, like the moving fog ebbing and flowing and gnawing into the landscape, hung and floated and seeped the rumour that Miss Hsu was leaving the hospital in order to marry a widower, a small official, the relative of a warlord of the Liu clan.

My involvement with this project came about when Miss Hsu coaxed me into acquiring a small piece of land outside Chengtu in the spring of 1941. Inflation, which had started in 1940, was getting very uncontrolled, and whereas a good restaurant meal had cost $3.50 in 1939 it now cost $50.00, and it was going up and up. The class worst hit by inflation was the peasantry because they paid their land rent in grain, and then they had to buy everything they needed, and had no money. The usurers exacted grain in repayment, and hoarded it, or took the land from the peasants for debt. Small farmers who owned a piece of ground, a half to one and a half acres (the average size of a 'farm'), now sold it and went to the cities. There were peasant risings every year from 1940 onwards in Szechuan, both because of this and because of pressganging into the armies and into road-building, without pay, for the government.

Meanwhile, people from the city bought land as security against inflation, as they bought and hoarded firewood, cloth, straw, medicines, tiles, bricks, shoes ... anything that could be hoarded and kept. Speculators were building wooden houses, rickety structures which occasionally collapsed, for the families of officials, who were being evacuated from Chungking because of the bombing. These sold swiftly, then were resold, the price going up and up by the month. When the orders for the evacuation of families and all non-essential persons were given – which some said was to avoid riots in the cities due to food shortages – many families with children went to the countryside to live, rather than starve in the cities, and this gave rise to land-buying by real-estate companies from destitute peasants.

Now Miss Hsu also talked of the necessity of buying land as a buffer against inflation, and of building a small house to escape the bombers. I, being naive, saw no further, until I heard the gossip about her intentions, which were marriage. Marian Manly confirmed it, though soberly. She deplored what Miss Hsu was set to do. 'I feel she's giving in to her environment.'

The person who had cajoled Miss Hsu into pre-marital pecuniary preoccupation was a lady with eight children, a frequent visitor to our hospital and enthusiastic about the whiff of anaesthetic which banished all pain. She brought, sometimes by main force, pulling them by the hand, many a reluctant mother to the outpatient clinic. On her days off Miss Hsu played mahjong with her and other friends. Miss Hsu had delivered her last little boy, and this had made the woman gratefully devote herself to Miss Hsu's change of status. She promoted herself matchmaker to such effect that very soon Miss Hsu blossomed into a fuzzy permanent, put rouge and white upon her face, encased her half-bound feet in altogether hideous modern shoes, talked in a distracted manner and, what was worse, began to lose her mild, equable temper.

Before her spirit had begun to dwell upon the importance of being wedded, Miss Hsu had been the most unruffled person one could meet. Now she began to throw tantrums. Marian Manly did not approve of the project, because the man whom Miss Hsu was going to marry was 'old-fashioned', and not a Christian, and Miss Hsu would not only no longer be able to practise midwifery, nor to teach; but also might lose her Christianity. She would have to adapt to that soul-eroding idleness which was the life of the better-off women, busy with a thousand trivia, yet with a host of servants: lengthening each task to make the day seem shorter; filling the hours with gossip, smoking the water pipe, playing mahjong, breeding children, then immediately giving them to wet-nurses to care for; and to express all this was the word *Shua,* which meant that there was always time to dawdle away, a doing nothing, a loitering, bland and formless, and no counting of the drifting hours or the days.

Miss Hsu would be clasped into these longed-for fetters, day-long week-long mahjong parties, and these would take the place of useful hours of midwifery. In our Chou family mahjong parties were ritual, occurring at stated celebrations or when the calendar, compendium of auspicious or luckless days, stated that these were good hours for a mighty cascade of the game. They went on for two, three, five, ten days; whole clans gathering in one or the other household to participate, with forty, sixty players, four to a table, at once. Sometimes a person would withdraw briefly to sleep or to eat, and the place would be occupied by a replacement. I remember a scene in the courtyard of Third Uncle's house where a young woman at play was brought her three-year-old son to breast feed. With one hand she opened her dress and extracted her breast, long and pendulous as so many breasts were from over-usage. Even at twenty-eight or thirty, most of the women had had six or seven children, though half might have died in infancy, and breast-feeding went on for two years or more, as this was supposed to ward off another pregnancy. She thrust the nipple in the toddler's mouth, while a servant held the child; meanwhile the mother's other hand never stopped flicking the ivory and bamboo-backed chips upon the table. Most of the players did not need to look at the chips to tell what they were, but felt them with the finger as they picked them up, and knew them by touch.

Miss Hsu was palpably unsure, in dread, weighing the loneliness of the older woman coming upon her, against the unbliss of marriage and living with a man and having to endure not only intercourse, to which she professed repugnance (as all women did, for what 'moral' woman would confess to *liking* sexual intercourse?), but his certain infidelities; for if he did not continue to frequent brothels or indulge in a concubine, that would prove that he was 'wife-fearful' and his male friends would jeer at him. Hence those moods altering her former self; but relentlessly she was being borne every day nearer to matrimony; her hair now became blacker; her heavily plastered face showed more wrinkles than had ever been perceptible when it was lightly powdered; she smiled at mirrors, talked of black-market gold for teeth-fillings, essayed a youngish gait, resurrected some influential relatives.

And then it turned out that Miss Hsu was very worried about one thing, which was her virginity. She had, it was known to only very few, been raped when a child of thirteen by her maternal uncle – a by no means uncommon occurrence in large clan families – and now wondered whether the warlord would mind ... certainly she would never tell him ... Marian suggested that she should not tell the warlord anything. 'Anyway he has not been a saint,' said Marian, who always became very angry at the double standard. But this point of view carried no weight. A man could do what he liked, a woman never; and if she had been raped she was spoilt for ever, and had better die.

But then Miss Hsu's friend thought of an obvious way out, which was to stain a towel beforehand, and place it where post-wedding inspection would effectively prove pre-marital intactness, a device which had been used in an old Chinese novel. Preparations now went ahead, subtly and underground, for the not-yet-announced betrothal. Miss Hsu did not meet her husband-to-be; it was all done by the marriage-broker, her garrulous, enthusiastic and determined sponsor.

How this match-making came to be tied up with buying land later became obvious; in the general turnabout of her personality, Miss Hsu was capsizing, throwing overboard the sober ballast of her life as a midwife, a salaried teacher, a respected member of a hospital, a spinster, and plunging into the oceanic muddle of money-caring, security-riddled gentry wifedom, with its cortege of valuations and worth; and the most important asset was land. Miss Hsu's status in the world would depend on the number of silk dresses, fur-lined dresses, coats and shoes she owned, the number of times she could afford to have a permanent for her hairdo, the servants she would be able to commandeer and keep, and above all whether she was a 'landed' person or not. In fact, this purchasing of land, the sudden rapacity accompanying this purchase, were all part of the new image in order to make Miss Hsu acceptable even unto herself.

And this destroyed the pleasant sweet Miss Hsu we had known, and out of the wreckage was born a shrewish small person with rouged cheeks and screaming voice, a metamorphosis achieved not at once, but in several stages, of which one was buying land.

Miss Hsu therefore pursued me with talk of buying land, land upon which I could build a house. I did not want to build a house, but she worried me until I weakened and we went to see the land. I had two thousand dollars, considered a large though now dwindling sum in the spring of 1941. This sudden influx of money I had earned by my own exertions, giving English lessons to the Soviet military mission in Chungking the previous year. I told Miss Hsu that I would consider lending her half the money, but she insisted that I must be co-owner, that together we would build a house, a refuge from bombs, which we could either rent out or inhabit. She coaxed me into inspecting 'our' piece of land. It was some way out in the countryside, an unkempt sand-and-water moundiness where nothing grew; it was being sold by a village clan in debt, and that night there was a dinner at which the clan and the brokers foregathered. On our side came Miss Hsu with

Miss Wang, someone's elderly male cousin, and myself. By the flicker of the oil wicks we saw a table of mute and suspicious peasants, in rags, sitting in the dancing shadows and nursing their bamboo pipes and not saying anything; they were the owners. The middleman on Miss Hsu's side began to exhort them to accept the price, pointed out that they could not do anything in the way of planting rice or beans or rape seed there, and that the money offered was a large sum for such land. Suddenly, apropos of nothing, for the peasants never uttered, Miss Hsu managed a small raging whirlwind scene, shouted that it was far too much money for such a piece of land ... She seemed almost hysterical, screaming and pounding the table with her little fist. I never quite understood what had gone on; some days later, pertinacious Miss Hsu came back with many papers, and I could hear her discussing them, in her room, with her match-making friend.

In the end I paid one thousand dollars and I received a piece of paper in which Miss Hsu engaged herself to share with me the land and whatever building would be erected on it ... And now I think what she obtained was, indirectly, the protection of my name – that of the Chou clan (since I was of the Chou family), and that of Pao, as I was his wife. For no deal or venture of any kind was ever straight and simple in those days, everything was tortuous and crooked and had repercussions beyond conjecture. Such tangling tactics of influence and string-pulling have always been beyond my perspicacity; even today I remain innocent of subtleties. So I lost one thousand dollars, then I lost the piece of paper, or tore it up. A few months later Miss Hsu wrote to me once to give me news of 'our house' and the cost of the tiles. Whole villages were now selling the very small fields they owned, but money went down and down – soon that thousand dollars I paid for an eighth of an acre of land would not buy a bowl of rice ...

Miss Hsu duly entered upon marriage. Though I missed her wedding, I heard about its aftermath from others: that Miss Hsu was giving mahjong parties, that Dr Manly had not attended the wedding, which gave Miss Hsu no face and much anger, so that she eschewed coming to the hospital, but invited the midwives to her home instead.

Miss Hsu must be an old woman now, but the fixity of images once perceived does not allow me to modify her round face with the frizzy permanent, nor the rich pigeon-murmur laughter which was hers. And with these come to mind the voice of the doorkeeper calling the midwives to go out on a case, the wooden stairs creaking as they go down heavily loaded with the kitbags. I see my friend Huang Seyuan, so good, so sad and so quiet; Shen so wizened, whose bed I slept on one night when she was away, and all the bedbugs of Chengtu came to bite me. I remember pockmarked Miss Ma, strong and garrulous; able and clever Miss Wang who did everything well, whether it was knitting, pickles, midwifery, playing volleyball or making cloth shoes. I smell the smell of the operating room, disinfectant, sweat, hot wet dank birth; hear the smart slap of the fly-swatter and the voice of Marian Manly with its American-Szechuanese accent; babies, babies bawling their way into the world; the mothers, the talk, the laughter, the tears; and at night the smart click-click of Marian's typewriter, moulding my chapters into a book.

Marian liked to read out aloud the chapters that she had ended to an appreciative audience, and that meant to other missionaries; occasionally she took me along to dinner with one missionary family or another. After dinner Marian would settle happily to an hour of reading, and the others listened. I was detached from it, sometimes recognizing my sentences, but not always. I admired Marian, who did not mind reading out loud; the act of writing, so public, is also so intimate, that though others read me, I could not read myself to them. Sometimes, as she read, my mind wandered out to Pao; then fear would sweep its coldness over me. But there was something very soothing in Marian's determined voice, her air of assurance. I knew that I could not have spun out every detail meticulously, as she did, until it became so beautifully inset, a gift of magnification which in my own writing later I was to handle differently, striving on the contrary to give the feeling of a scene in as few words as possible, not building up, but stripping down.

Thus I met, through Marian, a few missionaries, American and Canadian. All of them have since left China; some have written books to describe their stay in China and how the Revolution, when it came, changed their lives. One at least helped many of the progressive students hunted down by Tai Lee's secret police; others believed in Chiang and were afraid of or hostile to political activity, because of the ambivalence of their position in China.

Chengtu West China University at the time housed six universities; five of them had trekked there from other provinces. Secret police agents abounded, kept watch on the professors, lecturers and students. The missionaries felt the pressures, took no sides and few risks; except for the very few.

I met an English medical couple, the Parfitts. Jessie was a tall handsome woman, a gold medallist of London University; she represented all that I wanted to be – a doctor, a capable woman, a confident person. Her husband was a pacifist; a sincere man who got into long arguments over non-violence because he hated war so much. I remember Jessie well because in May 1940, when the phoney war in Europe, that had smouldered since September 1939, finally broke out, and the Hitlerian Blitzkrieg rolled over France, it was she who came to my room in the hospital one evening and said: 'France has given up, the British Army is trapped at Dunkirk, everything is finished ... ' The Parfitts had heard the news over their radio; news of the fall of France, of the disaster at Dunkirk. To them it seemed the end of their world. To me it was a far-away episode in a war which for us had started so many more years ago ... 'What will happen now?' I asked. 'I don't know,' said Jessie, 'England is all alone now.' She was really upset. I had not seen her so upset before. 'Oh, I don't think it will be so bad,' was all I could manage. 'We can't have Hitler in England. We just cannot,' said Jessie. I thought, 'Look at China, so much of it gone, so many Japanese in it, and alone for so long and still it goes on, and on ... '

This world of missionaries continued to be half familiar, half alien to me; as in Yenching University, there was certainly a 'relationship' they entertained with their Chinese colleagues, but again, the startling and by now even more acute difference in standards of living made all pretence at being a united intellectual community on equal terms a sham. The Westerner was so much better off – with a far larger salary, beautiful brick house, servants – than his Chinese counterpart, even if the latter was better qualified. And this really divided the campus into two strata, with the Chinese staff progressively less well nourished as the war went on and inflation played havoc with their salaries, so that they became less and less able to afford even the necessities of life. Whereas Western missionaries were receiving foreign exchange money, and were thus not affected, the others began literally to starve.

At our hospital all meat dishes disappeared, as did chicken and eggs, in 1940. Soon the midwives were eating brown rice, coarse kidney beans in their husks, pickles; if I went to an American missionary home there was meat, and cake and rich sweets, and butter and chicken.

Under such conditions no Chinese could entertain a Westerner to a meal, and though the opposite could be done, it happened very rarely, for as things became harder to obtain, missionaries hung on to what they had, to parcels from abroad, for themselves and their children, and to their privileges. Already very early in 1940 malnutrition was making its inroads in the student body. Pretty soon there were two grades of students, those who could afford, and paid for, dishes with their rice, and the others who could only afford rice, and what remained in the dishes after the first batch had eaten. Tuberculosis became alarmingly widespread, and this was due to the food situation. A few years later, students, lecturers and professors were dying of hunger.

After the May 1940 debacle in France, there was contempt for England and France in Chinese military circles, a feeling that they had richly deserved this humiliation. Their lordliness and arrogance in Asia, in China – where was it now? Ho Yingchin, the Defence Minister, was certain that Germany would win: 'The British are finished, the French too.' No longer could an Englishman look down on China, on the mess and chaos or retreat and defeat; there had been more chaos and mess and rout all the way in France in 1940, and the shambles of the armies of the Allies were littering the Dunkirk coast like tide-lapped debris. Naturally the humiliations inflicted upon those who once had humiliated us evoked no sympathy; on the contrary, it gave rise to smugness, even among those who liked the British and the French. But to most of the missionaries, only the war in Europe seemed to matter. They were a great deal more concerned about it than about what was happening in China. Churchill's fighting speech was the subject of their after-dinner talks; and when I told one of them that what happened in China was important, he said that no, the future of the world was being decided in Europe.

On July 17th, 1940, came the news of the closure of the Burma Road, a decision taken by the British government which was a direct encouragement to Japan. This infuriated many of us in China. Churchill, the man who seemed best qualified to represent an indomitable fighting spirit, at the same time ignored China's fight against Japan, and closed the Burma Road, through which went the supplies for the war in China. It seemed an unbelievably cynical act. For three months that summer the road was to remain closed; and this ignoble gesture only further diminished the prestige of Britain in Asia. By closing the Burma Road, the British sought to detach – or so they thought – Japan from Hitler Germany. They hoped to come to an agreement with Japan on the sharing of the markets in China, and to avoid a thrust by Japan into South-East Asia. However, they only succeeded in making the Japanese invasion programme more definite. Whatever Churchill's qualities in Europe, he remained singularly unwise about Asia. To Churchill China was a motley collection of warlords and beggars; as Gandhi was a half-naked fakir and India a land where violent repression could go on for ever. Though he embodied Britain's desire for national independence against tremendous odds, he seemed incapable of comprehending that same desire in Asians and Africans.

After the closure of the Burma Road, a sharp feeling that China should 'negotiate' with Japan swept through the missionaries. What China needed most of all were trained people such as doctors, professors, engineers; this long-term view would do better in the end than 'political agitation'; better to study and leave politics alone ... In spite of outward calm there was much underground dissent on the campus. Meanwhile military clashes between Kuomintang and communist troops were on the increase, as were also the arrest and putting into 'thought reform' camps of left intellectuals.

Many of the missionaries did not want to fall foul of Tai Lee's Blueshirt spies ... Yet it was in the home of a missionary that I began to attend the weekly 'Bible Study' discussion meetings.

It was forbidden to teach or to debate on the economics of the countryside, or the meaning of fascism, or what was going on in Yenan, on the other front. It was also forbidden to discuss inflation. All these forbidden subjects, however, we began to discuss, which was already treason. This was done quite simply, by taking a Bible text, and then going on from there. There were always students present, also some lecturers. The presiding missionary always uttered some reassuring little generalities at the beginning and end, but the implication was *criticism*, not total acceptance; as such, our meetings, if reported, could have been very dangerous, both for the missionary who sheltered us and for the Chinese students and lecturers there.

At one of these meetings we met Jack Belden, then a journalist, writing for an American newspaper. He had visited the liberated areas under communist rule, and was later to write that very fine book *China Shakes the World*. He had been a sailor, a working man; had arrived in China in 1933 and stayed nine years. He talked to us about

Yenan, about the 8th Route Army, and what it did to fight Japan. With extra-territorial privileges no foreigner could be touched by Chinese law and Jack Belden would not be molested, but had some-one betrayed us, there would have been much trouble for the few Chinese present. At another meeting I met David Crooke, today teaching in Peking; he was then lecturing in Chengtu. David partici-pated at these meetings and his clear mind, his quiet arguments, made a deep impression. He was one of the chief movers behind these study groups.

There was also Ruth Weiss, a most courageous personality. An Austrian, she married a Chinese somewhat younger than herself, and bore him two sons. Some years later, it was not she, but her husband, who went off to the United States, although he had always appeared the more 'progressive' of the two, and Ruth was left alone with two children to rear through the difficult years of the downfall of Chiang Kaishek. The Revolution found her in China, and there she remained, saying that both her children were Chinese and must stay in China. At the beginning it was very difficult for her; no one knew the hardships she went through, always with smiling face and a wonderful good humour. I have seen her again in Peking. Her face is as unlined and smooth as a quarter of a century ago in Chengtu, when gay, and full of life by the side of her husband, she asked me to dinner.

There was Liao Hungying, a Chinese girl, a lecturer in chemistry. She had great integrity and was therefore offensive to many bureau-crats and hypocrites. She had been studying in England for some years, and returned to teach in Chengtu. She was a friend of Huang Szeyuan, the midwife with whom I was friendly, and later married an English-man, who was studying Chinese, and she is now living in England.

These meetings and these people affected me, although at the time I argued against David Crooke, retailing some of the nonsense that Pao had infused in me, for we are not immune to brainwashing, and I was too insecure and too candid, good faith to the fore always, believ-ing people's words too readily. They provided a pause and a counter-poise, a strengthening of my opposition to Pao, to the ideas of his system. They enabled me to survive; but their total effect would not be apparent for a very long time.

Together with Liao Hungying, Huang Szeyuan, little Shen, and clever

Wang the head midwife, I ambled in the streets of Chengtu, Silver-smith Street and Silk Street, Pewter-makers' Street and Book Street. We went to eat *lamien* (small bowls of noodles smothered in chilli sauce and brown sugar) at a stall in Little Heavenly Bamboo Street. We made pickles. My friends taught me Szechuan riddles, and those ways of speech which make Szechuanese dialect so full of fun and humour. Thus the expression 'a spinach and beancurd dish' meant a spotless family, untainted by evil deeds. To 'deafen one's ears and steal a bell' was applied to people who had self-delusions, and whose talk was all of themselves. To 'beat a dog with a dumpling' was Shen's pithy way of huffing off someone trying to bribe her, and 'a buddha of mud crossing a river' meant someone who was not qualified for an enterprise yet attempting it to his detriment.

On my days off I returned to Third Uncle's house in Sheep Market Lane, and Third Uncle was always ready to talk, for when I went to see him he was provided with a willing audience to lecture. My interest in Szechuan proverbs delighted him. 'The down-river people don't talk in our way.' To say that a man 'had a parrot's beak' meant he was all talk and no performance, and this was peculiar to Chengtu, where parrots swung on wide rings in front of many shops. 'Your essay is like the footclothes of a lazy woman', indicating a confused, verbose style, was heard about the literati, and Szechuan literati were notorious for the profuseness of their literary pieces. 'A cucumber on a wall' meant a double-faced acquaintance. When a guest overstayed, Third Uncle would mutter that he 'wore a felt hat in June'.

Some expressions which might sound critical were actually praise. Thus 'a hairless toothbrush, down to bone and eye', meant a good opera singer, one whose voice, pure and clear, did not need a pretence of embellishing, extra trills and fancies.

When we went on visits to patients' families the children would crowd around us, and a favourite pastime of Miss Wang, while we waited (and midwifery is hours of waiting and then a tremendous frenzy in minutes), was to play at song riddles with the older children.

I wish now that I had collected this children's talk, and also the lulla-bies and baby songs I heard the mothers croon, for Chengtu women were full of such old, old tunes. Alas, memory is not so accommodat-ing, though I can still hear, when I go back to Chengtu and listen under the hum of traffic, a familiar warble, a mother, from one of those lath-and-plaster houses (now also disappearing, for they are very insanitary), crooning to her child; and on the streets the children playing at cat's cradle, or at hopscotch, still set song riddles to each other.

Then there was Szechuan opera, so much more shrill and less stultified than Peking opera; the movements less impassively determined, the women's roles more lively. One of my cousins, Teng Wenhu, was an opera lover and with her I sat through many a five-hour performance. After that we would wander in the street, select a small eating shop and eat *maotutze,* the famous Szechuan hotpot of spice, liver, kidney and giblet, while Teng Wenhu and her friends indefatigably discussed the finer points of the opera we had seen.

In 1964 I was to see Szechuan opera change, and the Chengtu theatres begin to show new themes, discarding the old subjects of poor scholars marrying wealthy princesses, but keeping the techniques of song and gesture, and the underlying vein of humour, so strongly part of its enduring worth. And I am waiting now for a good Szechuan opera on one theme, the Long March, when it went through the province, and changed the lives of so many people.

Eight

BESIDES THESE days in Chengtu, with midwifery and writing, there were also the weeks and months in between spent in Chungking with Pao; and that was another life, morsels of existence which I never discussed in Chengtu, so that I was able to divorce those areas of being from each other.

The bombing by the Japanese which began in 1939 continued in 1940 and in 1941 with increasing ferocity. As soon as the winter fogs lifted the planes came, and through the gruelling hot summer, until late in autumn, being bombed was part of the normal process of living. Our daily activities were geared to this predictable occurrence: one rose early, and since the nights were an inferno of heat and sweat, the rock exuding its day-stored heat, it was easy to wake when the sun rose, for dawn did not mean coolness, but another raging hot day. Quickly the fire was lit with sticks of wood and a fan to spurt the flame, water boiled for morning rice, and by nine o'clock the day's first meal (the before-the-bombing meal) had been consumed. The first alert then started. One went to the dugout, with some luggage in hand, kettle and iron pan (irreplaceable after 1940, as metal became almost non-existent); and there one spent the day. Sometimes the bombs fell very near and we came to know the peculiar whistling sound they made. At other times the drone was farther away, and the explosions faint. Sometimes the bombers came over five or six times, on occasion up to twenty times a day. And once, in 1941, they continued without let for seven days and nights, and many people died, both in the bombings and also in the air-raid shelters, especially babies, from heat and exhaustion and diarrhoea.

The shelters were scooped-out tunnels in the rock, and since Chungking was all rock, with juttings and small hollows and hillocks almost everwhere, the bowels of these promontories could easily be utilized. But some of the common shelters had been dug in softer earth, and were unsafe. They caved in after a while. There was no ventilation in them, and the people who sat deep inside, away from the one and only outlet, the mouth of the tunnel, became anoxic if the raid was prolonged. They started to thresh about, or to faint. In between the explosions, there was respite. While awaiting the next batch of bombs, everyone would come out of the dugout, sit round the mouth of the cave, fan, gulp the hot air; but this was almost as gruelling as sitting inside the dugout because there was hardly any shade, and if there was a single bush, it was monopolized in its thin narrow coolness by some police squad or some self-important official and his family. The heat pounded upon the rock, the day wore on and on, the hours were a casque of hot lead, were sweat, were suffocation and thirst; a single large wooden bucket was provided for the men to relieve themselves at the mouth of the shelter; nothing was provided for the women. The children could and did squat about, and the area became noisome with smell and flies.

After 1940 it became dangerous to use a pocket handkerchief to wipe one's sweat during the air raids. There was a rumour that 'spies' had been caught, signalling to the planes with white handkerchiefs. Anyone 'signalling' was to be executed immediately ... I was witness to one unexplained episode; going to the dugout in our neighbourhood a little late (I always postponed going till the very last minute), I saw a man, hands bound, face covered by a black cloth, with two slits for eyes, being marched off by three soldiers. Behind them came a plainclothesman holding a revolver loosely, muzzle down. The prisoner would probably be executed in a small private shelter, shot through the back of the neck, and why I did not know. This was another method devised by the secret police for getting rid of 'communists'. The executioner usually took the victim's shoes, after death, to prevent the dead man's ghost running after him.

When we sat outside the shelters, therefore, we had to refrain from showing anything like white cloth, and in the collapsing heat, which never let up, one's skin was always pouring; so we bought towels of grey or blue. When I stood up I would sometimes leave wet marks on the rock where I had been sitting, and that was sweat.

Often, returning home, I found there was no water. The bombings broke the water pipes, and twice hit the Chungking electric plant. Most of Chungking anyway depended on the water-carriers, bringing water from the few mains or from the river two hundred feet below us. Down, down, down and up, up, up, to get a pail of water ... and this yellow, turbid fluid, the sap of the Great River, cost five, ten dollars a pail. In bad periods I learnt to drink, cook, wash, clean, with only one pail of water a day.

We lived in 1940, till we were bombed in summer 1941, on the rented first floor of a house in the Chang Family Garden. This was not a garden, but the name of a long narrow flight of steps, a ladder-like street, paved like a mountain pathway, going from the main road down to the river. The houses on it were built on one side only, the other side was a deep ravine. Across the ravine another slope, another ladder-street with houses could be seen. They were para-military installations with a training camp, possibly a Blueshirt institution. A public privy was almost opposite our house; convenient for emptying our toilets. The Soviet military mission's office was on yet another promontory sloping down to the river, visible to us and only about half a mile away.

The relations of the Chiang government with Soviet Russia were at the time better, in a factual way, than with America, because of the Chiang stance of resistance to Japan. Diplomatic relations had been restored in 1934, a non-aggression pact signed in August 1937; loans and military supplies began to come through the newly constructed 1,700 miles of road running from Siberia through Urumchi and Lanchow to Sian in 1938. It was the presence of this road which prompted the opening by the Americans of the Burma Road, six months later. The Russian Ambassador Paniushkin, when he came to Chungking, refused to take a huakan to be carried up the steps from the river to the main road level, and this democratic gesture made him widely popular with the people of Chungking. Soviet military missions kept strictly to themselves, and there was no special guard on them, whereas the Chinese communist liaison group, headed by Chou Enlai, was kept in restricted conditions. They were virtually prisoners; the small house in which they lived was encrusted with special agents. The concentration camps were filling with people accused of 'dangerous thoughts', found reading in bookshops, or caught on the road to Yenan. The Soviet mission in Chungking had nothing to do with the Chinese communists. Throughout the war all Soviet military supplies went to Chiang, and until 1941 they were his major suppliers. The aeroplanes which repulsed Japanese bombing attacks were Soviet planes, manned by Soviet volunteers, and the anti-aircraft guns came from Soviet Russia.

By the end of 1940 inflation was so bad that it was difficult to get meat in the Chungking markets, and some men went out with their wives to shop; they carried choppers, hacked off portions of meat themselves at the stalls, and carried them away, for there was no orderly queueing and people clawed at the food, knowing that as the counters emptied, the prices went up.

Stabilization of the currency, price controls and punishment for shops which raised commodity prices were topics which found expression in editorials, but the finances of the Kuomintang were in a constant state of muddle; the black-market outflow of the legal tender to Hongkong and Shanghai for the purchase of luxury items, by the commercial monopolies, had the backing of the Finance Minister and members of his family, so that edicts forbidding such practices did not apply to the very government which promulgated them.

Besides the Finance Minister, H. H. Kung, there was also Tai Lee's organization and its monopoly companies; there was the Kuomintang Army, trafficking directly with the Japanese. Frugality drives were started, but no one paid attention, least of all the higher officials. A credit of U.S. $50 million was granted that summer by the United States, but there was no exchange control, as the Finance Minister and his wife were opposed to it. They, and many government officials connected with them, were benefiting from this freedom by buying foreign exchange at the pegged rate of 20 to 1. Thus each loan, each grant, was channelled away into the pockets of officials, and by 1940 the purchasing power of the legal tender, the *fapi,* went down to one-tenth of its 1937 level. By 1941 it was one-fiftieth of that level.

In order to avert a crisis in the administration, the Kuomintang government began to pay its officials partly in rice, at the rate of 16 catties for a woman, 12 for a child and up to 28 catties for a man, depending on his importance. This measure made it possible for salaried clerks and employees barely to survive, but meat, eggs, even beancurd disappeared from their fare. For those who were not employed in government offices the hardship was much greater, and they had to buy on the black market. During 1941 money was depreciating on average by ten per cent per month, and the 'fixed prices' of essentials, such as rice, could not be maintained.

I bought as little as I could. The searching for food, the haggling, were beyond my capacity. Pao was well fed, as he got one meal a day at his office canteen, and the office canteen was on a priority basis. I hired a servant; a hefty country woman whom I sent to market to buy food. The chicken she brought back was swollen with water, its weight farcical for it had been made to swallow stones and grit; more often she returned empty-handed and grinning. All the best supplies went to the South Bank, to the restaurants, and at times there was fighting at the markets for the food there. Enterprising people went to the countryside with large baskets to buy vegetables, eggs or meat directly from peasants. Others began to keep hens or ducks or pigs, some even on rooftops fenced with bamboo when space was lacking, and there was a story about an official who slept with a litter of piglets under his bed ... Only those who had 'government rice' could afford the grain to keep poultry, and hence the competition for extra supplies, by way of reporting extra children or relatives, or by judicious bribery, was lively. Since birth certificates did not exist in China at that time, the number reported could not be checked.

Our landlady, the owner of the house at the Chang Family Garden, was a very efficient woman, rapacious and capable; and she had a little adopted boy who later died of meningitis following whooping cough. I tried to board with her, but it became too expensive. My succession of servants ate from the dishes they cooked until scarcely anything was left when it reached me, for I did not have my landlady's knack of watching the servant, standing over her, nagging her, preventing her from tasting; her servant was hard at work all day, ate what was left in the dishes after the landlady had done, and did not, like mine, look fat and rosy. But I had to get rid of mine the day she achieved the feat of leaving us absolutely nothing but the neck and the rump of a small chicken which had been obtained with much difficulty. Another servant could never be bothered to empty the toilet (a jar in the Szechuan manner); yet the public cloaca was across the way. Instead she used mine freely when hers was full, until the contents reached the wooden lid.

As the difficulties of housekeeping increased, so did my unwillingness to become a model housewife. I could see around me women whose lives were the perpetual drudgery of housework; harassed and unkempt, they were unable to become interested in anything but the cost of firewood or rice, or oil and vinegar; they extracted the last ounce of strength from the servants, the porters, the water-carriers; they went about with keys in their hands; and these were the good ones. But good or not, efficient or not, I could see that if I let Pao have his way I would be nothing but a household slave. I decided therefore that I would never, whatever happened, become efficient. I would not cook, for this was the key to man's paradise and woman's hell. No matter how much praise was showered on those who could turn out excellent meals, I saw there the beginning of my own destruction.

As a result we spent a good deal of money in restaurants, and I was able to keep this up because, as prices went up, salaries became insufficient and shortages augmented, and it became obvious that even the best housewife could no longer manage. I saw our next-door neighbours, who had eight children, eat spinach soup and rice and very little else day in and day out. And Pao was a gourmet, who loved good food – he could not put up with the things I managed occasionally to produce as food, hence he was obliged to let me work – and I gave English lessons to the Russian military mission in Chungking. The way in which this happened was rather curious.

As a student at Yenching University in Peking, from 1933 to 1935, I had known a girl whom I shall call Yuenling. Yuenling was Manchurian, tall, fair-skinned, very good-looking with long fine black hair. An orphan, she had been brought up by a Russian family in Harbin, and spoke Russian fluently. Perhaps this gave her a reputation for being progressive. She was active in the Students' Union at Yenching, and in the students' movement against the Japanese in 1935 and 1936. I had seen her again when we were in the mountains at Nanyu in October 1938. She was walking through the village with some foreigners, the Russian aircraft technicians employed by Chiang Kai-shek, and she stopped to speak to me, in a most friendly manner. She was working as interpreter to the Russians, she said, who had followed the Kuomintang government to Nanyu after the fall of Wuhan.

Yuenling told me laughingly that she had heard of me; everyone had said to her that I cleaned my room assiduously. She did not seem to think this odd, however, and on the contrary praised my neatness. When I met her in Chungking, again it was on the street ... I saw her, but scarcely greeted her, for I had become morbidly suspicious, thinking everyone against me, thinking everyone talked about me. Pao steadily cultivated this in me, and he had just told me that a Chinese student from Belgium (who one evening in Brussels came to my lodgings to borrow money never returned) was saying malicious things about me. Yuenling, however, stopped to speak with me, in her engaging, smiling manner, both kind and civil, and with a warmth and quickness of sympathy which was balm, precious and seldom received, so that I went home for once light, not in dread and heavy-footed.

Yuenling did more; came to see me, one day cooked noodles for me, and sat down and ate them with me; and was altogether so nice, so kind, so friendly, that I was immensely grateful, hung on her every word, thought her wonderful and stood by the door long after she had left, waving goodbye, or going halfway back to her own rooms with her, for the pleasure of her company. And Pao did not seem to mind this friendship, which was strange, since Yuenling had a reputation as a progressive, was independent, earning her living, going about with foreigners, acting as interpreter and also, because of her Russian upbringing, suspect by some of affinities with Russia ...

I thought, perhaps Pao did not know that she had been active in the student movement. Or perhaps he was changing ... I was so afraid to lose this friendship that I did not speak to Pao of my feelings.

What I did not know was that Yuenling, whom I thought so progressive, was also working, though possibly unknown to herself, for Tai Lee.

It was twenty-six years later, in 1966, that I was told, by another Yenching ex-schoolmate, that Yuenling belonged to what was called 'the false left'. The false left was a product of Tai Lee's 'thought re-education' department, one which utilized the services of Chang

Kuot'ao, a defector from the Communist Party, in order to study communist methods of education in Marxism and to apply them for anti-communist purposes.

Chang Kuot'ao, who now lives in Hongkong and has published his memoirs through the courtesy of the U.S. Information Services, was one of the two delegates from Peking to the first meeting and foundation of the Chinese Communist Party in 1921. Later, when Chiang Kaishek in 1927 turned against the communists, Chang Kuot'ao fought against him, and established a Red base known as the O Yu Wan soviet in Central China. In 1932 he retreated with his army to a border area in Szechuan, and established a base on the Szechuan-Shensi border. He had there an ideal hideout; at his back the great Tibetan ranges, round him the Miao and Lolo national minorities, with whose chieftains he came to an understanding.

Thus protected Chang waxed great and wealthy, his army a private army, with no political education, until he was confronted, in spring 1935, by the arrival of Mao Tsetung and the Red Army during the Long March, at that time down to 45,000, 'ragged bands' as Chang called them, never stopping to consider that their incredible epic, the constant fighting they had gone through was proof of a marvellous endurance.

Chang Kuot'ao was against what was called 'the northern policy', which was the name for Mao Tsetung's decision to establish a base in the north-west to fight Japan. He was not in agreement with the results of political education: peasant uprisings in Szechuan, farmers flocking to join the depleted ranks of the Red Army. 'New volunteers by the thousand join us' was one of the songs of the Long March, when the Red Army went through Szechuan. Afraid for his own well-established position, Chang Kuot'ao violently opposed Mao; suggested that the new arrivals should withdraw to Sinkiang 'to await better times', arguing that Chiang Kaishek had thrown 100,000 troops across the route of their march. He also suggested that Mao Tsetung and Chu Teh retrace their steps, and go to take the city of Ta Tsienlu, in Sikang, on the borders of Tibet, as a 'safe' base for the Red Army.

But he was voted down, and the northern policy reaffirmed by the majority in the Red Army.

Later Chang Kuot'ao was criticized at a Party meeting, and did his self-criticism. However, he then had a change of heart; he fled, arriving in Wuhan in May 1938, and was received by Chiang Kaishek with great honour. For three years he was employed to train cadres against communism. In 1943 Chang became acquainted with the American Major Miles, head of the Office of Strategic Services in China. Chang's training helped to produce agents of psychological warfare, known today as the 'false left', 'false' guerrillas, 'false co-operative movements', all borrowed out of the communist ideological arsenal. Even today, in Taiwan, there are thought-reform camps, self-criticism meetings, mixed with a jargon of moralism, calculated to imitate what happens in China. Perhaps it was true that Yuenling also was a trained agent ... or was she merely an innocent, like me?

I told Yuenling that I wanted to work, to be useful, and it was she who suggested that I should give lessons to the Russian advisers. It would give me something to do, at the same time it would ease our financial condition; she herself, as an interpreter to the Russians, was well paid. She spoke of this project to Pao, who, to my utter surprise, agreed immediately. Within a fortnight I was going three times a week to the Russian mission compound; that massive-looking building which we could see from our front window, two gullies away. The pay I received for these three weekly lessons of two hours each was phenomenal; I averaged about five times what Pao received in a month. And now I did not need to cook any more. I was both excited and terrified, searching for another view of the world than the Chiang view, but secretly I longed to know more now about the Soviets, about Russia. Was it really true, all that was said about Stalin?

I had three men and one woman students, a happy memory, for they were nice, cheerful, kind and unaffected. One was a huge happy Siberian, full of stories; in the winter, he said, he carried an icepick to the lake (Baikal, and the memory of the beauty of Lake Baikal glimpsed one morning during my trans-Siberian journey had begun our conversation) and hacked a hole in the thick ice to draw water in which to wash. He called himself a Siberian bear. 'I am a Siberian bear,' he said, flexing his muscles and laughing in a gigantic ecstasy of good health. The other two men had less of everything, bulk, laughter and muscle. One was a dark man with eyes of piercing melancholic fervour, who spent hours telling me with great passion about the crimes against Stalin perpetrated by those who had been executed in recent years in Russia; their putting poison into food, on walls, in wallpaper, their treacherous activities as spies for Germany. In autumn 1941 I met him again and he told me with even more concentrated fury about more crimes, committed by certain agents who had put arsenic and other things into the paint of walls and thus tried to kill 'many people'.

The other was a curly-headed, blue-eyed young man, very clever with his hands, whose father had been a wood-worker; he learnt at first painfully, but got on very quickly, more than the Siberian giant who preferred to laugh and tell wonderful stories in his own way. My only woman student was handsome, with green eyes and decisive copperish curly hair. She showed me pictures of herself as a general of the army, and of course she learnt best of all; she had great vivacity, and spoke of Stalin with obvious reverence and admiration. 'Our great beloved leader Stalin,' she said, her eyes moist. All four radiated robust health. All four nourished me with tea, *piroshkis* and laughter. There was a wonderful cherry jam in the tea, and the lessons were enormous solace, and I was sorry when they ended. It was through them that I saved two thousand dollars, of which one thousand went to help Miss Hsu to acquire her land, and with the remaining one thousand dollars, I was to buy a little girl in the autumn of 1941.

Pao's temper did not improve in spite of the fact that he was now doing very well. Contrary to his gloomy predictions, he was rapidly scaling the various steps towards a secure place in the 'Obey and Serve', which he had entered by the summer of 1940. Meanwhile he did not need, as so many others did, to take two or three jobs at a time in order to make enough money; for my teaching the Russians much improved our financial situation. At the time the administration was in such chaos that it was quite possible for an official with the right connections to have three jobs at once in three departments, and not spend more than ten minutes a day at each of them, meanwhile engaging in more lucrative black-market deals elsewhere. And there was the story of the officer who had seven jobs, and managed them all by farming them to seven relatives, who were each provided with a seal in his name.

Pao did not need to indulge in black-market deals, or take extra jobs. He was not burdened with debts; we lived well. But he went on ill-treating me, and there was never a week without his finding fault with me, enough to vent his temper in physical brutality. One evening I met a friend, a social worker at the Young Women's Christian Association, and accompanied her home. I returned a little late to find

Pao had already returned and was in bed. Before I could explain he had jumped up and started striking me; opened our room door and pushed me down the stairs. The wooden stairs were not too steep, and I broke nothing but the banister as I fell. The next day I rose as usual to give lessons to the Russians. Then Pao felt remorseful, and was charming (until he began again a few days later). And to make up he took me that evening to a good restaurant, and then to a horoscope man to have our fortunes told.

In Chungking during the war, going to the *K'an Hsiang,* the 'looking at physiognomy' man, who could tell fortune by features; or to the sage who from the eight ideograms, the zodiacal sign, the year, the day and hour of birth, could discern fate; or to the mole-removing man to improve one's destiny; or to the bone-manipulator, whose fingers, touching the bones of one's skull, or kneading one's hand, could thereby counsel what tactics of social dexterity would procure official advancement; all these were involved, grave, serious consultations, in which important and not-so-important officials of the government indulged steadily, not to mention housewives, clerks, bankers, pimps, agents, generals of armies, Hu Tsungnan, Tai Lee, and Chiang Kaishek himself.

This passion for astrology was not Szechuanese backwardness, for the Szechuanese had their own horoscope men and fortune-tellers; in Chungking officials from down-river, from Shanghai and Nanking, were the ones who consulted and were closeted with astrologers and diviners and other sages, demanding repeatedly that the future be revealed to them. Side by side with medical doctors *K'an Hsiang* men advertised their skills in the newspapers. Some became so famous that only the highest could consult them, and they lived among the elevations of the South Bank, safe from bombs, in close proximity to their important clients. Chiang had his favourite 'looking at physiognomy' adviser; whenever he was perturbed, and wanted to calm his spirits after slapping a few subalterns, breaking crockery, or condemning someone to be shot, he would make a great effort to collect himself, shut his eyes and 'cultivate the spirit' by repeating to himself some calming phrases. Or he would play his favourite record, which was the Ave Maria of Gounod; after which he would ask his favourite 'looking at physiognomy' man to inspect the weather of his soul upon his face.

Many jokes were also current about Ho Yingchin and his favourite bone-kneader; it was said that the latter had had great difficulty in finding anything resembling a bone in Ho's fat hand ... But no one joked about Tai Lee and his horoscope-gazer. Tai Lee was extremely superstitious, extremely vindictive. He believed firmly in physiognomy and in handwriting as keys to the soul's scrutiny, but would not hear anything unfavourable to himself. Like the examiners of Imperial days Tai Lee was influenced by a man's calligraphy, and advancement sometimes depended upon assiduously cultivating a good hand to write to Tai Lee.

And now Pao, too, was infected by this credulous bigotry; and would consult one or another soothsayer, mole-remover and physiognomy scanner, both for himself and for me.

My fate was to become subject to the ministrations of mole-eradicators. These were long-robed and amiable strollers carrying in the one hand a banner, hoisted on a pole, which represented a face covered in moles. Each one of the spots was labelled with a name, and its peculiar influence upon the lives, destiny, feelings and fortune of the owner were vividly described in a 'mole almanac' which the mole-eradicator carried upon his person. Moles on cheeks were either vastly beneficial or of particular malevolence; moles on the neck were mostly detestable; they indicated hanging, decapitation, or other ways of losing one's head. Moles on the forehead and on the chin were in general of good augury. And a mole on the left lower chin would be, by the standard of these mole-eradicators, a most precious and fortunate mole, located in a most favourable position ... There were moles for men, and others for women; on the other side of the banner was usually painted a woman's face, with her constellation of pigmentary luck. Pao consulted bone-feelers, *pakua* or eight-character fortune-tellers, face-scanners, graphologists, for himself, but it was the mole-eradicators that he chiefly consulted for me.

The mole-eradicators also carried, in a wooden box slung over the shoulder by a canvas belt, the apparatus for removing ingrained ill-luck, and this consisted of a mirror, a little bottle of acid, and some blunt metal needles. My acquaintance with the mole-men had started after a bombing, while going up the steps of the Chang Family Garden, on a stroll, when one of them advanced upon us, and with a flowery speech, redolent of Szechuan flavour, exclaimed upon Pao's excellence, his fortunate and heroic physiognomy. We stopped, and Pao immediately asked the mole-man whether he was able to predict the future. 'Certainly,' was the grand reply; 'I can even alter destiny, by my art at removing nefarious moles.' He professed, however, to have nothing to alter in Pao's face, where he discovered only signs of uncommon nobility and good fortune; 'assuredly the highest seats of office are within the eye-sweep of such features.' He then turned to me, espied in me 'great grace and many sons, but alas,' said he, 'that such good fortune and perfection should be marred by a weeping-tears-of-sadness mole under the left lower eyelid!'

I had not noticed a mole under the left lower eyelid, but now, impressed with this hint that I overwept, Pao desired a reconnoitring of my face's potential; and the mole-man beamed his approval of this wise decision which cost us a dollar, for, said he, moles were infectious in their influence and a single bad mole on me might affect Pao's rising expectations.

Pao was now determined to remove such obstacles to his advancement; at the same time, because he was, by fits and starts, in love with me, he desperately sought for an explanation which would place the responsibility for my vices, crimes, and other calamitous traits upon fate, or the stars, and not upon me. Were these adverse features to be proven part of an unfortunate mole-galaxy which would now yield to the administrations of this expert, he would be much relieved ... We bargained for a 'distant and general view' of my character and physiognomy; and then a more detailed aspect of my moles, with removal of the two more obnoxious ones the mole-man had discovered – the weeping-tears-of-sadness one below the eye, and one on my cheek, which I claimed was a freckle but he said was a mole; and which, he averred, showed I was prone to offend my mother-in-law, and a more heinously uncomfortable misdeed could scarcely be imagined.

The mole-man then opened his box, extracted the little bottle of acid and a small stick of wire with a knob at the end; this he dipped into the bottle, and dabbed carefully upon my moles. 'It will whiten, harden, then drop off, on no account must it be picked off; in ten days' time your luck will change.' This was only the first of a good many mole-eradicators who all discovered on me moles to be removed, two on the neck, four on the cheek, forehead, temple, chin; thus I was made immune to hanging, drowning, quarrels with in-laws, and having only daughters; and as summer advanced my moles, which had dropped off, reappeared. They were freckles, after all.

One basic defect of mine, however, could not be altered, and that was my ear lobes. Ear lobes also played a prominent role in one's destiny. Pao had already been discontented with my ear lobes for a long while, for they were puny. They neither looped, nor protruded gently, nor hung low and full; everyone knew that a long, fleshy, thick ear lobe, well furnished, was a sign of good mental and physical health and fertility; while a thin, small one, or a practically midget lobe like mine, meant a short life, much worry and bitterness. Because of these appendages I was certainly fated to an ample store of sorrow; and 'there you are,' Pao said, 'your ear lobes prove it.' The sooth-sayers also found my ear lobes inadequate, and Pao, showing off his knowledge, talked of Liu Pei, emperor-hero of the Three Kingdoms, whose lobes had touched his shoulders. As for Pao himself, not one of the many fortune-tellers we consulted ever had anything but praise for his face, his nose and chin and forehead, and augury of brilliant fortune and a long life for him.

With such consultations, seducing time and thought, we loitered away some of our whiles between the bombings; some of the hours of comparative peace between us. Since Pao hated to see me book in hand I could never read when he was present. So it was either the mole-man or listening to him talk about himself, and that was better than when he talked of me.

Then there was the training camp, across the road from us. We could not escape it. Every morning before the night yielded altogether to the dim fog-bound cold, or in summer when, like a blast, the fierce sun came up while we were still gasping from the unrelenting night, when the stone gave off its stored heat and even our mats, soaked with sweat, laid on the floor, were hot to the touch, the bugles blew, words of command stabbed the air, and the shuffle and clink of men on the parade ground, the tramp of feet, made a morning ritual, repeated at night. But often, very often, there was noise. Screams. Unbearable screams. And the dull thud of beating. Only once did I see what was going on; a man stripped naked to the waist, his back a mess of blood, being walked by two men supporting him, and then screams again. Another time, one evening, there were more shouts, a trampling, and cries *t'ao pin, t'ao pin* (an escaped soldier), electric lights stabbing the darkness, and the panting of men running about. All, the landlady, the servants, the neighbours and I, we all went on, as if we neither saw nor heard ...

Another event sticks to my memory. And it concerns Caroline, whom I called Lisan in *Destination Chungking*. Lisan was not Caroline, just as *Destination Chungking* was not what happened but an attenuated, transformed version, all unpleasantness eschewed.

Caroline came to stay with me at the Chang Family Garden; recommended by a friend at the Young Women's Christian Association Hostel, which was so crowded that she lived with four other girls in a stifling small room, and sought one on her own, with board. I had an extra room, for besides our large room upstairs, and next to it a small boxlike recess (which for a while served as refuge to a woman friend of mine who was pregnant and abandoned), there was another room, on the lower floor, which the landlady also let us have, and which we could use for a guest.

Caroline was a small-boned extremely pretty girl, with long hair bobbing down her back and on her shoulders, an oval delicate face, a beautiful voice. She wore red leather shoes made in Shanghai, her clothes though worn were smart, and she was utterly different from the squat Szechuan girls with their round faces and thick legs. She had that air of breeding which the girls of Soochow carry so well; her English was as beautiful as her Chinese; she had been educated at a Protestant missionary school and then at a university in Shanghai; in her spare time she wrote love poetry. She was gifted, intelligent, and told me that she suffered from tuberculosis, for which she ate eggshells which she powdered fine with a spoon, because, she said, they contained calcium.

Caroline was a most outspoken, candid person; she was so certain that nothing could happen to her that it was frightening to hear her prattle, in serene unconsciousness, of all that one was forbidden to mention.

Caroline went off every morning, hopping like a small cheerful bird, her hair bobbing and bouncing, full of joyous life; sauntered back in the afternoon, always with the same carefree air, contrasting so much with all that was round her. An inner fortitude sustained her, and though she was peremptory and short with the servant (who terrorized me), hers was the unconscious arrogance of one used to giving orders in a well-to-do household. She told me that she was on her way from her Shanghai college to Yenan, the communist base. She denounced

195

in a loud and delicate voice, ringing like a small chime of silver bells, Chiang Kaishek's government. She told how she had escaped from her Shanghai college and her family. Her father was a wealthy man, but had ill-treated her mother; she took her mother's part. At the college she had met a young Englishman, a lecturer there; a communist. From him she learnt about Yenan and began to read and to think. She showed me his picture, told me his name, Jonathan. He had left Shanghai, he was now in Chengtu, and she was on her way to Yenan, hoping to meet him in Chengtu, and perhaps to go with him ...

On the cross-country journey from Shanghai to Chungking she had no trouble passing through the Japanese lines; as I knew, there were 'open' crossings at certain well-determined points. Once in Kuomintang territory, however, she had had a difficult time. A good many other passengers, in the truck in which she travelled to Chungking (along the same road which I had travelled eighteen months earlier), had heaped lewd comment upon her; the petty officials thought she was a young prostitute, and she repeatedly found herself having to repulse them almost physically. When she arrived in Chungking she went to the Young Women's Christian Association, and there learnt, after a few days, that Jonathan was engaged to another girl, and was soon to marry her. She mourned, wrote love poems, read; had introductions from her missionary school in Shanghai and got a job teaching Chinese to some American and British diplomats, in the diplomatic enclave of the South Bank.

Caroline gave me small panics with her frankness. I begged her, first indirectly, then directly, not to talk so much. Things happen to people, I said, you must not tell everyone what you are going to do. Caroline laughed, 'What does it matter? I am not staying very long in Chungking ... and besides I have FRIENDS. No one will dare to do anything to me.' But I was worried, and the reason I was worried was Pao.

Pao was following 'the military road' through Hu Tsungnan to a good job under Tai Lee. In Chengtu, in Chungking, Pao spent much time calling on people who could help him with these two all-powerful pillars of the Chiang regime. At home Pao had practised for many days a letter to Tai Lee, begging him to vouchsafe his favour to 'pluck him up', and promising devotion and loyalty should he be thus chosen; he wrote and rewrote drafts of this letter, so that he might impress Tai Lee with his calligraphy.

Other young officer friends of Pao also came to our house, to practise writing with a bold yet modest brush stroke, or to compare their efforts with Pao's, or judiciously to advise him on the quality of the specimens he produced. How ardently they discussed the strokes, how long, long and tedious the hours spent retailing stories, gossip, gossip about this, that and the other, how to get on, how to get on, what to do, what not to do. I never heard them discuss any war problems, or the front, or anything resembling a logical assessment of the financial situation. Their total passion was climbing, and to climb one had to make a good impression upon those crafty and credulous masters whose whim was more than law, Chiang Kaishek, Tai Lee! And one thing sure to doom a man was ill-omened calligraphy, showing icono-clastic tendencies, irregularities in spiritual 'breath', weakness of character ... Pao strove, holding his brush lifted in a masterly way, to produce strokes and style which would inspire confidence in Tai Lee's soothsayer, so that he might be 'plucked up'. I found the drafts in the waste-paper basket.

And it did happen. All at once the other officers were congratulat-ing Pao, and Pao, well pleased, filled pages and pages with his own signature, Tang Paohuang, Tang Paohuang. And now Pao, flushed with arrogant success, went on a witch hunt, denouncing 'perverted thoughts', exalting 'virtue', more than ever. He threatened that he had power to do anything he pleased. 'Don't think you can ever run away; within an hour, you would be brought back.' But describing the hours and weeks and months which I endured is tedious, and explains only the commonness, almost the universality, of wife-beating, so profoundly encrusted in the Chinese customs of that time. Seeing him so tormented with ambition, contemplating himself in the mirror, striking poses, going about well groomed in boots and swagger stick, mouthing 'benevolent brother' to so many, writing letters with an important look, it was obvious that he was now heading upwards; and the benevolent brothers who came to the house had a cosily fawning friendliness in their voices.

Pao's buoyancy had been reinforced by an episode which happened during the bombings that summer. A certain official had tried to make fun of Pao; and (according to Pao) had hinted at my being a 'mongrel' to taunt him. But the next day, the same official, trying to go to the toilet (he was suffering from the usual loose bowels which afflicted nearly all of us at one time or other in Chungking), did not return in time to the dugout when the Japanese bombers came over. One bomb did fall where he squatted. All that was found later was a pair of legs hanging in the small bush behind which he had concealed himself ...

Pao felt that this man had drawn Heaven's wrath by his loose-mouthedness and was awed by Heaven's favour so obviously showered upon him. For some days the friends of the dead man came to pay court to Pao, and mourned by reciting his foibles, 'You see, Heaven punishes those who try to do me ill,' said Pao to me. Was there really a Heaven caring about such small things? But such omens and portents, signs and wonders, were so important to Pao, and now there was no stopping him. No more talk of dying on some front line, unknown and anonymous, sacrificed for his country; but much talk of spiritual mobilization, stopping communism, and becoming a leader. He anxiously scanned his forehead one day and asked me whether I could see 'the light' shining from it. Apparently some soothsayer had discovered it. I burst out laughing and laughed so hard that my stomach ached and I had to rush to the public privy (my private jar being in its usual state of overfulness).

And now there was Caroline, come to us; living so near to Pao, and Pao so dangerous in his new megalomania ...

'Please, please be careful,' I told Caroline, but could not tell her it was my own husband she had to be careful about. Caroline looked at me with some contempt. I think she felt I was not courageous. I was not, and hung my head, ashamed of my lack of bravery. 'You are afraid, but I am not afraid,' said Caroline. Bone-frightened, I waited, and sometimes I think the picture of a cowed, overbeaten dog, who trembles at the sound of a whiplash, is an appropriate description of myself in Chungking.

Pao knew that the room was rented to Caroline. He had met her; a small gathering, with Caroline, a neighbour and his wife, some brother officer; an impromptu affair, so many people now dropped in on us. The summer was waning and in the slight coolness of evening many people liked to sit and talk, and sip tea. In the middle of this particular gathering my landlady asked me to extract a kitten which had fallen into her rain pipe. I did it by breaking the clay rain pipe, which greatly angered my landlady. Twice afterwards, Caroline came to chat with me in my living-room; once Pao returned suddenly, and began to talk with her, or rather he talked about himself, about his being simple-hearted, about his devotion to Leader and country; about woman's purity and secondary status, 'solely dependent on her husband's status and position in life'. Caroline listened with a sarcastic smile, but did not contradict him except to pass a humorous remark; she smiled so sweetly, and was so clever in avoiding a direct reply, that Pao did not appear angry. However her irony, though light, was potent. He felt bested, and he was adept at detecting non-conformism, even in its most subtle disguise.

Caroline had been with us about five or six weeks when I returned early one afternoon from an errand to find Pao unaccountably back; unaccountably early. It was not more than three o'clock; his cap and stick were thrown on the bamboo settee, yet he was not in our room. Where was he? I felt the usual grinding and weight in my chest; the usual suffocation as before and during a scene, premonition of disaster. I went down the stairs, not daring to hurry. Caroline's room had a big window opening on the garden of the house. The window was open and I saw Pao in her room. I walked to the open doorway and said rhetorically: 'What are you doing here?'

I could see what he was doing. The drawers had been pulled out of the small desk; their contents, letters, papers, some photographs, spilled on the floor; he had also ransacked the small wardrobe, pulling out the dresses and the shoes, piling them in a heap on the bed; the suitcases had been opened and their contents turned over. Pao was standing by the ransacked desk, reading some letters; letters of Caroline; the notebook with its leather cover in which Caroline wrote her poems was placed on the desk, she usually kept it in the drawer that locked. The lock had been forced.

'What am I doing? Are you asking? You see what I am doing. I am doing my duty as a Chinese and as a patriot,' he shouted.

'But these are her private letters, this is her room, you have no right to come here,' I said, losing my caution. 'This is ... '

He came towards me and hit me then, knocking my head against the door. 'You cheap bone-heap, you dare, you dare, you dare tell ME what is private? There is no such thing as private. No one has a right to keep private such disgusting things ... this girl is a communist, do you know it? And she is in love with a foreigner ... she has probably had an affair with him, and she keeps his photo, here, in her drawer, she has letters ... '

I stood there, my lip was hurting and I would later have a swollen mouth. I muttered, 'It is not fair, not fair.' I went upstairs to our room and sat down. I suppose I should have twisted my hands, but to what avail? Pao came in, and sat at our table, and grasped his brush, opened the ink box, his back straightened and he began to write a letter. He looked like a young scholar doing his exercise in calligraphy, and I suddenly hated him with all my spirit and for a moment dreamt of going to the kitchen and getting the knife, and ... As usual he was not pleased with the first draft and started again. Then he put the letter in an envelope, placed his cap on his head and walked out. I took out the draft from the waste paper basket. It was addressed to Tai Lee, under his honorific of Yunong, and it was a denunciation of Caroline; saying that he had 'investigated' her, that she had a conduct and behaviour 'which is not that of our virtuous Chinese women', that she had had 'commerce with a foreigner', and that her case should be taken up.

Three times in the next hour I walked to the street, scanned its upward steps towards the main road to see whether I could perceive Caroline. I wanted to meet her in the street, to warn her there ...

Supposing Pao came back with plainclothes detectives, supposing when she returned she was arrested; I went up to the main road, and for a short while considered going to the ferry to meet her. Returning from the South Bank where she was giving her lessons to diplomats, she would cross the river on the ferry, and if I went and waited at the landing quay I could warn her ...

But I was also afraid that Pao might return, and not find me, and guess what I had been doing ... Only a few days before there had been a scene in a small restaurant where, in one of his more charming moods, he had taken me to eat, late at night, that Szechuan speciality, *maotutze*. And there a man had come up to me, an erstwhile student at Yenching University, who had recognized me, and wanted to shake my hand. I forgot Pao's peculiar temper (I kept forgetting), greeted him, shook his hand, and introduced him to Pao, only to receive all the contents of the boiling soup bowl upon me, and blow after blow all the way home, where I arrived vomiting because of the emotional shock.

Up and down, and again into my room, and at the window to watch for Caroline. I sat down, stood up again, and of course missed her. She was back, in her room, when I ran down for the last time. I saw her standing, her arms folded, looking at her desk ... 'Caroline, it's Pao who has done this.'

She gave me a haughty, contemptuous glance. Then her eyes went back to her desk. 'Of course I can see, your husband is ... '

Then in strode Pao, with his jaw set, and that peculiar pallor which indicated that he had worked himself up in an inner fury. Oh my God, I thought, he is going to hit her ...

But he did not. He stared at her and she stared right back at him as I used to, before I had been beaten down into a wreck. She started: 'Mr Tang, who has given you the right ... '

'I have done my duty, as a Chinese patriot.' His voice was controlled, not shouting as he used to shout at me. 'Believe me, it is not with a light mind that I have done this. But you are in my house and I have a right to see that nothing that is dangerous to the country is done ... '

'Dangerous to the country? What can I do that is dangerous to the country ... '

'You are a young Chinese woman, and you are all the time with foreigners. You have even written love poetry about a foreigner. You have thought of marrying him. You are now teaching foreigners. It is my duty to investigate what you are doing ... '

'Please,' I said, 'please.'

He pointed at me: 'Ask her. Ask her how I beat her. Do you know that?'

Caroline's lips curled with disgust. 'You are really ... ' Pao then launched into a tirade; chastity, honour, tradition, that medley of nightmarish virtues, the way of salvation for China dependent on each individual, keeping the Four Virtues and the Five Cardinal Principles that made for harmony in society. Caroline stood there, and from time to time tried to speak, but he went on and on and began to threaten: 'Do you know who I am? Do you know I could kill her?' (pointing at me). 'But my heart is kind; I decided to save her, and you, if you repent ... ' On and on, this by now, to me, unbearable moralism so ingrained in the Chinese mind and Chinese language that even today in China faint whiffs of it come through. After an hour of haranguing Pao left; Caroline sat down exhausted; I stayed just long enough to say to Caroline miserably: 'Don't worry, please don't worry.' And I went back to my room.

The next morning I had to go to the market and when I returned she was gone, so I did not see her, but her room was neat, I could see that through the window, which she had bolted as well as the door. Pao was in a very good mood, and even affectionate, when he returned from the office that night.

The day after, Caroline came to me to tell me she would soon be

moving, she had found a room. 'I have asked my friends to find something for me. I think your husband is completely ridiculous.'

'He is dangerous,' I said. 'He has written a letter to denounce you.'
She tossed her hair, contemptuously, 'Oh ho, is he so terrible? He cannot do anything to me.' She behaved as if she was quite sure that
nothing could happen to her. 'I have told the British diplomat whom I
am teaching about your silly husband, he will come to see me. Your
husband will not dare to do anything.' She turned her back on me,
behaving as if it was my fault.

The Englishman of the British embassy whom she taught had
already come to visit her once. I was going up the steps, he was coming
down, and I had recognized him immediately; he was no other than
the little Scotsman who had been so nice to me in Peking at my first
and awful Christmas party at the Grand Hotel de Peking, Mr Smith.
I walked past him, straight-faced, fearing above all that he might run
after me, stop me and recognize me. What would Pao say or do then?
I kept praying I would not meet people I knew, it was so tiresome to
be beaten for it afterwards ...

I was not convinced that a British diplomat, or anyone else, could
save Caroline, though it was true that to know Europeans was some
sort of protection, for the government did not want a bad press abroad.

Caroline returned to tell me that the British diplomat had now told
the story to an American diplomat, and they had both taken her to
lunch, laughed cheerfully, told her not to worry; that they would protect her. They had also offered to put her up. She also knew a famous
American journalist, a woman named Emily Hahn. Emily Hahn
would write an article about her if something occurred. 'If anything
is done to me it will be written about in the Western press and your
husband will lose a lot of face.'

The next morning, as I returned home from the market, there was
a stocky, bespectacled, short-haired young woman in trousers in front
of our house. She was talking with our landlady. When she saw me
she greeted me in a most friendly manner, and tried to talk with me.
She followed me up the stairs, into our room. I told her I was busy;
she said, 'Please do not misunderstand me. I have come to speak to you
about this young lady. We would like to see her.'

I felt the chill of dread once again creeping up my spine, clawing at
my throat. Down, down, hysteria, don't scream. The woman went
on, garrulous, talking too much, repeating herself. 'I am a student my-

self. In the Three Principles Youth Corps. I am a graduate of middle school. Unfortunately I am too poor to attend university. But everyone must do what he or she can to save the country. We have heard about Miss Caroline. We would not like anything to happen to her *near your house*. We would not like you and Colonel Tang who are respected people to be connected with this. Perhaps you could tell me about what time Miss Caroline returns. We knows that she wears red shoes. But we have no photo of her. Have you got a photo of her? Or can you obtain one?' (So Pao had not been efficient, he had not taken a photograph of her and she must have removed all her private papers.)

'No, I have no photo of her.'

'Can you tell me what she looks like?'

'She is rather tall and strong. Yes, it is true she wears red shoes. She is neither fat nor thin. Her hair is curled.'

'We think if someone could stand in the street and identify her; if we could arrange ... does she go to the cinema? Perhaps you could suggest a film to her. About what time does she return from work?'

'Always late,' I said promptly.

'Well that makes it difficult to look at the colour of her shoes ... and we would not like to meet her in your house or anywhere near. It would not look good. We are told she goes over to the South Bank to teach.'

'Yes, she teaches important diplomats. She knows a lot of important foreigners. American, English, newspapermen. She is very well known.'

The girl sounded regretful. 'That is somewhat troublesome. It must not happen here. Perhaps on the South Bank ... or at the ferry, or on the way ... '

I was glad of the woman agent's stupidity in talking to me. I told her, 'I will obtain a photo ... you had better move slowly in this affair. There is no hurry. Come back in a few days.'

Then I had some hours of anxiety. Suppose someone smarter than this girl had waited at the ferry ... there might be more than one flat-footed female agent sent to investigate ... there were so many people at the ferry ... they would not dare to kidnap her in broad daylight. Not on the South Bank. Not near the embassies.

Pretty soon I saw Caroline return, bouncing as usual from step to step, her hair bobbing; her red shoes appeared to twinkle, an illusion due to my state of mind. Now I was happy every time I saw her still safe, and I rushed at her. 'Look,' I said quickly, 'you must change your shoes. They know you wear red shoes. You must take them off and buy ordinary shoes ... you must never wear those shoes again.'

'I'll wear what I please.'

'I tell you, the secret police came here, my husband had written to Tai Lee himself about you, I saw the letter.'

That seemed to make a small impression. 'You are trying to scare me, you are trying to scare me,' she said, still defiant. 'You are very wicked.'

I was in despair. 'I am telling you the truth. You can do what you like, you can think what you like about me. It is true I am frightened, I am not brave like you, but they are thinking of doing something to you far from here, on the road, or at the ferry, they don't want anything to happen in this house. Please, please be careful.'

Caroline looked a little shaken now. Her off-and-on hostility towards me was understandable. Perhaps she thought me responsible for what had happened. But this did not matter. I had the most terrifying visions of Caroline being kidnapped; being beaten, being tortured; in the camps for 'moral rehabilitation' of students with dangerous thoughts, was applied the regime of what was called 'family correction'. Family correction was what I myself endured; which meant being beaten into submission; in those camps were mostly students and young people caught on the roads, in the buses going to Yenan, to the Red base ... like Caroline.

Then one day Caroline came in tears, holding in her hand a copy of the *New Yorker*. The magazine had been given to her by an American diplomat. Inside was an article about Caroline by Emily Hahn. But it was not a pretty piece of work. It made deft fun of Caroline, of her ideas, of her candour.

Caroline never mentioned her 'friend' Emily Hahn again. Perhaps it is wrong to expect writers always to be aware of the anguish and sufferings of the people they write about.

Caroline left us; later she did get to Yenan. In 1967, twenty-seven years later, I heard of her again. She had married a Chinese intellectual who later became eminent; the marriage had not been happy, however, and there had been a divorce. Someone told me Caroline had been criticized during the Cultural Revolution, but then everyone was criticized; the massive movement, like a purificatory flame, must have seared countless people. I hope to meet her again one day; and perhaps we shall laugh together, all suspicion spent?

Nine

THE BONE-POUNDING heat of summer and the Japanese bombers left us; the great clefts of the mountains let go of their swollen waters, the sky's dismal glare gave way and the Chialing river sparkled like a new sky; a small fine evening rain laid the dust low and cooled the rock and we began to sleep again. All about Chungking, after the summer destruction, there was the hammer sound of rebuilding as new shacks and new houses went up. Inflation also took a new leap; rice was in short supply, unhusked and brown; it was said that Sir Stafford Cripps, on a visit to Chungking, had recommended to Chiang Kaishek that rice should not be polished, to conserve the vitamins; it was difficult to get white rice except at special black-market rates, or in the houses of the wealthy, or the expensive restaurants.

On September 23rd, 1940, the Japanese had walked into Indo-China, and there was no resistance from the French there, whose Vichy regime collaborated with the Japanese secret police. Then the Americans became worried about Japan's intentions; did they not have a plateful with China? Would they, could they want more? The Burma Road was reopened in October, and in December a loan of £10 million was made to China by Great Britain, and 100 million U.S. dollars' credit extended for general purposes by the U.S.A., half of it being for 'currency stabilization' because of the inflation. The U.S. government prohibited the export of iron and steel to Japan, but this embargo was not successful; iron and steel continued to be sold by American companies under various chartered flags until Pearl Harbour in December 1941.

China was now increasingly a factor in the spreading conflict; and military missions to China, and visitors, came in and out. A British military attaché, General Dennys, a cheerful man with a handlebar moustache, pleasant, a keen observer, was now sent to Chungking; it was he who arranged for the visit of a Chinese military mission to South-East Asia. He was to be killed in 1942 in an air crash in Assam. The Americans had a gunboat, the *Tutuila,* anchored in the river facing the South Bank, where the American embassy occupied a large stone mansion with terraced gardens. There were parties on board the *Tutuila* to which Pao, now doing liaison work with foreign missions (he was at the time under Cheng Chiehming, subsection intelligence affairs), often went, and always without me. The American military mission had a Colonel David Barrett as assistant military attaché. Barrett knew Chinese well and liked to make puns in the language; Pao made fun of him because he was corpulent. Barrett once called on Pao at his office and was given the smallest stool to sit upon; a silly joke from which the officers drew much laughter, but which expressed their inner hostility, while outwardly they fawned upon the Americans. Barrett later went to Yenan, where he spoke with Chairman Mao, and in 1965 he was to write me a long letter about this meeting and his impression then.

Like many other Americans in those days he was not enthusiastic about Chiang Kaishek, and abhorred Tai Lee. It was he who was later to send me Randall Gould's book, *China In The Sun,* where the following passage occurred: 'Certainly there was some gang group, close under Chiang, which was implacable in pursuing all his political foes – but Tai Lee is not a man to ask about or try to see ... Boo!' However, later Barrett was to rally to the American choice, which was to support Chiang, though for some time he struggled within himself, and was unhappy over the events which occurred. But he was not strong enough to stand against McCarthyism.

Another visitor was Henry Wallace, whom Chiang disliked on sight, and who was responsible for urging that a small U.S. observer group be posted in Yenan. The Whangpoo officers were pleased at American interest in Chinese affairs, but sought to discourage American visits to the other front by all possible means. Chiang thought of the Americans chiefly in terms of his ulterior aims, getting America to back him (Chiang) exclusively, while he fought the communists. Now he expected American dollars and aid to flow towards Chungking, and for the next few years was to play his main card, which was threatening to negotiate with Japan whenever he wanted anything from the United States.

That winter my social life took an upturn. We were invited to lunches and dinners. Some I attended, though in great fear of doing or saying something which Pao would dislike. Thus I met Sir Archibald Clark-Kerr, the British Ambassador, and the American Ambassador

Nelson Johnson just before he left Chungking and was replaced by Gauss. Clark-Kerr was a shrewd and forthright person, not much liked by the Chiang entourage because he expressed himself forcibly about such things as the black market in goods, the poverty, and the corruption of certain high officials.

There were many policy talks, mostly inconclusive, at the end of 1940, between the British, the Americans and the Chinese. A Chinese military mission to South-East Asia was now prepared, under General Shang Chen, Director of the Foreign Affairs Bureau of the Chinese General Staff; a smooth-looking, able man, whose personal dexterity as a diplomat was impeccable. Everyone tried to be included into the mission, in order to get out of Chungking; Pao was early nominated to it. It was in late January 1941 that the mission, comprising fourteen people, left for a tour of Malaya, Singapore, Burma and India, returning at the end of May. The 'impregnable' fortress of Singapore was shown them, and almost exactly one year later it was to fall to the Japanese in a few days. The mission toured India, inspected military installations and shopped in Delhi. They returned with forty-eight trucks full of silks, cosmetics, shoes (for women and men), cameras, suits for men, watches, gramophones ... one officer wore four men's jackets, one on top of the other, and sixteen watches strung up his arm. This orgy of buying, due to the foreign exchange allotted to the mission, was possible now that the U.S. had made a loan to 'stabilize' the currency at the rate of 20 to 1, and the scarcity of goods in Chungking made anything brought from outside eagerly sought after. Shang Chen alone brought five trucks back via the Burma Road. Pao was still the most modest buyer of them all, with only seven suitcases full.

Pao was angry with me when he returned from this mission, for I was not at the airport to meet him. I should have been there; but it was more dishonesty than I could succumb to, to pretend that all was well when I was suffocating inside myself with all that I could not say. 'Here I have brought so many things for you, and you are not even there to welcome me back.' I could not welcome him; could not, with the new load of disgust and weariness which the new year 1941 had brought to me. For January 1941 was the beginning of my slow understanding; a revolt personal, incoherent, frustrating, but still a point of no return. It was in that month that the massacre of the communist New Fourth Army by Chiang Kaishek's orders occurred, and that massacre was a turning point for me.

☆

Besides the main Red base at Yenan, other seedling bases, nuclei of future communist areas, underground partisans scattered in regions where previously Red power had held dominion, had remained in many provinces. The famous Long March, whose success was entirely due to Mao Tsetung and no other, had planted many new seeds of revolution in its passage, even among the non-Han national minorities, the Miaos, Tibetans, Lolos. In previous Red areas, in spite of the White Terror and the massive scorched-earth policies initiated by Chiang, underground cells had remained.

Thus in 1964, I met in the Old People's Home at Chingkangshan, Well Ridge Mountain, where Mao Tsetung had established his first base in 1927, a very old peasant who for years had kept buried in the mud floor under his bed a jar full of salt. He was waiting for the Red Army to return, having been one of those who supplied it with salt, of which the base was being deprived by the Chiang blockade. For twenty-two years this old peasant had waited with the jar under his bed ...

In Szechuan, most feudal province of all, when the Red Army passed through villages and made propaganda, it was the women, the downtrodden women of Szechuan, who were the first to revolt, to organize women militias, to raid the landlords' houses and their hoards of grain.

Many of the women walked miles to collect food and bring it to the armies on the Long March. And when the soldiers left, the women would give them shoes; not only those straw shoes used for padding about the mud roads, but also the more precious cloth shoes, made of slabs of cotton cloth felted together layer by layer with glue for the sole, and stitched evenly, through and through; and which they would embroider with the name of the soldier stitched on the inner sole:

> Using my needle, as a pen
> To write clearly, in stitches
> Your name and my thoughts ...

they sang, and this was not romance, but revolutionary love, greater than romance.

And the soldiers would carry these shoes, fastened round their necks, and never wear them, but keep them clean, in memory of the peasant women who had stitched them, asking the names of the soldiers and painfully copying down the characters, for they knew not how to read them ... In the reprisals which followed, the landlords and warlords killed both men and women. Here, too, in the so quiet-seeming countryside of Szechuan, people waited for the Red Army to return.

It was among such groups, silent and waiting, that volunteers were found and went into action. Later these nuclei gave rise to many new Red bases, which operated behind the Japanese lines all through the Sino-Japanese war.

At the famous Well Ridge mountain, Chingkangshan, under-ground partisans remained active throughout the decade from 1927 to 1937, in spite of repeated onslaughts. In 1937 when open warfare began with the Japanese, and the United Front came into being, it was Marshal Chen Yi, the present Foreign Minister of China, who was sent to this area to tell the partisans about the United Front with Chiang Kaishek, and to reorganize the scattered volunteers into a New Army group, to become the core of the famous New Fourth Army.

Chen Yi, born in Szechuan, joined Mao Tsetung early in 1928, to-gether with Chu Teh. In October 1934 when the main communist forces began the Long March, Chen Yi remained behind to cover the withdrawal, and to develop a clandestine base of operations in the lower reaches of the Yangtze river. This he did till mid-1936, fighting against the much stronger Chiang forces.

In the summer of 1937 Kuomintang pressure on the partisan under-ground lessened, due to the military hostilities with Japan. Chen Yi, who by that time had gone to Yenan, now returned to rally the guerrillas, reorganize the troops left behind, and to tell them about the new situation brought about by the Japanese invasion; the United Front with Chiang Kaishek ...

Because he came in a gentry-type robe (to avoid being murdered by the Kuomintang), the partisans took him for a traitor when he started talking of 'united front with Chiang Kaishek'. He was severely beaten, and it took both time and stamina to persuade the suspicious fighters that he was telling the truth, and that the policy of the Party was now an alliance with Chiang. 'What, united front with that son of a turtle, Chiang!' they shouted. So many of their fellow partisans and relatives had died, or been tortured, they could not believe that now they should co-operate with Chiang. Finally they accepted Chen Yi's word and his explanation that the main problem was now resistance to the Japanese. Chen Yi's return journey was as dangerous as his

209

going. At one time he had to hide in a small cave when pursued by an animal, either a leopard or a bear.

Chiang wanted these reorganized partisans, guerrilla units, to be incorporated into the Kuomintang armies. But this Mao Tsetung refused, holding out for autonomy with co-operation, for as Mao was to put it later: 'We must not be naive ... about this question of power ... ' Knowing Chiang's ultimate aim, the annihilation of the Red Armies, to place the partisans in his hands would have been sheer murder.

The build-up of such scattered units in Central China thus resulted in the New Fourth Army, established in January 1938, with headquarters at Nanchang in Kiangsi. Like all the communist forces using the pattern set down by Mao Tsetung, it not only fought, but provided political instruction; it was an ideological instrument of education, as well as a physical weapon for battle.

There was no dearth of volunteers, for 'like a spring wind blowing' the news that 'the Red Army is back' made the peasants come to it; bringing old flint-locks they had buried, knives, spears, cudgels, salt, food ... It was a great gathering. In a short time the New Fourth Army grew from 13,000 to 30,000, then to 60,000 men.

The triangle formed by the cities of Nanking, Wuhu and Chingkiang, which was Japan's sealed zone of operations and one of the most populous and fertile areas of the lower Yangtze basin, became the New Fourth's hunting ground. Its successes, so near large and important cities, greatly worried Chiang Kaishek, who now accused the New Fourth of 'enlarging and consolidating arbitrarily' and without orders from the Defence Council. Chiang cut off all supplies of arms, ammunition and money; forbade the New Fourth to organize the village masses; forbade the establishment of people's councils and peasant militias. As a result, and also because certain commanders in the New Fourth were inclined to give in to Chiang, dissensions occurred. Not all the units were politically strong; nevertheless in 1940, according to Agnes Smedley, they had the best medical team and workers, ten hospitals, two medical training hospitals, and three hundred company first-aid groups.

Within a month of reaching their operation terrain in April 1938, the guerrillas of the New Fourth were already striking. In eight months they fought 231 battles, captured 1,539 rifles, 32 light machine guns, 48 sub-machine guns, and 50,000 rounds of ammunition. They inflicted 3,000 casualties and destroyed 200 enemy trucks. By the middle of 1939 they had secured the countryside. The Japanese could only garrison the cities and fortify them, and all cross-country roads were impassable to the Japanese.

Because the New Fourth was spread out over a vast territory, part of it was north and part south of the Yangtze river. It had already come into armed conflict with troops of the Kuomintang in the summer of 1939. During 1940 relations between communists and Kuomintang deteriorated severely. The area in which the New Fourth Army operated was infiltrated, by order of Tai Lee, with 80,000 secret society men belonging to the Shanghai Triads. A full-scale attack by 200,000 men under the Kuomintang General Tang Enpo was launched in October 1940 against the north of the river columns of the New Fourth under Chen Yi.

But it was in January 1941 that the New Fourth Army 'incident', as it was called, happened. Between the 7th and the 13th of January the New Fourth was ordered by Chiang Kaishek to cross the Yangtze river and 'reorganize', several hundred miles to the north, to join forces with the 8th Route Army. When some units carried out this command (and this in itself was a mistake), 12,000 of them, including the medical corps, were ambushed; 8,000 were murdered, among them the majority of the medical personnel …

This massacre (for it was no other) was perpetrated by 60,000 Kuomintang troops. It was claimed by the Kuomintang that the New Fourth had attacked their headquarters; that this was 'insubordination', and that the action taken against them was 'restoration of military discipline'. Yenan denounced the fiction. Mao Tsetung named Chen Yi acting commander of the New Fourth Army.

The massacre of the New Fourth Army shook a great many patriotic Chinese, who suddenly realized that Chiang had not changed; he was still the Chiang of 1927; as soon as he could, he would begin civil war again. Indeed, in 1943, Chiang tried to start an all-out offensive against Yenan. But he could not get the support of the Szechuan and Yunnan provincial warlords, and had to give up until after 1945, when he was able to persuade the Americans to help him in this enterprise.

A torrential, massive indignation swept over the people of Chungking, the people of China, at the massacre of the New Fourth Army. Even Western correspondents were badly shaken. 'It's a dreadful business,' the forthright Archibald Clark-Kerr said to Pao. As for me, it was such a shock that I could no longer contain myself. I shouted at Pao, 'This is awful, awful.' I felt suffocated, walking up and down Chungking's ladder streets – oh how suddenly I saw, clearly, too clearly, that Chiang would have to go! From that day on, I was convinced inside myself, morally certain, that Chiang would go, and that there would be a 'great change' in China, a big, wished-for, longed-for change ...

I was not the only one to shout: 'This is awful.' Many more, afraid to talk, harboured in their minds an anger which would end their tenuous clinging to a vain hope, Chiang Kaishek. I confronted Pao, 'This, this is your virtue ... killing one's own countrymen ... and while the war is going on ... ' For three days Pao looked sheepish, his glance wavered, he replied in a hesitant voice: 'It's not at all like that.' But later he recovered his equanimity. 'How many of ours have not the communists killed? This was insubordination ... the New Fourth did not obey the orders of the Military Council ... the Leader has said ... even the communists have acknowledged ...' But voice and demeanour were still unsure, not the usual arrogance, though he quickly assumed the stance of outraged sincerity, his refuge when he was caught lying.

And some nights later, walking in the street, I met Kung Peng.

Kung Peng was also, like Yuenling, a student at Yenching University when I was there; however, unlike Yuenling, I had never actually met her at that time. She had an outstanding role in the student movement in December 1935 and in 1936, and then she went to Yenan. I had met her in Chungking once before, with another schoolmate, and had the impression that she was a secretary of the Young Women's Christian Association. I do not know why I had this impression; perhaps because the other schoolmate was actually working at the Y.W.C.A. hostel. But Kung Peng was then the secretary of Chou Enlai, who was in Chungking, representing the liaison committee for the United Front. Chou Enlai was almost a prisoner there, living with his wife and two secretaries and three aides in a small house, in a narrow street, a house infested with Tai Lee agents on the floors above and below the three rooms where the seven communists lived and worked.

That night, walking back from visiting my cousins at the Meifeng Bank, I met Kung Peng coming towards me from the opposite direction, and we both stopped. Kung Peng was always a very quiet, self-possessed person, radiating an intense thoughtfulness; her intelligence, poise, and inner beauty made her the most fascinating person I ever knew, and yet she herself has remained, even today, completely unaware of her own charm, the power of her good looks and deep intelligence. Suddenly upon seeing her my tears began to flow; I told her how horrible it all was, the New Fourth Army, Pao, everything, it tumbled out of me and how I could see it was horrible and I did not know what to do.

And Kung Peng stood there and said not a word, but I had a strange impression of comfort from her. I walked home and when Pao asked me why I was late, I said: 'I have been to see my cousins at the bank.' And perhaps some of the strength in her had now passed into me, for he did not get up and beat me, but lay quiet and wordless.

Many years later Kung Peng was to tell me that, that evening, she almost decided, after talking about me with Teng Yingchao, the wife of Chou Enlai, to ask me to join them ... But I might have been pretending, I might have been trying to insinuate myself among them ... I might have been, like Yuenling, a 'false left'. They had to be very careful ...

Had I been offered the choice then, the other side, that other front; had it been suggested that I go to Yenan, would I have gone? Was not my head still fettered, my mind battered by Pao into confusion, myself too timorous, too discouraged, to decide?

I shall never know whether, had Kung Peng taken the risk then, my whole life could not have been totally different ... But Kung Peng did not speak, and I never knew that this could have happened, and I remained alone, and afraid. It was not until 1956 that Kung Peng told me about this possible choice which passed me by. A very long time – fifteen years – too long ...

But I can understand that Kung Peng could not take the risk of trusting me; too much was at stake. And I was too ignorant then, trusting Yuenling (although I never talked to Yuenling about Kung Peng – was it an unconscious sixth sense, or simply that this meeting was too precious to share?). In the end it does not matter, but understanding acquired so painfully itself becomes a constant reminder of pain.

The attack of January 1941 on the New Fourth Army was the culmination of a series of such conflicts, which had not been written about in any of the Chungking newspapers. Already in July 1940 Mao

Tsetung had called for 'unity to the very end', for maintaining the United Front, in spite of the constant attacks by Chiang's troops and the actions of the Blueshirts. Resistance to the Japanese to the very end of the war came first, but this did not mean capitulation to the Kuomintang. In December 1940 Mao had written: 'In the present high tide of anti-communist attacks, the policy we adopt is of decisive importance ... *in no circumstances* will the Party change its United Front policy for the entire period of the war of resistance against Japan ... ' And it was a garbled version of this statement which Pao had produced as 'evidence' that the communists had acknowledged that they were wrong ...

In March 1941, when the shock and indignation over the January massacre had somewhat subsided, Chiang Kaishek made an openly anti-communist speech, and the People's Political Council passed an anti-communist resolution, blaming the Communist Party for 'lack of unity'. Voices were raised from the extreme right wing, demanding the banning of 'alien parties'. Some of the Kuomintang officials gloated over the cowardice of the members of the People's Political Council (chosen and appointed, in the main, by the Kuomintang government save for one communist representative). 'You only have to push these people a bit and they fall.' They told how many of the members had been 'pushed a little', and how, when Chiang had said to them: 'Well, of course you agree,' they had agreed, shaking with fear. The sole communist delegate to the People's Political Council, Tung Piwu, had walked out.

The Communist Party sent a telegram on March 6th, refusing to attend the session of the People's Political Council before redress had been made, and measures taken for a 'provisional settlement' of the New Fourth Army massacre. On March 18th Mao Tsetung wrote an inner party directive, analysing what he called the second anti-communist onslaught; noting that this was 'the renewal of armed hostilities in a civil strife ' ... But in spite of the intense provocation, for the general interest, a policy of conciliation would be followed, because the conflict with Japan was still of primary importance, and the internal struggle still subordinate to it.

In April 1941 Japan's world peace plan appeared in the *Japan Times and Advertiser*. In the Pacific Ocean, Japan demanded demilitarization

PART ONE: 1938–1942

of all British and American naval bases and that American influence
go no farther than the Hawaiian Islands.

At the same time Japan signed a non-aggression pact with the Soviet
Union; thus Japan had her landward flank guaranteed against Russian
attack while she proceeded with her plans for launching her invasion
of South-East Asia.

On April 6th, 1941, Germany invaded Yugoslavia; on April 27th
Greece fell to Hitler. In late January of that year the Chinese military
mission to South-East Asia (with Pao one of its members) had begun
its tour, and in April it was in Delhi, being assured by the top British
military authorities that all plans to meet all contingencies had been
drawn up, and that Hongkong, like Singapore, was quite impregnable ...

For me, the outstanding event of that spring of 1941 in Chungking
was the speech made by Chou Enlai. The place chosen was a small
hollow between two hillocks. On either side had been dug air-raid
shelters. It was crowded with people two hours before Chou appeared,
some of them climbing on poles, or erecting platforms of tables and
chairs they brought out of their homes, to see him.

This was the first time I had seen Chou Enlai. A slim, thin-faced
man with an abundance of black hair, very calm, very handsome, all
his gestures supple, he is perhaps the most intelligent statesman living
today, with the greatest capacity for self-abnegation, with subtlety,
patience and vision. What one felt on seeing him was an almost
physical impact of sureness, of self-control and intelligence. And
indeed I was to find out in later years that he has one of the very best
minds in the world, able to think of several alternatives and at many
levels at once; able to deliver, with very small hints, the result of many
hours of thought in a minimum of words. When he stood on a table
so that he could be seen by the crowd, his eyes went calmly from face
to face; all of us were caught, waiting for his words. He spoke for
almost four hours, and we listened, untired. He could have gone on
for ever. It was one of the simplest, least complicated, most un-
rhetorical, almost painstakingly basic speeches one could have heard.
But each word counted.

Chou explained the attitude of the Communist Party towards the
assaults launched upon it by the Kuomintang, and made very clear
the issue that all was being subordinated to the national struggle. At
the same time there would be no capitulation to 'those who were bent

215

on capitulation to the enemy, in a sell-out of the true interests of the
Chinese people'. The precision and clearness with which he defined
this policy of subordinating temporarily certain issues to the overriding issue of the war of national salvation was a masterpiece of
understatement, yet of uncompromising principle. Afterwards I
wanted terribly to go up to him, but I was too shy, and the crowd
jostled, and though I followed him, along with others, I could not
reach him. I saw in the crowd Paohua, Pao's cousin, standing a few
paces away from me. He looked at me, and I at him, and both of us
kept quiet. I went home as if walking on clouds, all fear removed,
luminous with logic, reason; Yuenling came to see me and I said to
her how much I liked Chou Enlai's speech and she agreed, so that I
believed in her more than ever.

During the four months of 1941 that Pao was away I went back to
Chengtu, and returned in time to be at home for Pao's return. Once
again the dreary round of bombing was upon us; the heat of summer
was upon us. This time we moved some of our belongings to the
Meifeng bank, so that when in August our house in Chang Family
Garden was hit, most of the things that Pao had brought back were
saved. And such pitifully silly things they were, but in Chungking
incredible, unseen luxuries. Inlaid carved boxes of sandalwood and
ivory, carved ebony elephants, yards of sari silks, velvet, veiling
material, five pairs of high-heeled shoes (none of which I ever wore),
two saucepans, nail polish, alabaster lamps, plates of nacreous mother-
of-pearl ... A profusion of bazaar shopping, with that Indian touch of
glitter which in a glitter-starved city was so tempting. Now I can see
that what Pao bought did not cost very much, but at that time it
seemed the height of extravagant folly. And I was morose, derisive.
What was the use of pretending? I told him I did not believe in the
'mission'. 'Mission' for what? I gave away most of the materials
except one length of brown silk with a woven pattern of roses, and
one of black velvet; those two became dresses which were to last me
all through the next eight years, till 1949.

It was in that spring also that I met Cecilia and Francis Pan. Though
today our inclinations (the Pans remain with Chiang Kaishek) are
wide apart, yet in personal kindness to me the Pans have been different
from many others. They not only helped me in times of hardship, but

actually came to see me when I was without any means. However much I cannot agree with their loyalty to an order that is gone, their staunch and unchanging personal friendship is part of that same creed of loyalty. 'I have only one heart,' says Cecilia Pan fiercely, meaning she will never change. I who have changed, because I realize that it is not a class, but a *people,* the people of China, who deserve a loyalty and a love which must forswear all smaller dedications – I can still understand her attitude, though I do not share it.

I first met Cecilia Pan when Pao made me call on her and her husband, who was an important official in the Ministry of Finance. I duly went to their house, to find Cecilia Pan standing, very dignified, in a fine gown with a high collar, not a hair out of place, her face serene, in the middle of the debris of her living-room, whose roof had collapsed due to bombing. Always I would see her thus, with a graceful gesture, offering me a cup of tea as we sat in the chairs, which had been well dusted; around us stones and mortar and chunks of plaster seemed to regard us with desolate surprise.

I invited her to lunch in our living-room which, though much plainer than her luxurious one, boasted a large woven red mat, covering the floor. Everyone was bemused by my huge red mat; no one ever had anything but blue or grey or tan mats, of small dimensions. My mat was a folly, ordered from and made and dyed by one of the innumerable Szechuan craftsmen, and costing so little; I slept on it on very hot days; on sombre, foggy ones it made the room look pretty and warm. I had this passion for things made in Szechuan, the handprinted flax cloth, the blue cotton, all things the Shanghai ladies despised as coarse were for me beautiful, beautiful, great with life and talent, so much more so than the vulgar copies of Western pottery, the cheap glassware, the artificial silk so highly priced, imported from Shanghai through the monopoly agencies of Tai Lee. I found so much beauty in the bamboo chairs and settees made by local craftsmen, in the bamboo baskets and barrels which the poor made and used, that I bought only these things, and Pao was ashamed of my bad taste. Cecilia said she liked my red mat; this may have been exquisite courtesy, but it was also courage; for even the word 'red' was shunned then. A red mat, spread all over the floor – did not this indicate dangerous thoughts?

☆

In June 1941 Pao and I were back in Chengtu with Third Uncle. After his exertions in the military mission to South-East Asia, Pao had a short holiday, and to escape the heat and the bombers for a while we went to Chengtu. On June 22nd, while I was paying a visit to Marian Manly at the hospital, I heard a rumour, laughter, the shouts of newspaper boys on the street; the animation I felt as I crossed the streets was not clear to me until I had returned to Third Uncle's house in Sheep Market Lane and Sixth Brother had brought the newspaper back, with the news that Hitler had invaded the Soviet Union.

In the next few days the newspapers printed maps showing the territory into which German troops were arrowing in blitzkrieg. Pao was jubilant, so were his friends; Ho Yingchin was certain that Hitler would win. In the evening Third Uncle, fanning his chest with a palm-leaf fan in the courtyard, made talk with Pao. Pao lectured him on the 'strong nation', meaning Germany; and how purity of race kept people strong, and how the Russians were too weak. Third Uncle nodded and nodded and asked what was the population and size of Russia; I could see he was not convinced.

Pao followed the war with happiness, for the German advances were indeed very swift. I thought of my friendly Russian students, all three of them, and longed to express to them my feelings, which were all on their side. And as day after day there was news of German victories, my gloom increased; finally Pao, overjoyed, left again for Sian and Hu Tsungnan's headquarters. I went back for a few short weeks to the hospital at Little Heavenly Bamboo Street.

Life was getting much harder. On the university campus, because of the inflation, many students were affected. Rice was unhusked, and that and kidney beans and chilli, the only diet, made many suffer from enteritis. The strong odour of the brown rice was not pleasant, and a bowl of white rice was a luxury, for the rich, and in the restaurants. Though Chengtu would always be better off in food than Chungking, the rice was being mixed with stones to give it weight. There were two kinds of weight, big and small, the latter half the former, and so one cattie of rice could be a big or a small cattie. This was done to beat the price-fixing which was attempted, and which was of course a failure, no 'big' or 'small' being specified.

The harvest had not been good that year, but still rent-collecting in kind was done, and now the government also did it. The grain was supposed to go into government granaries, but of course it went to a host of hoarders, many government officials.

The Army and certain organizations, such as Pao's, were being paid in rice, in order to ensure a basic supply to the administration. A bag of rice on the black market was soon worth three times Pao's salary for a month.

There was no salt and no soap; the ever resourceful Miss Wang, the midwife who did everything well, taught me to wash my hair with a special kind of bean which made the water soapy. And for salt people burnt green twigs, collected the ash, and used that ...

One evening, there was much excitement at the university. General Feng Yuhsiang, the stalwart northern militarist whose popularity rested on his having first resisted the Japanese in 1932, was to speak to the assembled students on the sports ground. No one would miss hearing him, and with Huang Szeyuan, Shen, Wang, and other midwives we went early, but already there was a large crowd. In the darkness, with only a few hurricane lamps, the tall, square-headed, burly Feng Yuhsiang, in a simple cotton uniform, in his beautiful northern burr, spoke of fascism attacking the democratic peoples of the world; predicted that China would win over Japan, and Russia over Hitler. We clapped and clapped, and on the campus there was much excitement, so many of us wanted Russia to win. A while later the Catholic bishop, Yupin, also made a speech. Bishop Yupin was very active collecting money in America for Chinese Catholic missions. He too was from north China and this gave him authority. He was an extremely astute and wily person, with a great deal of self-confidence and a gift of oratory. He asserted that Germany and Russia would mutually destroy each other, for they were the same brand of totalitarianism.

We returned to the midwifery school and spoke about Napoleon and winter in Russia. Someone said that was a long time ago and the Germans were strong; but we looked forward to the winter.

Meanwhile, the newspapers went on describing imaginary victories on 'the front', meaning Chiang's front, but did not publish any maps. Everyone made fun of these victories; even Pao. Actually there had been in May 1941 an attack by fifty thousand Japanese in the Yellow River Area. A quarter of a million Kuomintang troops were there; the Red Army fought in support of these troops, but Chiang withdrew his troops deliberately, after three weeks, leaving the area to the Japanese and abandoning the communists ... his plan unchanged, attrition of the communist forces ...

☆

In that summer of 1941 Chiang's government announced that China was 'at last' being recognized as a great power, of equal status with the others. Both the United States and Britain had at last stated their intention to relinquish their extra-territorial rights, which had lasted since 1842, a hundred years. For a hundred years no Westerner or American in China came under the jurisdiction of Chinese law. They could enter China without a passport, stay as long as they liked, rob, steal, murder, run over people in their cars, bring in narcotics and opium and guns without being punishable by law. This privileged exploitation was practised not only by civilians, military men and businessmen, but also by the missionaries.

Now the Kuomintang government proclaimed that the Western powers were 'voluntarily' relinquishing these 'rights'. The internationalization of the war was drawing China into a world role; and Chiang was eager to play the world statesman. Actually, the promise to consider relinquishing these rights was made in order to keep Chiang in the fold of the Allies; for as 1941 wore on, Chiang bluntly asked for more money, otherwise, he said, he would negotiate a separate peace with Japan. One billion dollars was what Chiang wanted now. And he had chosen his time well, for all pointed to a growing concern and disquiet in the United States about Japanese intentions ...

All through that summer of 1941 the Red armies launched attacks on all fronts in North China on Japanese troops, whereas Chiang maintained a stalemate. Right up to November 24th, two weeks before Pearl Harbour, negotiations between Japan and the United States were still being dangled before Roosevelt by the Japanese envoy, Kurusu. Yet both sides were also preparing for war. By September the Japanese had already planned their attack on the U.S. fleet at Pearl Harbour, a fleet which had been there since May 1941, poised either to pounce on Japan, or to protect the American colony of the Philippines.

In Europe, America had recognized Pétain and the Vichy regime. The Free French and de Gaulle were to be permanently cold-shouldered, for Roosevelt had the intention of dividing France in two ... This ambiguous policy of America also extended to Indo-China, which, Roosevelt was to declare to Stilwell, would have to become a 'trust territory', ostensibly under international but actually under American domination. But in summer 1941 the Japanese were already solidly established in Indo-China, with bases granted to them by the Pétain government ...

By the end of summer 1941 much of Chungking had been flattened
by bombing, including our own house in the Chang Family Garden,
which was knocked out in late August. We dug in the rubble and
rescued half a bottle of brandy (from India) and the bed frame. Third
Uncle once again offered us hospitality; this time at Ta Er Wo, the
house belonging to the Meifeng bank, outside Chungking. Here there
was an abundance of hills and trees, the soil was thick, as we were
farther inland; and on the slopes among the trees were erected quite a
few 'villas' of the wealthy, who could sleep here in peace, away from
the bombings.

Across a small valley we could see another wooded slope, and halfway up it stood the imposing mansion of General Shang Chen, the
leader of the Mission to South-East Asia, later to become Ambassador
to the U.S.

There was also the house of a Szechuanese warlord, who had placed
four of his wives in a large and dizzy palace full of servants, spittoons,
and orchid pots. The number four was deliberate, they could occupy
themselves playing mahjong, whereas with three, or five, it would
have been difficult to make a game. The four wives played mahjong
every day, all day; they looked as if they never washed, their clothes
were always crumpled as if they had just got out of bed, uncombed,
to play, and would return to bed, fingers still upon the ivory and
bamboo chips.

We had not been there more than a fortnight when we went down
with malaria, both Pao and I. Pao began with an attack of tertian, and
then it was my turn, with attacks of excessive cold, vomiting and
fever. My malaria turned out to be the malignant type which was
coming into China from the Burma Road. Some people died of it
quickly, in twelve hours, others took a week, or more. At first I
thought mine was tertian too, and took the quinine pills Pao had been
given by the medical department of the Military Council. These pills
were genuine, not the fake ones that were being sold in the pharmacies
to the ordinary people.

But the pills were ineffective, and within three days of the first
attack I was almost unable to rise, and could only vomit and shiver,
shiver and vomit. Pao was on guard duty for a week at the Obey and

Serve and I was alone with Yao Niang the concubine, who took malaria as a matter of course. Fortunately the wife of General Shang Chen came to see me, on what impulse I shall never know. She was a buxom, energetic lady with piercing eyes and an active body. I went to the living-room to greet her, staggered and could not speak. She immediately took action, sent me a good physician, German-trained, in attendance only for important officials such as General Shang. The doctor told me it was malignant malaria and gave me two injections of atebrine, which cost fifty dollars each. Three days later I was much better and went across the hill, with a servant to help me to walk, and up to the Shang mansion, to thank Mrs Shang Chen; but there I met the other Mrs Shang Chen, not the brisk, nice woman to whom I owed my life and a courtesy call, but a thin, waxy pale person, utterly unlike the first Mrs Shang. In great confusion, after some polite phrases, I withdrew.

In September of that year a big tragedy occurred, when about twelve thousand people were suffocated in a public dugout in Chung-king (some reports said twenty thousand). I have already told how defective these dugouts were. This horror happened in one of the last air raids of the year, on a Saturday afternoon. No planes came over, but the all clear did not sound for hours; the armed guards locked the people in, and then went away themselves to the South Bank, to play mahjong, to see a film ... The idea of locking people in the dugouts was a madness, thought up in the name of 'order', to prevent a constant to-and-froing at the mouth of the shelters, for air; instead of improving ventilation, iron-barred gates had been erected and these were now locked during the time that the alerts were on. In this particular and very large dugout the people began to batter at the gates, trying to get out, but no one was there to let them out and the gates were too strong. The guards were away altogether for ten hours.

It took more than a week to clear the dugout of its corpses; whole streets were unpeopled, whole families died together. Throughout the nights of the beginning coolness the lorries came and went, carrying the corpses, and masked men worked with spades removing decomposing debris ...

Perhaps it was inevitable that in autumn 1941 we should be invited by

Tai Lee, and this was a 'supreme honour'. Pao was not only a member of his clique, but a favourite now; his calligraphy and physiognomy had made a good impression; he was being 'lifted up' so rapidly through the hierarchy that people began to speak of him as 'the young stronghold' ... More than ever Pao consulted astrologers, and now that military and diplomatic missions abroad were being supervised by the Tai Lee organization, it was certain that Tai Lee had in mind to send Pao as military attaché either to England or to America. Hence we were invited to have dinner with Tai Lee.

'I don't want to go,' I said, 'I've heard too much about his doings. I don't like him.'

'But you must go,' said Pao, all charm and cajolery, even bringing me flowers. I had heard nonsense, he said. Did I not know that politics were ugly, yes, and ugly things had to be done, but even the communists agreed that the New Fourth Army was in the wrong; they had accepted Chiang's reprimand, and now all was over. 'Believe me, you must not always think the other side of the fence is the better one.' This he said because an astrologer to whom he had shown my photograph had exclaimed that I was the type who always thinks the flowers on the other side of the wall are more fragrant, which had an illicit, immoral implication. Pao now applied it to what he sensed was becoming political opposition in me. Chou Enlai had made a public speech in Chungking, had he not? He had been allowed to speak, was this not benevolence towards the communists when they had done so much harm? Pao could be immensely persuasive; reasonable, dignified, patient, he pleaded: 'You do not understand politics, why not have a look at Tai Lee? How can you judge a person without seeing him?' Then Pao lost his temper and said he would shoot me if I did not go. He took his pistol and banged it on the table. And then he threatened my family. 'Take care,' he said. 'Where would your Third Uncle be without me? I can have him jailed again.'

He said this because Third Uncle had been recently kidnapped by Tai Lee's men, shortly after Pao's return from India, for playing mahjong. The issue was not the mahjong playing. It was an attempt to blackmail some of the Szechuan gentry and capitalists, such as Third Uncle and his friends, by claiming that they infringed the edicts against 'spiritual mobilization' (which precluded whoring, gambling and opium-smoking). It was part of the pressures brought upon them to acquire local produce for the Blueshirt monopolies.

223

No one paid any attention to the edicts on 'spiritual mobilization'. There had never been more prostitutes in Chungking; inflation drove even respectable families to encourage their redundant female members to go on the streets. With the increase of Western military missions in 1941, and the rumours raised by the Chiang government that the Western powers were now going to abandon their strategy of Europe first, China second, large contingents of American airmen and Marines were expected any moment. The prostitutes were getting ready; some had even dyed their hair a startling yellow colour. The city of Kunming was designated as an air base for American airmen; buildings were going up for them, and bath tubs and water closets flown in. The girls were moving, moving from Chungking to Kunming, in order to be at the disposal of the Americans ...

The only people who were hit by the edicts were the Szechuan 'locals'. Hence they played mahjong in shuttered rooms, on green baize bridge tables, so that the sound would not carry. Meanwhile, in the streets outside prostitutes calling themselves students, and carrying textbooks as they walked about, were being actively plied for 'overnight chats' by Chiang's military bureaucrats.

When Third Uncle was taken away at night for gambling, it was Second Brother from the bank who came to tell us. Pao went to the police, and they immediately released Third Uncle and his friends, saying that it had all been a misunderstanding. Pao, of course, was pleased with his own influence; now he reminded me of what he had done for Third Uncle. 'You need not say a word to Tai Lee; but I swear to you, he is a good man.'

I put on my black velvet dress and went to the dinner with Pao. I thought: 'There are so many evil people about, and we eat and drink with them, and smile with them ... this is only one more.'

There was a long black limousine to fetch us; one of those limousines that are always associated with the secret service. A bodyguard saluted us with a flourish of cape and felt hat. It was fashionable for men to wear those knee-length capes, since Chiang Kaishek wore them. The face of the bodyguard was severe; pale hands, rather flabby, protruded from his cape. Pao had brought back from his travels some gramophone records, among them two of the Ave Maria of Gounod; and a gramophone to play them. Hour after hour he played the Ave Maria, to demonstrate his devotion to Chiang Kaishek. Now Pao was taking with him one record of the Ave Maria to Tai Lee, as a present.

The car drove to Fu T'u Kuan and beyond, to one of Tai Lee's residences, on a cliff with a dugout shelter; we were ushered through two or three doors by young men of severe mien in black uniforms and white gloves; we went down a staircase and were in the presence of Tai Lee. I have always thought since that we must have been below ground, not on street level, since we went down instead of up. But it is also possible, since in Chungking so many houses perched on steep cliffs, that the large mansion began at one level and went down to another without being below ground. However, this descent empha-sized the awe and importance of the meeting; the King of Hades could not have stage-managed it better – the silk curtains, the glowing red lanterns, the forbidding silence ... Tai Lee's appearance as he stood all in black, short, thin, with very thick eyebrows, so swarthy that he had an Arab look, was also of a piece with the theatrical setting. The sombreness of his cheeks and chin, the heavy eyes with their piercing look, the black uniform, combined to create a feeling of actor's villainy, but as he moved one knew him dangerous, a coiled viperine menace.

Tai Lee shook hands and motioned us to sit; we sipped tea. The conversation consisted at first of commonplaces, with Pao talking in his best 'good family' manner. Pao told Tai Lee that I was recovering from an illness (my malaria). Tai Lee added brusquely how many children we had and Pao said one daughter in Chengtu. Of course I was supposed to have a child, a convenient fiction to account not only for my frequent disappearances when Pao did not wish to exhibit me in public, but also for my trips to Chengtu. But there was another reason for the answer, which at that time was not clear to me.

Tai Lee asked where I had studied and Pao said in England. Tai Lee nodded approval, as if making up his mind over something. Then Pao talked about the situation in England, and in South-East Asia, and in India. He said that Britain could not fight, England was finished but was trying to get America to help her. Tai Lee said England was going bankrupt, selling all her assets in the world, but she was getting Lend-Lease, and no Lend-Lease was coming China's way, which was true. He did not like the pro-English Foreign Minister Quo Taichi; and at that moment a feud was going on between them; a cabal would be raised against Quo in order to pull him down. Tai Lee hated the British because he had once been arrested in Hongkong when he was

225

only a small crook, and kept in jail for two days, then released with an apology. Pao's mouth uttered beautiful sentences, all sweetness and quiet flattery; he had on his most 'sincere' look; not a word out of place. He listened attentively when Tai Lee spoke.

The meal came, delicacies, sea food – so scarce in that inland province, a thousand miles from any sea. Tai Lee's chopsticks hovered over choice morsels for me. Pao and he got up and drank to each other; Tai Lee's brief questions kept the talk going. For a wild moment I wondered what would happen if suddenly I pretended to go berserk, slapped Tai Lee, rolled on the floor. I thought of my hand meeting that cheek and it was repulsive. Through a raised silk curtain one could see, in another room, some lacquer vases, some pink lampshades with fringes and two bodyguards, in black uniforms, supervising the servants bringing the food in and out. Tai Lee then asked me if I knew a cure for sore throat, he was subject to it. 'She is a doctor,' Pao had said. Then abruptly the talk went on to astrology, and fortune-telling; Tai explained some abstruse and delicate point about the blind fortune-teller who felt one's bones ... Then the meal was over, and after a cup of tea it was time to go, since in China courtesy forbids one to linger long after a meal. We left, again in the same car. And the next day Pao told me I had done well. 'You did not speak too much.' I had not spoken at all.

Ten

SOMETHING WAS worrying Pao, and now it came out. For some months we had been drawing rice rations. Rice was distributed to all government officials to 'stabilize' prices (it did not), and Pao had drawn rice rations for three, not two. I think he gave the supplementary rice to Paohua, his cousin, who either sold it on the black market, or gave some away in return for 'services'. Pao had claimed as part of his family a child born in Chengtu, and thus obtained rations for three.

Now a good many of his benevolent brothers were saying they had never seen a child, not even a photograph. Pao was intensely preoccupied with an impending change in his career, and that was to be sent abroad as military attaché. He feared that an insidious accusation might disqualify him for the post.

Pao's great reproach to me was my childlessness. If only I could become pregnant, if only I had a son, all would be well ... His superior officer, General Hsiung, whom I was obliged to meet at a reception, had a great many children; other officers boasted of their reproductive capacities, as they boasted of the numbers of bowls of rice they were able to eat – six or seven at a sitting – or of the 'artistes' whom they invited to 'a chat overnight'.

This constant demand of Pao's for a child was not peculiar. It is normal for men to want children. And it kept me in a constant state of tension. Consultations of astrologers, fortune-tellers, invariably produced the story that I would first have a daughter, then two sons. And hence Pao had invented a female child, hoping that the wish might father its accomplishment.

Another handicap of Pao's was that he had never been in active command on a battlefield and so did not possess a situation in which he could bribe some useful underlings with posts. And they were useful. There was the story of one minor officer who merely by adding one stroke to a man's name, had sent the wrong person to death ... and another who, asked for files concerning a certain embezzlement, simply mislaid them for four years. In the same way, a clerk, by placing Pao's name well in front of Chiang's eyes in reports, could obtain the High One's attention ... and he would not be forgotten. A growing anxiety pervaded Pao; would he have enough support to ram his way through the tangle of rivalries which engrossed all the energies of the Chiang officials? Would he escape the thousand snares, made up of petty gossip, which could destroy his best laid plans? Had he been agreeable enough, had he impressed his superiors enough? He tormented himself with all this. If only he had a son, he would feel so much strengthened – he clamoured for a son, a son, a son, as if he were forty-five instead of twenty-five, and hit me in his frustration. And then this question of the rice rations – supposing it became evident that there was no child, secure in the bosom of my family in Chengtu?

In the autumn of 1941 I returned to Chengtu to bid goodbye to Third Uncle and Third Aunt, to my relatives, my friends, and to acquire a child.

Marian Manly had known of Pao's wish for a child. She had tried to help me; had examined me, and found nothing wrong. I was also examined by another woman doctor in Chungking, who gave me electrical treatment to stimulate the womb, this being a current (and

227

futile) fashion. Tests during the previous two years had proved negative for disease or block; but psychological factors were not taken into account as they were to be later; and although Marian did talk of tenseness and nervous strain, no one really knew the extent of my distress. Hans Selye's studies in psychosomatic diseases, and the effects of mental anguish on the body, had scarcely reached medical circles. Marian told me of other couples who had become fertile after the adoption of a child, and she was sure that, should I relax, as she put it, I could become pregnant. But how could I relax with Pao?

In that autumn inflation played havoc with the livelihood of many salaried clerks, small shopkeepers and all those who lived on salaries. They found their purchasing power reduced to almost nothing, their savings vanishing. They sold their clothes, their furniture; many people were doing two, three jobs, at a time, in order to earn more, but their frantic efforts could not keep up with rising prices. Restaurant owners throve, as did landlords and usurers, hoarding rice, textiles, fuel. In Chungking there was the crying scandal of fresh butter and American oranges being imported by air for members of the Kung and Soong families, while hungry people fought over some cabbage stalks in the markets, and babies died of beri-beri. Many people began to starve, lost weight and became listless, stayed home, too weak to walk, lying down, unable to work. Beggars abounded, and in the cities there was an active market in female children for sale to the wealthier families.

There were riots, revolts among the pressganged peasants. Some years previously, in Mienyang on the road to Sian, the peasants had been impressed into forced labour. All the material had to be provided by the people in the districts through which the road passed. Some twenty thousand had been recruited and sent to work, without food. Now the same thing happened again, but on a larger scale; the peasants had no time to do their harvesting, and revolted. About two thousand were killed, and others were sent off into the army. Out of six thousand thus sent to the north-west as 'recruits' only seven hundred survived.

One of the midwives I knew in the hospital had a relative with four daughters; the fourth born only three months before. The mother wanted to sell the third daughter, because she felt the first two were too old, and would know enough to weep and scream; the youngest, the baby, she could not as yet bear to part with, though she would also sell it later, 'for it is better that she should live than die of starvation'. The third, the in-between, at the toddler's stage, was only a year and a half old. She had asked the midwife to help her to find a buyer for her.

The midwife told me that the little girl was not very pretty, and also had a bad temper ... but perhaps I would like to have a look? The price was one thousand dollars, which was high; one could get a small and sturdy little girl for five hundred, or even three hundred. Some of the midwives thought I should bargain for five hundred; 'the mother does not expect a thousand, it's only the asking price.' But that price was because the mother was educated, and could read and write. The child had previously been sent to another family on a trial basis, but after a month that family had returned her, saying she was too head-strong and not pliable enough.

One morning Huang Szeyuan came into my room carrying a little girl. She was in rags, and so very frightened that she looked frozen, with a big tear slowly beginning in each eye. I fell in love with her. She had sores on her face and body, it was obvious that she had been cruelly treated; fine blue veins ran under her fair skin which was just begin-ning to wrinkle; in a fold under the left ear there was a small patch of ringworm. She had an adorable baby face with big round serious eyes, the roundest and brownest I had ever seen, and she looked at me so seriously, with such a solemn and candid stare, while the tears con-tinued to roll slowly and silently down her cheeks. My heart turned over at all the suffering this self-controlled weeping in a little eighteen-month-old represented. She was frightened of noise and loud voices and she whimpered 'Don't want, don't want' when she saw strange faces crowding around her. She did not scream when I took her in my arms, but let me carry her, and I got some hot water and washed her and dried her. I examined the terrible sores and she let me do it. Then the servant came in with a bowl of soft cooked rice with liver on top, and suddenly the tears on her face changed; she was now crying with joy as she screamed 'fan, fan,' which meant rice, rice, and nearly threw herself on the rice, and ate up the whole bowlful.

I paid the thousand dollars without bargaining, without insisting on a trial period, while Huang Szeyuan tut-tutted between her teeth and said I could have had her for less; and everyone else said what a lucky child, and I said I was the lucky one, for she was the most beautiful child I had ever seen – had people no eyes for beauty?

This was more that I had ever wanted, this lovely little girl who now stared thoughtfully at me for two days, only interrupting her solemnity to leap at food, every time weeping with joy. On the third day, suddenly, she touched me lightly on the face with her hand, and smiled.

I was so happy that I went to Huang Szeyuan's room with her, shouting 'Look, look, she is smiling.' All the midwives came to see her smile, and now they said how pretty she was, and one of them blamed the mother for parting from her, but she was not to blame or to condemn; for she had done this to save the child, and only despotic injustice, the inflation, the misery, the war were to blame. There were millions of such cases all over China; millions of such children, so common no one even thought it anything but normal that children should be sold in times of famine ... And I knew the mother was not doing this gladly, but because she had to, and it was better than killing the child, as some did, so that it might escape misery ... And this little girl had a very strong character, which was the reason why one family, only wanting a slave, had rejected her; she was not cowed and submissive. She had a mind of her own, young as she was ...

All the midwives now made clothes for her. Huang Szeyuan knitted her a cap, Miss Wang stitched cloth shoes; Shen made her a top and trousers, Marian Manly cut up an old woollen dress and sewed a lined winter coat. Miss Hsu bought her a doll, a very expensive object in Chengtu.

Perhaps Miss Hsu wanted to say thank you for the land, which cost as much as the child (but already that land had doubled in price in the past six weeks). The little girl stared at the doll for a very long time, touched its nose and her own, and the doll's eyes and her own; it was her first toy, and she kept it tight against her, slept with it and held it in her arms and never threw it about as other children do, and it had to be taken away from her when she was washed or dressed. And then Marian produced a children's book with big letters, A, B, C, that a missionary family had discarded, and the little girl stared at it solemnly, then pointing to the letter T she said: 'Airplane, bang, bang,' which showed that she knew about bombings.

Later I bought her another toy, a small bear. This was also terribly expensive, worth about six yards of cotton material. When I returned to Chungking I sold the rest of the useless things which Pao had brought back from India, those I had not given away, and found eager customers among some of the wealthy Chungking ladies; one pair of high-heeled shoes now sold for the equivalent of Second Brother's salary at the bank for eight months; and a ridiculous artificial pearl handbag fetched five hundred dollars, or half the price of the little girl ... Thus I had some money and bought toys, shoes, a few clothes, and did not have to ask Pao for money.

The little patch of ringworm by the child's ear soon became a dull red blotch, spreading with a sharp advancing edge. 'It is erysipelas,' I said to Marian, and she agreed. Soon half of the face was dull red, and also the whole of her back, and she was feverish. We had to get sulphonamides for her, which was difficult, the price of one tablet being then twenty-five dollars, but we managed to obtain some from the hospital and Marian helped. This patch and the other sores on the child's body and head I washed, and now all the skin of the buttocks and legs began to peel off, pus-filled blisters forming. She never cried as I washed her.

The piece of paper on which the sale was recorded was handed to me. 'You ought to have asked for some clothes with the child,' said Miss Hsu, 'you don't want to be cheated.' But I felt rich now, rich with this beautiful little girl with the lovely eyes, and the serious face, and I would have paid many times more, most cheerfully. Miss Hsu wagged her head over the terrible expense of a child that was so sick, that had come in such a bad state. But her prompt recovery astounded everyone.

Now the child began to smile more frequently and at more and more people, and the news went right through the school of midwives. 'She has smiled at me today, Meimei (little sister) smiled at me.' Two dimples formed in her cheeks and she was less thin. In about two weeks her sores cleared and I took her back to Chungking by air; small and now confident, pointing at things in sudden trust, talking, and occasionally wilful as a baby should be, but in distress, patient and silent, and looking at me, waiting for me to notice ...

In Chungking I found that Pao had moved from Third Uncle's house and rented a room for us near the centre of the city; it was a good room, with a wooden floor, a bed, a chest of drawers, a table, in a flat belonging to an official who some years before, when land and houses were cheap, had built this house. By great good luck it had not been bombed.

Offers of rooms to put us up, invitations to eat in expensive restaurants, were now plentiful, because Pao was so successful. The wife of the official, Mrs Ling, a thin and remarkably competent woman, had given us her best front room and withdrawn to a smaller, closet-like space near the kitchen with her two children. But there was no bed for the child I had brought back, so I pulled a drawer out from the chest of drawers and it became her bed. I placed it on the table, so that the rats might not get at her, and strung in place some wire netting, securing it with strings and nails on top of the improvised bed, as I had seen done for the baby cots in the hospital. It was comfortable enough; the baby moved very little during her sleep. She was putting on weight, always ate ravenously, and one day, when I had given her a small tangerine to play with, ate it up entirely, skin, fibrous under-skin, pips everything. Now the sores were healing and the ringworm had also gone. She took little walks with me, and her hair, which had been too pale and fair due to lack of vitamins, began to thicken.

I had not told Pao which day I would return because the obtaining of air tickets was so erratic, one had to pay bribes to get them from the clerk who registered one's name, bribes when paying for the ticket, bribes to the controller who stamped the ticket ... I arrived in the afternoon and Pao returned in the evening and saw the child eating her bowlful of rice and liver. She loved meat, ate very neatly, never left a grain of rice, fishing it out with her finger and sucking her finger clean then licking the inside of the bowl with her tongue. He said in a loud voice: 'Ha, the little one,' for now that the child was here he could not deny her; had he not drawn rice rations for a child for several months already?

After two or three days, seeing her so quiet – for she made no noise at night, and looked at him with big unblinking round eyes – he too was caught by a wave of affection, for he was not a hard man, only a lost one, lost in his own ambition; no worse but perhaps slightly less calculating in his misguided loyalties than many others of his age, caught in that hallucinating system which drove us all mad.

Pao said to me: 'What are you going to do with her?' I said, 'We are taking her with us.' He said, 'Well, we can bring her up to become your *yat'ou* (slave maid) later,' thus reverting to the tradition which was to buy little girls and turn them into handmaidens, slaves, or sell them to older men as concubines. I tore up the little piece of paper which was the deed of sale. I would never let her be a slave, never any-thing but herself. The warm little body, so precious, so lovable, so full of trust, would never be sold again. I was not going to do as Chinese tradition demanded, use her as a prop for my old age, as a servant, as an insurance ... I did not reply to Pao.

And now I was so glad, so *happy* that I had no child by Pao, no child of my own. For misery would have been perpetuated into another generation. With this one not mine, yet all mine, by love and will; not a haphazard event of biology, engendered in darkness, unwished, unpredictable, but mine by choice and intent, so much more than any flesh and blood could be, I was content enough, I was content for ever.

For only love is the true bond, and there are no children and no parents, save where there is love. And to this day, I am glad that I have no child of my own, for I think I could not love it as much as this one, not love without worrying, worrying about it all the time, and half hating it ... I would always wonder what part of me might lead such a child to self-destruction. I did not want a reproduction of myself, difficult and self-castigating and self-ruinous ... *this* child would be my love. And so it has been.

Early winter brought its cannibal fog, swallowing houses and ruins and hills. The turbid Great River heaved into subsidence, its pace slackened as the heavy waters lowered. All about was the sound of hammering, and on the cliffs one could see small men putting up short limbs of wood for new houses. The tiles that had been blown off roofs by the bomb blasts were again rearranged in neat rows upon new roofs. From the eaves swung out bamboo poles on which were strung the winter clothes, to air in the last gasps of the choked sun. Winter. Chungking rebuilding – but this year things were so expensive that whole areas laid waste, remained waste. Prices rose, up and up – a restaurant meal was now a hundred and fifty yuan; it was seventy-five three months ago ...

October 1941. The American military mission in Chungking was much reinforced; more riots in the countryside; labourers dying of hunger and malaria and cholera while digging ... Another anti-communist drive. Another 'spiritual self-reliance' drive. In Kunming a hotel and several residences were being made ready for Americans; a set of advisers, also Air Force technicians and Marines ... Paper currency printed in England came in by the ton over the Burma Road, later it was to be flown over the Himalayas, when the Burma Road fell to Japan in May 1942. A hundred and fifty tons of paper currency were flown into China in 1942 ...

In Chungking an American colour film was shown, all girls and lingerie, so different from our lives that we gasped, and the nakedness of the girls drew shouts of derision from the crowds.

New edicts appeared against the rise in prices, against corruption; but still they rose. Forced evacuation of families to keep city prices low ... and still they rose. Newspapers even dared to criticize 'certain high officials' for their luxury in the middle of want ...

But in that early winter attention was diverted from the real issues, the inflation, the hunger, the dugout deaths, the corruption, the riots, by a piece of trivial gossip: a personal scandal. That is perhaps the most effective diversion when a tyranny is beset with troubles.

A cabal against Quo Taichi, the Foreign Minister, whom Tai Lee and Hu Tsungnan both disliked, took shape. Quo was anti-Hitler, anti-Japan, pro-British; that was not enough for Tai Lee to 'haul him down'. Quo was accused of having misconducted himself with a young lady not his wife ... there was no scrap of evidence, there never would be, but rumour reported that he and an attractive and able young girl, about my age, Miss S, a student in the same year as myself at Yenching University, were interested in each other ... of a sudden Chungking 'society', the higher echelons of government, talked of nothing else. Not of the famine, the riots, the censorship, the witch-hunts, the inflation, the corruption, the concentration camps, but of the imagined affair of a minister! 'Such nonsense,' I said when I heard of it. Floods of virtuous vituperation poured from Pao as if this petty private fabrication was the most disastrous, unheard of, shocking thing that had ever occurred, threatening to throw our virtuous government into disequilibrium, threatening the outcome of the war!

Meanwhile Tai Lee (and others) were having a succession of affairs; Tai beat up a girl he had seduced and sent her to one of his 'schools'; even the High One, Chiang, was reported to have had his face scratched over a certain 'No. 3' ... The tales of what had happened when the military mission was in Singapore begin to filter back. Twenty years later, in 1962, in Singapore, I was to be told of Pao's affair with a Singapore beauty, now the owner of a successful restaurant which I, all unknowing, patronized – and continued to patronize.

But all this disappeared in the noise made about Quo and his imaginary dalliance; and though Mrs Quo strenuously denied her husband's interest in someone else, this only added more zestful indignation to surmise ... All of a sudden every woman was a paragon of prudery, indignantly condemning Miss S. Sex was ever a safe topic, whereas peasant revolts, corruption, inflation, are not ...

On December 1st Pao came back with the news that he was promoted acting military attaché to London for three years. He was elated at the prospect, though he would have preferred Washington.

We were to leave for London on December 9th via Hongkong, Honolulu, and the United States. The only thing that worried Pao was that the consul-general in Honolulu was the very same Dr Yang who had been Press Information Officer and whom I had met in Brussels; would Dr Yang recognize me, mention knowing me as a Brussels student, when Pao had told everyone that I had studied in England? I was cynical: 'Why tell so many lies?' I packed while Pao ranted on about Dr Yang; at the last moment Pao wanted to leave the child behind, and went into another scene about it; wearily I cabled Jessie Parfitt in Chengtu to ask whether she would take the child, but Jessie wisely refused; and I expected her to.

And then on the morning of December 8th came the news of Pearl Harbour.

It was Pao who returned, almost as soon as he had left for his office that morning, and told me; bringing the newspaper with him. Almost immediately there were noises in the street; newsboys shouting extras, people surging out of the houses to buy the newspapers, crowding together, the sound of their voices above the hum of traffic.

Pao was radiant; the Military Council jubilant; Chiang so happy that he sang an old opera air, and played the Ave Maria all that day. The Kuomintang government officials went about congratulating each other, as if a great victory had been won. From their standpoint it was a victory, what they had waited for, America at war with Japan. At last, at last, America was at war with Japan! Now China's strategic importance would grow even more. American money and equipment would flow in; half a billion dollars, one billion dollars ... Now Lend-Lease would increase from a mere 1.5 per cent (England got 95 per cent). America's navy had been partly destroyed and the next Japanese targets would be Hongkong and South-East Asia.

That Japan was doing this, that Japan had knocked out the Great White Fleet, made the Whangpoo officers almost delirious with pleasure, both because Japan had delivered a big blow to a White Power, which would enable the pro-Japan clique to emphasize the failures of the whites, and because the telling criticisms of Chinese chaos, inefficiency, and defeat, could now be shrugged off with a triumphant 'And what about you?'

'America will no longer be able to play a double game,' said an official at dinner that night to the circle of beaming faces round the table. This he said because the Kurusu mission to Washington – which was devised to convey to the State Department an illusory impression of hesitancy when already the Japanese military were ready to attack – had greatly worried Chungking. How the Chinese now laughed at the Americans! For it was a Sunday, the week-end, when the 'fat boys', as the Americans were nicknamed by the Japanese, had been caught. 'They were too busy drinking and whoring,' cried a very drunk Chinese brigadier, raising his glass to toast the future. Now America would *have* to support Chiang, and that meant U.S. dollars into the pockets of the officials, into the pockets of army commanders, and guns to Hu Tsungnan, for the coming war against Yenan ...

The joy over Pearl Harbour was even more ample than that over the German victories in Russia, though Pao duly looked solemn and commiserating when he saw David Barrett. The Kuomintang had looked forward to an alliance with the Axis powers, and the entry of America into the war did not modify these long-term views. It was conceivable that Japan might need Chiang's invisible co-operation more than ever. It was Quo Taichi who urged Chiang to declare war on Japan and Germany, promising that Chiang would then get a £100 million sterling loan. On December 9th war was declared on Japan and Germany, and Chiang obtained a loan of £50 million.

The Asian battlefront, it was thought in Chungking, would now become the Americans' primary concern because of America's situation as a Pacific power. This hope was soon dashed; Frank Knox of the State Department made a speech saying that Hitler should be beaten first. Hard upon one another came the Japanese advances, at a speed surpassing all conjecture. Hongkong was attacked two days after Pearl Harbour, and fell on December 25th. Some hours *before* Pearl Harbour Japanese war vessels had steamed out of Cam Ranh bay in Indo-China to hit the British Far East Navy; Guam, Wake, the Marianas were attacked.

Our plans were changed; we would leave by air for Kunming, then over the Himalayas to an airport in Northern Burma, from there to Calcutta in India. From Calcutta Pao would fly to London, while the child and I would proceed by train to Bombay, and from Bombay take a ship to London. And since the Suez Canal was closed to ordinary passenger boats due to the war in North Africa, we would have to round the Cape of Good Hope, and sail across the Atlantic ... A long and roundabout journey.

In January 1942 the Japanese land onslaught against Malaya and Singapore began; England was at war with Japan, and Pao's nomination took on increased importance.

In early January, we left Chungking for the air trip across the Himalayas to an airport in Northern Burma. We rose at two in the morning, and reached the landing strip of Shuang Hu Pa by three thirty. It was a deep fog we waded into, going down the steps to the river, now at low ebb, and crossing by ferry to the elongated island in the middle of the river. Mat sheds served as waiting-rooms – there was no permanent structure for an airfield under water half the year.

Two Americans, one Englishman and a few Chinese officials were going on the same plane as we were. I carried the little girl in my arms, bundled up in a blanket. By the light of paraffin lamps we waited, and then Tai Lee arrived, in black cape and mole-coloured felt hat; with bodyguards before and behind him, he swept in, and everything went hushed. His hat, tall-crowned to give him more height, was almost surrealist in its live malice. Hatted, Tai Lee reminded one irresistibly of a half-comical and totally sinister film gangster. The Chinese officers, including Pao, clicked heels, saluted. Orders were barked, tea poured. Tai Lee inquired when the plane was leaving; he had come to say goodbye to the important officials going with us, and also to Pao, and he was not going to wait. One moment he was smiling, with that pulling down of his lower lip and chin which was his smile, and the next he was a hurricane of wrath, his cape sweeping the air, his short body hurtling this way and that, froth on his lips. But the hat remained a theatrical headgear, detached from that maelstrom of fury which was its wearer. Pao and the bodyguards followed Tai Lee up and down as he paced, and ranted, and screamed.

The reason for this fury was that the flight was delayed. The meteorological service had warned against attempting to leave, a storm was brewing in the mountains, the pilots had decided to wait another two hours ... Tai Lee suddenly took by the middle the cane he carried. It was a long smooth-knobbed sword-cane, whose top came off, and the blade sprang out. Tai Lee had had two such canes made, and one of them he had given to Chiang Kaishek. He started whirling it around, slapping it on the wooden table, which served for customs examination.

Disregarding the weather reports the pilots started the engines and our plane took off, Pao waving and saluting. In February 1946 Tai Lee was to die in a plane accident because he would not heed the storm warnings, and forced the pilot to fly the aircraft despite adverse weather reports ...

Our journey to Kunming was wind-tossed and the storm-bearing black clouds bumped the plane ominously; at one moment our plane fell about five hundred feet; we laughed to find ourselves alive. But Kunming airport was accessible; we rested there for an hour and then took off for the flight over the Hump, as the crossing of these mountain ranges was called. Such journeys have now become more commonplace, and the hazards of those days are wearisome to recount; but in those years there were no jets, and only inadequate pressurization in the plane cabin. We flew high and felt quite sick. Through the plane windows we saw the mountain ranges below us, about us and above us. Snow peaks, ice blue, pink, violet, glaring white, would rear their gigantic shapes as our plane seemed to bear down upon them. Avalanches of sunlight rushed at us between clouds, ink black on one side, glowing rainbow on the other. Vast abysses of darkness, in which our tossed plane plunged opened in front of us. And then, pure and taking away all fear, as if death itself were but lightness, again snow peaks, incredibly pure and still, watching us with the distant look of gods as our plane skimmed their hallucinating splendour and left them. Everything in the aircraft, seats, wings, was jerking and quivering, and groaning all the time. All of us kept silent: we were very frightened and also very sick.

Then we came down at Lashio, so hot, so hot and so green, and me with two padded gowns on, the exterior one filthy with the child's vomit. The child had become pale with heat, dripping with sweat. Pao removed layer after layer of clothing, but I could not remove more than one padded gown. Then we re-entered the plane, and in a green evening haze arrived at Calcutta, hot, steamy, with cattle in the streets and clanking trains, and dust, and clamour. By that time we were in a trance of fatigue.

The Great Eastern Hotel gave us a palatial room, with enormous beds, mosquito nets, a bathroom like a dim cavern. But it was not possible to fall into bed and sleep because there was a dinner to attend. The Chinese Consul of Calcutta and his pretty wife had come to greet us, and insisted on our eating dinner. I had to dress the child and take her with me; I could not leave her alone in the room. English people in evening dress tutted and passed loud remarks about the unnatural mother who was forcing the darling little baby to have dinner with adults. She was so tired she would not eat. In the morning she would not eat again, she was not used to the strange food, she did not like bananas, or milk, all she ate was rice.

Three days later Pao left by air for London.

He was happy, full of confidence. Malaya, the Philippines were attacked, were falling ... The *Prince of Wales* and the *Repulse* had been destroyed by the Japanese. Pao told me as he got ready to leave for the airport that the last fortune-teller to read his face was right: greatness would come to him. 'He saw the light shining from my forehead,' said Pao, inspecting his mirror face with deep satisfaction; a long life, a brilliant future, for the most chivalrous and loyal 'reliable stronghold' of Chiang's power, Tang Paohuang. How good Tai Lee was at picking the right followers! This pleasant prospect moved Pao to his most affable and charming mood. In three short years he had climbed to the top – he was the youngest military attaché ever known, only twenty-nine years old. The suddenness with which he could switch from one mood to the other, from fury to gentle, wistful tenderness, never ceased to baffle me, until I realized that many other Chinese men of his class and upbringing exhibited the same talent.

On leaving Calcutta Pao named the little girl, giving her a poetic name, Yungmei, Plum Blossom of Chengtu; for she had been born on the third day after the Chinese New Year, when the plum blossom adorns every household. Wistfully he said: 'Maybe she will bring us luck.' I did not reply, but clutched Yungmei to me as I waved him goodbye at the airport, and made her wave. Then we went back to the hotel, Yungmei and I, and I tried to feed her and I said: 'Now Yungmei, you and I are going to see this through together' – for I could no longer think of my life as separate from hers, and I would never give her up.

Part of the steps up from the river, Chungking.
A fairly recent photograph.
(Popperfoto, London)

A street in a Chinese city in 1939.

Third Uncle, Third Aunt, and their offspring and relatives in 1956.

Visiting friends in the English countryside.

Yungmei, aged three.

Pao and the Chinese Military Mission in England, winter 1943–4.

Part Two (1942–1948)

Eleven

YUNGMEI and I remained almost four weeks in India, in January and early February of 1942. We stayed at the Great Eastern Hotel in Calcutta for a fortnight, and then took the train to Bombay where we stayed at the Taj Mahal Hotel. Twenty-five years later I was to find both hotels almost unchanged, with their marble pillars, lofty cupolaed ceilings, and inimitable Victorian ponderousness relieved by ineradicable dust. I am always bemused by this mixture of imperial decay and slapdash toil; armies of bearers, waiters and untouchables, sweeping and cleaning for ever – with that air of fatalistic wisdom accepting the eternity of their gestures – those massive marble edifices pinioning them to their servitude.

I do not remember meeting any Indian who was not a servant, a bearer, a something-wallah; in those days, Indians existed merely as functions of service, and 'educated wallahs' were upstarts, hot-heads, better off in jail. In the hotels no Indians stayed as guests; these edifices were only for the British, or diplomatic guests, such as us.

The Chinese Consul in Calcutta, and later the one in Bombay, and their wives, looked after us painstakingly well; with gifts and solicitude, with indefatigable courtesy and tireless smiles. They shopped with us, fed us, entertained us. I needed chiefly summer clothes for Yungmei, for on the steamer crossing the Equator it would be very warm, and I had only a few winter clothes for her. To cut the cost of shopping I reverted to a student outfit for myself – shirts, shorts, pants – hoping to buy in England what I would need, and only purchasing enough to last me the sea voyage. I bought a small coral necklace for Yungmei and a pair of milk opals to make into ear-rings for myself; I thought they might function as 'jewellery' in my new status.

Yungmei became quite difficult, and this was understandable; there had been too much change in her baby life. She was bewildered and tired, ate badly; I did not know what might suit her, I tried everything, and found her staring at me reproachfully over milk and bananas. Then I discovered that she had worms when in the warm bath water, as I washed her, I saw one waving its blind end slowly out of her anus and back again.

Ascariasis, roundworm infestation, is very prevalent, even today, in many countries of Asia. The infestation rate was ninety per cent in rice-bearing Szechuan, where the use of human manure and especially the eating of pickled vegetables, which are not cooked but plunged in a salt solution, promoted its spread. I should have dewormed her, but with all her other illnesses had omitted to do so. I went to the chemist and bought the appropriate vermifuge, with stupendous results. The next day she passed about twenty-five large worms, in coils; I had to extract them manually, they were so enormous, some still feebly writhing, and the wonder was that such a small body could have harboured so many. After that her health improved, but she still could not be left alone, and screamed and screamed if I went to the bathroom.

I tried hiring an Indian ayah to look after her; the hotel procured an oldish, gaunt woman, with pendulous lobes drawn thin like string by heavy brass ear-rings in clusters, large as curtain hangers. She started dandling the child and singing to her. Yungmei shrieked, would not stop shrieking; within an hour I had paid off the ayah. Then I took her everywhere with me, since she refused everyone else, and having won the battle, she consented to eat.

In the afternoon, I took Yungmei to the Calcutta Maidan, the large open space, where one could walk about in the mild winter, warm as early summer in Chengtu. There were Indians in groups, white-clothed, astroll. They made a faraway, unapproachable frieze. There was little evidence of Indian art about, so deeply anchored was the possession of the 'superior' race, the rulers. The clatter of the trams, with bells ringing, and jarring wheel-changes, the unkempt and desultory appearance of the crowds, made no sense because their actions were not understood by me. The irrelevance of the British walking on Chandni Chauk, the ambling cattle, chewing, relieving themselves, the hordes of beggars, mutilated, whining, with their persistent extended palms, constantly pushed back by white-gartered policemen with black sticks into intestinal, fetid back streets; the smells, the smells which today I know and love – all this made strangeness. Only the poverty, which I was accustomed to, provided a link with China ...

British India was stranger by far to me than Europe was. At that time many of us in Asia, because of the orientation of colonial power, because of our westernized education, were more separate from each other, more ignorant of other Asian countries and conditions, than of the Western powers which held us in subjection. Immured by prejudice, I could not connect the great stirrings, the massive seething discontent under all this impassivity, under this apparent acceptance of inhuman misery, with the revolutions already germinating in Asia.

On the main streets, at the railway stations, were daubings and posters: V for victory, Talismanic V, in brown on whitewashed walls. But in a back street of Calcutta, just behind the hotel, where ambulant Muslim pedlars sold roasted cow udders (a delicacy I ate without knowing what they were until 1957), I saw scribbled upon a wall 'Long Live Subhas Chandra Bhose.' Chandra Bhose was head of a Japanese-sponsored Indian National Liberation Army. A surreptitious half-effaced 'Long Live Congress' stood out. Gandhi was in jail, and Nehru, and many other 'hot-heads'.

The Calcutta English newspapers – *The Statesman*, the *Hindustan Star* – wrote of battles in Europe, of the Russian front, of Africa and Rommel. On the back page some brief reference to a speech by an Indian babu pledging 'loyalty', saying 'the Allied cause is ours', urging an increasing 'war effort' from India, received three paragraphs. At the bottom there was a line about a famine, and relief projects. The social news included a New Year charity ball which was 'a great success', *almost* three thousand rupees being collected to relieve 'the sufferers from starvation'.

The Chinese diplomats in Bombay harboured contempt for the Indians; 'They have a slave mentality.' They said the British put down revolts massively; the jails were full, new jails were being built. Their wives told of Indian dirt, inefficiency and thievery. Could they not see that the same conditions obtained in China? That we, too, were almost slaves? That the flaming misery of India, spread out in the sun, was the same as ours in Chungking? We saw it not ... In none of us was there any prescience that things would ever be different for India, so strong was the myth of Indian fatalism, hopelessness. And yet there had been risings, and there was the beginning of a huge famine in Bengal, which was to kill two million people, a man-made famine, due to the requisitioning of rice by the British authorities, without regard for Indian suffering ... And the half-erased name of Subhas Chandra Bhose meant something deep and much more lasting for India that the good child handwriting, V for Victory signs, on new whitewash in each railway station.

No one I met then believed in Gandhi, for those we met were not Indians, but Chinese diplomats and, in Bombay, one American woman, a very devoted missionary, who felt Indians must be 'prodded' into doing things for themselves. I spoke to only one Indian, not a servant, during those weeks in India. As for the English there, they simply stared through us, assured gods and goddesses on their way to the Gymkhana Club, to the season's balls; vivacious and certain, even their laughter had the ring of command.

The Bengali on the Maidan who came towards Yungmei and me in a circumspect and gentle sidle was haloed by birds; crows, their immense web swooping over the city, glossy and fat; Yungmei ran among the alighting crow throngs, hand extended, crying 'ducks, ducks' in Chinese, and one of them snapped her finger in its beak. 'Good evening, madam,' said the man solemnly, and a long and dilatory conversation about crows followed; and 'we believe they are the souls, madam ... we believe that all lives are sacred.' The magenta heaven, that marvellous sky of the Indian evening, replete with the splendour of the dust, hung above his disapproval that I should allow Yungmei to chase after crows. He spoke of India too, 'this land of the Gods', and 'Mother India', and there was no core or substance to our talk, which remains a fugitive without face. Only the tone of his singsong voice and the strange, affected, duteous English, which made me strain my ears, remains. It was not until evening when the Chinese consul's wife with careful indignant persuasion told me that one must never speak to strange Indians met accidentally on the Maidan, for 'they all want money, or to read your palm, or they will even attack you' that the old man came alive to me, his humanity mine. And then I knew him as wanting to say so much, as straining for expression, and in his stiff English finding only the stilted formulae coined by the British about his own country, and the words he used emptied his soul of meaning, for he could not tell what he wanted in the words of others.

And the great night of India, so gladly dolorous, came majestically with its smell of dust and dung of bats, tangled in the trees that held it captive. The strange hotel with its chandeliers, its deep halls full of English men and women dancing to an English orchestra which played 'Me and my shadow' and 'Alouette', shut out the Indian night.

In Bombay at the Taj Mahal Hotel (more marble pillars, white-and-scarlet-clad servants) I met Miss S., the attractive young girl who for a while had been the subject of so much malice in Chungking.

. She was suffering from typhoid, and stayed in bed, waiting for the same boat as I. She was going to Canada. The consul's wife looked after her; brought her fruit and chicken broth cooked at home. I found her sweet and sad. She got up one afternoon to come shopping with me in the bazaar. She was an extremely good shopper. Jewellers brought her gold necklaces, precious stones which she looked at critically, twisting the chains and turning the stones about in her hand. I felt overawed by her calm, the equanimity with which she treated me, and though according to Pao her whole life was ruined, she seemed very unruined to me, and made no reference to the vileness from which she had suffered. Only once did she break down, and that was some weeks later on the boat. I then realized she was not suffering from typhoid but from a nervous breakdown; and wisely healed herself by staying in bed. She stayed in bed the whole time we were on board ship, only getting up to use the bathroom.

I became convinced that she was the victim of Tai Lee's hatred for Quo Taichi, for she was certainly neither ambitious nor full of intrigue. But she had savoir-faire when I had none, poise where I was brusque or shy; taste and good clothes, while the camisoles I had bought showed and my shoes did not fit. And so I felt more inferior than ever when finally our ship docked at Bombay and we went on board. We shared a first-class cabin for the next seven weeks.

Much had happened since that Sunday morning on December 7th, when three hundred and sixty Japanese planes took off from six aircraft carriers to destroy the American fleet at Pearl Harbour. On December 16th the Japanese had landed in Borneo. A few days later, the Japanese forces crossed from Siam into Burma. On January 7th, Kuala Lumpur, the capital of Malaya, was taken. By January 25th the Japanese had conquered Malaya. Singapore, the 'impregnable fortress', fell on February 15th. By March 1942 all of the Dutch East Indies, today's Indonesia, was under Japan. MacArthur and ninety-five thousand men were besieged on the Bataan peninsula, locked in the enormous tunnels dug under Corregidor Island.

The rumour that the Japanese would launch an attack on India at any moment had caused an exodus from cities such as Madras and

Bombay. The Indian Ocean was reported to be infested with Japanese submarines.

Our ship, the *Tjiluwah,* sailed from Bombay in early February. It was crowded; missionaries, businessmen, Americans escaped from the Philippines, refugees from Hongkong and Shanghai, Dutchmen from the 'Dutch East Indies'. Chief refugee and most deferred to was Sir Victor Sassoon, of the Shanghai Sassoons, owner of vast wealth. He came on board with a limp, a monocle, and that Shanghai brand of arrogance which by now seemed almost a parody.

We sailed a zigzag course, the ship creaking, all hatches fastened and blacked out at night. It was suffocating. The Americans on board argued back and forth, endlessly, about Pearl Harbour, berated their own government for unpreparedness. The British did not discuss the war, but read the daily news bulletin silently. One American woman remarked on this reticence. 'They pretend nothing has really happened ... they talk about bridge and the weather, and they make *Punch* jokes, but the world will never be the same again.' The cabins were crowded; water was rationed; there were scores of children on board, each missionary family had at least three, and the majority seemed under seven years of age.

After the *Tjiluwah* reached the Atlantic, the fear of Japanese submarines was replaced by that of German submarines; our zigzag course accentuated. I watched the trail of sharp-angled twists and turns we left on the ocean. Yungmei got a heat rash. The toilets were inadequate, and water was further rationed. To promote friendship and goodwill a bridge competition was arranged; I did not know how to play bridge, having only played twice before, but participated, and was eliminated very swiftly, and watched the post mortem rancour, some of it lasting the whole voyage through.

The peculiar mania of ship travel had taken hold; the ship one's universe and all else put away, filed as dreams in the stores of the night. Only the ship, and all that happened on it, however petty, took on the dimensions of Event. Amateur theatricals were started. A young American teacher and I collaborating on a dismal play insufficiently rehearsed but politely clapped, for everyone would have been as bored without it. Victor Sassoon was provided with a large armchair in the middle of the first row, swept regally in and just as regally out again after twenty minutes. There were three or four ruptured marriages and the same number of illicit love affairs, and all of it was real and unreal, the creation of a small water-hemmed world, where a squabble about a deck chair became epic. And the fixed points, lodestars of the hours spent crisscrossing the waters, were the daily bulletins scanned with great fervour, the conversations round the bar, or on deck.

I met and talked with a young American newspaperman who gave me a long lecture on the (to be accomplished later) partition of India; he was a devotee of the Muslim leader Jinnah, hated Nehru, but he also hated the British, and thought it would be a good thing if the British lost their empire, and the United States took over to show what could be done in India, in South-East Asia. He was all for a U.S. trusteeship of these territories, and suggested giving parts of French Indo-China (the north) to the Chinese 'under American knowhow'. I regret that I did not listen more carefully. Much of what he told me was serious stuff, actively debated in Washington then ...

When we arrived at the Cape of Good Hope we had two half-days on land, at an hotel where we were well received, though 'coloured': the special beach hotel reserved for diplomats of non-white races. We saw Table Mountain, the brisk sun and air revived us, for once we could wash ourselves properly.

Through the Atlantic, with the soliloquies of the ocean round us, world without end; each creak, each pound of the engine a second of time's needle stitching, hemming, binding us to each other; Mrs Jones and Mrs Wells no longer on speaking terms; their children do not play together any more; the blonde is going to divorce her husband and marry the other man as soon as we reach Miami; everyone talks, talks and talk makes the ship creak. I talk to the ship's doctor and tell him I want to go on with studying medicine – he laughs and tells me that that's impossible, I shall have to do everything over again from scratch. Love and hate know the dimensions of the walk without end curving round the deck; class hatred is first and second class; passionate and undying transience wreaks its shallow havocs and all is more important than anything yet gone before. The daily bulletin is contemplated by Victor Sassoon's monocled haughtiness, who says peremptorily, 'We'll be back in Shanghai next year.'

From all this Miss S. and I were almost immune; she because in bed the whole journey through (except for one evening when she came down to dinner but gave up after one sip of the soup), and I because of Yungmei, who stood up in her cot and yelled if I left the cabin. I read steadily through the ship's library, a book a day, and because of Yungmei I read in our private toilet, sitting on the floor. Because of her I escaped the adults' dinner, a strut and parade occasion, the time for preening. I hear the others, loud voices asserting, striving, I see them changing and changed, moulded by the ship into other beings they will deny one day ... I too have a different self here; all mother, I eat at the children's table with Yungmei and a few missionary matrons who relay each other at the children's meals, and two Chinese amahs brought out by American families to look after their children ...

We landed at Kingston in Jamaica, and were entertained by the local Chinese, the Lim family, the Tai family. Miss S. dressed, sedulously brushed her long, beautiful hair. Two or three hours on the sun-dazzled island with the passion flowers thrusting out at us from the lush greeness were too much for her weakened condition. After tea under the furling rain trees holding promise of wind in their clusters, she became ill again, and had to go back to bed.

The Chinese in Jamaica were very well off, they took us in their cars to their hill slope homes, to show us the beauty of the sea-girt land, the jacaranda blossoming in the velvet warmth of evening gardens. They were, like so many overseas Chinese, intensely patriotic, asked many questions about China. Some had Negro blood which im-proved their looks, but to my surprise, others were ashamed of it and spoke deprecatingly of the darker-skinned among them, and did not see the extra vitality and good looks it gave them. They sent money to China, and sons and daughters, and even though some could not speak Chinese, all that pertained to the ancestral land was of concern to them.

On to Miami, and thence to New York, to the cold of late March, a hotel too expensive for my budget and also inconvenient with a child, the Waldorf Towers. Fortunately the American woman with whom I had become friendly on board found me a small hotel with apart-ments; a bedroom, bathroom and small kitchenette, the price four-teen dollars a day, one half of the Waldorf prices. The same woman gave me the address of a firm where I could hire a nanny, and I hired an English one, prompt, competent, neat. She came from nine to five and I paid her fifty dollars a week. Thus I was able to do a little of what was expected of me, pay calls, go to lunch, do a little shopping, for by now my dresses no longer held together.

Nanny knew where and how to buy clothes for children: at Lord and Taylors. Yungmei looked beautiful in her new clothes. 'They are British clothes,' said Nanny proudly. All the best things came from England, and everyone told me to buy all I needed in America, for in England they said there was nothing left. Americans were sending food parcels and clothes parcels to penurious bombed England. I bought three dresses, two suits, three pairs of shoes and some stockings, a fur coat and a fur jacket, an evening dress and an afternoon dress; apart from one more black dress which I bought in London, all this served me well for the next six years.

The Chinese we met in New York and in Washington were mostly diplomats, hospitable and kind. They arranged parties and I was in great difficulty because I could not leave Yungmei alone at night. I remember one such occasion I had to leave Yungmei alone, and take a taxi; I arrived to find forty people in a spacious flat, with seven mahjong tables going. Suddenly I was transported back to China, to the rhythmic click click of the chips, thrumming the seconds, the minutes of our time of decay, nail blows in the coffin of our system. The atmosphere was not America but Shanghai, gracious, scintillating, heartless, a brittle crust of plenty, a surface pellicle ignoring its fundamental bog. It hit me in the stomach. I could not take my mind away from the war; huge battles in Russia, also in the Pacific. From the kitchen, delicious flavours; my hostess, rosy-cheeked, bent over a saucepan sauté-ing some large prawns ... Yungmei in her baby bed, perhaps awake, waiting with those large round eyes burning the semi-darkness. I left after ten minutes.

And another time, I went downstairs to have a drink with the American correspondent from the boat, who like the American woman, in the typical American way, had looked me up and asked if he could help. We had just ordered one drink, when the waiter appeared to tell me Yungmei was walking in the corridor, without any clothes on. She had taken off her nightgown, slid down the bed, and was running about in her skin. Thus my evenings were imprisoned, and since the institution of the baby-sitter was not mentioned to me I did without. Only twice in a five-week stay did I get away for a concert and a ballet, when American women friends offered to watch her for me.

We visited Washington, the cherry trees in blossom round the

White House, paid a call on the British Ambassador, Lord Halifax and his wife, both immensely statuesque: tea and small talk in a great, grave manner. Returning to New York I found American friends trying to give parties for me; I did not know that they so much enjoyed giving parties. To me, Chungking, the privations of Chengtu, were still vivid, and everything that was done here seemed sheer extravagance. But the American women I met all wanted to do something to help; one woman volunteered to stay with Yungmei while I went to the first Russian ballet shown in America for a long time. Just before the curtain opened, Helen Hayes came onto the stage and announced the disaster of Corregidor; the house stood in silence for the dead of the Pacific. The Russian ambassador Litvinov and his wife rose to the applause of all; Litvinov was a glint of spectacles and a round face above a black evening suit. Someone told me, quite erroneously, that his wife wore the diamonds of the late Tsarina.

In that April of 1942, not only the Java seas but also the Indian Ocean had now come under the sway of the Japanese. The Royal Navy bases at Trincomalee in Ceylon and the last of the British fleet in Asia had been subjected to massive Japanese aerial onslaughts. The Japanese were expected to sweep on to Suez, to effect a junction with Hitler's North African armies there. But this did not happen. Instead they turned back, because they wanted to consolidate their gains in South-East Asia, and in that same April the defeated MacArthur, who had flown back to America, leaving his troops in Bataan to capitulate, returned to Australia to head the defence of that (at the time) jittery island, and to form an extensive rampart of islands, beginning with New Guinea, north of it. Then followed the battle of the Coral Sea, where American losses were greater than the Japanese; and the battle of Midway Island, leading to Guadalcanal in August 1942. And slowly, slowly, the tide turned. The battle of Midway Island was the turning point of the Pacific war. After that the Japanese began to lose.

There was, in America, an almost hysterical fear of attack. Reports of Japanese submarines off the Californian coast; vociferous clamours that the Nisei* be jailed, dumped into the sea. This was a big, raw, lusty, shouting nation, tremendously emotional, irrationally impatient and profoundly indignant at what had happened. Pearl Harbour seemed to them the most horrifying, unforgivable thing. And hearing them descant, I kept thinking of China and what the Chinese people

*Japanese established in U.S. for generations and U.S. citizens.

had suffered and were suffering – so infinitely more.

China was extremely popular now; Eleanor Roosevelt presided over a meeting for Help to China. But the conduct of the Chinese diplomats in the U.S., who lived most luxuriously, was occasionally brought to my attention by Americans; for the graft and corruption of the Kuomintang were also to be found in the diplomatic missions abroad.

I received a letter from Marian Manly, giving me the name of her agent in New York. I rang them up and went to see them, as I had not been told about the publication of *Destination Chungking*. They gave me a copy of the published book to read. They had done a good bit of editing on their own, and I was not altogether happy with it. My mild criticism in the last chapter had been cut further. But since they had dealt only with Marian, they were not at all convinced that I had anything to do with the book, and were very suspicious of me.

Of those weeks in the electric spring of New York, no cohesive picture remains except the nervous brilliance of Americans, their high-powered and explosive way of talking, lack of reticence on all subjects, resilience, emotionalism; they would become thoroughly involved, and just as thoroughly disengaged; the rawness and the energy, the contradictory moods and statements, the wealth and (even then) the poverty and squalor of the Negro districts (I visited Harlem once); exhilarating and exhausting. They were eager, generous, yet also intensely self-centred, exorbitant and strenuous and always trying to convince themselves of their own goodness.

But after Chungking, what flabbergasted me most in America was the talk. Being able to say anything, hearing people say things which in Chungking would have meant being shot. I had forgotten the very notion of free speech, and in New York it confused me. But above all, astonishingly, I found an uncommon fear of physical distress, perhaps because people like myself, who have been bombed, are no longer afraid of bombing. The hysteria about the bombing of London was more intense in New York than I would ever find in London or anywhere in England. Some even tried to dissuade me from going to England. 'They're all coming over here or going to Canada,' they said, speaking of the few thousands (and the children) from the well-to-do class, as if it was a massive exodus.

· A woman who lived in the same hotel as I did in New York moved from the eighth floor to the first floor, because she feared that bombs

253

might be dropped upon the eighteen-storey hotel. She asked me how tall the buildings in Chungking were, and when I told her that the highest was three storeys, and they were mostly wood, she could not understand how we had survived.

America was rich, beautiful and mighty, and the war made for more wealth; only one person spoke to me of the Depression days, how hungry he had been then, and that was the lift man in the hotel. He shook my hand and said he loved Russia and China.

One morning in May we took the plane to England. Our first stop was Bermuda, where we stayed for two days. I became acquainted there with a Doctor Wilkinson, who took Yungmei and myself for a drive in his horse-drawn carriage, a lovely drive on a lovely afternoon. Twenty years later, in 1962, I was to see Dr Wilkinson again, in Singapore, at a meeting of the World Family Planning Association; as spry, quick-witted and kindly as he had been in Bermuda, twenty years before.

From Bermuda we sped across the Atlantic for another stop in the Portuguese-owned Cape Verde Islands, waiting with the sun and the sea wind battering us, taking long walks round a sun-baked, white-walled town. From there to Lisbon, and another flight in a rainy squall along the Portuguese coast, flying low and the plane bumping so that everyone was sick, while we were being informed that we were in the country of port wine, and small bottles of the local pride were distributed to us.

And finally England, rainy, late afternoon, and Pao, slightly fatter, ebullient, who drove us to London. He had taken one of the best rooms at Claridge's to welcome me back; a mausoleum, with black marble facings in the immense bathroom. The day after that we drove out to Egham, where he had found a small house for us. Pao was full of plans concerning his career and the future ... he was the youngest military attaché, everyone was impressed with him; we would now begin a new happy life. He would be a success ... I must help him.

Yes, I would help him, I would do my best ...

On New Oxford Street, looking at the calm, orderly people in London – so calm with the war going on, so huddled and orderly and patient, with the bomb craters all over London, with the posters:

Is your journey really necessary? – I began another existence. And first of all, I understood that the picture of fear, hunger and want that had been painted in New York, was untrue. Compared to Chungking, London was comfort, was orderliness. At Claridge's and the Dorchester a lot of wealthy people still dressed and dined. Was this really the war?

At Egham the small cottage, rented furnished, was comfortable, and an elderly maid was available who could also cook. Now all I had to do was to stay in the cottage, help with the housework and the cooking, look after Yungmei, and be happy. Perhaps I could also help the war effort by planting some vegetables, raising chickens in the back yard? Next door to us was a retired couple, the husband had been in the Army and gave riding lessons to the few children in the neighbourhood.

Every morning Pao drove in his car to the Embassy in Portland Place, to the military attaché's office. 'All you have to do is to be happy,' said Pao. His job was a responsible one: to consolidate (that was the word) the ties between fighting England and fighting China. I looked through the windowpanes at the lush green grass, the spring leaves, the hedges foamy with may. There was plenty of milk for Yungmei. We had diplomatic extra rations, we would fare well. Pao was sure that the Germans would win in the end, that Russia would crack, but meanwhile here we were in England.

May 1942, and the British had suffered a total rout in Burma. The Burma Road was cut, only the air route remained from China, over the Himalayas to Assam, to India. An aerial bridge, seven thousand metres up.

By the end of May the Burma campaign was over, the British and Indian forces withdrawing over the border to India.

Pao and his Chinese Embassy colleagues were busy, for there were plans, American-inspired plans, for the reconquest of Burma, for the opening of a second front in Asia. An American general, Stilwell, was in China, to build up a new Chinese army – in this grand design Burma was of supreme importance. The second Burma campaign was being prepared; and from the start, due to the different aims between the 'Allies' – the United States, the British and Chiang – it was foredoomed to failure.

☆

Thus we began the next three years, and they went no better than the time in Chungking, for the same reasons; that Pao sought to mould me into what I could never be.

I do not blame Pao for this, his persistence was admirable in its own way. But the unpredictable iconoclast could not be tamed, though I put myself to it with will and docility, strove to become what I was not, partly succeeded, for a short while – but it did not stick.

Had Pao allowed me to work half a day at something useful, constructive, as I asked him to do, perhaps things might have been different. If he had talked things out with me, perhaps we might have influenced each other beneficially. But Pao never wanted me to be anything but an adjunct to his career, a useful object in his plans, and his career made no sense to me now, his plans I could not understand. His dreams of personal glory were alien to me, their aim, his becoming a second Hu Tsungnan, another replica of Chiang Kaishek, to me absurd.

I felt that, after the war, there would have to be a great many changes in China, and was now pursued by the urge to understand the meaning of events, yet far too ignorant to see the whole picture. All I knew was that I no longer believed in Chiang Kaishek; Pao's career, therefore, seemed to me a waste of time and effort. His work in London appeared to me to have little bearing on the war situation. Had someone asked me then: What, basically, do you want Pao to do? I would have answered: 'To leave the government, to become a private person, and to work ... '

And yet how busy, important, grave, were the military, air, naval attachés, the diplomats of the Chinese Embassy, with talk of a second front in Asia; with demands for supplies, loans, equipment; rushing to and fro, in an expense of muddled activities, in a waste of confusion! For just as Chiang Kaishek sent orders and counter-orders to his generals, by-passed the regular chain of command to issue contradictory fiats to junior officers, so a stream of contradictory telegrams, as well as Chinese missions, flowed from Chungking to London and to Washington, all peremptorily demanding instant obedience. There was only one consistent core to the clash and jangle of this dazing surfeit of orders and their instant countermanding, and that was the demand for money.

In this connection, it was primarily the United States, rather than Britain, to which Chiang looked for help; and prying loose some of the priorities assigned by Washington to London, for the war fronts in Africa, became the main preoccupation of the Chinese Embassy in England.

Pearl Harbour had brought America into the war against Japan; and Hitler, foolishly declaring war on the United States, brought it (though a strong pro-German element agitated for neutrality in the European war) on to the side of Great Britain. The chief concern of the British was that the resources of the United States should not go to an Asian theatre of operations, but to the European one, to Great Britain herself with her great needs of food and supplies for the forces in the Middle East.

In early 1942 the question of offensive action, either in the Pacific, or in the Euro-African theatres of war, was the constant underlying problem. Which should it be first? Which would America consider the main priority?

In January 1942 a conference in Washington established a combined American-British Chiefs of Staff Committee, at which it was agreed that an invasion of Europe would be essential to defeat Hitler, and that this aim was of 'overriding importance'.

Chiang Kaishek, when he learnt of this, was very angry; in February 1942 he toured India, on a visit arranged the previous year, and made a speech in which he stated that China and India had 'a common destiny', thus baiting the British, who knew how restive the Indian masses were, and who, because of Gandhi's call for non-cooperation in the war, were keeping Gandhi in jail.

Throughout the war years, a basic opposition in plans between Chiang and the British government was obvious, and one of the more evident points of friction was the Burma front. Never was any territory, never were any forces, any campaign plans to suffer from so much bungling, indecision, and sudden change of plans as the unhappy Burma front, until Mountbatten came along and changed the situation.

Thus Pao, and other diplomats, rushed to and fro, busy and important. I was bored. And today I can say that even had I lived up to Pao's expectations, been a satisfactory wife, housekeeper, to serve his career, the end result would have been exactly the same for Pao. Popular or not, able or not, there was nothing any Chinese diplomat under Chiang could do to influence the shape of the tremendous historical forces at work in the world, during the war. No amount of American-infused money, equipment, goods, would prevent the downfall of Chiang. But I could not voice these things, even to myself, for I had no exact knowledge, I had only a belly feeling of emptiness, as if all that we did was worm-hollowed even before it was done. And so I tried to be happy, tried to think that being a diplomat's wife was important, and was utterly bored.

Class feeling was very striking in England then. As an attaché's wife, moving in diplomatic circles, I was struck by the invidious subtleties of class differentiation, so different from the chasmic gaps which separated classes in China. Here innuendo, accent, attitude, were the signposts, not clothing. I was at first unable to understand the fine gradations of the social hierarchy; to use the correct and appropriate distance with shopkeepers, with the gardener who came twice a week (and soon found out that I was frightened of him), with the char who came to clean, and went away with the meat from the food-safe ... I did not know the kind of conversation that was appropriate for each class.

In diplomatic circles, my voicing of unorthodox opinions, my inability to sustain small talk, my neglect of hints which permit to assess and delimit a person, my lack of discretion, my inability to say nothing with gay intensity, my failure to voice exaggerated professions of enthusiasm and interest, all, all combined to make me feel entirely odd and out of place. Even though social graces were at a minimum in times of war, meeting the British upper class was like learning another language, another code of signals.

Fortunately London was full of foreign diplomats, the Free French, Poles, Czechs, Norwegians and later Americans, and lapses were not uncommon, the presence of many beautiful young girls of obscure parentage in secretarial jobs (the prettier they were, the more they seemed able to escape being recruited into the services) also facilitated the throwing of large parties where diplomatic alcohol made behaviour a secondary issue. When the Americans came in large numbers, in 1943, their appearance signalled the mushrooming of private clubs, dozens of them, in beautifully appointed houses, safely a distance from London (but easily reached by car). To these clubs diplomats also were admitted, and there was much gaiety and dancing, to keep up the morale of our brave fighters.

In the end England remains for me, not those dinners at the Dorchester, or at the Czardas restaurant; not the dressed-up affairs at the Allied Club, but first and last the wonderful people of England, whom I finally did get to know, in spite of this curious (and to me boring in the extreme) diplomatic life. I began a series of visits to factories in the Midlands, to the A.T.S. and the W.A.A.F.s and the barrage balloon service. All of this was sustaining, nourishing, because it made sense. I saw the ordinary working women of England, streaming to work in the dank, stark mornings, working at night, manning their machines, hair tucked under caps. I visited their canteens and had cups of tea. And I would have loved to go on and on with this, for it was so interesting, so instructive. Bombed sites, nurseries, a university or two; the massive recruitment and utilization of women everywhere to do very hard jobs; the organization and the cheerfulness, the stolidity of the women on the night shifts; this was the true measure of the English people, and not the cocktails at the embassies, nor the drawling women with precisely dyed hair and indistinct age, doing a job I could not quite understand. But there were of course splendid exceptions, women of great wealth and beauty, who really scrubbed the floors of hospitals, manned engines, did dangerous work and never spoke about it – and these I yearned to know. And some of them spoke of the social injustice which existed in England, and which the war had revealed.

The evacuation of three-quarters of a million slum children from London and the larger cities to the rural areas had uncovered rottenness, squalor, under-nourishment; deformed and stunted children, physically and mentally conditioned by an environment little better than in any Asian country. Two women I met, aghast at the revelation, spoke to me of their efforts to abolish these conditions. 'After the war the slums must no longer exist.' In all these things, the names of women, the actions of women, held my attention; as a result I fretted more, condemned as I was to what seemed a purposeless life. And such was the persuasive strength of my feelings that for a short while, even Pao appeared shaken. He even went so far as to suddenly consider giving up his post, and studying ... economics!

Someone then introduced to us a man named Owen, a short, bespectacled man, with great sense. We contemplated taking extracurricular lectures at the London School of Economics, and Owen seemed to encourage us. But Pao was not really able to study; he never read for pleasure, or to instruct himself, but only with the aim of making an impression, or advancing his career. Very soon it was obvious that he would not change course. I never tried to change him again; but in me the desire to become a doctor, never more than in abeyance, gave me no rest. I was almost obsessed now with a compulsion to end the medical studies I had begun; and all that I saw round me only increased this urge.

And so once again I was disjointed in time and place, in what I wanted to do and what I was doing; and there was no reconciliation within myself. Only Yungmei, her growing up, was a sureness, a fixed responsibility, understood and accepted. The other duties of my position augmented daily in futility. I saw myself captive of these tremendously absorbing and irremediable trivia to be performed, social·calls to make, teas to be taken, small talk to be exchanged. Eating and drinking at Prunier's, the Savoy, the Ritz, the Dorchester, with other diplomats, hearing Lady Thus and Lord So declare that I had been perfectly charming, with that gracious patronizing air and tone I was becoming allergic to – unreal, absurd hypocrisy! I felt bleak and dazed: 'What is the purpose of all this?' A party with its loud haw-haws flattened my spirit, increased my restlessness.

After the first two months at Egham (where I took riding lessons twice a week from our neighbour, to master some craft other than party-going), Pao insisted that Yungmei should be put into a nursery – for he said another Chinese couple had done so with their child – in order to free me adequately for social functions. Also he wanted to be more in London. We sought and found a flat in Welbeck Street, a grand affair on the seventh floor of Welbeck House, fairly cheap and all furnished at considerable expense with heavy, gothic furniture, all genuine carved oak, with velvet draperies, a grand piano, carpets on the floor. And only two guineas a week more than the cottage at Egham.

There was a host of problems. I was servantless, unable to clean and cook and queue and look after Yungmei, and attend to diplomatic life as well. I could not find anyone to look after her. This Chinese Embassy couple had suggested a nursery. Their child was in one, and very happy; London was unhealthy for children 'with the bombings'. I gave in, and we put Yungmei in a nursery school a little way out of

London. She had been there a fortnight when I went to see her, for I could not sleep, thinking of her boring the night with wide open eyes. I found her playing in the small backyard of the nursery, which was really a small cottage taking about a dozen children. She had become fatter, and looked well. She stared at me, and then I took her hand and the matron said: 'Show your mummy your room.' We went in to look at her little cot, along with two other children's cots in a room, and Yungmei opened a drawer and said, 'Look, Mummy, I put my things here ...,' and then suddenly she began to weep and clung to me, crying 'Mummy don't go,' and I too began to weep, and I took her back with me. Bombing or no bombing, whatever happened, her weeping was more than I could bear. 'You'll stay with me, you'll stay with me,' I said, 'don't cry, I'll be there, you'll stay.' There would be no nursery school as long as I could manage to have her with me, whatever other people did or said. But my Chinese friends thought this strange; their child loved the nursery school and it was very difficult getting someone to look after a child in London. And indeed it was.

Soon it was autumn, and then winter of 1942. News of the war in Africa superseded everything else. There was El Alamein. I cooked and cleaned and queued, and Pao brought his friends to the flat and they left glasses all over and asked for food at midnight. I became gaunt with tiredness, and also with the deep restless anger within myself at the pointlessness of my life. I was not a good housekeeper; I did not *want* to be; once again, my instinct told me that this was *not* what I ought to do, and that I was losing myself doing it. Today, I am a very good housekeeper, because there *is* meaning to it, I do it as a corollary, a hobby, now that I can also do the work I want to do.

I kept on advertising for a nanny, for a cook. None was to be found. They were either in the services, or in the factories. Finally I obtained a very old nanny, who insisted she must spend the summer at Bognor Regis. She did nothing but dress Yungmei, take her for walks, put her to bed. I had to cook for her, bring her her breakfast in her bedroom. After three weeks she told me she was used to better things. I got another one; she whispered to herself as she paced the rooms, and boiled carrots in milk. At night I could hear her outside my bedroom door, shuffling and talking to herself. She was going to take Yungmei out for a walk without a coat; fortunately I saw her come out of the house with the coatless child and stopped her. 'The child is cold, you must put on her coat.' A little while later, I heard her run a bath and rushed into the bathroom in time to stop her lifting Yungmei into a scalding bath full of almost boiling water; then I knew she was insane and fired her. A week later I saw her, in her nightgown, pacing in front of Selfridge's. I hope someone did realize that she was insane, and took care of her; but in those cold, hard days of early winter everyone was so busy, there was so much tiredness along with the fortitude. Life was hard in London with its dull skies, its blackouts, and I could no longer laugh at the protective balloons of the barrage, dancing their static ballets in their thousands in the sky.

After the crazy woman went I was again without anyone to look after Yungmei; and since I could not leave her alone at night I could not go out; yet Pao wanted me to go with him to receptions. In those early days no one had as yet commented on my looks; with perfect politeness the British accepted everything Pao said, even if they knew it was quite untrue. Even if they could *see* I was Eurasian, they did not say anything. Hence Pao was convinced that he was believed, and since I was accounted 'decorative', in spite of my sometimes inconvenient forthrightness, we were 'popular'.

It was, of course, nearly *de rigueur* for Pao to call on many of the British military, and thus we met many a household name, pleasant occasions. One of the more exciting ones was Captain Liddell Hart, a tall gangling man who spoke quickly and well and was utterly without self-consciousness. It was impossible to have only a casual acquaintance with Liddell Hart, for he tore right into one, impetuous, discursive, arms and legs flying – with unconcealed fire and swift, biting arguments, he would talk passionately of his favourite subject, war. We also called on the far less popular General Fuller, who lived in semi-retirement, because his ideas were accounted too near to those practised by the military in Germany, and who had a German wife. Fuller was very highly regarded by Chiang Kaishek, probably because of this alleged affinity; Pao called on him, and told him that Chiang had been given his books to read by his German advisers.

It was while I was floundering in a quandary of domesticity, unrelieved by social scrambling, that, miraculously, Mabel Marcham-Gillam, to be known as Gillie, materialized. She had been recommended to Pao by an English officer, a Sandhurst classmate. Gillie had looked after his children. And it was Gillie who for years afterwards cared for Yungmei when I could not. She was, could only be, the product of this class-ridden English society, where the nanny, the governess, is an indispensible adjunct whose place is determined by all that was unwritten yet practised in an England still imperial until 1945. Gillie's whole life was given to other people's children and when she came to me, I had no idea that she was, also, an essential part of the educational system for the young of the ruling class.

'I hope you don't walk the corridors at night and I *do* hope that you don't talk to yourself,' I said to Gillie at our first meeting. By now nannies, with their navy hats and coats and flattish shoes and gloves, looked to me potential for repressed insanity. Gillie said no, she didn't walk the corridors at night. 'When do you take your bath?' I asked next. (The crazy nanny had run up to three baths a day.) Some years later, Gillie was to remind me of this, saying she thought me very odd; but she decided to give me a try, and this was because she saw Yungmei. One look was enough for Gillie, as it had been for me.

And this indeed saved Yungmei; for she was getting malnourished, her appetite poor, eating at all times of the day, recalcitrant and whining. The two unsatisfactory nannies had almost deprived her of food, I was not always there to watch. When Gillie came everything fell into place; Yungmei was well looked after, her clothes clean, she was happy, and she began to speak the careful, pretty speech of the top social set. Gillie did more: she helped me with the cooking and the cleaning and the marketing; through her stabilizing presence I at last also got a char, a very good one, who did the whole flat three times a week, and was the most honest and hard-working person one could find.

And now, bouncing up again, to occupy my mind I started taking Russian lessons twice a week for an hour at the Berlitz School in Oxford Street near where we lived. And this was because of Stalingrad, the enormous and heroic defence by the people of that great city, which fired my imagination. Avidly I read, devoured all I could about the Russian campaigns.

There were three of us in the Russian class, two men and myself. In the reticent British manner we sat round the table and never spoke to each other, and I never knew the names of the other two. One of them dropped out after a few weeks.

I remember our teacher well, he looked so much like Lenin's pictures of Lenin, but with a pair of glasses added; he had a small beard, fiery white; he was in love with his own language, and became

263

very irate when we stumbled; I learned quickly with him. However, when Pao heard that it was a MAN who taught me, he put an end to Berlitz.

Through a notice in *The Times* I then obtained a woman teacher, Mrs Kirilova, a dumpy, charming person, extremely untidy, but bursting with high spirits. We spent much time reading poetry, and I went once or twice to her small, overfurnished and very dusty flat. I did not learn much Russian, but I did learn to laugh in instalments; she was the instalment, and I had my twice-weekly light-heartedness, away from the obsession of Pao's now returning gloom and rages. It was at Mrs Kirilova's that I met a very nice Scotswoman, Mrs Cluny, who owned an enormous castle and lands near Aberdeen and took ballet lessons in London. Some two years later, after Pao had left England, and for a short holiday, I was to take Yungmei and Gillie up to Aberdeen for a fortnight at Mrs Cluny's castle.

Mrs Cluny was tall, lean, blonde, with a marvellous figure (due to the ballet) and a whimsical, uncommon mind. Altogether kind, wealthy enough to do what she liked, she loved animals and kept a mob of them in her park; Shetland ponies, any number of dogs and cats, turtles, peacocks, turkeys, sheep, and a favourite duck, with only one leg, who slept on a satin cushion in her magnificent bedroom. Mrs Cluny also bred bulls, and won prizes. Our stay in Aberdeen coincided with the University of Aberdeen Students' Rag Day, a gay rampage of the streets in which we got whirled off into the crowds. It was so much like the Brussels University of my youth, where on one day of the year, St Verhaeren's Day, the city came under bondage to students, some of whom broke a few windows, but apart from a great consumption of beer, did little harm.

I have some photographs of this happy fortnight at Aberdeen, and one of them is of Mrs Cluny with her duck, both sitting up, she in her bed with its lofty canopy and draperies, a regal affair, and it sitting up straight on its blue satin cushion by her side.

Though the stipend of a Chinese military attaché was small, we managed at first quite well, and even gave large and well-attended cocktail parties, but could not manage more than two a year, for it cost something like £150 to £200 every time. The Chinese diplomats mostly preferred to live in Finchley or cheaper districts, and did not entertain lavishly. Most of them saved as much foreign exchange as possible (which later came in handy when the Chiang regime crumbled and they were left to fend for themselves). However, in our urge to do well I went to great pains to entertain properly. A dinner in honour of General le Gentilhomme, who represented Free France, cost £70 and was an utter disaster, due to the weather. That day the thick brown peasoup fog, which, with its shades of gold, gave one a warm womblike feeling of enclosed solitude, chose to come down upon us. There were to be sixteen for dinner, round the enormous carved oak table with its gothic chairs covered in *petit point*. I had hired a Chinese cook, the best in London; one who cooked delicious food but left a vast mess in the kitchen. That night the gas, always at low pressure in wartime in London, was uncommonly unco-operative; scarcely a blue flicker issued from the enormous gas cooker. In order to make the living-room less austere, I had tried to get some sort of fire going in the vast marble chimney; and had been sold some pebbly coke pellets which, I had been told, would give a splendid flame; there were no logs to be had.

Hopefully I piled the fuel in the grate, hopefully lit the accumulated newspaper and coke. The first guests began to arrive; despite the fog, all had found their way; the Chinese ambassador, Dr Wellington Koo, the French guest of honour, General le Gentilhomme, other distinguished guests ... There were drinks; and then we proceeded to the table. The soup came, and slowly the fog and the smoke from my coke amalgam, instead of going up the chimney began to seep out into the room. By the first course not only was everyone coughing discreetly but we could only perceive each other dimly through the sleazy smoke and fog mixture; by dessert time, even the valiant and expert General le Gentilhomme's conversation began to flag as he stabbed at the *bombe Général de Gaulle* (a confection of the Chinese cook) with unsure hand. Dr Wellington Koo, whose eyesight was poor, when we went into the living-room for coffee, rose to shake my hand again; he had mistaken me for a new guest. After that gruesome experience, we tried to entertain at restaurants; but the bills came very high.

Not all my parties were disasters, some were even accounted outstanding successes. But the sensation of utter futility remained and grew. I was being thrust away from thinking into a bedlam without end (even if it was polite bedlam, all noises offstage); all I did was a waste of time, irrelevant to the real issues. This despondency became worse and worse, and finally unbearable. The war in the desert, Tobruk, Stalingrad, the carnage and madness, and China, the China of 1942, in which only inflation grew, and famine – all this came true to me, pricking my conscience. Only when I got away from being 'diplomatic', in the overcrowded slow trains, always late; among the roar of machines, with the hefty working women in rows, like automatons, and the syrupy music dripping upon them; in the freezing weather in the Manchester slums, where I was walked round to see a university resettlement scheme and a factory, and some A.T.S. units, did I feel real. And this unrest, this growing trauma, what was it but the hiding capsule of an inarticulate truth? To use an American expression, I could not identify with the self I gave an imitation of being, and the harder I tried, the more intolerable I became to myself.

Wellington Koo, who had been Ambassador in Washington, had now been transferred to London. His wife, the daughter of the Sugar King of Java, followed him after a few months. Her first appearance in London, in a Fifth Avenue hat and sables, was startling. Huilan Koo, for such was her name, was informal and therefore controversial. She had great spirit and temper, and had collaborated in a book, her autobiography, published in the United States, which her husband spent a lot of money to withdraw from circulation.

She was our Ambassadress, and for a while we came together fairly often. I was very taken with her dogs, and on that account some sort of friendship grew between us. Huilan was entertaining and had a great fund of stories about people and places. When we were together the Pekinese dogs, restless and full of fun like children, kept us amused. They awoke in me a great childhood nostalgia.

Every afternoon in the Central Park in Peking where my sisters and I played as children, a large, stout eunuch walked past along the sycamore-shaded avenue, carrying the smallest of his Pekinese puppies, while a dozen others frolicked about him.

One spring he was there with three new puppies, a tiny one like a flame, all bronze and red-gold, with a tail like a goldfish, and two black-and-white ones; marvellously they pranced about, how brave their bark, as they worried with diminutive mouths the legs of the benches! Old men carrying their birds for a saunter stopped to admire them. They were worth a lot of money; perhaps two or three hundred silver dollars each. Intelligent as a monkey, brave as a lion, with the paeony-in-full-blossom tail of a goldfish and eyes like crystal balls, such was the Pekinese, a hunting dog for the Manchu emperors. And such was our childish enthusiasm for the puppies that the next day, which was a Saturday, my father was persuaded to come with us to the park, to see the dogs. We awaited the eunuch, and he duly appeared, portly, courteous, in a long blue robe, with his diminutive and wonderful and precious dogs gambolling about him; all three puppies ran about, bouncing like feathers, their tails flowing. Tiza and I could no longer contain ourselves and ran forward, with hands outstretched, to caress them. Pekinese are indomitable dogs, and these were not afraid of our carrying and hugging. Meanwhile Father spoke with the eunuch, who told him that he was going to sell one of the black-and-white ones to an English lady. 'She is the Englishwoman who goes by past Tung Chang Street every afternoon in her landau,' said Papa.

This was one of the sights of Peking: every afternoon, in a landau, with coachman and grooms in green-and-white livery, the Englishwoman, hatted, veiled and upright like a queen, went for a drive; and in the carriage with her were her pet Pekinese. When the carriage arrived near Hatamen Street one of the grooms took the dogs out for a walk to relieve themselves, and then the cortege went home.

I never knew the name of this Englishwoman, for she belonged to another world, but was reminded of the Pekinese in the park, and the landau, and its occupant, when with Huilan Koo and the Pekinese in London we sailed majestically about Hyde Park in the magnificent Rolls-Royce of the Chinese Embassy. Huilan Koo told me about her grandfather, who had been a Taiping, had revolted against the emperor, and to escape being flayed alive had escaped to Java in a junk, there to make a fortune. His son, her father, was now the Sugar King of Java, and had so many children he could not count them, nor could he count his money, and he had bought a palace for Huilan Koo in Peking. All this she had written in a book, and all this her husband, Wellington Koo, had suppressed by buying up and destroying the whole edition ...

In the autumn my friend Liu Hualan came to stay with me.

Hualan's mother was Polish, her Chinese father a lawyer who

lived and worked in Russia for many years. Hualan was in England now, studying. Later she returned to China, and when Liberation came, remained there, where I have seen her again year after year.

Hualan was short, had a strong Russian accent to her English, always dressed in black or grey suits with a white blouse, wore severe low-heeled shoes. Her hands were rough with cold, she had a low-pitched voice, always a book in her bag. She smoked a good deal; her fingers were brown with nicotine.

We had been at school together at the Peking convent, although not in the same class; now there was about her the same seriousness and solidity as she had had at school. We went to Regent's Park to sit in the summer sun while the children played around us. Several times she went with me to the Allied Circle or to parties; but she disliked these occasions, at which she was stone mute.

Hualan lived by night better than by day. With the blackout curtains well drawn she would read until three or four in the morning; in the ashtray by her side the stubs heaped up; in the morning she would get up and make coffee for all of us.

One night round about two a.m. there was some pretty bad bombing; I prepared to go downstairs to the basement with Yungmei wrapped in a blanket. The janitor thought it best, as the flak was rather impressive, and he had come to tell me so. He was a dour Scotsman with a moustache and a military bearing. I knocked at Hualan's door, light peered from under it. 'You must come down, Hualan, we are going to the basement.' 'I'm washing my hair,' she replied. She had started the habit of washing often, face and hands and hair; she complained that her skin and hair were dirty or greasy or both. 'Don't wash your hair so often, Hualan, it will make it worse.' 'I've got to, it gets so greasy,' she replied. She continued washing her hair throughout the bombing, which was very intensive that night. She was utterly fearless, completely dedicated.

Another visitor to our Welbeck flat was Yeh Kungchao, George Yeh, then councillor at the Chinese Embassy, in charge of Press and information. He was English-trained, a scholar in both Chinese and English. He had been refused a room in Singapore in 1941, at the Raffles Hotel, because he was Chinese; and this he often referred to, for as a Cambridge Blue, with a double first, the humiliation had been telling. He retaliated with a mordant, biting, sarcastic manner, which delighted the British. He drank whisky with Pao and the hours of night went by. One day I asked him if it was true that everyone at the Chinese Embassy talked ill of me. 'Are you crazy?' he said. 'Why?' 'Nothing,' I replied. George Yeh made fun of everyone, including himself, but also at times struck the attitude of the man with a secret wound; I liked listening to him, but in the end he was to let me down, refusing to talk to Pao as a friend and ask him to desist from his campaigns (there is no other word for it) against me.

In 1948, George Yeh went to Formosa, following Chiang Kaishek. An English friend who was with him wrote to me: 'The precious antiques taken from the Imperial Palaces in Peking in 1932 by the Kuomintang are also being packed. "We are taking them to Formosa with us; we might need to sell them, who knows," George Yeh told me, grinning.' In 1949, in a bitter letter which I preserved, George Yeh wrote to me: 'All is lost ... I now have to eat and drink with, and serve, people I profoundly despise.' But he had made his choice, and continued in it. Thus each of us fashions his own fate, and to blame others for what happens is otiose and useless.

The writer Hsiao Chien, who later returned to China, and whom I met in Peking in 1956 (he was denounced as a rightist in 1957, and has since been living quietly in a provincial post), was also an occasional visitor to Welbeck Street. He had published *A Harp with a Thousand Strings*, and used in it an excerpt from *Destination Chungking*. He gave a copy of the book to Pao, with a dedication, asking for Pao's 'valuable criticism'. He forgot to give a copy to me. His book is still in my collection today.

S. I. Hsiung, who wrote *Lady Precious Stream*, was also about, in a long gown with a mandarin look, and Chiang Yee with his *Silent Traveller* series and their delightful water-colour drawings. All these writers came at one time or another, but I never became very friendly with them. Hsiao Chien was a great favourite of Dorothy Woodman of the *New Statesman*, who thought a great deal of him. Hsiao Chien's way to her heart had been a stray kitten which he told me he had rescued from drowning in the sea, swimming with the kitten on his head to safety. It was, he averred, an 'oriental' kitten. In reality he had bought the kitten in a shop to present to kind-hearted Dorothy, who loved animals so much that she had become, and remained, a staunch vegetarian.

In the summer we were presented to the King and Queen at Windsor Castle, together with the Czech Ambassador and his wife. We did not

know we were to meet King George VI and Queen Elizabeth until
after a lunch to which we had been invited with some friends in
attendance upon the Royal Family. When after lunch we were told,
the Czech Ambassador's wife became slightly nervous and whispered
to me, 'I have no gloves ... Can you lend me gloves?' 'Only one,' I
whispered back, 'can you manage with one?'

I owned no jewellery except the opal ear-rings purchased in India
and mounted in New York, and a wedding ring. For formal occasions,
however, such as parties at the Allied Club, or to go dining at some
embassy, I was able to borrow the diamonds of my friend Phyllis Tai.

Phyllis was a Chinese girl from the West Indies. Her sister, Eileen
Tai, was a ballet dancer in London. Epstein had immortalized Eileen
in a bronze later exhibited as part of a collection in an Aid to China
Fund drive. Eileen was to return to China, and today is a director of
the ballet school in Peking.

Phyllis was a superb dancer, a wonderful hostess. She could make
any party go. She had a luxuriant sense of small talk, an abundance of
very black and slightly curly hair, a tall lithe figure, wonderful legs,
lovely Chinese dresses. She had married a Singapore Chinese, a very
wealthy man, and lived there until the fall of Singapore in February
1942. She was one of the very few Chinese who escaped on the boats
'reserved for the whites', and just in time. This was possible through
the sacrifice of an English friend, who gave up his boat passage for her,
and then was never heard of again. When Phyllis left Singapore she
took with her a small face towel and her diamonds.

She landed in England, found some relatives, and now had become
a great ornament of the Allied Club parties where diplomats of all
nations congregated.

I fell under the spell of her gay chatter, her willingness to entertain
everyone, to listen to the most doddery general with beaming face. I
did not have to talk or to pretend interest when she was there; I could
leave my more testy guests to her and know they would be enchanted
by her attention to their witticisms. With Phyllis even Pao was amiable,
although later he turned against her, accused her of 'unvirtue', and
forbade me to invite her; but Phyllis laughed and dropped in all the
same.

It was Phyllis who suggested that I should wear her diamonds.
'You're too severe-looking,' she cried. 'All your clothes are too strict.
I'll lend you my diamonds for parties.' And in a little cardboard box,

she left me £12,000 worth of gems to use when I wanted. For a whole two weeks I wore her diamonds and felt matchless and different. 'Are you sure you don't want to keep them longer?' said Phyllis. 'They are yours any time you want to borrow them.' And so I wore them when we went to Windsor Castle.

On our return from Windsor, Pao was elated; he had many photos printed and sent to China. The idea that shaking hands with a constitutional monarch indicated a personal success in his career was emphasized, and perhaps it was true that this presentation was, socially, a great step forward. But I could not think of it in that way; for when thought of in such a manner, the agreeable afternoon, the sun, the delicate pastel of the Queen's coat and hat, but above all, the very natural sweet smile of George VI became effaced – and for me it was this very nice smile, the pleasant way in which the King had asked, 'How do you like our weather?' which I was happy about, and not the thought of success.

My first meeting with Jonathan Cape, who later was to become a very staunch friend as well as my publisher, was one afternoon in late 1942, when after receiving a letter from him, I went to 30 Bedford Square to see him. Jonathan was tall, white-haired, and extremely handsome. In his office with the fine ceiling, the walls panelled with books, I felt relieved for a short while of the enormous tensions building up in me.

Jonathan wanted to talk to me about publishing *Destination Chungking*. I told him that I had not actually written the book all by myself, that it was a collaboration. He replied that most first books were collaborations of one kind or another. I gazed at the shelves behind him loaded with authors' works; was I really to take a place among these? 'But I can't write,' I said, 'I am not a writer, all I want is to be a doctor.' 'So long as you feel at times inclined to put things down on paper,' replied Jonathan, who then took me to lunch at the Étoile restaurant, which he favoured. I was very nervous; I was lunching alone with a man ... what would Pao say if he knew? I had told Pao nothing of this, and I begged Jonathan also not to write to my flat, that I would ring him up if I wanted to discuss anything. But it was over a year before I saw him again, as I did not dare to ring up.

As in Chungking, a captive of words, haunted by imagined ghosts of rumour, bent on doing himself evil, Pao began again his wayward, contradictory, almost psychopathic persecution of me.

As Chiang would order a general to advance, and two hours later tell him to retreat, and yet another few hours later tell him to prepare to attack, so Pao bellowed wrathfully at me: 'You must not talk to these people' – 'I don't want you to laugh' – 'You must not look so sad' – 'You must refuse to dance' – 'You must dance' – 'Why don't you talk?' etc. etc. Thus, once again, he fashioned a world of phantasms about me. He also now began to take offence at imagined slights offered to him, and on the grounds that my English was better and that I could 'translate' his grievances for him, sought my collaboration in pursuing grudges. He had been placed in a lower position than his rank warranted at a party; I must write a letter about it for him ... When the British officer, all unsuspecting, came to apologize after receiving the letter, Pao told him, 'My wife was offended,' which was untrue, for I had not even noticed. I therefore began, once again, to keep the most innocuous things secret. My lunch with Jonathan was certainly a secret, but the very fact that a harmless lunch had to be kept secret made me tense, nervous; and thus from small episode to small episode, the phantasms grew to monster proportions. By the summer of 1943 I was heading for a total nervous breakdown.

Twelve

DESTINATION CHUNGKING was published in England in autumn 1942. Pao was told of it by Major Kerr, one of the British liaison officers, who praised the book. It was in keeping with the times, the war, the 'allied solidarity' – all those formulas by which it was possible to toast Chiang Kaishek, Stalin, and His Majesty the King of England without incongruity. It drew favourable reviews. The book's publication coincided with a renewed interest in China through the China Campaign Committee and the Aid to China Fund, and it was in this connection that we became acquainted with Stafford Cripps and his wife Isobel, with Kingsley Martin, Dorothy Woodman, and Margery Fry, all involved in various activities concerned with China. They were rather different from the Marchioness of W ——, Lady F., Lady B., the military brass and the diplomats whom we met sedulously and *de rigueur*. The Marchioness terrified me, Lady F. and Lady B. crooned over Pao, and the Dowager Lady M. was to play a rather odd godmother role (though with the best will in the world) in my relationship with Pao.

There was for me much more immediate sympathy with the Cripps, with Dorothy and Kingsley and Margery Fry, than with the others; they had a social conscience, were not afraid of intelligent conversation. Stafford Cripps was still considered, and spoken of, at that time, in the very conservative circles in which we drifted, as an almost irreligious extremist, a 'left-wing' man. But with the strain of war, the changing times, and the talk of the Beveridge plan, this reputation was giving way to appreciation. Stafford had been to Chungking to see Chiang; he was probably better able to judge events in China than many other visitors. Pao warned me at first not to have anything to do with the Cripps. 'They are communists.' He then realized that in English society, the Cripps could by no means be called such, and suddenly decided that we should know them. As for Dorothy Woodman and Kingsley Martin, Pao disliked them, made fun of them, and was charming to them.

The first time we went to see Stafford and Isobel Cripps was at their flat in Whitehall Court, in the winter of 1942. It was an enormous flat, well furnished, but it had no kitchen. This did not inconvenience the Cripps; they were both vegetarians, did not believe in cooked meals, and kept their food in a safe in the bathroom.

The Cripps had asked us to tea; Isobel opened the door. Tall, ample but graceful, soft-treading. Isobel achieved the harmony of very blue eyes and a mild voice; she was the most self-controlled yet tenacious woman I ever met in England. She was always dressed in greys and blues, and her apparent lack of warmth, which was shyness, put off people, who thought her forbidding; but she was actually so scrupulous that she was given to withholding judgment and expression of emotion, sometimes too long, in a strenuous search for impartiality. Isobel believed that the emanations of thought, like radio waves, could in themselves promote soothing and healing influences from afar, and she held that the spiritual component of all illness was of enormous importance. In this she was probably instinctively right. The Cripps believed in health foods, and in proper posture as remedy for chronic disease. To me Isobel was always warm, understanding, and kind. Her letters, full of wisdom, reflected her steadfastness. Her tenacity, always dispassionate, got the better of opposition to her well-balanced aims.

I also liked Stafford, tall, carrying his head very high (or so it seemed to me), almost near the ceiling, with its elongate features and great stubborn chin. He was even more shy than his wife. Brilliant in talk, with bright concise shafts of wit, he had a scientific approach to facts which did not yield to other interpretations; and he was unbending and rigorously exact in his statements. From him emanated a total integrity and therefore a slight greyness, because his earnest endeavour was sometimes misunderstood and his uncompromising sentences were repeated without embellishment. He had thus told Chiang Kaishek, on his visit to China, a few coldly severe truths, and thereby became thoroughly unpopular with Chiang.

Archibald Clark Kerr, the British Ambassador in Chungking, was a friend of Stafford, and he too came to tea, that day. The conversation was about the Commonwealth and its future, about a projected international organization (later the United Nations), about the war in Africa; Stafford repeating that things must *not* be the same, and talking about the social iniquities which the war had brought out in England. In Asia, too, there would be challenging situations after the war. 'Who do you think is going to win?' Pao asked, with his eyebrows up as if this were a bona fide question. 'Oh we shall win, of course,' Stafford replied very casually, and Isobel poured milk into Pao's cup of tea. But this was not what Pao had meant at all.

Isobel Cripps was active in the Aid to China Fund, of which she was President. There were such functions as speeches, bazaars, exhibitions and collections of money on the streets; but there were also internecine disputes. How much of the money should go to the Chiang side for medical ambulances and aid, how much to the Yenan side? A more militant organization, the China Campaign Committee, with Dorothy Woodman, allotted part of the money to a hospital on the Yenan side. Isobel told me how difficult it was to remain 'impartial'. A great variety of people were in the Fund, duchesses and mayoresses, as well as trade union members and Labour politicians; the fear of 'communism' was strong among some of them and all through the years the question of allotting funds was a difficult one.

Kingsley Martin, Dorothy Woodman, Margery Fry, J. B. Priestley and his wife, invited us to dinner at a Chinese restaurant in Soho. Before meeting Dorothy, I had heard about her from Pao. She was intensely interested in Asian affairs, whether it was China, Indonesia, Burma or India. This immense zest for our enormous continent, her pertinent and outspoken defence of national causes against diehard colonialism, was to earn for her the nickname of Mother Asia. She was a splendid, big person, and though a vegetarian, a cooking one, and she cooked magnificently. She was inclined to put on weight, and would then go on a dieting spree and reappear twenty pounds lighter. At the restaurant, she congratulated me on *Destination Chungking*. 'Who told you?' 'A little bird told me,' Dorothy replied in that mock coy manner which she used to disguise her probing intelligence. I liked her very much.

I was also happy to meet J. B. Priestley, having read *The Good Companions*, and our talk was easy. For a short while I was unimpeded by self-conscious restraints and covert looks towards Pao (wondering what would happen when I got home if he had not liked my behaviour). We talked, and soon Kingsley Martin with his wit charmed all of us. His Mephistophelian looks, and the goodness of his heart, his sensitive and immediate recoil from any ugliness, endeared him to me. For some years, both Dorothy and Kingsley were placed in a small pantheon of my own, composed of superior beings, whom I would never catch up with, whose opinions on art, music, gardening, politics, I retained to mull over in the distressing agonized hours of my inadequacy – and they were the majority of my waking hours.

No such feelings however, haunted me with Margery Fry; and this is a tribute to that great woman, whose approach was so lively and unaffected that one only discovered her gradually. She was, of all present, the least pontificating, the least impressive at first sight. Sitting opposite Priestley, eating her rice and spring rolls, with application, if no appetite, Margery spoke mordantly and kindly, grey-brown eyes twinkling, peering in the dishes, an ageless young girl, an elfin with blazing grey hair aureoling that remarkable face. It was only much later that I realized the quality of her conversation as a continuity of small masterpieces. Twenty-five years later, I was to note the resemblance between Bertrand Russell and Margery Fry, when I went to call on the Earl and found him, at ninety-two, nimble and full of talk. It was a kinship not of feature but of spirit; a cherubic uncompromising candour.

I blossomed, spoke with no preoccupation or fear of 'what would Pao say', or what I would have to pay in ill-treatment for being myself,

275

and I remember that party as sparkling, and it was only as we left the restaurant to return within that jail of cowed and sullen hours, when all depended on Pao's frown, that my thoughts and desires fell back, became once again insubstantial shadows, even unto myself.

I re-entered that twilight region of morbid suspicion which gradually, massively, cut me off from the real world. With obsessive terror, hour upon hour, I doubted, suspected, felt that what had happened had not happened. I knew the felted, fetid otherness that haunts, the havoc without cause, that makes one not quite there, the compunction at every step, the hallucinations of half-heard sentences, the nightmares. I saw people's mouths move, heard words, shook hands, answered, laughed at some remark, and all the time between the actions, gestures, words, was this glazed substance called doubt. Unreality. Was this *really* being said? Had I not *heard* wrong? What would be the *right* answer? Was there *another* meaning, one I had not fathomed? I would lie awake for hours, going over and over again all that had been said because Pao would ask me to explain this or that, and I knew that if I did faithfully retail to him what was said, what was answered, he would pick a quarrel, find something suspect. He would ask me why I had said this or that, and there would follow hours of cross-examination, and later I would refuse to see people again ... And so I went out in terror, returned in terror, hesitated to take part in any slightly more intelligent conversation for fear of the reprisals, later ...

At the end of this particular occasion, however, Margery had asked me to her house at 48 Clarendon Road, Holland Park.

When I rang the bell a week later Margery was already peering through the large bay window giving on to a small garden at the front. The house was narrow, with many doors, embellished with paintings of Chinese landscapes with tall pagodas and hills; two Han bronzes on the mantelpiece, many books about. Margery, exuberant in her dateless dresses, with a brood of necklaces and the lock of steel-glint hair falling forward over her eye as her head moved with that prompt birdlike jerk, thawed me, though the house was cold. We walked on the large green behind the house where she watched birds in their due seasons; the gas fire was of medium size and inefficient in the hearth, but Margery radiated vibrancy, life.

She knew both Liao Hungying, my friend in Chengtu, and also Miss S., had discovered in both of them treasures of charm and goodness; for she was ever immensely interested in people as they were, and loved their foibles as well as their virtues. Her enormous vocabulary range, the way her mind rampaged boisterously, going from one topic to another but always keeping to the main endeavour of her talk – back to the fundamental, precise beginning, whether art, literature, birds, China, but anecdoting endlessly as she went on – cast a spell upon me. Prison reform, the education of women, Margery's undiluted China experiences, all went through the room like a flock of happy ponies through the mild landscapes painted on the doors. I was more than captivated; I knew this to be the kind of talk and doing which, like a transfusion of blood, exalted me. Margery was my kind and from her I could learn so much ...

And yet, it was not so; there was an essential difference; but the approximation seemed to stir me into telling her of my ambition to study medicine – an ambition only increased by time and difficulties.

After that I began to drop in at 48 Clarendon Road about once a fortnight, to have tea with Margery, or lunch. All she said was beautiful to listen to, gorgeous sentences flowed from her, she solaced and soothed me with stories of all kinds; about her Free French friends, her sisters, her brother Roger who had died, and whose books she loaned me.

From these sunlit hours of friendship I returned to the flat in Welbeck Street, to the point where I decided against opening letters, for fear of I knew not what; where at six o'clock my heart began to beat wildly and strenuously, waiting for a footfall, booted, coming towards the flat; when even Margery became, suddenly, not Margery, but some uneasy presence, who had drawn things out of me I should never have said ...

No one knew then, not even Margery, that Pao had started ill-treating me again. The common hell of married life can only bore others. According to Pao, Isobel, even Stafford, even Kingsley and Dorothy Woodman, now made remarks to him on my behaviour ... The only one he omitted, ignored, was Margery Fry.

And now, as our circle of acquaintances and friends solidified, Pao gathered about him a group of venerable, respectable, middle-aged or slightly above middle-aged ladies, all insistent on our relaxing at week-ends in their country homes, all very fond of Pao.

The mother-to-son relationship thus established was altogether in the feudal Chinese tradition, but the unconscious identification by these respectable dowagers with a Mother Figure was never obvious to them, and neither was it to me until many years later.

The dowager Lady M. was one of these. She lived in a flat in London, surrounded by Victorian furniture, plates, silver; she gave us tea in old Georgian silver; wore a hat with feathers and beads, a distinguished, affluent and influential figure. Pao often came back from tea and a chat with Lady M. (or other, similar ladies) to tell me how much they disapproved of me. Thus he reproduced the strict pattern of the mother-in-law, who makes the life of her son's wife pure hell.

One day, he told me that Lady M. had used the word 'half-caste' about me. Greatly angered, without reflecting on Pao's mendacity, I sought out Lady M. and conveyed to her my view. The dowager was more than puzzled; I am now certain that Pao had either invented the story, or exaggerated a chance remark. Lady M. became in turn irate; she concluded that I was 'a very upsetting young woman'. If anything could convince her that I was 'not quite balanced' it was this meeting I had myself so foolishly initiated.

Yet it was true that, unconsciously, there was in many of these ladies a built-in apprehension of the 'half-caste'. The Anglo-Indian, the chi-chi, the not-quite, with its innuendo of a half-world, castigated and repelled, its wrong-side-of-the-blanket connotations ... twenty years ago this was a very prevalent feeling. The contempt for Eurasians was much more pronounced than now. All the exceptions glibly produced ('delightful fellow, his grandmother was Anglo-Indian, I believe, but he's charming, *perfectly* charming, a perfect gentleman') only confirming that cast in their eye, nuance, distance, distaste, over-compensated by extra jollity, heartiness, a determined showing that one was *not* a racialist ... The Eurasian woman was a danger: the mistress, the interloper, shame-bred-in-the-night. And when today in England people deplore miscegenation as likely to produce 'half-castes' and 'misfits', they are voicing precisely that same attitude which twenty years ago was current and outspoken. It is this prejudice which produces the misfits, and the misfits are not the Eurasians, but the others, the racialists.

The next time we went to see Lady M. she blushed with happiness at seeing Pao, and never said a word to me. The instinctive class bond, which this Kiplingesque society knew so well, made Pao more acceptable than truant-capricious me, with my odd remarks, absent-mindedness, and the label of Eurasian tagged on to me. Unconsciously,

Lady M. (among others) helped to push me into the course I was to take.

Pao brought home one evening a young woman; a Canadian, red-haired, green-eyed. He had met her at the Allied Club dance where he had gone with George Yeh. They came back and I made dinner, and while I was cooking in the kitchen he came to see what I was doing, and said: 'You must cook a good meal, because she is a woman doctor.' She was not a doctor, but a nurse, and he spent the next week-end with her, without telling me where he was. I stayed awake most of the two nights, wondering whether an accident had happened; wondering and worrying where he was; I rang up his secretary, and the Chinese naval attaché. They both assured me that they would try to find out what had happened to Pao, but I heard no more until Monday afternoon when Pao returned and fell into a rage when I told him I had rung up the naval attaché (whom he particularly disliked). Later when he had gone out to dinner (while I dissolved in tears), I discovered the photograph of the girl, with an inscription: 'From a very happy little wife', in his coat pocket. I think he had left it there deliberately.

I wept some more; it was not the fact of physical unfaithfulness, but the whole pitiful comedy it represented which seared me. And I was so tired. In the next few days the girl reappeared, had coffee with us, was taken out by Pao, and always it was impressed upon me that she was a doctor; whereas I had not been able to finish my studies.

A week later I called her on the telephone and told her that I would complain about her if she went on. She assured me that 'nothing had happened' and that it was just fooling; yes, Pao had spent the week-end with her, but nothing had happened; she had threatened, she said, to set her dog upon him; no, she was not a doctor, but her father was. And then she turned round and threatened me; her father was a very influential person and he would take steps against me ... 'you dirty Eurasian'.

She did not come again, and Pao for a few days made remarks about the weather; asked what I would like to eat, as he wanted to give me lunch. To this I opposed only silence, and he gave up, sitting on the sofa, his brows puckered, pretending to read; or closing his eyes, putting his head back and pretending to doze. We moved within the same house in a spectral aloofness, slept side by side in the large bed with its draperies and satin pompoms: rose, without saying a word to each other. And there was no way to each other, for we were frozen, each one of us acting out his private nightmare, and no deliverance in words.

And then the Dowager Lady M. came to teach me my duties as a wife. 'He has not complained, not said a word, but I can see he is very unhappy,' said she, eyeing me frostily; I replied that I wanted to study medicine and be a doctor. Her blue gaze sparkled with icy disapproval. She asked me to pray with her to God that I should 'know my duty and do my duty above all else'; she said it was the lot of Woman to put Husband and Children and Home first, before any other desire. So we prayed, or rather she did, and then she went home.

After her visit I began to measure heights, gazing from the windows of the flat down to the courtyard below. Should I kill myself? Should I leave a note? People might think that Lady M. had driven me to suicide, her reputation would suffer ... such nonsense went through my head, querulous and childish, that I laughed at it, for a moment freed; I moved away from the window, saved by that other-me for ever questioning my every word and action. For in spite of the deepening terror and incoherence (and I could feel the darkness invade me, it was there, just waiting at the corner of my eye, the monster, horned fear in a great black cape of madness, hovering) there was Yungmei, and she was life and love and beauty. I turned from the window and suddenly began to plan, collecting what shreds of coherence remained to plan well.

I arranged for Yungmei and Gillie to be away on holiday, by the sea. Gillie did not like staying in London, she was very frightened of the bombing; at night when the bombers came over she would get up and take Yungmei downstairs. She had been hinting for a good while about moving to the country, talking of those families whose children she had looked after, and who were safely away from the bombs ... and one of these kind and wealthy families did ask her to go, with Yungmei, as paying guests; and of course Gillie more than paid her way through anywhere, since she not only looked after Yungmei, but took charge of the other children as well, thus blissfully relieving harassed mothers, dazed and energetic grandmothers left alone to 'cope' with progeny, when husbands were away at war and they battled, womanfully, with rations and queues and servantless houses.

Yungmei was very fond of Gillie, happy with her, and I felt my mind so rapidly folding up that I wanted, quickly, to make Yungmei safe, even from me, to protect her, while I finally worked out my own nightmare with Pao.

Thus relieved, for a few weeks, of the worry of Yungmei and Gillie, I could now afford to be ill, afford to let go. But I waited, grappling with myself, waited for the last drop, the event which would finally precipitate me into action, and such guile and cold planning was mixed with my decision that I can never claim to have had a real illness; I was too aware at all times of the phantasmic side, but it had to be done.

And it came. Pao now demanded that the English edition of *Destination Chungking* should be stopped. He kicked and beat me for days, shouting: 'Stop it, tell the publishers to stop it.' But he did nothing himself, preferring that the onus should be on me. There was the precedent of Wellington Koo stopping his wife's book. I rang up Jonathan Cape. He had married again, and invited me to tea with his wife, Kathleen; they were putting a big brass fender, hand-beaten, round their fireplace as a fireguard. Jonathan said: 'How long has your husband been cruel to you?' I wept and wept. I was in a trance of weeping when I left. But Jonathan laughed when he heard about Wellington Koo stopping his wife's book, and of course he did nothing about mine.

It was Margery Fry whom I chose to go to, perhaps because she had said one day that if I needed rest I could come to her; she had a spare room upstairs. I rang her up. 'Margery, I am not well. Can I come to you for a few days?' She said, 'Of course, bring your toothbrush.' It was not surprising to Margery that I should say 'I am not well.' I could no longer stop crying, and the last time I had seen her the tears had rolled down my cheeks; later I would not be able to stop laughing. I remembered Miss S., and her self-cure, lying in bed for weeks until she healed. I knew that if I slept and slept, I would be well again, without doctor or pills. And this I have since practised twice in my life.

I took my toothbrush and a nightgown, but forgot a towel and a change of clothes. I left a note for Pao, saying 'I cannot stand it any more and I am going away for a few days, for rest', and left it on the table in the hall. I put the key under the mat. The janitor with the little moustache touched his cap and took me down in the lift. Pao would return, any time between five and seven, or late at night; I would not be there. I stopped myself from thinking whether there was

281

food in the ice-box. And then I was in the Tube to Holland Park, and walking up Clarendon Road, and in front of Margery's tall narrow house. And Margery was there, behind the large window, the rocks in her little rock garden seemed so familiar, and there was tea ready on a tray, and the gas fire which could not fight the cold.

I could now tell her, with big gulps of tea and milk and much incoherence, a little of everything that had taken place, and it all sounded disjointed and silly, a stream of nonsense, so that I nearly went back then, but the tears would not stop flowing.

Margery put me to bed. 'You look a wreck.' For the next week, I was to stay in bed, not getting up except for an occasional bath, and after the first three days for meals. Fears and terrors assailed me, so that I wanted the curtains drawn against the day. I would not even go downstairs to Margery's drawing-room. And Margery, that splendid and wonderful person, let me stay in bed, insisted on bringing dinner up to me that night – a mighty effort for a woman in her late sixties. And thus, selfishly, I gave in, let go, reverted to a state of childish dependence, slept.

The next afternoon, Pao arrived at 48 Clarendon Road. It was easy for him to find me; he reasoned that I could have gone only to three or four people: Isobel Cripps, Dorothy Woodman, Margery Fry. He rang Margery up. She invited him to come and see her; he came, talked with her; after he left, Margery came up to my room. 'My poor legs,' she said, for her house was all stairs and she had only one very old cook. I stared at her weepingly – there she was running up and down for me. She told me how reasonable Pao had sounded. 'Well my dear, he has agreed that you should rest here for a few days and he's promised not to bother you – he was actually quite sensible,' said Margery. He had also told her about Yungmei not being my daughter, which I had not, for I did not want to bring the child into any of this, I wanted her safe from my own woes, sheltered both from Pao and me.

I wept again. How noble and good Pao was, to allow me to rest! I would sleep a few days, get back my strength, then I would try again ... I wrote a postcard to Yungmei, as well as to Gillie.

The next morning there was a ring; it was a bouquet of flowers, yellow daisies, a splash of some red-dyed autumn leaves, from Pao. I wept again, and Margery snorted; she had recovered from what she called Pao's soft-soaping. 'I have an idea his feelings are about as genuine as this foliage,' she said. 'Tell him I am at the end of my strength, all I want is a few days' rest,' I supplicated, needlessly, and rose to put the gift in a vase by my bed.

Margery gave me books to read, those of her brother Roger Fry on Chinese Art, to take my mind off things. I refused to see a doctor, but she insisted. 'I am not ill, just mentally upset, just very very tired.' I wrote another postcard to Yungmei; every day I wrote one to her, a practice which I continued for years, whenever she was not with me.

That afternoon, rolling back on the pillows, I thought of the past. Of Pao coming back to Wuhan to fetch me; of Pao saving me from being pushed into the river in Kweilin ... he was good, noble and kind, everything was my fault ... That evening, about eight o'clock, the door bell rang. Margery was in my bedroom having an after-dinner cup of coffee with me. The blackout curtains were drawn. She went downstairs to answer the door. Then I heard a noise, heavy footsteps coming upstairs. Margery reappeared, behind her were two men in white uniform. They were male nurses, with a doctor's signed note. Upon request from Pao, I was to be consigned to a clinic for observation, as mentally deranged ... Behind the two stretcher-bearers, pink and well scrubbed and bursting with energy, precipitating himself upon me and saying in Chinese, 'Get up, I'm taking you away. Get up,' was Pao.

'Colonel Tang, you promised, you promised me to leave her in peace for a few days ... ' cried Margery. The stretcher-bearers came into the room, carefully holding the stretcher sideways, taking care not to knock the door, and stood there, with the white canvas frame between them, while I sat up in bed and started to howl. 'Take her away,' Pao ordered. He told Margery not to interfere. 'Do you know that I can have you arrested? She is my wife, I am taking her away, I can look after her.' The nurses came nearer. I cried, 'I don't want to go I don't want to go ... please don't take me away, I am so tired.' One of the male nurses said to Pao, 'I am sorry, sir, but we can't remove her against her will.' Margery said to Pao, 'Colonel Tang, let us go downstairs and talk this over.' The male nurse turned to Margery and said, 'She doesn't look crazy to me.' He spoke to his companion and they started to go down again with the same careful, heavy-treading deliberation, saying to Pao on the stairs, 'Sorry, sir, but we can't remove her, it's not right.' Then Margery said to Pao, 'Follow me, we must talk this out.' 'Is this a case of ill-treatment?' one of the male nurses asked Margery on the stairs. I did not hear her reply.

Pao started to shout at them: 'I order you to take her – I am the military attaché.' Then a policeman appeared, and he filled the door with his overcoated bulk. He said to Pao, 'Come on, please sir, let's go downstairs and talk things over,' and Pao said, 'But she's my wife, she's my wife,' and the policeman said, 'That's all right sir, but you can't take a person to hospital without her consent,' and then it looked as if Pao and the policeman would begin arguing, and I said to the policeman, 'Oh please, please, don't arrest him, he doesn't know what he's doing,' and Pao came to me and said, 'Dearest, dearest, all right, just rest here,' and tried to kiss me and I turned my face to the wall and said: 'Oh, why do you do these things, why do you do these things? It is so stupid.' And then I was laughing and could not stop and he went away. Half an hour later all was quiet, and Margery came up-stairs looking tired and strained, there were two dark folds from her nose to her chin.

The next day Margery told me that Pao had misrepresented the facts to a doctor in Wimpole Street. He had got him to sign a certifi-cate to have me removed for observation, as mentally deranged; but what Pao did not know was that English law does not allow such re-movals: although his status as diplomat had persuaded the doctor to go ahead without taking the necessary step of seeing the case (me), the male nurses used their knowledge to prevent a miscarriage of the law.

And now Pao tried to start a legal action against Margery. He had an uncanny knack for ferreting out gossip, probably helped in this by one or another of his fond dowager ladies. It appeared that some de-cades previously there had been some rumour about one of Margery's relatives, and her friendship with another woman; Margery was certainly not involved, but Pao brought the matter up as if it were Margery, and threatened an action against her, after taking 'legal' advice. 'But he is mad, your husband is quite mad, he is truly a very wicked man,' cried Margery, astonished at this viciousness.

Now Isobel Cripps, alerted by Pao (who complained to her that Margery had 'abducted' me), came to see me; this was only two days after the scene with the male nurses. The speed and the energy with which Pao pursued these activities was truly astonishing; had he nothing else to do? queried Margery. Isobel at first did not realize what had happened; and not knowing the background, she sounded (according to Margery) both annoyed and reproving on the telephone, for as president of the Aid to China Fund, and with a deep sense of responsibility, she was aware of the scandalous ramifications of what was happening. She had heard only Pao's side, and speaking to Margery on the telephone had been both stiff and cold (Pao's fatal charm again).

Isobel came to see me, and I told her my side. I said that one of the main things I could no longer stand was having to lie to everyone: for I was a Eurasian, and not pure Chinese, and Pao had made this into a shameful thing, and I could no longer live this lie. And Isobel thoughtfully said: 'But you mustn't say Eurasian, dear, it's not a nice word.' 'But I am,' I protested, 'I must say it, I am.'

That Isobel should say this, that the very word was something to be ashamed of, so strong were the feelings of caste and the racism inherent in the British upper class, I was always to remember, especially since Isobel herself was completely free from any racialism. Never was there a woman more aware of the evils of it, more strong to combat it: but she was soberly apprising me of a fact, of a prejudice that existed. 'I don't care,' I said, 'I want to say it, I want everyone to know it.'

Isobel heard me through quietly and then she said she would go to talk with Pao, which she did; and she said I must not stay at Margery's house, since Pao had started this evil, and one never knew to what lengths it would go. Margery was threatening to sue Pao for slander, and this would only complicate everything. I was to stay with Isobel's sister and brother-in-law, who lived in a large house in the countryside. And this I did.

I must confess, to my shame, that I was unaware of the gravity of Pao's action, for the (at the time) very grievous implications in Pao's charges were not understood by me. I wondered what exactly it was that Pao tried to accuse Margery of. Only some years later, when I became a medical student, did I begin to understand. And then I was distraught that Margery's integrity and kindness in aiding me should lead to such vicious distortion ... and she was then well into her sixties.

The house of Isobel Cripps's sister was a halt, a rest, but not the only one. Another friend, Margaret Godley, whose temper was impetuous and kind, who took up causes and cudgels with courage and pertinacity, also asked me to stay in a quiet country house, as a paying guest. I owe a great deal to those who put me up, and put up with me. Yungmei now joined me, and Gillie. Away from Pao-induced hysteria, I began to heal. In the meantime Pao had long talks with Isobel Cripps. Isobel wrote to me: 'He is so mixed up in his mind, it is quite unbelievable,' and another time, 'He makes up things in his mind, then makes himself believe them.' And soon, after six weeks away, I was out of tears and into laughter, so that every time Isobel mentioned Pao I had to giggle.

Isobel held us apart till one day she told me that she had arranged a meeting with Pao, with Stafford present. Would I come? Since she had taken me in hand I could only say yes.

I was much stronger, had begun to eat and to read again, still laughed nervously at words like sincerity, virtue; sometimes became light-headed with laughter. The countryside was so lovely; why had I not noticed how beautiful England was until now? This was a sure sign that I was healing, getting away from madness, which is hyperconcentration on self. Every day became a new discovery, both of people and of things. Of things, the pleasant grace; of people, the long, deep, enduring steadiness. And I began to dream again, in front of trees, to look at the sky, to read. The desire to do something came back stronger than ever. And now I knew that I would have to become a doctor; come what may.

As a preliminary to the meeting with Pao, Isobel took me out one day to dinner with Myra Hess, the great pianist, who in her large and beautiful flat full of flowers, where an enormous piano centred all attention, played Mozart, with that exquisite knowledge and care which is creator of enchantment, and thus opened a whole new world to me. The tears flowed again, but it was joy, discovered happiness, floating on a great stream of sound. And later, when I became once more a student, I went to the National Gallery concerts and to the Albert Hall to hear her and others play. But I could only do this alone, and not for more than one hour at a time; after longer than one hour I became tired, and could not take in any more.

And now vociferous, clamourous the desire to learn, to know – I would break this slavery, this doing of things I did not want to do, wasting away time, precious time, the only thing one ever owned and spent ...

One afternoon we met again, Pao and I, for tea with Isobel Cripps and Stafford; it was December, two days before Christmas. Stafford was a little embarrassed, puffing a pipe and then knocking it empty and filling it again. And Pao came in, open-faced, candid, spick and span in his uniform; at his most handsome and charming. He talked very

286

well; saying it was all his fault, promising to reform. Gravely, he spoke of China; of the need to put away our private feelings for the sake of China; for now China was fighting for her survival; and Isobel and Stafford were greatly impressed by all this. Of course Pao was playing on the patriotic fibre; which was then, and would remain, for me, for so many of us, a call to sacrifice, to abnegation.

It was on this that I said yes, I would come back; then we were left alone and Pao said that he loved me; and there was, it now came out, a Chinese military mission recently arrived to discuss military matters, under General Hsiung; that very night a dinner with them had been arranged ... would I come? He had told everyone I had been very ill but was now better. I stared at him; his face lit up with youthful ardour, so false, so real unto himself; and I thought wearily, 'Why do you always do this?' and then I said, 'Yes, I will come. But I am going to study medicine.' He said: 'Of course, everything you wish.' It would now depend on me, to do the single thing I wanted to do.

So I attended the dinner. There were seven or eight military men; they brought with them the flavour of Chungking and its odour of corruption; they talked of non-existent victories. General Hsiung said: 'Let me see the British officials and I will turn them round my little finger,' and boasted how Chiang was handling the Americans; and how it was all over with Stilwell. A game was going on, the same weaving, subtle, insidious game of power, which I had seen before. And all was as before. But now I was no longer vulnerable.

Winter 1943–4. Stalingrad's heroic defence; the war in the desert, swinging to the Allied side, with Montgomery in command. Much talk of a second front in Europe; and Chiang at Cairo with Roosevelt and Churchill, and then Teheran, which reversed the promises made to Chiang at Cairo ...

In August 1943, with Admiral Lord Louis Mountbatten as Supreme Allied Commander, the South-East Asia Command had been established. Mountbatten had flown to Chungking to see Chiang, arriving there to find, as he wrote in *Paris-Match*, that Stilwell had just been fired by Chiang Kaishek.

That testy general, Vinegar Joe Stilwell, had been stationed in Chungking by Washington since 1942. American strategy then (later abandoned) was to organize the enormous Chinese manpower, to equip and train it, to command it (through American commanders) and to use it for massive land campaigns in Asia, against Japan.

One of the great campaigns thus planned involved Burma, and it was the series of Burma campaigns, from May 1942 till May 1945, which provided one of the areas where the clash of aims among the Allies was exteriorized in what was called 'the forgotten army' on 'the forgotten front'.

Stilwell's grand strategy, where Burma was involved, was to train thirty Chinese divisions: the famous forces X, Y, Z; one at Ramgarh in India, one at Kunming, one at Kweilin. The three forces would, when ready, perform enormous marches, join, and establish a line from India to the eastern seaboard of China, thus cutting right across all Japanese communications, and clearing Northern Burma. This done, a road was to be established, linking India through Assam and Northern Burma to China. Variously called the Northern Burma Road and the Stilwell Road, it was to replace the other Burma Road, lost to Japan in May 1942.

Even before Pearl Harbour, in the summer of 1941, the Chinese Military Council had agreed to make available to the Americans thirty divisions. But when Stilwell wanted action on this, Chiang used Ho Yingchin, who was an absolute wonder at the art of not getting anything done, to oppose Stilwell by evasive promises, for ever unfulfilled. Since half of Chiang's divisions existed only on paper, and none of them had more than half of the men listed as alive, it is not surprising that they did not materialize.

For morale purposes an air raid upon Japan was staged by Doolittle in April 1942, and this led to a retaliation by the Japanese, who destroyed the airfield on the China coast in Chekiang and then withdrew, thus showing their awareness that America intended to use Chinese airfields, ports, and manpower for an attack on Japan. Chiang, dissatisfied at the priority given to other fronts, did his usual trick: he gave orders to his troops not to do anything to stop the destruction of the airfields by the Japanese. Stilwell, who would never understand the motivations behind Chiang's actions, or lack of action, was furious, and complained that he was bogged down in what he was to call 'the cesspool', Chungking. He called Chiang whimsical and flighty, self-contradictory and Old Peanut (Old Peanut actually was the name coined for Chiang by the American-trained Chinese round T. V. Soong, his brother-in-law). Finally Stilwell wrote that the only way that China could progress would be if she were delivered from Chiang

Kaishek. At the Teheran conference of December 1943, which followed the Cairo conference in November, Roosevelt and Stalin forced a drastic alteration in the American strategy on which Stilwell had laboured so fervently for two years. Thus the projected Burma campaigns were only showpieces, a useless sacrifice of men, whose equipment was deficient, in a useless 'show of force'.

The Allies had now reneged on the half-commitment made to Chiang at Cairo in November 1943, by a basic alteration in strategy. Stilwell was sacrificed, not by Chiang, but by his own government, before he knew it, since the whole plan of a land attack on Japan was now to be dumped. Some say that this abandon antedated the Teheran conference and was actually decided upon in early 1943.

Stilwell's plan, if carried out, would have placed American and Chinese armies in British colonies, in South-East Asia, in Burma. Chinese armies, equipped and trained as Stilwell wanted them to be, would be a challenge to British domination in South-East Asia. The overt ambitions of America to replace Great Britain in Asia caused the British to drag their feet, and for good reason. Not only did they not want Chinese power there, they did not want American power either. They confidently expected their territories to be handed back to them after the war. This ambivalent game was well known in London Chinese circles, and there was mounting covert hostility between the Chinese and the British establishment.

When Mountbatten went to Burma after August 1943, he found an appalling situation. As he tells so vividly, the rate of hospital cases was one hundred and thirty-five per cent of the troops, due to malaria; for one man wounded, one hundred and twenty were out of action due to the disease. The appalling mess of the 1942 Burma campaign was vivid in the minds of the British officers, and the mess was continuing. The Burma front was still the very last on the list of priorities, and remained so for another year. There were no planes, no material, no equipment. Ships sent to it were taken away; only Wingate and his Chindits, whose operations, like those of Force 132 in Malaya, were undertaken for psychological reasons and also for intelligence gathering (ascertaining the degree of local communist influence, to be actively combated later, as in Yugoslavia and Greece), kept Burma from being altogether forgotten in the Press, by the people ...

Mountbatten tells how he persuaded Chiang Kaishek not to fire Stilwell that year (September 1943) by promises of a speedy second front in Burma. But two-thirds of Mountbatten's fleet was abruptly taken away again, after having arrived in Indian ports, and sent on Mediterranean operations, after the December 1943 Teheran conference.

Chiang learnt about this from Roosevelt, of all people. At Cairo Chiang had asked for a billion dollars. 'I'm not going to give that b—— a billion dollars,' said Roosevelt, and let out that the Mediterranean was a top priority. This gave Chiang a wonderful excuse for getting rid of Stilwell. If other heads of State did not keep their promises, why should he? And Chiang once more threatened to make peace with Japan, and so got half a billion dollars.

Chiang asked Mountbatten who would be responsible for the civil administration and maintenance of order in the Burmese territories, where the Chinese troops would be utilized; Mountbatten replied that the British would be. This to Chiang meant that the Chinese would really be fighting to restore British rule in Burma. The British suggested a Civilian Affairs mission whose officers, accompanying the 'Allied' forces, would take all necessary measures to 'canalize communications' between the people of the country and the Chinese. Thus Chinese troops would be doing the fighting, but would be isolated from the population in whose territories they found themselves. Lieutenant-General Sir Adrian Carton de Wiart, v.c., was to work out the arrangements; there would be a liaison office in Kunming. Carton de Wiart came to dinner, and was charming; he lunched with the Chinese mission at the War Office, and General Hsiung, draped in his cape, was taken round to inspect military establishments ...

Chiang refused to let Chinese forces operate under Mountbatten, except for the Chinese divisions already at Ramgarh in India. Orders and commands, counter-orders and counter-commands flowed to London, as they did to Washington; Wellington Koo was so overworked that he appeared stuporose; the naval, military and air attachés were being bypassed, both by Chiang, in his usual manner, and by the British who were seeking to establish their own liaison office in China.

From November 1943 to May 1944, the Chinese troops did not move; and no one could make them move. This procrastination, Chiang's 'shiftiness', infuriated Stilwell who seemed unaware that his own government had changed its mind and undercut his plans.

In May 1944, Chinese forces began to cross the Salween river, but no previous communication was forwarded to the British about this move. A disquieted Carton de Wiart reiterated his demand for permission for the immediate dispatch of the British civil officers' mission 'to accompany the Chinese forces' in Burma. There was a proviso put up by the British that 'civilian offenders of British nationality' (which meant the Burmese, who as a colonial people came under this definition) should be tried exclusively by courts set up by the British military administration which had been created in anticipation of the re-occupation of south-east Asian territories after the war.

In June 1944, a few British officials were given permission by the Chinese to fly to Kunming; but no acceptance of any of the provisions, nor formal permission for sending the mission, could be obtained at any time from Chiang Kaishek.

Meanwhile, in January 1944, the Japanese had launched a major operation across the Chindwin river into Assam with large forces, and there was a critical period in March 1944 when it looked as if Assam would be taken and Calcutta threatened.

If the Japanese had succeeded, they would have cut the lines of communication to the airfields operating the airlift to China.

The Japanese also reinforced their propaganda by promising India her independence. Subhas Chandra Bhose, whose Indian Army of Independence they supported, was from Bengal, and they hoped to stir up a movement for independence in Bengal.

The first half of 1944 thus saw the collapse of the Second Burma campaign, all plans for using China as a base of attack abandoned, and the American strategy changed to one of island-hopping, attacking Japan direct from Pacific islands conquered one by one. But the United States was also intent on keeping China in the war, to make maximum use of her military potential and strategic geographical position, for the purpose of building an American-dominated political post-war order in the Far East. The realities pursued were the introduction of the American presence as the dominant power in the Far East, replacing 'colonial' Great Britain, France, and Holland, both economically and militarily. The deeper involvement of America in China, starting from that year, was a product of this vision, whereby the Kuomintang, increasingly dependent upon and subservient to America, was to become an instrument of American policy.

But China could not fulfil the role assigned to her if she was to continue weltering in civil war; hence the grand design of a 'coalition' government, in which both Kuomintang and Communist would 'co-operate'; in order to introduce reforms which would make Chiang's set-up more viable, and dilute the communist strength in a hash of pseudo-democracy.

Roosevelt became increasingly amenable to Chiang's blackmail, in the belief that China would support U.S. policies everywhere. Chiang and his wife did all they could to reinforce this belief; Madame Chiang on her visit to the U.S. in the winter of 1942–3 having assured Harry Hopkins that 'China would line up with the United States' at the end of the war.

The battle of Imphal, in June 1944, broke the Japanese offensive in Burma. That battle was due to the reorganization of the Burmese forces by Mountbatten. Chiang once again put up no resistance to a Japanese sweep in China, timed to coincide with another desperate Japanese assault in Burma.

Mountbatten realized that Chiang had to be kept in the war at all costs; but Chiang was now mounting a general offensive, mobilizing all his troops against Yenan, against Mao Tsetung's Red Base. Mountbatten flew into Chungking to talk to Chiang.

The third Burma campaign gathered strength. By January 1945 Northern Burma was at last cleared of Japanese, and by June the reconquest of Burma was achieved.

The paradoxical results of these shifting events and shifty plans are enlightening.

Had Stilwell's ideas for a Burma campaign been carried out, and the Stilwell Road cleared earlier, Chiang's regime would have been much strengthened, for the Burmese offensive as planned by Stilwell would have secured for Chiang an enormous rear, very rich, where communist bases were non-existent.

This did not happen, and by early 1945, when at last North Burma was cleared, Chiang's economic and political deterioration was such that it left him far weaker *vis-à-vis* the communists than he had been in 1942. Yet he had done his share in the sabotage of Stilwell's efforts.

But had these efforts been successful, American military might in China would have been far greater than it was at the end of the war in August 1945.

And it was in those years that the communist forces increased enormously, both in strength and territory, not through inertia but through continuous, strenuous, relentless fighting, mobile warfare, guerrilla warfare in the rear of the Japanese lines, so that by the war's end the balance of power in China was irreversibly changed.

I was persuaded to go back to Pao; Margery thought that Isobel's advice was faulty, that I should have made a clear break, struck out for myself.

I went back to the large Welbeck Street flat. Isobel advised me to find another place to live in, 'this flat has been an unhappy place', as if changing house could change us ...

For some weeks all went much better, we could even talk, carefully. I told Pao that I wanted to study medicine, because now was the time for me to complete my studies. 'Great changes will come to China, the people can't go on being as miserable as they are.' I thought of myself as working as a doctor, and this was not a new idea but a very old one, and the stubbornness and tenacity which I had put in abeyance all these years now made me drive on, to the end of re-entering the university and completing my medical studies; as I had wished to do when I was twelve years old; I was now twenty-seven years old.

Pao too seemed now swayed; the news of the inflationary situation in China made Chinese diplomats uneasy; directives for thrift and a cut in expenditure were relayed from Chungking. George Yeh's acerbic criticism of the regime, held in the privacy of our flat, may have influenced Pao.

Isobel now recommended me to the Hunter Street School of Medicine for Women. I had my certificate from the University of Brussels (which Third Uncle had kept for me).

In the spring of 1944, I received permission to enter the London School of Medicine for Women, Royal Free Hospital, provided that I could pass the entrance examination to be held at the Hunter Street School of Medicine, in March 1945 ... That meant going to Hunter Street for refresher courses in anatomy, physiology and especially biochemistry, of which I knew nothing. Biochemistry was not included in the curriculum of the Faculty of Natural Sciences at the University of Brussels; the course was given later, in the fourth year.

It also meant re-doing, in English, the whole of anatomy and

293

physiology and chemistry, in addition to biochemistry and another subject, pharmacology. I would have to do all this between spring 1944 and March 1945 and I would have to study at home to begin with, until I could attend the lectures and anatomy classes full time in autumn 1944.

Could I do it? It was seven years since I had left Brussels University to return to China – a decision which had given me many not exactly happy days, but which I did not regret. They seemed worth while, and today, three decades later, even more so.

I was to start again in 1945, at the point where I left off in 1938, but with seven years of experience stored, and I did not allow myself to think how difficult beginning again would be.

I made no plans which took into account any difficulties; only set my mind on what I wanted. And what about money? What about Yungmei, Gillie, Pao? It sounded unfeasible that the wife of the Chinese military attaché should suddenly take up studying medicine.

The inflation in China now seemed astronomic; twenty-five thousand Chinese dollars to the U.S. dollar on the black market; it was to become much worse later. Average prices in February 1944 were two hundred and fifty times those of summer 1942. The presence of increasing numbers of American soldiers and other personnel in China between 1941 and 1945 had a very bad effect on the inflation. American military activities in China were to be financed in Chinese dollars: the Flying Tigers of the American General Chennault and the 14th Air Force, Stilwell and his staff, American training and support of Chinese troops, the air route over the Himalayas, bombing operations – these additional demands on the currency for paying the Americans could only be met, wrote Arthur Young, the American Financial Adviser, 'by running the printing presses harder'.

Since autumn 1942 American personnel in China had been paid in U.S.$ notes, which they could sell freely on the free market; this gave another spurt to the depreciation of the Chinese dollar. There was considerable friction between the U.S. and Chiang over money problems, and the Chinese were stubborn on insisting on the rate of twenty to one instead of a rate of hundred to one because, says Young, there had been an 'undefined promise' by Roosevelt to pay the whole cost of the American military effort in China; a promise which was not kept, since food, lodgings, amenities, roads, the building of airports (for which three hundred thousand men were pressganged at a time) were paid for by the Chinese. In mid-1944, China was paying $200 million (local currency) per month for the food and lodging of American forces. In 1945, prices had inflated enormously and the cost was twenty-five billion Chinese dollars per month ...

Because of the inflation, I knew I would have to find my own financial resources. I had an idea that, pretty soon, I would have to provide for myself, for Yungmei and Gillie – how was I going to manage? I did not want to ask Pao for money, I wanted to be on my own.

I applied, through Isobel Cripps, to the British Council. Would it be possible to obtain a scholarship? The notion of a diplomat's wife applying for a scholarship may have sounded ridiculous, but actually a few junior members of the Chinese embassy were already getting out very quietly, applying for jobs as lecturers, or for scholarships and fellowships.

The British Council reply was that if I succeeded in passing the entrance examination in March 1945 I might be favourably considered, and with this I went ahead.

And then, with the doodlebugs coming in over London, we found a house outside London, Barney Cottage, Maiden's Green, near Winkfield. A small house with a garden, neat if nondescript. I began packing to move. It was then January 1944. In March, I found I was pregnant.

Pregnant at last. Pregnant, at the worst time. Now what would I do? The child would come, I would take care of it with Yungmei; I would manage. And study. I did not change my plans.

After a visit to the gynaecologist, Mr Green-Armytage, who confirmed my pregnancy, I came home to the flat in Welbeck Street and told Pao. I thought he would be happy, but he was not, because of the inflation, and perhaps he was now resigned to a period of calm, without any added difficulties. The euphoria of early pregnancy was filling me with new energy. Nothing seemed out of reach or impossible. I was no longer afraid; it was Pao who went around with a disturbed look, and he was angry with the British because he had applied to attend a course at the Staff College and not been accepted. Increasingly, too, he and his friends talked, briefly but significantly, of civil war, of the 'red-banditism'. 'There will be big changes,' I repeated, 'after the

295

war.' 'If the Americans back us, all will be well,' said Pao.

One afternoon, returning from the laundry with some sheets and two suits, I felt a sudden tearing pain inside me as I walked up the steps of Welbeck House – a pain so agonizing that I nearly fainted. I managed, however, to take the lift, to open the flat door, and then I went to the bedroom and lay on the bed. But the pain became more acute, indescribable in its tearing quality. 'Something is bursting in me, perhaps it is a miscarriage.' I dragged myself to the telephone and telephoned Pao; I said, 'Please come, I think I am having a miscarriage.' The pain was so very bad; I had to go to the toilet with it. 'Telephone to the gynaecologist, please.' Pao did. Green-Armytage sent an ambulance and I was taken to the London Clinic and put to bed. Pao had a party that night and he went to it; I told him that I could manage.

Green-Armytage came and asked me what had happened. I told him about carrying the laundry, and the pain. He put a nurse to watch me and left me in bed, and I thought, this is fine. I want to keep the baby. Lying flat will help me ... I was not bleeding. Only a few drops staining my clothes. I told the nurse I wanted to keep the baby and then gave myself up to pain. And all the night it kept on, went to my right shoulder, which became acutely painful too. I vomited repeatedly. The nurse was an Irish girl, endlessly patient. Towards morning, I could not breathe well and was gasping. The nurse took my pulse every half-hour. Then at five in the morning I said to the nurse, 'I am much better now, there is practically no pain in the tummy, I am better; only in the right shoulder, very tiresome.' I became quite euphoric and started to laugh. 'You see, Nurse, I shall be all right.' 'Yes dear,' she said. She began to shave me and said, 'Now we are going to do a little examination, Mr Green-Armytage is here.' 'Good, but I want this baby.'

In the operating room there was Green-Armytage in sterile clothes and mask. Now I breathed in great gasping sighs; I did not know that my pulse was up to 160 and my temperature had dropped to 96, the signs of internal haemorrhage. The anaesthetist handed me a mask and off I went, into oblivion; but had no fear, for I trusted Green-Armytage completely. When I woke up, I was in bed, there was a bottle with blood running into me, and my stomach was bandaged. Later Green-Armytage came in and told me that I had had an ectopic pregnancy which had burst; that I had lost a lot of blood but I would be all right now. 'But don't worry, you can be pregnant again, there is another tube, you know.' I laughed and said yes, and then went off into sleep.

Convalescence was wonderful; I had a radio and I listened to Ben Jonson's play *Volpone*; I was hilarious and happy most of the time. Outside there were doodlebugs roaring and suddenly shutting off and within the London Clinic no one worried. Pao came and I tried to explain to him what had happened, but he marched up and down the room and told me that he would have to return to China at the end of his three-year term, in order to 'lead armies'. 'You mean fight the Japanese?' 'No,' he said, 'fight the communist bandits.' After he left I read the poems of Aragon, the French Communist poet, which I had obtained from Bumpus in Oxford Street, just before going to the laundry on the day I had burst my tube. Now I read what I wanted; Pao could no longer frighten me into not reading this or that.

After a week, I left the London Clinic. Meanwhile Pao, Gillie and Yungmei had moved to Barney Cottage and I went there directly. It was still very cold, but spring would begin soon. We were far from the London alerts. For another week, I had another Irish nurse, a very nice person, whom a friend had recommended to me. I looked at the scar on my stomach and worried that it would leave puckers; soon I was walking about; and then it was English spring; a heyday of may and honeysuckle scent, and I began to read anatomy, took long walks with Yungmei and Gillie. Then it was June 1944, and the Second Front in Europe opened, on a blazing and beautiful day, when we could see the planes in their hundreds and their thousands crossing the sky towards Europe, and their screaming filled the air, and Gillie waved at them and so did Yungmei and our neighbours came to us and we to them, and all of us were happy, for soon, perhaps very soon, the war would be over ...

The summer of 1944 was one of continued excitement, news of great battles, victories in Europe, a lovely summer in England. Pao and the other military attachés were busy with the brisk war pace, with many briefings by the War Office. The attachés were keen to get to Europe, in order to view the war at close quarters, and conducted tours of the battlefields were arranged for them, the War Office punctiliously sending photographs, as mementos of these visits. One of them shows Pao with some captured German soldiers, very young, fifteen to sixteen, recruits of the last desperate months. Pao's face began to look lined. He had hoped for a German victory. The Chiang regime viewed with great disquiet the defeat of Germany and the possibility of a strong Russia to face on an enormously long frontier, actively helping a subversive Chinese Communist party into power ... And all that summer in Barney Cottage, I rested and studied; and grew strong; preparing for the life to come; but I never discussed this with Pao. And though he saw the books about, he pretended he did not see them, and the days went, and morose silence between us drew its night curtains, and neither could speak to the other.

Thirteen

IN SEPTEMBER 1944, I entered the Hunter Street School of Medicine for women and began another life as a student, though not altogether relinquishing, since Pao was still there, my life as the wife of the military attaché.

Thus, for a while, I was two distinct people, but soon these two lives, by the hazards of circumstance, got in each other's way.

I would be seen in Bond Street in slacks and mackintosh with a fellow student, and greeted with a mixture of dismay and surprise by one of Pao's amiable dowagers. I would take one of my new acquaintances to tea at the Dorchester Hotel, together with some diplomatic acquaintance. This was disconcerting to many. As for myself, I was past caring unduly.

Precisely because I had at last breached the closed walls of the life I was supposed to lead, I had also put behind me rancour or resentment. I had no feelings of revenge, either towards Pao, or towards those kind friends of his who had contributed to making things more unpleasant for me. The dowager ladies, the honourable so-and-so, that well-meaning group so fastidiously clutching their conventions – I could now feel almost condescending about them. They still contrived, by gushing over Pao and nodding icily to me, to convey their disapproval, but it no longer hurt.

My first impression when I became a student was my own terror when, walking into what was called the quad, a large courtyard with a conventional arched cloister walk around it, I found myself in the midst of girls, girls in bevies, in clusters, all boisterous, all knowing each other, all stridently talking in full-lunged voices a lingo I could not understand ... student English.

In that first terror-stricken half-hour, someone came up to me and said: 'I say, will you share my locker?' and that was Cherry Heath, who was to remain my best friend. I followed her meekly to the locker room and the first expression she taught me was: 'I must see a man about a dog.' Two other girls, friends of hers, came up and were introduced and with them I ate lunch at the canteen, queueing up for the soup and the stew and the saccharine-flavoured sweet.

Cherry proved invaluable; a staunch friend, an able girl, resourceful, energetic, with all the know-how of student life at her fingertips. No one was better than Cherry at finding digs, discovering cheap but good meals, 'buttering up' suspicious landladies, wheedling hot water and cups of tea out of them, and making a shilling go a long way with the small all-purpose gas rings that are found in most student bed-sitting rooms.

The second impression of this new person I was to evolve into, me as a medical student, was the smell of the anatomy room, soon to become not only familiar but inseparable from my clothes and my belongings. A third impression was the sight of the grey silvery balloons, in a web above London's many-millioned chimney pots, hovering over us in ominous blessing when we were busy dissecting in the anatomy laboratories.

I had inspected the Balloon Command the year before; had seen the way these were handled; I had also visited the girls who made the parachutes for the R.A.F. pilots; I told Cherry that to ensure efficiency, one girl was occasionally picked out and dropped by parachute, so that no minute defect would be due to negligence. Cherry later told me she had not believed a word of what I had said. 'We all know married bods make up stories,' said she. Cherry and her mates were convinced that I·was odd in a nice way (so they said) and amusingly naive, but they did not believe I was the wife of a diplomat until, one day, I took them to Gunthers for tea ... They were convinced that 'I would never make it', which meant that I would fail my examinations. Cherry even opined that it was 'money down the drain' for me to register for the hospital entrance examination.

Gradually, and without compunction, I borrowed the notes of fellow students and picked their brains, taking short cuts everywhere, painstaking, apparently stupid ... They were generous, Cherry and her friends, instructing me, telling me the gist of lectures I had missed. And in this way, very quickly, I managed to pick up the work, and to make up for lost time.

Like them, I became a little unwashed, a little careless about spots on my clothes; in exchange I was at last in England at war; at last with the real England, with the English people, their true hardships and inconveniences, the drudgery of no warm water, very little soap, making do, queues at canteens, the cold and wetness and the trudging and the terrible meals and no cigarettes and how I loved every minute of this austerity time!

Now the doodle bugs came over in the sky and crashed upon London, but no one was afraid. We continued to work although the enormous glass windows of the lab, right on top of the building, were somewhat dangerous. I carried the smell of Chanel Number 5 (brought by a friend of Pao, a U.S. colonel with two ladders of medals, back from the continent of Europe) to the dissection room, and the reek of preserving fluid to receptions at Claridge's Hotel.

Rome had fallen in June 1944. The allied offensive in Italy, clawing its way up the peninsula for twenty months, had gathered heart from the Normandy landings on June 6th. Paris was liberated on August 25th; the newsreels showed the flowers, the crowds, the triumphant heroes in their tanks; some time later we also saw on the newsreels French women having their hair shaved because they had collaborated with the Germans, but uglier features of the revenge of the French people against the collaborators were not shown, though we heard about them.

Then Montgomery, for whom Cherry, like many of the English, had a great affection, was made field marshal after his victory over Rommel, in North Africa, and drove the Canadian First Army and British Second Army two hundred miles in four days in the Ardennes, and Brussels was liberated on September 3rd, Antwerp on September 4th.

From the Russian front, too, came the news of victories, victories; in the newsreels, the German captive host treading through the streets of Moscow, von Paulus and the nervous tic on his face, the Germans captured in the desert, endless rows of men singing 'Lili Marlene'. And as total victory came nearer, Pao became more gloomy. It was now certain that Germany would lose. Pao was to return to China 'because we are now going to have to fight the Reds.' The civil war Chiang had prepared for many years was going to break out. In early 1945 it was clear that American involvement in China would continue ...

I had to wake early to get to classes in time, and from Barney Cottage, Winkfield, to Hunter Street in London took over two hours. I bought a motor cycle in order to get myself to the railway station, about eight miles away, from where there was a direct train to St Pancras; from St Pancras I walked to Hunter Street. It was often difficult to return at night.

After December 1944, Pao sold his car; his hours were erratic, he went (alone) to many parties; getting washed and dressed for a diplomatic party, straight from the lectures and laboratory sessions at Hunter Street, was increasingly difficult for me. At week-ends I returned to that other life of dinners, parties on Saturday nights at posh 'exclusive' clubs. I spent most of Sunday studying (or 'swotting', as I now called it), reading for the examination to come far into the night.

I was not the only married student; in my year there was another one, Sanchia, with three children; a vivid and beautiful woman with long fair hair and undiminished zeal who regularly failed her examinations. She was quite determined to go on for years and years if necessary, and she has finally become a very good doctor. I discovered the general opinion of the unmarried majority at the School of Medicine was that the married few were 'a pain in the neck'. This was probably also the opinion of some of our lecturers and teachers; though they never voiced it and were most punctiliously polite to all of us. Married Sanchia brought her baby to classes, fed it behind a kind of screen made by herself, described the joys of matrimony lengthily to her own côterie of admirers. I kept quiet on matrimony since I was almost unmarried by now; not only sexual desire, but even the notion of sex and love had been effectively murdered in me, and this frozen state was to last four years. I who had been healthily normal could not even call to mind the notion of love without nausea. I suffered badly, but in silence, from vaginismus, that tightening of all the muscles, that shrinking of the flesh, defined so gravely in gynaecological textbooks. And though I endured the sex act, it was extremely painful, almost unbearable. But Pao was going away soon, he was going away and I would be patient, it was only a matter of holding out a few months, a

few weeks more ... never did I add refusal to my other acts of independence, because I not only pitied him now, knowing I had won, but
I also did not wish to give him any opportunity to make a scene. The
reek of disinfectant from the anatomy laboratory, however, occasionally neutralized Pao's inclinations, as did the sight of bones and a skull
spread out on the dining-table ... and there was a pickled brain in a
saucepan under the bed; there were also my hands, vari-coloured from
chemical experiments.

These four years in the summer of my life, twenty-eight to thirty-
two, I merely note down as a clinical observation. It was a period endured, one which has helped me to understand so many other women
when I became a doctor. I was not pursued by erotic fancies or dreams.
The whole idea of sex and love simply ceased to manifest itself, buried
so deep in healing non-existence that it took four years to resurrect.

One day I compared notes with M., a woman friend of mine, on this
topic, both of us detached enough to be able to talk about our lives.
Cruelty in her first marriage had had the opposite effect on M.; she
had become a nymphomaniac. 'I don't know how many men I've
had, literally hundreds, it lasted three years.' Then brusquely the driving urge disappeared, she was no longer spurred by the necessity to
prove herself desirable. She remarried and has remained completely
faithful to her husband.

In me the total smother of libido involved both body and mind; I
was bored by films depicting romance. The incomprehensible ab-
surdity of love's frenzy also extended to novels. Where I was concerned, it was much ado about so little, and all of this little extremely
repulsive. I read detective stories, technical books. One man tried to
get me out of this frozen sleep, and failed even to begin awakening my
interest. All my energies were focused on study, work, getting qualified
in the shortest possible time.

In spite of my friend Cherry's dire predictions of failure, by the end
of four months I was coaching at least one other girl in the intricacies
of biochemistry, because the best way to learn anything is to explain it
to someone else. I invented for myself tasks and problems, set myself
questions in anatomy and physiology and answered them aloud. Then
I discovered with dismay that I would not have finished revising all of
anatomy in the time allotted, there was too much to commit to
memory. I decided to leave out one item, the leg.

As winter deepened I wore a mackintosh all the time because I was cold with chronic tiredness, and went stockingless in slacks: I found out how good hot tea with milk and sugar was when tired and hungry, and consumed vast quantities of it. I ate fish and chips at cheap restaurants, because to return to Barney Cottage on an empty stomach in the cold made me giddy.

During the Christmas holidays another Chinese military mission came and I had to cook for them, to go to parties with them. Fortunately my culinary efforts were appalling, and the mission quickly left Barney Cottage to eat at some choice Chinese restaurant in London.

So went the icy winter of 1944–5. Diamond hoarfrost sparkled on the dark-boned trees, the roads were slippery and dangerous. I rode my motor-cycle, Gillie cooked and cleaned and kept house (the gardener's wife coming in for the rough), and always had something in the oven for my return at night.

The brain I kept for study purposes under my bed in Barney Cottage, in a large saucepan full of preserving fluid, was a subject of great interest to Yungmei, now a vigorous four-year-old. She took a special delight in leading her friends to the bedroom, to lift the lid and peer. 'These are Mummy's brains, she keeps them under her bed.'

The general disapproval of my behaviour by the more respectable among our neighbours did not long remain unspoken. One nice woman asked me to tea and lectured me on the duties of wife and mother, saying that I must devote myself to my child and not 'gad' about in student slacks. I stared sleepily at her, too tired to explain and too near dangerous laughter. There was something eminently laughable in those pompous women delivering their lectures ... They did not know how insecure the future was for Pao.

Pao himself did not know it; he could not believe in the downfall of Chiang. But my bones were alert to the Revolution to come; I felt it, the Great Change, coming, coming ... One day Pao would not be so successful; there was no future in his stale and narrow ambition ... I had told him so, but he did not listen. One day I would have to feed Yungmei; I did not want Yungmei to be sold again. I would rely, for both of us, on my own strength.

My total lack of reliance on Pao could not be better expressed than by my never asking him for money. Once I told another would-be do-

303

gooder (there were so many of these about!) that the price index of
goods in China if quoted at 100 for 1937, was now, eight years later,
125,000, but it simply did not register with him. This lack of understanding, so common among so-called 'informed' people, the refusal
to see the shape of events, to think ahead, infected and still infects the
upper class, the so-called intellectuals of England, to a greater degree
perhaps than anywhere else. Perhaps because of the conviction that
'muddling through' will always succeed in the end? No wonder the
B.B.C.'s most up-to-date programmes on current political events are
often spoilt by commentary from which anything not outdated has
been expunged.

By February 1945 Pao's three years as acting military attaché were
up; the preparation for his return to China involved packing a good
many things, attending parties, giving parties in return ... Our diver-
gent views became expressed more clearly. He said he must engage in
the coming civil war. 'Because we must fight the communists now,
and I must make up for not having led troops in combat.' I said: 'You
never fought the Japanese, now you want to fight other Chinese. This
is bad. I am sure that the communists will win. There is going to be a
revolution in China, you will see.' The year before, such words would
have brought upon my head his great wrath, and many blows, but
now he was too defeated, too discouraged. He sometimes watched me,
while I was studying and one day he said: 'I did not know you well,
I am finding out how stubborn you are ... how hard you work, when
you really want something.' Now he knew in his heart that all along
he had never thought of me as a *person,* only as something belonging
to him, and the extent of my victory became daily more obvious to
him, so that during the last few weeks of his stay, all was very brittle
and fragile between us.

Selfishly I did not want Pao to break down, to be on my hands, to
elect to remain in England; what would I do with him hanging
around me? Two years before I would not have been so determined
to get him off my back; I had tried to make him give up his job, to
study; now I was afraid he might burden me, for I knew that he
would never study, never work hard at anything. His mind was not
made that way. He could not think of knowledge, service, the joy of
creation, doing something because it was good to do it. Truth, to
Pao, was the explanation that would fit the aim he meant to achieve.
Knowledge was to be recognized; success meant reaching the heights

of power under the militarist regime of Chiang Kaishek, and service was 'loyalty' to a Leader.

Discussion, debate, cogitation, hard work in obscurity, unpopularity – these had no meaning for Pao. Even though he occasionally talked of retiring to a farm and living 'as a peasant', what he meant was living like a landlord where his family owned fields.

Pao could not believe that my aim in studying medicine was to slake the desire to know and to do; he could not understand that I did not wish to become Director of a hospital, or Health Minister ... And now I wanted him to keep his broken dreams and his broken heart to himself, that is, *if* he was conscious enough to *know* they were broken. And though I still felt that he could choose another way of life than serving Chiang Kaishek, I wanted him to do it alone. I no longer wanted to help him. Yet at times I felt more compassion than ever for him, but I hardened myself against it, for it would have interfered with my studies.

So Pao had himself photographed, had some suits and uniforms made to take back with him, and was painted by a war artist; the other military attachés gave him a party and a silver dish with their signatures engraved upon it. He gave it to me to keep for him and I have it still.

Some people invited us: the Cripps, Kingsley and Dorothy Martin. Others were not too kind: however, their pinched welcome, their curtness was all for me. Yet others invited only Pao, to tearful little farewell dinners. In slacks and a mac, running about London, looking like the poor student I really was becoming, and so much more me than the carefully dressed military attaché's wife, it was pretty obvious that there was something wrong with me, but not with Pao, always impeccable in his uniform.

Occasionally Pao would hint at his great love for me, so misunderstood ... and the tragedy was that he was completely sincere when he said this. For he did love me, and now that he had been beaten all he could say was that he loved me. But he could not say it to my head bent over books, to the me no longer there, with him, at his call, but gone, escaped, escaped with bones and books and glazed eyes that looked through him and saw him not, ears that heard him not. He took me out to expensive restaurants and I ate absentmindedly, not knowing what I ate, and not caring. I went to mean restaurants and for one shilling and elevenpence ha'penny got an oxtail soup which was horse, and beans on toast, and devoured them with gusto, and was ravenous.

At a diplomatic dinner party at the Dorchester I talked of pitted frogs; my hands, discoloured with chemical stains, looked out of place in the select luxurious 'clubs' a little way out of London, where food and wine were unrestricted and the attendance limited to Americans and diplomats. I often fell asleep at such gay parties. Even Isobel got a shock when I arrived for dinner at the Café Royal in my mackintosh, smelling of pickled cadaver, books under my arm, flat muddy shoes and no stockings. I did not apologize; I had sworn not to wear my fur coat, because I wanted to sell it, when Pao was gone.

Pao began to consider which way he should return to China. The option was his. He asked me whether he should return via America or via Russia. 'If I were you I would go back via Russia. Russia is going to play a great role in the future; I think you should have a good look at Russia.' But Pao decided to go back via the United States.

Some of the civilian staff at the Chinese Embassy were already thinking of settling in America 'should things not go well'. To say that the Chinese revolution came as a sudden peal of spring thunder, unexpected, may be true for the United States, so centred upon what America *wanted* to do with China as her greatest market and domain, rather than concerned with the realities of the Chinese situation. But it was certainly not true for many of the Chinese diplomats in London who already felt the earth quaking in 1945.

One cold, rainy, windy dawn in March, at 6.30 a.m., Pao took the train from Euston Station to a port whence a ship would take him to America – the name of the port, the ship, and the ship's sailing date were secret. We had spent the last few days at a certain hotel in London which had a dismal sepulchral dining-room, doddering waiters (only their age kept them out of uniform), and the most bread-packed and sawdust-packed sausages for breakfast (no eggs, no toast) that one could imagine. I remember protesting at mine and being told that I'd forgotten there was a war on, but by then some places positively enjoyed inflicting discomfort upon their guests, an English hospitable habit which I was to encounter even when the war was long over.

There was nothing we could say to each other, Pao and I. He was leaving, I was staying. Neither of us made plans, neither envisaged a decision, neither discussed the future, both too frightened to break the temporary harmony based on the knowledge that soon we would be parted. Pao said he would see how things went and then send for me; I said I would finish my studies as soon as possible. Our words were possibly false, possibly true; the times to come were not ours to decide. 'Who knows but that one day I may have to work as a lecturer in a university,' said Pao suddenly; glimpsing a future devoid of authority for him. I did not point out that he could not lecture on any subject. He had rung up Yungmei at Barney Cottage and wept when he heard her voice saying cheerfully: 'Goodbye Daddy.' His face was worn with the worry that he was no longer absolutely right in everything; doubt infected and eroded him; he could not bear to be unsure.

Handsome, well turned out, swagger stick in hand, Pao walked straight and confident-looking, with parade step, on to the station platform, me following in my student mac with books under my arm. After seeing him off I had to go straight to Hunter Street, for the examinations were beginning with a physiology paper that very day.

The platform was almost deserted, a setting for sadness and parting; there was a cold drizzle and the gathered dinginess so perpetual in London. I felt cold, a discomforted stomach. The rain whooshed on the platform roof; the horrible morning coffee made of dubiously ground beans was still with me. Pao looked resplendent with his shining shoes (shined by me) and new coat. We said goodbye, he climbed into the train, he was at the window waving his swagger stick as the train pulled out.

I went to Hunter Street; and that afternoon did the written examination in physiology. At St Pancras railway station there was a long queue for tea, and only one spoon tied by a string to the counter ... One queued to get a cup, queued to stir one's cup, put back the spoon on the counter, sloppy with wet tea; queued to pay for the cup ... thick cups warm and greasy with human use; I got back to Barney Cottage that night chugging on the motor-cycle up the steepish hill climb to Winkfield.

The next few days were feverish with anxiety and work; on the result depended whether I would obtain a British Council scholarship to continue my medical studies. Although Pao said he would send me money I knew this was only a bland statement with no root in possibility; by now a bowl of rice cost round about 6,000 Chinese dollars, or yuen as they were called , and one U.S. dollar was worth 100,000 Chinese yuen. By 1948 a U.S. dollar would be worth 10 million Chinese yuen. Pao would be back on Chinese money, not on foreign exchange, and though the traffic in gold bars and luxury goods which was the prerogative of military men might keep him well in funds, I could not visualize myself receiving any money from him, and in this of course I was right. He had gone out of my life, waving his ￿wagger stick and looking confident, and that was a job done; now I could drop that life completely. From that day on, I never went to the Chinese Embassy again, except once in 1947. Similarly I cut myself off from all my 'diplomatic circle' friends, simply disappearing out of that life, never to return.

The rent of Barney Cottage was paid for the next two months; we did not need to move from it till the first of May; then I would have to find a way to keep Yungmei and Gillie. How I would pay Gillie's salary, how I would pay for food and lodging, how I would manage, I did not know. Could three people live on £30 a month, which was what the British Council scholarship would bring me? Gillie's salary alone came to about half of that, not counting food, clothing, lodging. What about school for Yungmei? ... But first I must get through the examination.

One night during that week of examinations my motor-cycle failed to work; I dragged it back, walking it all the way home, and this took me three hours because of the uphill road and the heaviness of the machine. I arrived at Barney Cottage about eleven at night, tired out, and then at half past five next morning Gillie woke me up and I went back to London.

I scarcely slept that week, so overwrought was I ... failure meant so much. I regretted having turned down, almost a year before, in 1944, a sum of money which had been willed to me; all that Louis, my former fiancé in Belgium, had in the world ...

For Louis had turned up again; one afternoon, in 1943, when Pao and I were walking across Piccadilly Circus, I saw him standing by the boarded-up wall where Eros had been, in the blue uniform of the Royal Air Force, staring at me. For Louis had escaped the Germans, escaped to England, and enrolled in the R.A.F.

I looked through him, passed on; Pao was with me. It was all over. What could we say anyway? I felt very little. Surely, when a situation is empty of meaning the straightest thing to do is to treat it as such.

A few days later, a small tin of tea arrived. No name. Louis. He did not try to see me. In 1944, one afternoon, a telephone call, from a Belgian solicitor at the Belgian Embassy, relayed from Hunter Street.

Louis had been killed in Assam on a flying mission; one of those sorties of the 1944 Burma campaign. His plane had crashed into a mountain. His will left all he owned to me; the solicitor wanted to know how to send me the money. He was both prudent and discreet. I said that I had no use for money; it should go to Louis's sisters, in Belgium. About £640 were shared out between his two sisters.

Riding my motor-cycle, drinking hot tea to drive the cold away in dirty, tired station restaurants; filling sheets of foolscap with details about the parasympathetic nervous system, the reaction to acetyl-choline, and the functions of the spleen, I now worried about money.

On March 25th we assembled at the school to hear the results; they were announced by numbers, read out to us by a member of the staff, later posted on the bulletin board. If I failed perhaps I would find a job, work as a secretary. Could I find a bed-sitting room large enough to accommodate Yungmei and Gillie? Of course Gillie would not *like* being in London in a bed-sitting room ... If she left, would I have to put Yungmei back in a nursery school? The professor of anatomy walked in, read out the numbers of those who had passed, I was among them, Cherry was not. To celebrate, we ate an extra newspaper-wrapped portion of fish and chips, and drank three scalding cups of tea at the railway station that night; Cherry wept, and so did her friend, who had also failed. But they both handsomely congratulated me. They took the examination in October and passed, and both have since become brilliant doctors.

I would now have £30 a month from the British Council for the next three years; and what would I do about Yungmei and Gillie?

Meanwhile Pao had arrived in the United States; was there when Roosevelt died; wrote to me in grieved terms about the President's funeral, in enthusiastic terms about America. 'These people are so generous ... they are ready to help us to the limit ... so different from the pinchpenny British ... ' He sent me the book written by Mrs Wellington Koo which had been suppressed by her husband; a few copies had escaped destruction. Thus he sought to make amends for his previous behaviour.

Later Pao wrote me letters from Chungking. At first I wrote back brief notes to say all was well. Of course he did not send any money; I settled the bill for his photographs, something like £45. There was a tailor's bill for over £30. I sold my fur coat for £90 and it covered the debts.

Back in China, Pao immediately became involved in the negotiations between the Kuomintang and the Communist Party, with the Americans sitting in as 'arbiter'. There was much talk of a 'coalition' government; an idea in line with the whole American attitude towards China, stemming primarily from their consideration that China should become the greatest piece of real estate for American businessmen in Asia. The Americans wanted peace and reforms, but above all they wanted to be there ... and that was their greatest mistake. The time of White Power in Asia was over – but they still don't seem to know it.

Pao wrote to me in autumn 1945: 'We cannot trust the communists ... they deceive and they cheat us; what liars they are ... ' But since two years before he had already been speaking of annihilating the communists, with American help, this righteous outburst did not impress me.

I could not see the communists laying down their arms to please the Americans for the sake of a 'coalition' in which, inevitably, they would have been slaughtered by Chiang Kaishek. This had happened before; why should they be so criminally stupid as to lay down their arms for an unworkable legal fiction?

I did not reply to Pao, nor to another letter the following year, announcing that he was now promoted, and going north; and indeed he did go to North China, to Peking, where he saw my father. The way my father was to describe this meeting was quite different from the way Pao wrote about it to me.

'I saw your father,' wrote Pao; 'really he has no spirit at all. He keeps smiling and making small bows ... I wanted to reprove him for having brought you up so badly ... If I had known what kind of household you came from, I would not have soiled myself marrying you ... ' This he wrote because both my sisters had married American G.I.s, which awoke Pao's fury.

In later years, I read in my father's autobiography his own version of the meeting. My father, like every other civil servant when the old regime was destroyed and a communist government installed, had written his autobiography, not once, but several times.

I knew my daughter was married to a certain Tang Paohuang. In 1946 he came to Peking; I heard of it through my friend Ping Shih, who admised me to go to see him as he was a very important person; I hesitated to do so, but then received a note from the said Tang Paohuang giving me his hotel address. So I went to call on him. We did not say anything of great import-ance ... He later came to see me, but did not stay very long. I heard a rumour that he was going to marry a Miss Sun Chia-Huei, the daughter of a former warlord, General Sun. She had followed Tang Paohuang to Peking, and was actually residing in the same hotel. I knew that he and my daughter did not agree, but I did not discuss the matter with him.

There was a snapshot of Pao with my father and my mother, stand-ing on the steps of the garden leading to the veranda of our house. I found it, when I went back to China in 1956, amid many other photo-graphs, in the old trunk which my mother had brought from Belgium with her, so many decades ago. My father kept all these photographs, and sometimes spread them on his bed, and called, cried out loud in his loneliness to my mother to return to him, but she was gone and would not return to him. However, I returned to see him, and all these things at last came into my hands.

In early 1947 another, long-delayed letter arrived. It was a cry of pain and anger from Pao. It told an intricate story; how he and another officer had been on guard in Chiang Kaishek's service: how some remarks they had made had been overheard, misrepresented and twisted in a report to Chiang, how he had been degraded and was being punished by being sent off ... to Manchuria, to the battlefields ... poor Pao, who had so long avoided the battlefields ...

At the same time as I received this letter I also received a letter from my friend Yuenling in Peking. She wrote that she had met Pao, that he had complained to her that I was not writing to him, and she en-treated me to write to him, for he was, she wrote, a 'noble and fine spirit, one dedicated to his country'. I wrote back to her saying that I was well, that Yungmei was growing up, and not mentioning Pao. The civil war, which had started with a breakdown of negotiations in 1946, had now spread all over the country; I wrote one sentence say-ing I hoped there would not be bloodshed ...

Yuenling replied that it was necessary to 'fight banditism'. While I was still puzzling this out, the war burst into the news in England, at last making an impact. *The Times* pontificated; peace was desirable in war-torn China; this could only be achieved by a 'coalition'. There were many abtruse suggestions of reform; confidence to be placed in the small party of non-communist intellectuals who might 'save the situation' by judicious measures ... if only Chiang listened to them. But I knew there could be no middle way; and all the Western papers wrote was, to my mind, very near nonsense. I found myself following the campaigns, disregarding all hopeful talk of 'peace' and 'cease fire'. How could any of these palliatives work? In front of my eyes were the episodes I had seen; the files of dying men, tied with rope (sometimes with wire). Recruits for the army. The beatings, the brutalities – I saw again Pao one day in the street, rushing forward to seize by the back of the neck a young coolie so loaded with bales of cloth that he could not see where he was going, though he cried between gasps: 'A load coming, oh, give me a little way,' and had accidentally brushed Pao's arm. And Pao had knocked him down, and the bales spilled on the road, and he had pounded kicks in the young coolie's ribs – I still heard the screaming – and all I could do was to weep, yet Pao was only acting as so many did. I did not think there could be 'peace' or a 'coalition'.

I went on studying, stopped writing to Pao, and waited for the outcome of the civil war.

In 1946, when the Second World War ended, Third Uncle was able to send two of his sons abroad; his eldest son, whom I called Third Brother, to America, where he studied at M.I.T., and Fourth Brother, Kuangti, to London. Sixth Brother stayed behind in China.

Kuangti lived far from where I stayed; he studied at a technical institute in North London. I was posted to hospitals outside London, so that we met infrequently, but in the summer of 1947 I was doing a three-month course in ear, nose and throat diseases in London; Cherry and I and another girl called Betty shared a basement flat in Doughty Street. Here Kuangti came from time to time to see me, though the journey for him from North London was tedious. He gave me news of Third Uncle and Third Aunt. He also gave me news of the inflation. A bowl of rice now cost thirty thousand dollars; and in the restaurants if one sat down, one paid first, for often the meal would have gone up ten or twenty per cent in price by the time it was ended.

'People go about carting money in wheelbarrows and suitcases to pay for the bus fare!' said Kuangti, laughing as we all do when we see helpless misfortune.

On October 17th, 1947, three months before I was due to take my finals in medicine, Kuangti appeared one morning early at my basement flat. He said, 'I have bad news.' Pao was dead, killed 'with glory on the field of battle' in Manchuria, near the Fu Shun coalmines.

Of course I wept. I wept a good deal, felt utterly guilty; felt that it was my fault: all my fault ... rang up Isobel Cripps and told her. Margaret Godley came to see me, remained to comfort me. I went to the lecture and ward rounds at the Elizabeth Garrett Anderson and returned home to cry again. Pao was dead. 'Of course it is not your fault,' said Margaret Godley. 'I should not have let him go,' I replied. But within two days my remorse had ceased.

I had received no official notification from the Chinese Embassy – perhaps because they did not have my address. I had deliberately not been to the Embassy. Kuangti urged me to go and see the Chinese Ambassador. It was an icy meeting. The Ambassador – not Dr Wellington Koo, but a Dr Cheng – had not heard ... he did not know. In three minutes I was out again. A day later the Embassy did receive the news, and sent me a large certificate with red wax seals. It said that Pao had 'sacrificed his life nobly on the field of battle' and awarded me, as his widow, the sum of ten million Chinese dollars. In October 1947, I think this came to about £3 sterling. I did not bother to collect the money.

I then received from Third Uncle a letter in which he urged me to return for Pao's funeral; it was absolutely necessary that the 'hero's' widow should be there 'holding her child by the hand'. There was a hint in a postscript that 'a certain Miss Sun' was claiming to be the legal wife and that therefore 'the inheritance' was in jeopardy, unless I was present. I told Kuangti that I was not interested in the inheritance.

Kuangti sat in front of me, his earnest face puckered with the worry of making me obey tradition and carry out the suggestions of his father. Could I willingly let another woman follow my husband's coffin and perform the mourning rites of a widow? 'Yes,' I said, 'What does it matter?' Kuangti cabled my refusal by saying I was ill – a well-understood euphemism. Another letter, from my father this time, reached me, urging me to return and claim my 'rights' as Miss Sun was saying that I had been repudiated and that she was the rightful wife. But the slain birds of summer remained dead for me. I was not going to play the comedy of mourning. 'This is October and in January I am taking the final examinations, to become a doctor. Pao is already dead. I have no money to go and return to this country.'

Now the Chinese Ambassador, a venerable old man who was to end his life as an expert on China in the United States, summoned me. He told me that I was the wife of a hero and must act accordingly, returning with my daughter to the bosom of Pao's family, to Pao's mother. In true Chinese tradition it was now my duty to sustain her in her sorrow. I told him I had no money to go back: Dr Cheng saw in this a possible demand that the Embassy provide me with funds (after all, I still had a diplomatic passport), and hastily replied: 'You must be an exemplary widow. And you must write to your mother-in-law. You must write to your mother-in-law every ten days. This is tradition.'

The funeral would have to proceed without me; my duty as I saw it was to take my examinations due in two months in order to qualify as a doctor. I asked Kuangti whether he realized that with the civil war in China things would change very soon. But like many Chinese in London then, and possibly also in China, he was reluctant to comment on politics. Funerals were still funerals, and a widow should be there. Since I was Elder Sister to him and he, being younger, owed me deference, Kuangti could not object directly to what I said, but he was slightly put out: 'I shall write that you are unwell, unable to come, and that you must be represented by proxy at the funeral.' We discoursed emptily about someone in the family being delegated to represent me. And then all Manchuria crumbled, the communist armies swept on in triumph throughout China and I heard no more of funerals, or tradition, or Miss Sun.

Briefly, during my sorrow, I remembered that Pao had asked me, in case he died, to kill myself, in order to leave behind an honourable name as a chaste widow and to accrue virtue to his virtuous family. But I had never promised. Within a week I was hard at work again.

By the end of the month of November came a small parcel: Pao's diary, which he had posted to me. With it was a letter dated early October; about ten days before he died.

It was rather short: only five or six lines, and it said: 'I am going now to the front to fight; I do not know what will happen; but I think that all of us are lost. I have not treated you very well, but if heaven gives me life I will treat you better.'

There was the diary; without its cover, removed possibly to make the parcel lighter; only the pages inside; the close and even writing, the calligraphy he had practised for mastery of moral stalwartness and for climbing the ladder of success, the characters not sloppy nor mean, firmness in the upright strokes; evenness to indicate self-control ... I fingered through the pages; then burnt the diary in the kitchen stove.

Here and there I caught a word, a paragraph ... I knew that Pao had wanted me to read his noble thoughts; I thought of his tortured loyalty; of his love for me ... but the very word 'diary' threatened to upset my mental balance, to send me into gales of hysterical laughter ... and I had my final examinations to think about, I could not afford hysteria, upsets, sorrow, sentiment, memory, regret. Forward, hastening past myself, no time for tears, I must go on ...

Five years later, when I was in Hongkong, I was to receive a letter from Yuenling, telling me more about Pao's death. Yuenling was then in Taiwan; she had followed Chiang Kaishek there. She wrote to ask me to visit her. She had taken up landscape painting; had married and had a son; sent me snapshots of herself, tall, graceful, happy-looking ... She wrote to tell me how Pao had died.

Through the last twenty years I have collected, without seeking for them, four versions of Pao's death. The official one was that Pao had been killed in a battle, heroically resisting to the last, slaughtered by a hail of bullets.

Another unpublished report said that Pao's soldiers, like so many of the Kuomintang troops, deserted en masse to the Red Armies, and the engagement turned into a rout; Pao was left with one subaltern whom he asked to run his sword through him; the man refusing, he then killed himself in an unspecified manner.

A third, more flamboyant story reported that his own troops had turned against him and shot him.

Yuenling's version was the most gruesome. She had painted me a beautiful landscape, a picture of mountains and river and contemplative sage, inscribed to me 'with love', hoping I would join her in Taiwan: join Chiang Kaishek.

'These communists are savage beasts,' she wrote. 'They kill in a way unbelievably barbaric! Whatever you do, dear friend, do not trust them. I fear you may be tempted, they may be trying to seduce you ... Remember what they did to your husband. They caught hold of him, tore out his eyes, ripped off the skin, tied him to a horse, dragged him till he died ... ' But Yuenling had been some years in Taiwan when she wrote, and some tales do improve with time ...

In 1958 I mentioned all these variants to my friend Kung Peng in Peking, half in rueful reminiscence, half hoping to know at last exactly what had happened. But Kung Peng did not say a word.

So much blood had been shed in the thirty years ... so many dead in battle, in the long long strife, during the Long March, in the civil war; so many had never known what happened to wife, child, parents, lover ... others had seen their loved ones tortured in front of their eyes ... still others, like Mao Tsetung himself, had placed their children in peasant families during the Long March and never seen them again ... And just as going to Pao's funeral would have been a ritual empty of meaning, knowing the manner of his dying was a detail of no importance.

The military triumph of the Communist Party and its army, culminating in 1949, could be understood if one saw it as the continuation of the heroic, epic Long March.

The Long March had begun as a withdrawal, due to the encirclement of the main Red Bases in South China in 1933. Chiang had mustered almost two million men, tanks and aircraft for his fifth formidable annihilation campaign. He denuded vast areas, in a great pincer movement to drive the communists into the sea.

The Red Army broke through the concrete forts, gun emplacements and trenches constructed by Chiang in four rings round their bases. They fought their way out of the encirclement and began that stupendous trek called the Long March, in the autumn of 1934.

At that time Mao Tsetung, in spite of his successes, had been subject to criticism by some of the other communist leaders. The Central Committee, long in hiding in Shanghai, was much preoccupied with theoretical questions; but the concrete application of theory to practice in China escaped them. The influence and popularity of Mao Tsetung among the common people and the soldiers was enormous. Although he was unable, for about three years, to have his views adopted, he nurtured and perfected his ideas. The military techniques he had worked out were not followed, and great losses resulted; Mao Tsetung was to analyse later the errors committed; among them, a sectarian attitude towards the Fukien general Tsai Tingkai and his 19th Route Army, who had fought so bravely against the Japanese invasion at Shanghai in 1932, and had been betrayed by Chiang Kaishek. Mao Tsetung had advised the establishment of links with these patriotic, non-communist troops, but was overruled, the narrow 'closed door' view being then prevalent among certain leaders.

In October 1934, after terrible fighting, the blockade lines were broken, and the main body of the communist army and followers – 130,000 in all – surged through the breach and started trekking westwards.

On foot, in long files, they went through the autumn cold, going west, some said towards Szechuan. The women carried babies on their backs; pigs, rice, machinery (from the small arsenal of the Red Base), suitcases, a few carts for pregnant women, all was carried away. The column was three hundred kilometres long, the rearguard one week away from the vanguard. Attacked daily, hourly, nightly, strafed from the air, ambushed on all the roads, they went on.

Out of this trek was born the Long March, taking over a year, crossing eleven provinces out of eighteen, eighteen mountain chains by snowy passes, some 13,000 feet high; 7,500 miles on foot at a clip of 25 miles a day. Out of 130,000, 30,000 arrived: and all along there had been renewals.

Throughout the first two months of the Long March, there were severe quarrels in the leadership; on the routes to follow, on the aim of the multitude thus trekking, on the destination, and where this exodus would end.

In January 1935, thirty per cent of the front marchers (about forty thousand strong) had become casualties. At a place called Tsunyi a halt was called, and a conference took place. The two main factions were Mao Tsetung's, opting for a base in the north-west from which to resist Japanese inroads into China, and the 'Moscow' faction of returned students, such as Li Lisan and others, who wanted to attack and hold 'large cities' as 'future and safe bases'.

The Tsunyi conference was crucial: by then the commanders and the rank and file had realized that Mao Tsetung's ideas were right. He was elected General Secretary of the Party and the Central Committee, and his tactical line was adopted unanimously.

The first thing that Mao did was to order the abandonment of the impedimenta which slowed down the columns and thus made it vulnerable to attack. Machinery, money, clothes, even guns were discarded or buried. Even children were left in the care of the peasantry, including two of Mao's own children ...

Thus lightened, the Long March went on. Mao Tsetung's supple, flexible principle of operations earned a victory in February 1935, when four divisions of the Kuomintang troops were broken. And now the Red Army went on with the hardest, most arduous part of the journey, crossing the great mountains and rivers of the hinterland. In Peking I met a woman, one of those who survived the Long March; her very young baby had been placed in a basket on a mule's back, along with other loads. Crossing a very high mountain, crawling along a narrow ledge of rock, the mule slipped and fell with its load and baby into the precipice 5,000 feet below. There was no time to stop and search, for at their back was an enemy army ... Finally the Red Army arrived in Yenan.

From 1937 to 1945, throughout the Sino-Japanese war and the Second World War, the Red Army fought the Japanese and the Chinese puppet troops continuously. In this continuous fighting, both on the front lines and behind the front, in the creation through this fighiting of guerrilla bases behind Japanese lines, the Red Army grew strong, nourished on battle, sustained by the people in the areas where they moved; out of the nuclei they seeded everywhere rose more guerrilla units, new armies, new liberated areas.

Chiang's plan in organizing a stalemate on his front, letting the communists bear the brunt of the fighting,.to promote their attrition, failed totally. The strength of the Red Army lay precisely in its fighting, day in day out.

At the same time as they fought the Red Army *educated* the people, making the population round them politically conscious. The reminiscences of the Long March written by Teng Yingchao, the wife of Chou Enlai, described this process:

> The women comrades who took part in the Long March were as firm and courageous as the men ... In the First Front Army there were thirty women cadres – the stronger ones carried their own bedding and rice bags on their back. Wherever our troops stopped for a rest, they took the opportunity of carrying out political propaganda work among the people, looking after the sick and wounded, helping to cook the meals. All the women

comrades completed the Long March, none dropped out or died on the way. They reached their destination the same thirty.

Teng Yingchao, herself suffering from serious tuberculosis of the lung, adds: 'Strange to say, after a year's extremely strenuous life in the Long March, I was cured without any special medical treatment.'

By the end of the war, in 1945, Red power had grown from a territory of 1,500,000 inhabitants in a poor and drought-stricken corner of the north-west, to include 93 million people. The membership of the Communist Party had increased from 40,000 in 1937 to 1,200,000 in 1945.

The widespread mobile and guerrilla warfare produced its own recruits, peasants volunteering by the hundreds of thousands; military and political talent, a young, enthusiastic leadership of military commanders – all these the Red Army possessed. From 30,000 men in 1936, the Army grew to 910,000, with 2,500,000 auxiliaries in the people's militia.

Sixty per cent of all the Japanese troops in China, and ninety-eight per cent of the puppet troops (including those who went over to the Japanese on Chiang's orders) were kept in a constant and bitter struggle by the Red Army.

Chiang subjected the Red areas to a more and more stringent military and economic embargo, cutting them off from all sources of supply in their own rear. They were attacked by the Kuomintang on four major and dozens of minor occasions. They never received any supplies from the Soviet Union or from America.

What made possible this tremendous ability, after two decades of revolution, to organize a military apparatus, to maintain political control over it, and to win overwhelming popular support for it? The answer, undoubtedly, is Mao Tsetung's ideas and their application to the conditions in China. As John Gittings, an English scholar, points out, through the twenty-two years from 1927 to 1949 the model of a revolutionary people's army, which alone could guarantee victory, was created by Mao Tsetung, and it is this model which the proletarian cultural revolution today has again brought to the fore, against other conceptions of the army as a hierarchical instrument of power, a professional class which serves a ruling group.

It was the fundamental principles governing the functions, growth and purposes of the People's Liberation Army which assured its victory in the civil war against Chiang from 1946 to 1949. Today again, in another Revolution – the Cultural Revolution – it is the Army which must safeguard the principles upon which are founded the socialist state of China.

Hence what is called today the Thought of Mao Tsetung is indissolubly linked to the Chinese Revolution and its military and political achievements, to the organization and being of the Communist Party and its Army.

This identification took on further importance during the military campaigns of 1946–9: the civil war.

No sooner had Japan capitulated in August 1945 than the race to occupy the territory and the cities which had been occupied by Japanese troops started, between Chiang on the one hand, the Communists on the other. In this enterprise, from the beginning, Chiang obtained American help to place his troops in advantageous positions for the impending conflict.

The first step was taken in August 1945, a few days after Japan's capitulation, when General MacArthur as Supremo in Tokyo gave his first order (General Order No. 1) to the Japanese Army to surrender only to the Kuomintang, and meanwhile to 'maintain law and order'. Whereupon the Japanese, who had already evacuated parts of Manchuria, now fought the communist guerrillas in Manchuria, with the approval of the Americans.

Meanwhile, American air transport (directly under Washington's orders) was being organized for Chiang's troops: 235 Dakotas airlifted 110,000 of Chiang's men to Manchuria and Northern Chinese cities.

On August 12th, units of the Red Army marched out from Yenan into Inner Mongolia and from there on foot across North China to Manchuria, a move openly announced by radio, the objective being to dominate communication throughout North China and Manchuria before Chiang did.

The U.S. 5th Fleet then landed an extra 50,000 Marines. American troops in China increased from 60,000 to 135,000 *after* the Japanese capitulation.

One amusing story of the American airlift is told by Anna Louise Strong, the American correspondent then in Manchuria. While the

Kuomintang troops (and the Americans) arrived by air, the communist troops were slogging along on foot at a clip of 25 to 30 miles a day. Lin Piao was ordered by Mao to organize the Manchuria guerrillas. He reached Manchuria earlier by getting a lift, for part of the journey, in an American plane from the U.S. liaison group in Yenan, sent to pick up American airmen shot down over North China. 'Did the Americans realize how important this slim, intellectual-looking man was to be?' asks Strong. Evidently not, since they gave this meek-looking, quiet man a lift and thus, all unknowingly, doomed the Chiang armies to disaster in the subsequent battles for Manchuria.

The Manchurian campaign directed by Lin Piao owed its guiding strategy to Mao Tsetung's planning. It is not altogether surprising, therefore, that in the Cultural Revolution today – a struggle more complex, more difficult than any civil war – Lin Piao, the victor of Ping Hsin Kuan, the victor of Manchuria, the victor of North China, the man who led the crossing of the Great River into South China, should emerge as Mao's second, his successor, the one who has best understood and most faithfully applied the military thinking which had propelled the Chinese Revolution to victory in 1949.

At the end of August 1945 Mao Tsetung flew to Chungking; negotiations for a 'coalition' government, with the Americans present as 'arbiter and mediator', went on. Meanwhile all these troop movements were taking place and everywhere local clashes occurred between communists and Kuomintang, the latter deliberately attacking and provoking conflicts.

On October 10th, an agreement was reached, but the unilateral help given by the United States to Chiang went on. Chiang now filled Manchuria with his soldiers. Lin Piao organized the local guerrillas; together with the Yenan arrivals they were welded into a people's army of 300,000. The Americans placed 'truce teams' in the cities. The Russians, who had entered the war on August 9th, 1945, were also in some of the cities of Manchuria, and Chiang asked the Russians to *postpone* their evacuation of Manchuria, in order to prevent the penetration of Chinese communist troops into zones occupied by the Soviet Army ...

Meanwhile the U.S. continued to airlift troops for Chiang and on December 12th, 1945, the Russians allowed Chiang's troops entry into their zones.

Lin Piao obtained no help from the Russians. Anna Louise Strong is very clear on the point. To her question: 'What help did you get from the Russians?' 'None,' Lin Piao replied categorically. 'No troops, no weapons, no advisers, nothing. Whatever men and arms came with the Soviet Army into Manchuria, went back when the Soviet army went; whatever arms or war supplies they took from the Japanese they took into Russia or destroyed on the spot'.

The Soviet administrators protected Chiang appointees in Manchurian cities for many months. 'The Chinese communists were very annoyed', remarked a Russian major to Strong, 'when we threw them out of Mukden and put Chiang's men in. But what could we do? We had our treaty with Chiang.'

Meanwhile, on the United States side, General Marshall was now appointed as 'arbiter' to 'make peace' in China. On January 10th, 1946, another agreement was reached between communists and Chiang; but again fighting broke out, started deliberately by Chiang; even U.S. observers were categorical on this point. Even Marshall stated that 'the government was abandoning all democratic procedure and pursuing a policy of dictatorial military force.'

The civil war can be described in two stages: the first, corresponding to Mao's tactics, 'when the enemy advances, we retreat', broke out in summer 1946 and lasted till summer 1947. At first it looked as if the Kuomintang were winning everywhere. In Manchuria the major cities were theirs. 'All these towns ... will be burdens on Chiang's back,' said Lin Piao.

Kuomintang strength was dissipated by their occupying, garrisoning, and immuring themselves in the fortress-like cities, from which the generals refused to budge, refused to fight, and where corruption was soon rampant. Round them the communists organized the countryside.

During that year, the Red Army in Manchuria under Lin Piao spent as much time doing land reform, clearing the land, planting (so as not to burden the peasantry), harvesting, and educating the peasantry, as in fighting. This policy continued to be the mainspring of its success; not being an instrument of killing, but an ideological army, teaching and practising revolutionary ideas and methods, made the Red Army unconquerable.

Many foreign military experts spent time counting heads; five to one in favour of Chiang, three to one in favour of Chiang. The communists were in a minority – Chiang had more soldiers, American equipment. But there could be no comparing the dedicated, politically conscious, educational force of the P.L.A. with the pressganged, ill-nourished, ill-treated and betrayed armies of Chiang Kaishek.

During this year of tactical withdrawal, Mao Tsetung deliberately abandoned Yenan to Hu Tsungnan.

The retreat from Yenan was masterly; everything was taken away; the International Peace Hospital doctors and nurses carried the patients two days before to the hills. The mothers who had just given birth were brought in litters down the high ledges of the Yenan hill caves. Hu Tsungnan and his sleek troops, after many years of doing nothing, entered Yenan, two days after Mao had left; this was proclaimed a great victory, though Yenan was empty, empty when Hu came in. To celebrate this triumph, Hu Tsungnan got married – apparently he had vowed not to marry before he had taken Yenan ...

Only fifteen miles away at Wah Yao Pu, the Central Committee of the Communist Party learnt the news. 'Hu Tsungnan has fallen into the trap.'

After that it was a game; Mao's armies dragged Hu Tsungnan's troops in a wide, wide circle through North China. In hot pursuit, Hu forced his men; they were unaccustomed to fighting, to walking. 'When the enemy is exhaused, we attack.' Hu Tsungnan had over-stretched his supplies, his lines of communication were poor, his soldiers tired – the Red Army swooped upon him, and the end was swift.

In the summer of 1947, the People's Liberation Army passed to the offensive everywhere.

During the first three months of 1947 in Manchuria, Lin Piao launched five probing offensives in 'attack and withdrawal' tactics, with small forces of sixty thousand men or so. This tired out the Kuomintang troops; they claimed victory after victory when the communists attacked and then withdrew, but they were unable to pursue the Red Armies, and immured themselves again in their fortress cities. The fourth offensive, in May, perfectly prepared and executed, was a success; in this one Lin Piao utilized three hundred thousand men and also militia of two million in a classical people's war, with the active participation of the Manchurian people, against Chiang Kaishek's troops.

Then the avalanche started: the Red Armies swept on; Mukden,

Changchun, Kirin: encircled cities held by the Kuomintang. By July 10th half the territory once occupied by the Kuomintang in Manchuria was lost; and the number of desertions from the Chiang armies had reduced the strength of all Kuomintang units by over fifty per cent.

Tl. fleeing garrisons abandoned entire depots and supply trains, vehicles and weapons. The Red Armies now had (as the American Consul in Mukden reported at the end of May 1947) ever mounting numerical superiority, aid from underground units, while 'apathy, resentment, defeatism, an unfriendly populace, growing indignation at disparity between officers' enrichments and soldiers' low pay ... ' precipitated the Kuomintang failure.

Chiang persisted. He now sent his best troops to Manchuria; and it was in Manchuria that the battle for China was lost by Chiang Kaishek.

Lin Piao's sixth and seventh offensives took place in the last six months of 1947. In Manchuria itself, the incredible greed and rapacity of the Kuomintang generals and officials (they had even raided the dynastic tombs) had alienated the population completely.

The military leadership was in complete disorder, Chiang continuing his game of order and counter-order, by-passing or shifting commanders at will, in wild confusion.

The Whangpoo clique continued its shuffle for power. The rate of turnover in field commands soared, as general after general came in to get their share of the pillage of Manchuria ... 'Dissatisfaction', writes F. F. Liu delicately (he served with the Kuomintang armies and is now teaching at Princeton), 'filtered to the lowest levels.'

On September 15th, 1947, began the last offensive. The objective was the Peking–Mukden railway, cutting off Manchuria from North China.

The communist armies switched from guerrilla tactics to the use of tanks and artillery. Chiang recalled the general in command and put into Manchuria Hsiung Shih-hui, director of the Generalissimo's headquarters in Manchuria, who had headed the mission to England a few years previously, and Tu Yuming. The arrogance of these Whangpoo men was well known. It was under Hsiung that Pao had received a command in Manchuria.

Meanwhile in China itself the fighting, directed by Mao's strategic concept, led to the consolidation of great new Red bases in Shansi and in Honan. On December 25th, 1947, Mao Tsetung wrote: 'This is a turning point in history. It is the turning point from growth to extinction for Chiang Kaishek's twenty-year counter-revolutionary rule. It is the turning point from growth to extinction for imperialist rule in China ... The People's Liberation Army has turned back the wheel of counter-revolution, of U.S. imperialism and the Chiang Kaishek bandit gang – and sent it down the road to destruction.'

It was in the autumn to winter 1947 campaigns of Lin Piao in Manchuria that Pao's troops either abandoned him or killed him. By the division, the soldiers were crossing over to the communist side and, once there, they changed, they fought well, became transformed ...

By the summer of 1948, the Kuomintang army had three hundred thousand men tied up in Manchurian cities, entirely fed and equipped by airlifts (supplied by America), while the population of the cities starved.

The final stage came in four major campaigns, between September and December 1948, ending with the complete and total debacle of the Kuomintang armies in Manchuria.

After that, by forced marches of thirty miles per day or more, the armies of Lin Piao went into North China and the cities fell – Tientsin, Peking, in January 1949; then Lin Piao raced for South China, and crossed the Great River, the Yangtze, in April – three hundred thousand men crossing the mile-broad stream in two days – and thus came into South China.

By summer 1949, all was over; Liberation had come to China, the reign of Chiang Kaishek, of Tai Lee and his Blueshirts, was done.

Fourteen

THE SUMMER of 1945 in England was radiant with a great deal more sunlight than usual; and this impression perhaps is nothing but the colour of my mind, unblocked by sadness. I put my face up to the precious sun, the bird-crossed sky; there were hedges and fields with soft winds stirring, long grass in which, exhausted from pedalling my bicycle, I threw myself – the beautiful countryside of England, with its rich softness, all dulcet and depth; I smelt the little wild orchids of Dorset, and the honey slopes of Wiltshire, so sensuous in their deceptive mildness, mocking all grandeur with their sweet low curves.

Often the bombers went droning, singing their terrible song, back and forth in flocks through the summer air. I remember an afternoon bicycling down winding lanes heavy with may bushes and every blossom a new and radiant star; and overhead a doodlebug came droning; but the soft and limpid land took no notice. We shaded our eyes, munching our sandwiches, and looked up without anger or dread.

I had started my hospital training in April; since the School of Medicine in Hunter Street had been hit by a doodlebug, we had moved to country hospitals, at Arlesey, and St Albans; the next two and a half years saw me doing three-monthly terms in medicine, surgery, etc., at several hospitals outside London, and then back again in London, at the Elizabeth Garrett Anderson, at the Royal Free itself. I knew then the life of digs, the dinners cooked by landladies; putting shillings in diminutive gas-fires; bicycling in icy weather on icy roads; so often eating fish and chips, standing up; no stockings, wool socks taking a week to dry suspended on a string above the gas fire; a basement flat, where for nine months of 1947 I shared two and a half rooms with two other girls, and this was ease, comfort, luxury, costing only £2 10s. a month. There we had a kitchenette, a bath, and a cat called Minnehaha who found us walking in Gray's Inn Gardens, and adopted us. I had to drown most of her kittens regularly and we finally had her spayed, and then gave her away to another cat-lover when we qualified and could no longer keep her.

I went on rounds in a not-too-clean white coat with a stethoscope in the pocket; and now I could not think of myself otherwise. I saw myself slogging through the years, becoming a doctor at last, and all of it, despite the discomfort, was comforting. For all through I received much friendship, and best of all, I really did get to live as many of the British lived through the war and afterwards, on the same rations, with the same impecunious serenity. I sat in trains scheduled to start at 5 p.m. but which squatted at railway stations for hour upon hour before they deigned to budge; and one day I spent six and a half hours waiting in an overcrowded compartment, where no one said a word to anyone else. I was often cold and dirty, but all this was happiness – some of my happiest days, carefree and young; but others were not so happy.

For in that summer garden of my memory when my heart had

gone to sleep there was still one quiet terror lurking, and that was about Yungmei, who now became ill. I was not yet a doctor, and Yungmei was ill.

The thirty pounds a month I received from the British Council was to cover my living expenses; fees were also covered, but there was Yungmei, and Gillie. There was no provision for them. I had to find money by other methods; the sale of my clothes; book royalties; I became curator of the Pathology Museum at the Royal Free Hospital, which brought me five pounds a month. But the most important asset I had was Gillie herself.

Gillie, for almost two years, 1945 and 1946, was the mainstay of our existence. Her devotion to Yungmei, and her own ingenuity in devising ways and means of remaining with us – and considering how conventional she was, her staying with undoubtedly the curiousest, most controversial people (meaning me!) was incomprehensible to most of her friends – made it possible for me to study, to strain towards that goal, which was to qualify as a doctor in the shortest possible time. As long as possible I would provide Yungmei with a secure environment; I could not drag her with me in dingy bed-sits, from hospital to hospital. Yungmei's standard of living did not go down with mine; and that this was possible was entirely due to Gillie, who hired herself out to other people in well-to-do houses, taking Yungmei with her, and accepting only a pound a week from me. Thus Gillie worked, to earn Yungmei's keep.

I must emphasize that at any time Gillie could have left me, with a five-year-old Yungmei on my hands. But she refused steadfastly to be parted from Yungmei and stipulated that she could only look after other children if Yungmei came with her; and the scarcity of governesses, and Gillie's incomparable excellence (for she was, indeed, an extraordinarily capable person) made it only too easy for her to be swamped with offers. Our neighbour at Winkfield, Lady F., whose vast regiment of poultry Yungmei loved to feed, was delighted when Gillie accepted her offer, for she was very short-staffed (as everyone was, in England at war). Gillie thus obtained the rest of her salary from Lady F., whose grandchild she now looked after; but she took far less than she was entitled to, because of Yungmei.

Yungmei, however, drooped; became a little hostile, difficult, and ate very badly. There had been too many changes in her young life and this was reflected in her behaviour towards Gillie and towards her

327

hostess. She could not understand that she now saw me only occasionally, that I had to work so hard, that some people who came to visit Lady F. passed occasional thoughtless remarks. She became acutely conscious of being 'the little Chinese girl'; her proud spirit resented patronizing; she clung to me whenever I was there, refused to eat and was capricious when I was away. How could I explain to her that I was working for both of us, that I had to do this, so that I might earn enough for us two?

At week-ends I would try to see Yungmei. I would not dare to overstay, to abuse other people's hospitality. One day I took Yungmei away for two or three days, rented a room in a very small hotel, had her to stay with me. It was on this occasion that I found the maid of the hotel, who had 'asthma', fondling and kissing the child. And about two months later, Yungmei became ill with a 'cold', but the cold did not get better. She began to vomit, had fever, lost some weight. The doctor Lady F. sent for diagnosed bronchitis; but some dread presentiment made me take her up to London and put her in care of the pediatrician at the Royal Free Hospital, a specialist in child tuberculosis. I told the specialist I thought Yungmei was suffering from a primary tuberculosis complex.

'What makes you think that she has had a primary tuberculous infection?' The pediatrician was sceptical; for the inclination to believe that they or their friends are suffering from diseases which they are actually studying is well known among medical students, and we had been studying the primary tuberculous complex. It seemed just too pat that I should now want my child examined for this.

I told the consultant about the maid with so-called asthma, with a peculiar husky cough and husky voice, whom I had found kissing Yungmei and talking to her, face close-pressed to face. Yungmei was duly admitted to the children's ward for investigation; lay in a bed in a large, long ward full of other children; in forty-eight hours lost her careful sedulously acquired upper-class accent and acquired the most irresistible cockney twang.

When after four weeks she returned to Gillie's care, the latter was very upset by the language Yungmei brought back with her.

The X-rays did show a lung with a heavy primary infection; the specialist lectured on her case; Yungmei was very pleased: 'She's talking about mee – aintcher?' and made disobliging remarks about all the medical students, grouped in a semi-circle round her, to the little boy in the next bed.

The primary infection had undoubtedly been heavy, but with rest, food and care, natural resistance would overcome it; the specialist was optimistic. Yungmei went back to Gillie, to Lady F. They weighed her and found that she had lost more weight in hospital than before going, and this occasioned Lady F., slightly huffed, to point out triumphantly that her doctor was better than mine. But this was not the point of the examination, which was to ascertain what Yungmei was really suffering from. By now unfortunately both Lady F. and Gillie were taking it as a slur upon their care of Yungmei that I should have recourse to another doctor, and that I should have taken Yungmei to hospital when their local practitioner was so good ... It was little use explaining. Gillie was faced with a cockney-speaking Yungmei, who deliberately set herself to become exasperating; a child in rebellion, who vomited regularly every night, because she wanted to be with me. I told Gillie that the vomiting was psychological. Race was now invoked by certain well-wishers to explain Yungmei's misdeeds, for she now slashed one of Lady F.'s best antique chairs. Poor sweet Gillie, caught between advice from all sides! She in turn became upset, which was not surprising. After all, the child was in her care, was almost hers since she was with her most of the time, and I only appeared whenever I could.

I managed to spend a week with Yungmei in Dorset near Lulworth Cove; this took a bite off the preciously hoarded money from *Destination Chungking*. During those days no vomiting occurred and Yungmei ate voraciously. I was then convinced that the matter was deep-seated resentment; and was faced with the psychological problem of Yungmei deliberately damaging her health, turning to Gillie and saying: 'When my mummy is here you can go away,' becoming obstreperous because she was perfectly miserable. Poor Gillie, who had given her heart to Yungmei, was giving up her income for her, was doing all she could for her, and thus also for me! Poor Yungmei, a five-year-old wanting to restore the family pattern! I lay awake at night, thinking of all this, unable to find a way out – and again consulted the specialist. She now advised me to try the Caldecott School, in southern England. So I wrote to the Caldecott, and the next week the Director, Miss Rendall, came up to London and we met. Miss Rendall was a large, rather stout, infinitely energetic and intelligent person, and in a very short time we got on well. I told her about Yungmei, then went

329

down to see the school. It was a very fine house in the middle of a large park, with beautiful trees and enormous lawns. It had become a home for disturbed children, uprooted children, those whose parents led unhappy lives, and whose unhappiness was communicated to them. The children came from different communities and classes. I then talked to Gillie. This upset Gillie even more, for she had dreamt of Yungmei in a 'nice' school, the kind that most of her previous charges went to. But I was convinced that Yungmei must leave the refined and altogether unrealistic setting in which I had, perhaps foolishly, tried to keep her safe and happy; a milieu where children dressed for tea, and did not get dirty, and went to chapel on Sundays, and had nannies, and said thank you in just the right accent. So the Caldecott it was for the next two years, 1947 and 1948. And that meant really separating from Gillie, which cost me wakeful nights; but it was the best for both Gillie and Yungmei, for the emotional tensions, such as the climate of social hierarchy in England can generate, threatened to turn Yungmei into a child with a serious emotional disturbance. She had to find her own level, a level of common humanity. And this the Caldecott would give her.

The Caldecott School was from all points of view an admirable institution. There were many other children there, English chiefly but also French and Italian; some were from well-to-do families, many were not. It was good for Yungmei to be with such children; for all had suffered, and suffering is a common denominator; with them Yungmei would no longer feel singled out; having me as mother was no longer a disaster; on the contrary, in a world where separation and enduring unpleasant things were acknowledged – whereas in the good homes where she had stayed all these things were not supposed to exist – she would begin to open up to the world again, and stop that inward refusal to meet others, which she exteriorated in rebellion.

There is no doubt that the Caldecott saved Yungmei; she throve; she had no more trouble with her chest. I obtained special permission to come to see her once a month, instead of once a term as was usual; and once a month I duly made the (at that time) long journey, involving over two hours either way, by bus and train, and though we had only a few hours together, it made a great difference to Yungmei. For now she boasted to the others: 'My mummy loves me, she comes every month to see me,' whereas other children only received a visit once every term. To this visit we both clung, and also the postcards

I wrote to her, the letters, a constant stream which I tried to keep up, all the time, so that she should know she was wanted, she was loved, and that it was only circumstances which separated us. In about six months I felt strong enough to write to Gillie, and to suggest that she and I and Yungmei should meet for tea and a day's outing. Gillie showed the most remarkable perception and understanding, and also the most unfaltering generosity of spirit, accepting what had happened; though it seemed a hard blow after all she had done. She has thus continued as one of our very best friends, an unfaltering relationship, still enduring now that Yungmei is herself a mother (and a much better one than I could ever have been).

And thus we went on. But now I had to pay the fees at the Caldecott, and they amounted to something like four guineas a week all told, which took a big bite out of my £30 a month – but I contrived and stinted and saved and also managed the train fares, and taking Yungmei out to lunch on my monthly visit, and a toy or a book or a box of sweets. And Cherry helped; more often than not, she paid for the rent and the food at our lodgings.

In the summer of 1947 it became again possible to travel to Europe, though only with a five-pound allowance in British currency. Yungmei, who was on summer holiday from the Caldecott, myself and Cherry, sailed across the Channel to Belgium, to Brussels, and went to stay with Georgette Acker whom I had known when I was at Brussels University about ten years before; and who had actually found me through a persistent search via the Belgian Embassy in London.

Georgette Acker had been a communist, in the days when I was a student at Brussels University. When the war in China started in 1937, Georgette and her husband were in the Sino-Belgian Friendship Association, together with the priest Abbé Bolland, with whom I so often lectured on China. Apart from the Abbé Bolland, it was Georgette who stuck most in my memory because she was so indomitably persevering in everything she did. Ten years later, I found her the same amiable, sweet person, living with joy a life by no means easy, a sincere woman, whose abnegation was an intellectual conviction; a Marxist, who during the war had worked in the resistance in the Ardennes; and afterwards, returning to the Party, had found 'a lot of

331

young people in command' who had snubbed her. She remained staunchly convinced that only communism could provide a better future for all of mankind, and was scathing about the Belgian communist party, 'bourgeois counting their dividends'. 'The future of the world is in China, watch the Revolution there, it will shake the world,' she said almost laughingly.

I then saw again, with emotion, Abbé Bolland, who was much older, and whose high blood-pressure condemned him to an almost recluse life. He inquired eagerly about China. 'War again in that unhappy country,' he said. 'My God, how I hope for peace in China one day.'

We went to the sea at Ostend, for three days I hunted up some relatives, discovered their depleted ranks; and I saw Hers again. A friend of Georgette told me that Hers was in an office at the Banque de Bruxelles. I rang up the Bank and recognized his voice; he did not sound surprised to hear me, but somehow distant. However, he told me to come to the bank and as it was ten in the morning I went. Hers was sitting in an imposing office, all brown leather and polished massiveness. He looked just the same and said, 'Ho, ho.' 'You've gone up in the world,' I said to him, and he replied, 'I am married now, yes, I am married!' I said, 'Congratulations!' He continued with a window-panes look: 'I married a very young girl; very young; and she is insanely jealous. Someone has told her stories about you and she does not want to see you; she is infernally jealous of me, my past, all the people I have known; she is very young. So I will not ask you to meet her because I want to avoid a crisis in my family.' 'But she has no cause to be jealous of me,' I said. 'I know,' he said, 'but people have poisoned her mind. She detests you.' I laughed cheerfully, feeling it ridiculous that Hers, whom I had thought so independent, capable of imposing his will on anyone, should suddenly become so timorous. I said, 'You know I have never been interested in men unless they were the same age as myself.' The sentence came out of me before I realized its bitchiness, for in 1947 Hers was sixty, and his wife forty years younger than he.

Some years later I did meet his wife and found her a most beautiful, charming and intelligent woman, not at all as he had described. Hers became gradually excessively religious. ('The house is always full of priests and nuns,' his wife confided to me in exasperation, 'and I am in the kitchen cooking for three children and have no time for anything else.') She had a gift as a sculptress, which Hers would not let her use, by the simple device of keeping her tied down by domesticity, until she too erupted in revolt. And as I saw him, in 1947, embarrassedly stir papers on his desk, his eyes avoiding me, I almost burst out laughing. I told him I was studying medicine, that Pao was leading troops somewhere in China, that when my medical studies were over I would be going back. 'Back to China? You are crazy, you have always been crazy,' said Hers. 'And I don't think you will finish your medical course.' 'Too late for you to say so,' I said, 'I am finishing by the end of the year.'

Another visit I paid was to Louis's sister Jeanne. Correspondence between us, owing to the transfer of Louis's money, had continued. Jeanne invited Cherry and Yungmei and me to stay with her in the country, for a week's holiday. We went; a gaspy little train which hobbled all the way to the village in Wallonia where Jeanne was staying at a farmhouse with her son. The place was a manure yard; for there, as still today in some parts of Northern France, wealth was measured by the height of the dungheap in the front courtyard. However, we were told the well water was remarkably soft (which it was), and there was as much cream and milk as one wanted. There were also innumerable flies. Yungmei once again showed her gift for adaptiveness and she and Jeanne's young son ran about, watched a cow being serviced by a large bull brought for the purpose, fought the village children, and practised the local dialect with such success that I thought she would never utter in English again. She also promptly took over the most discouraging habits of Jeanne's little boy, such as nose-picking, and eating with the fingers and peering at people using the open toilet. Jeanne could not understand that I should not devote my life to the cause of Wallonia. Belgium, 'that hideous and idiotic confection', she called it, should not exist. There were Flanders and Wallonia, the latter to be reattached to France. Louis had been a fervent member of the Wallonia National Party which argued that Flanders and Wallonia spoke different tongues, had different people, that Walloons were becoming an oppressed minority. The Wallonia Party protested vehemently against the imposition of the Flemish language and against Flemish predominance in government. Today, twenty years later, the quarrel goes on; it has become much more acute; exacerbated by the very tangible material distress into which Wallonia is quagmired.

This cause Jeanne had now espoused with all the fervour she possessed. She could not see that there was anything else happening in the world, and thought it wrong of me not to give myself to it in memory of Louis. It was Cherry who became exasperated by the odours, the malevolence of the flies, the cows, the dogs (who all appeared rabid, and snarled and bit and had to be headed off with sticks), the soft water (but only one small wash basin for the three of us), the toilet – a shed in the field just beyond the cowshed, guarded by a ferocious hound on a long chain. It could almost reach the users if they did not squat well within the privy's recess, and always tried to, hurling itself forwards and barking and snapping. Cherry wrote to Georgette Acker asking her to send us a telegram calling us back to Brussels. We showed the telegram to Jeanne when it arrived. Jeanne was upset by our departure. The presence of another guest at the farm, a rather hefty young man covered in acne (he even had it on his buttocks, visible when he went swimming in very skimpy tights), also upset Cherry, for he frisked and gambolled round her with a persistence which made her push a chair against our bedroom door.

I too found these pastoral surroundings fraying; to the queasiness of a stomach averse to a mixture of cream and flies, was added the constant worry of seeing that Yungmei did not get her eyes poked out by the pointed sticks of the warlike little farm boys. With fervent goodbyes we caught the snail-paced train back to Georgette's friendly flat in Brussels.

When I next heard of Georgette Acker she was dead. She had told us, while we were there, that a small epithelioma, a skin cancer, on her nose, had been successfully treated; no one knew that this growth spreading into her body was to kill her, an uncommon thing for a skin cancer to do.

Fifteen

OF MY YEARS as a medical student, the gustiness, the splurging student lingo, the laughter, are resurrected when I meet other students of the Royal Free of those days. We then talk of digs and landladies, and call by their nicknames the consultants who taught us and awed us and passed or failed us. Being a student during those war years and soon after the war was being scruffy and messy and cold more than usual;

334

and hungry more than usual; and so accustomed were we to dirt that it was a year after the war when Mrs Lloyd Williams, the Head of the Royal Free, had to tell us to be a little more tidy and clean.

During those weeks and months I was always straining, straining, pushing ahead, incapable of understanding those who took the hours easily, who did not extract the last ounce out of the clinical round, the examination of patients. As soon as I was allowed, at the end of two years and nine months, I sat for all the branches of the medical examination together, in order to qualify at the earliest moment; and I did pass, thus qualifying in the least possible time.

This haste, this hurry, this aggressive pushing forward, did not endear me to all. That I was a demon for work could not be contested; but this energy did lead me, when I became house surgeon, to capture all the spare beds I could, so that I managed to have twice as many patients to look after as the other house surgeon, and this was certainly not fair to her. At my back, like the proverbial chariot, I heard not only Time, but Need driving me on, and besides Yungmei there was also something else, and its name was, once again, as ten years before, China.

Never for a moment did I contemplate remaining in England. I had to go back, I did not swerve from this aim; I would not sit back, dawdle, let myself live, take it easy – I would wrest what I could and go back, go back ...

No illness came to thwart my onward progress. My professors on the whole were very good to me, in particular the surgeon, Mr Shattock. The only unpleasant incident I remember concerned a Mrs Ledingham, the medical consultant, a tall and rather highly-strung person, whose richly adorned necklaces concealed a thyroid removal, and who at two afternoon sessions repeatedly and loudly drew the attention of the students to the fact that miscegenation often produced skin pigmentation ... a non-medical fact, which the presence of a Portuguese patient with negroid features had inspired. The quirks and foibles and fancies of our instructors and consultants who swept grandly through the wards while we trailed meekly or drooped fearfully about them formed part of our life; we nicknamed them and mimicked them. I think now they were some of the finest people I could have met.

In August 1945, the bomb on Hiroshima made me very unhappy for some days. We were then in Welwyn Garden City, and I remember

335

that splendid August afternoon, the hedges so green, and the big head-lines in the newspapers in everybody's hands. Years later, I read Kingsley Martin's reaction to it, identical to my horror, a consuming indignation which left me no rest. I walked Cherry up and down the sun-filled main street, telling her that this was the most criminal thing ever done ... I recapture that taste of horror, of something monstrous, fraught with doom for all of us; and Cherry's comment, as was the comment of nearly all the other students, that this 'shortened the war', made me incredibly angry. Whatever the Japanese had done, they did not deserve this; the people who died were the helpless men, women and children of a city; but the reaction of many around me was smug, or even joyful, one house surgeon going so far as saying that all Japan should have been bombed. My inexplicable anguish became muted as the days went by, but it never disappeared.

In September 1946 I did two months' midwifery in Ireland, at the Rotunda Hospital. We sailed for Dublin, Cherry and I. Coming from the 'egg a week' England, still on rationing, the abundance of eggs in Ireland (two or three for breakfast every morning) seemed to us in-credible luxury. The abundance of fleas in the homes of the poor also staggered us. Never had I seen such fat, large fleas. 'They are the Cabra fleas,' said in her rich brogue the maid who cleaned our rooms.

The Cabra district was four miles out from the hospital; to get to the cases on time one had to use a bicycle; and very often we were too late. No one was allowed a house in the Cabra district unless he was extremely poor, or unemployed, and had at least five children. Yet we were always greeted there with blessings, about our ears fell the throbbing, singsong Irish voices, bread (white) with butter and tea waited for 'the doctors'. So also did the howling new-born. 'So sorry doctor, I tried ... but I couldn't hold it for you any longer.' The mother apologized, as if for a misdemeanour; we sheepishly cut the cord, dabbed iodine on the stump ...

We were kept busy at the Rotunda Hospital, an imposing edifice both in and out. Inside a multitude of delivery wards, separated by screens, row upon row of women, all enduring the same pain and triumph. Participation in the perpetual, recurring miracle of birth was total once we stepped in. Baby-production went on all the time, behind one or another screen. We plunged into it, but it was there also that we learnt when not to meddle.

The Rotunda had a plentiful supply of male medical students only too ready to take girls round the Dublin pubs. My aversion to men was not dispelled by Ireland. It had been enhanced since, on the first night we arrived, we had forty-two beer bottles thrown at our locked door, one every ten minutes or so, all through the night. Cherry soon discovered a young doctor who took her out to Wicklow; but our best encounter there was dinner with the Irish Jewish family of an eminently respectable surgeon who lived on Fitzwilliam Square. The son, a non-drinking, hard-working student, was in our team of three, and took us home to his family. In their company we were amply nourished, told the history of Ireland with tremolo flourish and tears of indignation at the vileness of the English. And indeed the English 'limeys' were not popular in Dublin. Thus we saw something of Dublin, too little, alas, only enough to remember, with melancholy, how often its fey greyness, the unpremeditated twists and turns of its small streets, and the beautiful tones of its river we hurried by were discoveries unpursued while we raced into the overcrowded slums, to catch yet another baby born before our arrival. How often we were entreated by women to stop their becoming pregnant again, but were not allowed to teach them anything except the safe period, and that teaching was highly unsatisfactory. The fleas came home with us and we shook them off with anti-flea powder; they reminded me of the bedbugs in Szechuan.

While we were at the Rotunda John Coast, a young Englishman, turned up in Dublin because of me. In spite of my hostility to all men John Coast had tried to awaken my interest. I had met him through Dorothy Woodman, who after the war was organizing all sorts of committees for Asia. For ever generous, for ever expansive, a globe-concerned Dorothy had thrown open her arms and her house, and also the nice little cottage she had in the countryside, to many Asian students; landladies in digs being parsimonious about food, I repaired, when possible, to Dorothy's Thursday free-for-all when she cooked vastly, and well, incredible amounts of food (all vegetarian) for an army of vaguely leftist (some of them genuine leftists) Asian intellectuals.

Dorothy Woodman as well as Kingsley Martin are actually the product of the British administrative genius; the left wing of the Establishment. The ingenuity of the British, who nurture their future opponents and feed them carefully and listen sympathetically to their denunciatory abuse; knowing that in the fullness of time these kindnesses will be remembered! One could *talk* and *talk* and say such splendidly daring, non-conformist things in Dorothy's spacious flat, and some Asians were to remember those days as the best time of their lives ...

Clad in a vaguely Asian robe, Dorothy pressed upon us mounds of food, stimulated discussion with arch but shrewd remarks; and made appointments to take 'her' Asians to concerts and films and picture galleries.

I was not one of Dorothy's prize-winners, I was neither political, nor good for an argument. I had nothing to contribute to the meetings but an enormous appetite. Too busy eating to talk, and eating at great speed (my time was strictly limited) made Dorothy despair of me, call me a 'dilettante', surely an inappropriate word. 'You shut up like a clam,' said Dorothy. She might have added, 'upon a sandwich'. I nodded, too busy eating to answer. In spite of this, Dorothy was truly kind to me in a way which proves her goodness, since I gave back strictly nothing. I see her wearing Burmese *longyi* or an Indonesian sarong or an Indian sari or some *djellabah* with coral beads, dash from group to group, exclaiming joyously, 'I've taken off three stone.' Her weight went up and down, a topic of conversation.

Dorothy had great interest in China, and asked me to a meeting organized by the China Campaign Committee, at which Michael Lindsay was to speak on Yenan.

Lindsay, at that time not yet a Lord, had been for some years in North China, had gone to Yenan, stayed there a considerable time, and met Mao Tsetung and Chou Enlai and Chu Teh; had married a Chinese girl from Yenan. He was back in England, speaking about events in China and very favourably about Yenan.

It was too early to predict a communist victory, but Lindsay made it clear that he thought the communists did represent the aspirations of the Chinese people. Twenty years later, in 1966, I was to be with him at a teach-in on China at Toronto University, and he had changed altogether; he was now bitterly anti-new China, anti-Mao Tsetung, and so was his wife, the girl who had once followed Mao Tsetung to the caves of Yenan ...

That evening Dorothy Woodman introduced me to John Coast; he had been a prisoner of the Japanese for four years, had worked on the railroad they built in Siam, and was now back in England where his book, called *Railroad of Death*, was being published. John sat behind me in the row of seats; insisted on having lunch with me the next day and immediately proposed to me; he had, he said, fallen in love with the back of my head.

Since it was impossible for me even to imagine love any more, I was neither offended nor worried; I told him that I knew he was joking; that of course I would not accept, for I was not at all interested in men. This only made John more eager to pursue; he invited me to a ballet. For several months, once a fortnight, he took me to ballets or concerts, hoping I would change.

But he did not realize how tired I was; tired all the time, tired so that I nearly fell asleep at the ballets and did fall asleep at a concert. John would get irritated when I did not recognize a tune that had been played. I am so tired, I said. John could not understand the pace of my efforts; nor that at times I wished he would not take me out, for I would rather have slept. Unromantic, badly dressed, my hair badly done; I wanted to stay that way. He was sure he could improve me. 'You are so good-looking ... If you'd only stop wearing those boy scout clothes ... ' I stayed that way and he called me 'humourless'; and said I suffered from 'seriositis'. I did.

John brought an Indonesian ballet troupe to England. The compère of the troupe was a short, vivid-eyed young Indonesian, Suripno, who sticks in my memory, for he had a peculiar brilliance about him. Suripno was to be shot as a communist in the Madiun affair in Indonesia two years later, in 1948, and die shouting 'Long live the Revolution.' The Indonesian ballet was very successful in England; later John took another troupe to America.

John Coast came to Dublin for three days, while I was busy doing midwifery at the Rotunda. He took it in very good part, but now began to realize that transforming me into a well-dressed, relaxed, poised beauty was not going to be as easy as he thought. He then fell in love with someone else, and we stayed good friends. Later he obtained a job with the Foreign Office and went away, as cultural attaché, to Bangkok and then to Indonesia, where he was to write two more excellent books, *Recruit to Revolution* and *Dancing out of Bali*.

Dorothy had taken John Coast under her wing from the start; he was one of her special protégés, as was Maung Ohn, a young Burmese man with a bad hip. On the day John left for Bangkok we saw him off together; me still unsuccumbed, Dorothy clucking and worrying about John's welfare. I think she never forgave me for having proved so obdurate to John; and John confirmed this dent in our friendship by giving me an orchid as a parting present, and Dorothy a red red rose.

Apart from this anti-romance, nothing happened in that sector of living. The boon of a neutral state I took everywhere with me, whether London or Dublin, whether in digs or at Glyndebourne. I simply could not be moved, and remained undented for the whole four years of my medical studies and housemanship; my energies directed into one channel; all the love and care I was still capable of went to Yungmei alone. It was an arid season, not of nourishing torment and fertile fears, angers, passion and failure, but of hard relentless driving. Yet I was still affected by landscape, though I fought down the tendency to dream and threw myself upon a bicycle, till the land became miles of good road, wind in my face, sweat and exhaustion.

Only Yungmei was something quiet and sweet, like the pool of music that was live water in the Taoist temple in Szechuan. Only Yungmei's smile was more than gladness, it was a warmth about me, the stir of leafy trees as we went by the wooded lanes. Yungmei picking buttercups in the spring with grave intent, her legs now strong, her skin pink, was all joy to me. And sometimes I thought as I watched her play, looking so healthy, of the tuberculous complex in her, and wondered whether it would wake up stealthily one day ... and then I would become cold with fear, and watchful and tense. I would go back to work, work, work ... only my success could guarantee Yungmei against all evil ...

In January 1948 I qualified, first acquiring the L.R.C.P., M.R.C.S. degree, which allowed me to apply for a house job at the Royal Free Hospital. Besides working part-time in the Pathology Museum at Hunter Street I had also followed, during the last six months, courses at the School of Tropical Medicine and Public Health; for I wanted to prepare myself for diseases such as cholera and typhus, plague and leprosy, almost unknown in Europe but which I had seen in China. Later I received the M.B.B.S. degree, with Honours in surgery and pathology.

All through my medical studies it seemed to me that other interpretations were possible than those which we learnt and which were delivered with formal seriousness. And this applied as much to internal medicine, where there was a high degree of specialization, as to surgery, gynaecology, and obstetrics. In internal medicine I was not comfortable with those consultants who saw the whole patient from the standpoint of one organ alone. Everything within the body seemed to some of them to be governed by the functioning of either the heart, the liver or the stomach; and this natural penchant would have been funny, had it not also produced its crop of medical failures. In surgery it was possibly worse, and great was the number of stomachs, thyroids, and other organs removed in part for conditions which might perhaps have been treated differently.

But who was I to voice my doubts? I studied attentively Hans Selye's books on stress and psychosomatic diseases, which were now finding acceptance; and I was more and more inclined to feel that a study of 'the total person' was indispensable to good treatment, whatever the complaint. But there were many staid concepts, upon which reputations had been built over a number of years. Misconceptions were taught to us, based on partial knowledge. It was stated that acute rheumatic head disease 'did not exist' in Asian lands; and neither did high blood-pressure, because of the rice diet and 'the more passive' temperament of Asians; both these myths have now been abandoned. The incompleteness of many diagnostic judgments worried me. Later, during the fifteen years that I practised medicine in Asia, among Chinese, Malay and Indian populations, I was to discard a good deal of what I had been taught, having made my own mistakes, due to acting by the book rather than taking more time to see the person in his or her entirety. And mistakes, sometimes leading to the death or permanent crippling of the patient, remain with one, their guilt never dwindles. The mental component of every disease, the long deep roots of illness which reside in behaviour, attitude, reaction to events, in the person's acceptance or refusal to welcome suffering and dismay, failure and sorrow, as essential components of joy and happiness – this struck me as so important in the art of healing; and nowhere more perhaps than in dealing with women's ills, and also with children.

In the gynaecology wards of the hospitals there was one recurrent complaint which, I thought, was dealt with in a fashion calculated not to cure but to aggravate: vaginismus, the tense taut shutting up of the woman's muscles, refusing ingress to the male. Operations were done for this, to enlarge the passage, and after that, for a week, glass tube representations of the male penis were inserted in the vagina to accustom the patient to the normal process of intercourse. Having myself suffered from vaginismus in the last few years with Pao, but without seeking recourse to gynaecology, I knew the condition to be not inborn but acquired; and no amount of operative procedure, I felt, could remove the compelling mind, refusing the foreign body's assault. On the contrary, the pain and the trauma could only produce yet more psychic disturbance. At least one of our women consultants, a gynaecologist at the Elizabeth Garrett Anderson, realized this and used to murmur under her breath, as her hand plunged into examination: 'Now a good lover would make all that quite juicy.' But still the procedure went on. I felt like telling the patients that I too was like them; that a good talk with their husbands, or an act of revolt, might work wonders. But we were captive of a system where 'it doesn't work, so cut it out' still prevailed. And such was still the aura of reticence about sex, the general prudish squeamishness, that none of us discussed these operations even among ourselves.

Another feature of life during the war was brought about by conditions and not innate; emotional attachments, occasionally to a disturbing degree, between women. I had not been aware of this so-called deviation – which is a normal affective response – until after I had entered the Royal Free Hospital; which was an all-woman school of medicine. Such was still the prejudice against women in medicine, that few women doctors (and in some hospitals none) were allowed. The Royal Free had a long tradition of militancy behind it, and a splendid one. This, too, greatly appealed to me, as it would to any Asian woman. But it was at the Free that I understood suddenly the accusations formulated by Pao, and their baseness, when I had gone to Margery Fry, asking her to help me. For there, one night, when I had qualified as a doctor, and was doing my housemanship in surgery, a nurse, a very efficient and excellent one, came to my room, and talked of her life. She had become engaged, but did not know whether she would ever be fit for marital life, for, she said, she loathed men; had had only women friends, and fallen in love with some of them. She talked and talked, I think it did her good to talk, and perhaps verbal catharsis operated a transfer into what is called normality. During the war and afterwards with so many men away at war, in camps, in uniform, lesbianism seemed more natural than heterosexuality; and its counterpart in men was also extremely prevalent. The coy beastliness surrounding the subject of sex; the deprivation of any normal discussion or thought about the functions of men and women; the sense of sin, the hostility engendered in women by the social system, school segregation ... one could discuss many a factor making for these attachments; and today when they are almost normally accepted in the social context, perhaps at last the strenuous emotional upsets they engendered will also disappear.

After the First World War, with its uncommon carnage, many spinsters for life, having tasted independence, did not wish for marital fettering. But after the Second World War it was not so; far fewer of the male population had been slaughtered, and most of the young women would get married and live more or less happily for the rest of their lives.

As far as I was concerned, the fixed and frozen state in which Pao had left me worked for both male and female; my friendships were touched with resentful indifference. Like the Ice Queen, I knew that desire had been destroyed, and the knowledge was a strength; an imperviousness I was proud of. Would that Siberia ever thaw? Oh no, no, I thought, let me never again be so foolish; the menace of love, for ever unlamented love, let me in this summer season be delivered from its aberration, and for ever. I shall grow old and rejoice in solitary strength; the falling leaves of the leaf-bearing trees shall not stir my regrets; let it be winter always; never again shall I be defrauded, cheated, never go through the acrid corridors of delusive joy and despair ...

By the end of 1948 I had done a year as house surgeon at the Royal Free Hospital; and now I would either have to remain in England, take more hospital posts, or return to Asia. The first was a far easier and more reasonable course than the second.

For now the civil war in China was ending in the tornado of a triumphant Revolution. I was elated by the victories of Mao Tsetung, for anything was better than the Kuomintang; but on the other hand, also concerned, for no one knew what would happen afterwards. The real American tragedy, then, one which has actually doomed that country's ambitions for ever, was its folly in opting to support, with everything short of total involvement, what was already bone-decayed and hated and rejected by at least eighty-five per cent of the Chinese people, Chiang Kaishek. Yet great injections of money and

343

arms went on, and also pillage, for to get money and arms Chiang signed away the air above, and the seas and rivers of China, and all commercial privileges, to the U.S.A., and had he won, China would have been a permanent colony of America.

The introduction of an alien army into China, under pretext of help to the existing regime, only precipitated its downfall; it polarized resentment and hatred, identified America with Chiang Kaishek; had a traumatic effect upon the United States itself; for it kept an illusion of omnipotence, to be explained in lofty moral terms, and the paranoia of power could only swallow defeat and failure by loudly proclaiming that it had been betrayed.

The frenzy (there is no other word for it) of American activities in China during the civil war could therefore only be explained in terms of a vast scheme of domination; for up to the last day, eager and grabbing hands of American business were busy, among the debris, signing contracts, making schemes for monopolizing the market, making plans for flooding Chinese cities with American commodities. But this was not what the American people were told; today, with the Vietnam war the culmination of this disastrous policy of attempted domination in Asia, the American people are finally beginning to realize, on a large scale, that they have been lied to for a long time.

By late 1946, fifty-seven Kuomintang divisions totalling 707,200 men had been trained and equipped by the Americans for the civil war; and the training of secret agents continued. Thirteen Kuomintang armies of 473,000 men had been moved to fight against the Red armies by American naval and aerial units, of which eight armies, and twelve regiments of engineers and technical units, had been flown or conveyed to Manchuria for the campaign against Lin Piao. Between 1945 and 1949, America trained, equipped, and paid for 850,000 men to fight for Chiang Kaishek ...

As in all revolutions, the wave of anti-America feeling began with student movements, in all the main cities of China, in January 1947. The immediate cause was the rape of a young girl by some Marines in Peking, but this was only one of many incidents which had happened. Vivid word-pictures of the resentment against the Americans was given to me by my father, later.

'They could do what they liked, they called everybody names, they kicked rickshaw coolies and made them run races against each other, like animals.'

344

And from a friend, met again in Hongkong later: 'The Americans made a brothel wherever they went. They were an army of occupation, they behaved like one. There was always so much they brought with them and they wasted it all. They had too much of everything, and they made money selling it. The Marines would sell cigarettes, meat, stockings ... some women would go round with them to get lipsticks and silks and nylons and food. And they rode in cars while in the streets there were hunger riots. They did not pay for what they bought, they beat up anyone they did not like. All the cities stank. Everyone hated them, even those who made money out of them. An army of occupation.' And the G.I.s themselves knew they were hated: 'These people hate us. What are we here for, anyway?'

The students held big anti-American parades: 'Americans go home'. In Shanghai, in Peking, in Nanking, in Tientsin, 'G.I. go home'.

But right up till the end the Americans went on, neither deciding for an all-out Americanization of the civil war in China, which would have meant a million G.I.s to hold a few cities, nor deciding to get out of China.

In 1948, when Chiang left for Taiwan, he was able to take 450 million U.S. dollars' worth of bullion with him; for this enterprise the United States paid 5.9 billion dollars. And the bitterness of their defeat led to the witch-hunts and tragedy of the McCarthy period in America.

I decided to leave England, to go back in spite of much advice to the contrary. Isobel Cripps thought it a hazardous thing to do. I explained to her that even if I was not returning to China itself, I would like to be much nearer China than in London. I had now been away six years and I was beginning to feel much unease and restlessness, for I had not trained in medicine merely to have a good safe job in England. There was, of course, the problem of Yungmei. Miss Rendell, the Director of the Caldecott School, was indignant. 'There is a revolution, and you want to drag your child with you and throw her into the fires of this hell.' I felt perturbed. I was offered, by one of the surgeons for whom I worked, an excellent post as house physician at another hospital. The Burroughs Wellcome organization offered me a job in their pathology department, because I had obtained honours in pathology as well as in surgery. I went for an interview, and finally declined, explaining painfully, for everyone expected me to accept, that I was returning to Asia. The interviewer was exasperated. 'You cannot keep throwing your bread upon the waters,' said he. Other offers I refused.

In December 1948, two days after I had terminated my one-year housemanship, I packed, took Yungmei back from the Caldecott, bought with the rest of the money from *Destination Chungking* two airline tickets, and in early January 1949, we set off for Hongkong. During my year as house-surgeon I had received something like £2 a week at the Royal Free Hospital, but I had a room and free meals.

As the plane roared away (and how romantic, exciting, in those days air travel was, how awing to Cherry and Mary and Betty and other friends come to wave us away!) I felt at the end of a job completed, which could now be put away, to slumber in those harassed beds of memory where other selves, metamorphoses, transformations were also laid away. I thought suddenly of that self of mine in 1938, ten years younger, leaving Europe to return to China at war. I had then been so full of candour, fire, my eyes fixed on China – and I had been so badly treated ... why was I again leaving safety, gentleness, a certain career, and now dragging Yungmei with me – what was I going to? And why this inexorable push to go? And would it once again be hell? Had I learnt nothing?

But I put the thought away. For I had learnt something. I was much more cautious, much more suspicious, much less trustful now. And though I was never to commit the foolish mistake of thinking that all China was like Pao; and though that thing inside me, deeper than security or love, was dragging me back, yet this time I would play safe. I would not throw myself right into the boiling cauldron, but linger by the edge, and watch, and wait and see ... The last news I had about the Chinese Embassy in London was that some of the diplomats were buying houses and restaurants, and others packing, not to return to China but to go to America ...

'You're throwing yourself into the lion's den,' said Cherry. But I was not. I knew now that 'good will' was not enough; that 'I want to do something useful' was not written on my face; that the chances of there being quite a few Pao's around, even disguised under Marxist slogans, were fairly large ... I did not believe, even then, that a revolution is accomplished the day one power clique is overthrown – what would happen next?

I had believed too much in China at war; believed too romantically;

made myself believe that a just cause ennobled all those who participated in it. And now I knew that human nature can perpetrate monstrous crimes while mouthing great moralities – would this happen again?

Now there was a Revolution, triumphant militarily, in China; dedicated to sweeping out the viciousness of the Old Order – but was this true? Or would the old evils return, in new faces and new guises? And what is Revolution? To this I had no answer, save what I had heard, read, about the Russian Revolution. And this was not calculated to make me confident that I would be accepted. For I too belonged to the Old Order; I had been Pao's wife, and would a Revolutionary regime be so scrupulously exact, have time, with its impetuous storm sweeping hundreds of millions of people, shaking vast armies ... conquering many-millioned cities – would it have time for me? In the vast tidal bore that roared over China, in the hurricane that tore up by the roots so many institutions of the past decades, would one insignificant, ignorant person be spared?

But I could not contemplate living 'in peace' in England while tremendous China, like the phoenix, was being reborn from the consuming pyres of this massive conflict. I could not. At least I would be at the gates, watching and seeing, I would not abdicate, give up, turn my back on China ...

For China was not Pao, not the cruelty I had witnessed and endured, not the vile regime of Chiang and his administration. China was much more than this; it was the people I had seen, carrying their loads, sweating, starving, fighting, dying, the millions and the millions – the Revolution was for them ...

'Where are you going, Madam?' The steward bent to offer Yungmei, strapped in her seat, another sweet. 'Hongkong, we are going to Hongkong.' I held Yungmei to the plane window, to see the even fields of England below us. The seashore, white lipping the blue sea, stretched out, in the long afternoon speckle of the sun. I opened my passport and showed Yungmei her picture as a baby; on the passport I was still the wife of Tang Paohuang. It was still a diplomatic passport, valid till 1951.

Soon, within five days with all the halts, we would be in Hongkong, gateway to China. Hongkong, which was Chinese, though a British colony. And there Yungmei would go to Chinese school. And there I would watch, and wait, and make up my mind, for both of us.

347